Model A Ford
MECHANICS HANDBOOK

BY LES ANDREWS

Detailed Instructions for Servicing, Repair, and
Maintenance of Model A Ford Cars

Cottage Hill publishing
Grass Valley, California

Author
Les Andrews

Illustrator
John Dahle

Technical Advisors
Ed Coker
Lowell Jepson
John Stewart

Copy Editors
Glen Boire
David Hughes
Bill Gleason

Contributing Reviewers
Dick Johnson
Adrian Hemming

Photography
Ginny Gleason

Cover Design
Sugar Pine Studios

MHDC 990501-3

First published Aug. 1997 by Cottage Hill Publishing, 22126 Cottage Hill Dr., Grass Valley, CA. 95949

COPYRIGHT © 1999, LES ANDREWS
PRINTED AND BOUND IN U.S.A.

2nd Printing, Revised April, 1998
3rd Printing, Revised May, 1999

All rights reserved. No part of this publication may be reproduced without prior written permission from the publisher and author.

The information in this book is true and complete to the best of our knowledge. All recommendations are made without any guarantee on the part of the author or publisher, who also disclaim any liability incurred in connection with the use of this data or specific details.

All requests for information and comments should be sent to: Cottage Hill Publishing, 22126 Cottage Hill Dr., Grass Valley, CA. 95949   Fax (530) 268-3018

Visit our Web Site at:
www.ModelAMechanic.com

Printed and bound by
LectraMedia Printing
Nevada City, CA.

Library of Congress Cataloging in Publication Data

Andrews, Les
    Model A Ford Mechanics Handbook

ISBN 0-9658240-0-4

Foreword

IT is the purpose of this handbook to provide complete instructions for maintenance, disassembly, repair, and installation of the mechanical components for the Model A Ford.

The following pages show in a clear and concise manner the most appropriate way of performing the various repair operations. All procedures are fully illustrated to make them easy to follow.

The methods recommended have been carefully worked out for the purpose of giving definite and detailed instructions to the skilled as well as unskilled mechanics.

The first section contains removal, repair/overhaul, and reinstallation instructions for all mechanical components of the car. Illustrations provide clear definition of components, with a full description of all attaching nuts, bolts, and other hardware.

The second section outlines the proper methods of performing all service adjustments and alignments.

The third section details all of the points for lubrication and oil, and the maintenance interval for each point.

The fourth section deals with the diagnosis of car troubles and provides a complete troubleshooting guide of the most probable trouble conditions with an explanation of probable cause and correction.

The Appendix includes a preventive maintenance check list, a safety inspection check list, a cotter pin usage list, and torque specification data.

A complete list of Model A specifications, including engine numbers/dates and body type listing, is provided as the last page for easy reference.

SECTION CONTENT

SECTION I   SERVICE AND REPAIR

SECTION II   SERVICE ADJUSTMENTS

SECTION III   LUBRICATION AND OIL

SECTION IV   TROUBLESHOOTING

APPENDIX

SPECIFICATION REFERENCE CARD

MODEL A CAPACITIES

Crankcase	5 Quarts (Full)
	4-1/2 Quarts (at Oil Change)
Cooling System (Radiator)	3 Gallons (Water)
Gas Tank (1928-1929)	10 Gallons Gasoline
(1930-1931)	11 Gallons Gasoline
Transmission	1-1/2 Pints (600W Oil)
Differential (Rearend)	2-1/4 Pints... (600W Oil)
Steering (7 Tooth Sector)	7-3/4 Ounces (600W Oil)
(2 Tooth Sector)	4-1/2 Ounces (600W Oil)
Tires	34 Pounds (Air)

CONTENTS

SECTION I
SERVICE AND REPAIR

AMMETER 1-2
  Removing and Replacing Ammeter 1-4
AXLE-FRONT
  Removing Front Axle 1-4
  Installing Front Axle 1-8
AXLE-REAR 1-13
  Removing/Replacing Axle in Carrier Assembly ... 1-15
  Installing Rear Axle 1-16
BATTERY
  Removing Battery 1-18
  Battery Efficiency 1-18
  Installing Battery 1-18
BENDIX DRIVE ASSEMBLY 1-20
  Removing Bendix 1-20
  Inspection - Parts Replacement 1-21
  Installing Bendix 1-23
BODY BLOCKS 1-24
BRAKES 1-33
  Inspecting/Repairing Mechanical Levers 1-33
  Brake Actuating Arm Repair 1-34
  Disassembling Front Brakes 1-36
  Drums Inspected and Reworked 1-38
  Assembling Front Brakes 1-38
  Centering Front Brake Shoes 1-39
  Rear Brake Assembly 1-40
  Rear Drums Inspected and Reworked 1-42
  Assembling Rear Brakes 1-42
  Centering Rear Brake Shoes 1-44
  Installing Emergency Brake Band 1-44
  Installing Brake Rods 1-45
CAM SHAFT 1-46
  Removing Cam Shaft 1-46
  Installing Cam Shaft 1-51
CARBURETOR 1-57
  Removing Carburetor 1-57
  Disassembly 1-58
  Inspection and Repair 1-60
  Assembling Carburetor 1-61
  Assembly - Lower Body 1-62
  Assembly - Upper Body 1-63
  Installing Carburetor 1-64

CLUTCH 1-65
  Clutch Removal 1-65
  Inspection and Repairs 1-66
  Clutch and Pressure Plate Installation 1-67
CRANK PULLEY 1-70
  Removing Crank Pulley 1-70
  Installing Crank Pulley 1-73
CROSS SHAFT 1-76
  Service Brake Cross Shaft Repairs 1-76
  Emergency Brake Cross Shaft Repairs 1-79
CYLINDER HEAD AND GASKET 1-80
  Removing Head and Gasket 1-80
  Head Preparation 1-82
  Cylinder Head Installed 1-83
DIFFERENTIAL/REAR END ASSEMBLY 1-87
  Removing Rear End Assembly 1-88
  Rear End Disassembly 1-90
  Differential Inspection 1-92
  Rear End Assembly and Bearing Preload 1-93
    Carrier Bearing Preload 1-94
    Pinion Bearing Preload 1-94
    Ring Gear Pattern and Backlash 1-95
  Assembling Differential 1-95
  Installing Rear End Assembly 1-97
DISTRIBUTOR 1-101
  Removing Distributor 1-101
  Disassembly and Overhaul 1-102
  Inspection and Assembly 1-103
DOOR HANDLES 1-108
  Removing Door Handles 1-108
  Door Handle Cleaning and Repair 1-108
  Disassembly 1-109
DRAG LINK/TIE-ROD 1-110
  Installing Drag Link 1-110
EMERGENCY BRAKE HANDLE 1-112
  Removing and Disassembling
    Squeeze Grip Handle 1-113
  Removing and Disassembling
    Push Button Handle 1-114

CONTENTS (continued)

ENGINE OVERHAUL 1-115
- Engine Removal 1-116
- Engine Disassembly 1-121
- Engine Inspection 1-127
- Engine Overhaul 1-130
- Engine Assembly 1-135
  - Installing Crank 1-135
  - Installing Valve Lifters and Camshaft 1-138
  - Assemble Pistons and Rods 1-139
  - Wrist Pin Bushings 1-139
  - Ring Installation 1-140
  - Piston Ring Gap 1-140
  - Pistons Installed 1-141
  - Valves and Valve Guides Installed 1-143
  - Installing Original Mushroom Valve
    w/ Split Guides 1-143
  - Installing Modern Stainless Steel Valves
    w/One Piece Guides 1-144
  - Distributor/Oil Pump Drive Gear Installed ... 1-144
  - Oil Pump and Oil Pan Installed 1-145
  - Installing Pan Gaskets 1-145
  - Installing Flywheel Housing and Flywheel ... 1-146
  - Clutch and Pressure Plate Installation .. 1-148
  - Cylinder Head Installed 1-149
  - Thread Repair and Helicoil 1-159
  - Preparation to Install Engine 1-150
  - Engine Installation 1-153

FAN BELT 1-162
- Replacing Fan Belt 1-162

FAN BLADE 1-163
- Removing Fan Blade 1-163
- Installing 2-Blade Fan 1-166
- Installing 4-Blade Fan 1-167

FUEL SEDIMENT BOWL 1-169
- Flushing Cast Iron Sediment Bowl 1-169
- Disassembly and Cleaning (Cast Iron Bowl) ... 1-169
- Disassembly and Cleaning (Glass Bowl) ... 1-170
- Removing and Replacing Sediment Bowl ... 1-170

GAS GAUGE 1-172
- Removing Gas Gauge 1-172
- Gauge Repair and Assembly 1-174
- Installing Gas Gauge 1-175

GAS SHUT-OFF VALVE 1-176
- Removing Gas Shut-off Valve 1-176
- Disassembly and Repair 1-177

GAS TANK 1-179
- Removing Gas Tank 1-179
- Installing Gas Tank 1-184
- Installing Gas Gauge 1-186
- Installing Instrument Panel 1-187
- Install Gas Shut-Off Valve and Gas Line ... 1-187

GENERATOR 1-189
- Removing Generator 1-190
- Disassembly, Inspection and Cleaning ... 1-190
- Generator Assembly 1-192
- Installing Generator 1-192

HORN 1-194
- Horn Disassembly 1-195
- Cleaning 1-195
- Horn Assembly 1-196

HORN ROD 1-199
- Removing Horn Rod 1-199

IGNITION SWITCH (Pop-Out) 1-201
- Removing Ignition Switch and Cable 1-202
- Testing Switch and Cable 1-203
- Disassembly and Repair
  (1928 Through Mid 1930) 1-203
- Disassembly and Repair
  (Mid 1930 through 1931) 1-205
- Replacing Armored Cable Ignition Wire
  (1928 to Mid 1930) 1-206
- Replacing Armored Cable Ignition Wire
  (Mid 1930 Through 1931) 1-206
- Installing Ignition Cable and Switch 1-207

KING PINS 1-209
- Front Spindle Removal 1-210
- Removing Backing Plate 1-210
- Removing Spindle 1-211
- Installing New Bushings 1-212
- Installing Spindles and King Pins 1-212
- Installing Brake Shoes 1-215

LIGHTS 1-216
- Changing Headlight Bulbs 1-216
- Removing Lens 1-216
- Removing Reflector 1-217
- Removing Connector Socket 1-217
- Headlight Grounding 1-218

MOTOR MOUNTS 1-220
- Removing Front Motor Mount 1-220
- Removing Rear Motor Mounts 1-221
- Rear Motor Mount Installation 1-221
- Float-A-Motor Installation 1-222

CONTENTS (continued)

MUFFLER 1-223
   Muffler Removal and Installation 1-223
OIL PAN GASKET 1-225
   Removing Oil PAN 1-225
   Replacing Oil Pan and Gasket 1-225
OIL PUMP 1-227
   Removing Oil Pump 1-227
   Pump Design Changes 1-228
   Oil Pump Disassembly and Overhaul 1-228
PEDALS - BRAKE/CLUTCH 1-231
   Removing Brake and Clutch Pedals 1-231
RADIUS BALL CAP ASSEMBLY 1-234
RADIATOR 1-235
   Radiator Flow Test 1-235
   Overflow Tube and Baffle 1-235
   Removing Radiator 1-236
   Installing Radiator 1-238
RADIATOR SHELL 1-240
   Removing Radiator Shell 1-240
   Installing Radiator Shell 1-242
RADIUS RODS 1-243
   Removing Front Radius Rod 1-243
   Installing Front Radius Rod 1-248
   Removing Rear Radius Rods 1-253
   Installing Rear Radius Rod 1-254
SHOCKS 1-256
   Removing Shocks 1-256
   Disassembling Shock 1-257
   Assembling Shock 1-260
   Installing Shock 1-260
SPARE TIRE CARRIERS 1-262
   Rear Wheel Carriers 1-263
SPEEDOMETER DRIVE GEAR 1-264
   Removing and Replacing Reduction
      Ratio Case Assembly and Gear 1-265
   Removing Speedometer Drive Shaft Gear 1-265
   Removing and Replacing
      Speedometer Drive Gear 1-267
SPEEDOMETER 1-270
   Speedometer Removal and Disassembly 1-271
   Removing Oval Speedometer Indicator Wheels . 1-273
   Removing Round Speedometer
      Indicator Wheels 1-273
   Installing Speedometer 1-274

SPRING - FRONT 1-275
   Removing Front Spring 1-275
   Disassembly and Arching 1-276
   Front Spring Assembly 1-278
   Installing Front Spring 1-278
SPRING - REAR 1-280
   Rear Spring Removal 1-280
   Rear Spring Disassembly and Repair 1-281
   Installing Rear Spring 1-282
STARTER MOTOR 1-285
   Removing Starter Motor 1-285
   Bench Testing 1-286
   Replacing Brushes 1-287
   Disassembly, Inspection and Cleaning 1-287
   Reassembly 1-288
   Installing Starter Motor 1-289
STEERING ASSEMBLY 1-290
   Removing Steering Assembly
      (Through Engine Compartment) 1-291
   Removing Steering Assembly
      (Through Driver Side Front Door) 1-293
   2-Tooth Sector Steering Assembly Overhaul 1-295
   Assembling 2-Tooth Gear Box 1-299
   Sector Worm Mesh Adjustment 1-301
   Centralization of Sector to Worm 1-302
   Steering Column Housing Repairs 1-302
   Removing Control Rods and Upper Bushing 1-302
   Installing Control Rods and Upper Bushing 1-303
   Installing Column on Steering Shaft 1-304
   7-Tooth Sector Steering Assembly Overhaul 1-305
   Assembling 7-Tooth Steering Gear 1-307
   Replacing 7- Tooth Worm Gear 1-311
   Installing Steering Assembly in Car 1-312
STEERING WHEEL 1-316
   Removing Steering Wheel 1-317
STOPLIGHT SWITCH 1-318
TERMINAL BOX 1-319
THROWOUT BEARING 1-320
   Removing Throwout Bearing-
      By Removing Rear End Assembly 1-320
   Installing Transmission w/Throwout Bearing -
      With Rear End Assembly Removed 1-322
TIMING GEAR 1-324

CONTENTS (continued)

TRANSMISSION SHIFTING TOWER 1-328
- Shifting Tower Disassembly 1-328
- Shifting Tower Assembly 1-328

TRANSMISSION 1-330
- Production Design Changes 1-330
- Transmission Removal-By Removing Engine 1-331
- Transmission Removal-
  - By Removing Rear End Assembly 1-333
- Transmission Disassembly 1-334
- Assembling Transmission 1-337
- Inspection 1-337
- Assembley 1-338
- Installing Transmission-
  - With Engine Removed 1-342
- Installing Transmission-
  - With Rear End Assembly Removed 1-344

UNIVERSAL JOINT (U-JOINT) 1-347
- Removing U-Joint 1-347

WATER PUMP 1-352
- Removing Water Pump
  - (with 2-Blade Fan installed) 1-352
- Removing Water Pump
  - (with 4-Blade Fan installed) 1-354
- Water Pump Disassembly 1-355
- Water Pump Assembly 1-356
- Modified Pump Shaft 1-357
- Installing Water Pump w/2-Blade Fan 1-358
- Installing Water Pump w/4-Blade Fan 1-359

WHEEL BEARINGS 1-361
- Front Wheel Bearing 1-361
- Rear Wheel Bearing 1-362

WINDOW GLASS AND REGULATOR 1-363
- Removing Regulator 1-363
- Installing Window Regulator 1-364

WIRING 1-365
- Terminal Box-To-Generator Harness 1-365
- Instrument Panel Harness 1-365
- Main Harness 1-366
- Coil (Black) Wire 1-367
- Cowl Light Crossover 1-367

SECTION II
SERVICE ADJUSTMENTS

SERVICE BRAKE ADJUSTMENT 2-2
- Brake Adjustment 2-2

CASTER ADJUSTMENT 2-6
- Measuring Caster 2-6

CARBURETOR ADJUSTMENT 2-7

CLUTCH PEDAL ADJUSTMENT 2-8

FAN BELT ADJUSTMENT 2-9

FRONT WHEEL BEARING ADJUST 2-10

GENERATOR CHARGING RATE 2-10
- Power House Generator 2-10
- Cylinder Style Generator 2-11

**HEADLAMP FOCUSING
  AND ALIGNMENT** 2-11

HORN ADJUSTMENT 2-13

SHOCK ABSORBER ADJUSTMENT 2-13

STEERING ADJUSTMENT 2-14
- 7-Tooth Steering Shaft 2-14
- End Play Adjustment 2-14
- 7-Tooth Sector Shaft End Play Adjustment 2-15
- 2-Tooth Sector Shaft End Play Adjustment 2-15
- 2-Tooth Sector Steering Shaft End Play Adjust ... 2-16
- 2-Tooth Sector Worm Mesh Adjustment 2-16

IGNITION TIMING 2-18

TOE-IN ADJUST 2-19

VALVE GRINDING AND ADJUSTMENT .. 2-20
- Grinding and Seating Valves 2-20
- Adjusting Valve Clearance
  - (w/Adjustable Valve Lifters) 2-21

FLYWHEEL HOUSING VARIATION 2-22

CONTENTS (continued)

SECTION III
LUBRICATION AND OIL

SECTION IV
TROUBLESHOOTING

Troubleshooting Chart 4-1
     Major System Isolation 4-2
Troubleshooting Chart 4-2
     Cooling System 4-4
Troubleshooting Chart 4-3
     Ignition System 4-5
Troubleshooting Chart 4-4
     Fuel System 4-6
Troubleshooting Chart 4-5
     Electrical System 4-7
Troubleshooting Chart 4-6
     Engine Noises 4-8

ADDENDUM

Troubleshooting
     Generator (Charging)Circuit 4-9

APPENDIX

PREVENTIVE MAINTENANCE CHECK LIST A-1
MODEL A SAFETY CHECK LIST A-2
MODEL A COTTER PIN USAGE CHART A-3
BOLT - GRADE / TORQUE COMPARISON A-4

SPECIFICATION CARD

Ford SERVICE BULLETIN

A clean and attractive place of business attracts trade -- a dirty or dingy looking place actually drives it away.

Henry Ford

SECTION I
SERVICE AND REPAIR

INTRODUCTION

This section is intended as an aid to the mechanic in removing the various components of the Model A for repair or replacement. The following procedures and illustrations will enable the novice mechanic as well as the master mechanic to easily remove, repair, and replace all repairable and replaceable components of the Model A. Each removal procedure in this section starts from a fully assembled Model A. Both repair and overhaul procedures are included in this section. Any differences in the year model will be noted in the procedure. Adjustment and alignment procedures for replaced components are identified in Section II-Service Adjustments.

Before starting any removal of parts, it's a good practice to place removed components with attaching bolts and nuts in identified bags. This can be especially important in identifying nuts and bolts, and where they came from, when it is time for reassembly. All correct hardware sizes are identified in the reassembly procedures.

AMMETER

Removing and replacing the ammeter requires removing the instrument panel from the dash. Although the instrument panels for 1928/1929 are different in appearance than 1930/1931, both types of instrument panel and ammeter are removed the same way. Any time the instrument panel is pulled away from the dash, the battery should be disconnected as a safety measure to prevent an electrical short. If a fuse block (aftermarket safety item) <u>has not</u> been installed on the starter motor, a short circuit in the wiring behind the instrument panel could damage the wiring. If a fuse block has been installed, remove the fuse before working on the wiring behind the instrument panel and proceed to step 3.

Removing and Replacing Ammeter

1. Remove the bottom floor board [6 flathead screws] for access to the battery cable.

2. Remove the battery ground cable from the (+) battery terminal.

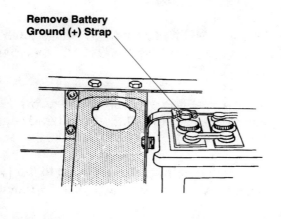

Remove Battery Ground (+) Strap

3. Remove the speedometer cable hold-down clip, located on the firewall next to the choke rod. This will allow the speedometer cable to be pulled up when instrument panel is released.

4. Remove four (4) 10-32 X 1/2 oval head screws from the instrument panel. Carefully pull the instrument panel away from the dash (gas tank) and unscrew the speedometer cable connector from behind the speedometer.

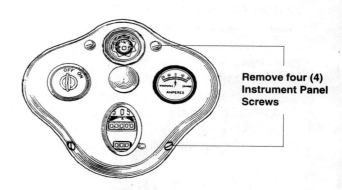

Remove four (4) Instrument Panel Screws

FRONT VIEW

5. Pull the instrument panel out far enough for access to the ammeter terminals on the back side of the panel. Remove the two (2) 8/32 nuts from the ammeter terminals and remove the yellow, yellow/black, and instrument light wires from the ammeter terminals.

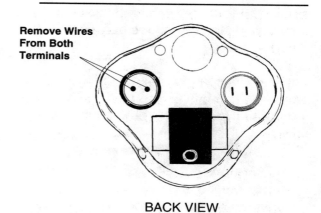

Remove Wires From Both Terminals

BACK VIEW

Service and Repair   1-2

AMMETER

6. Remove three (3) screws from around the original pop-out ignition switch to release the entire switch from the instrument panel.

   NOTE

   If a replacement type ignition switch has been installed, only the two wires (red and black) need to be removed from the switch, leaving the switch attached to the panel.

7. Move the instrument panel to the work bench for removal of the ammeter.

8. Bend the four (4) tabs up on the back side of the ammeter and push the ammeter out through the front of the instrument panel.

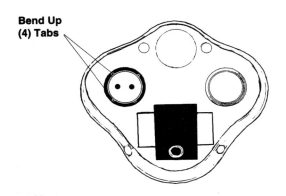

9. Insert the new ammeter through the front of the instrument panel and bend down four (4) tabs on the back side. Make sure the ammeter is rotated in the correct position. A few drops of silicone sealant may be needed to help hold the ammeter in place. The tabs may not hold the ammeter tight.

10. Place the instrument panel at the dash and attach the pop-out ignition switch to the panel with three (3) screws (6-32 X 9/32") and lock washers.

    NOTE

    Attach the red and black wires to the switch terminals (either terminal) for a replacement type ignition switch.

11. Attach the yellow wire to the ammeter CHARGE terminal post, and the yellow/black wire with instrument light wire attached to the DISCHARGE terminal post on the ammeter.

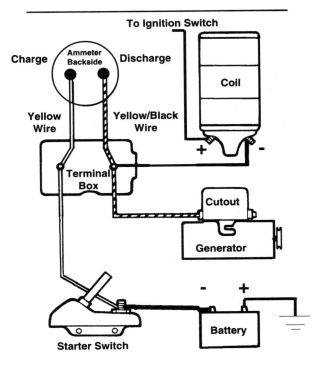

ELECTRICAL CONNECTION

12. Screw the speedometer cable into the backside of the speedometer.

13. Place the instrument panel against the dash and attach with four (4) 10-32 X 1/2" oval head screws.

14. Attach the speedometer cable hold-down clip on the firewall (12-24 X 1/2" round head screw and lock washer).

15. Reconnect the battery ground strap to the (+) terminal on the battery. Install fuse if removed.

16. Install the front floor board and floor mat. Secure the floor board with six (6) flat head screws [12-24 X 1-1/8"] and cup washers.

AXLE-FRONT

Removing Front Axle

1. Remove four (4) screws holding the front splash apron and remove front apron.

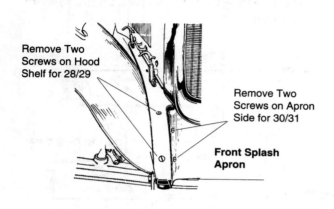

2. Jack up the front end and place jack stands on each side under the frame, just to the outside of the front radius rod.

3. Place a floor jack under the front axle and raise enough to allow removal of both front wheels.
4. On the left front side of the car remove the drag link from the spindle arm ball by removing the cotter pin and unscrewing the drag link end plug.
5. Remove cotter pin and screw out the top plug in both shock links. Remove both shock links from the spring perches.
6. Remove the clevis pins attaching the front brake rods to the actuating arms.
7. Remove the front wheel axle nuts, wheel bearings, and drums.
8. Remove the three brake shoe springs (1 long and 2 short) and remove the brake shoes.

NOTE
The brake shoes can be easily removed by pulling down on the bottom of the shoe, releasing it from the operating wedge. The springs can then be removed by hand and the shoes removed from the backing plate.

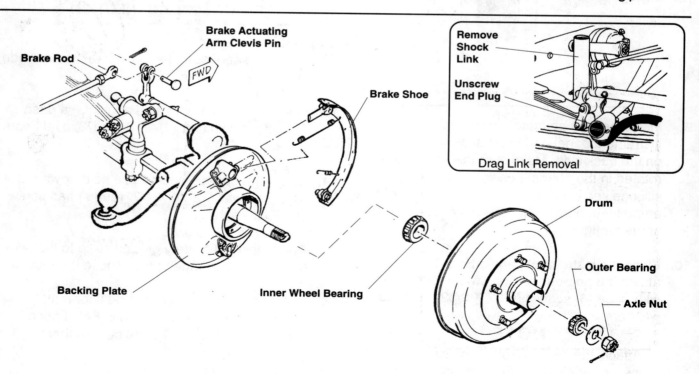

Removing Drum and Brake Shoes

Service and Repair

AXLE-FRONT

9. Remove the operating wedge stud nut [5/8 socket], located on the back side of the backing plate. The operating wedge stud and operating wedge can now be removed. The operating pin will then drop down out of the king pin.

NOTE
Be sure to retain any operating pin shims (pill) that may be in the operating wedge dimple, and the operating pin felt washer.

10. Remove the four (4) backing plate bolts (inside grease baffle) and castle nuts [9/16 socket]. The grease baffle and backing plate can now be removed from the spindle.

11. The tie-rod end can now be removed from the spindle arm. Remove the cotter pin from the end of the tie-rod and screw out the end plug. The tie-rod can then be lifted off the spindle arm ball.

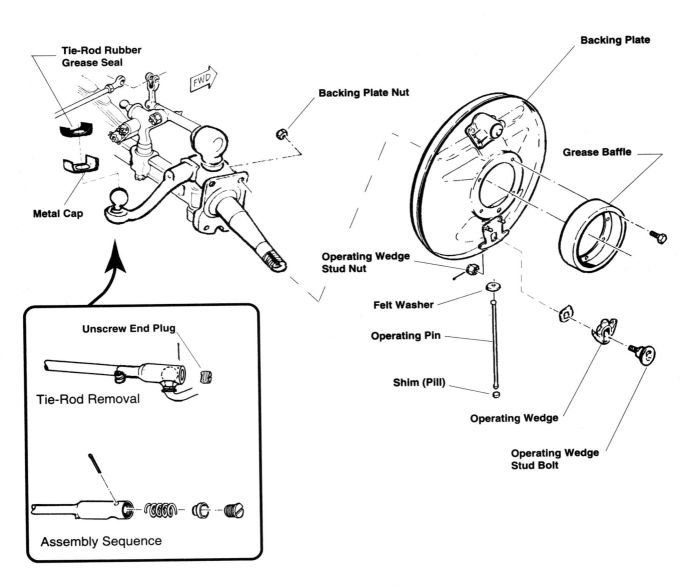

Removing Backing Plate

Service and Repair

AXLE-FRONT

12. Remove the spindle locking pin nut [9/16 socket] and lock washer. Reinsert the locking pin nut, screwing in only 1/2 the thread length. The nut is used to knock out the grooved locking pin. With a small hammer, hit the end of the nut to drive out the pin. A drift punch may be needed to completely drive out the locking pin.

13. Remove the actuating arm nut [9/16 socket] and lock washer from the back side of the spring perch. With large pliers or pipe wrench rotate the king pin cup (top portion of king pin) outward (toward front) a few degrees to release the actuating arm. Remove the actuating arm from the spring perch and king pin cup.

CAUTION

The king pin must be rotated outward slightly to allow the actuating arm bolt to release from the spring perch without damaging the threads on the actuating arm bolt.

14. Pull the king pin straight up and remove the spindle from the axle. Retain the thrust bearing, shims, and felt cup washer.

15. Repeat steps 8 through 14 to remove the opposite wheel and spindle assembly.

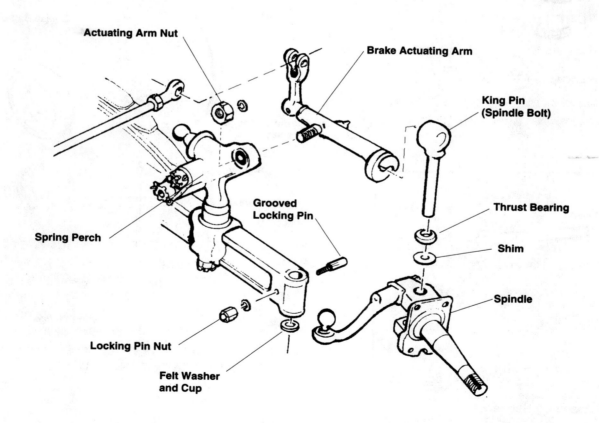

Removing Spindle

Service and Repair

AXLE-FRONT

16. Remove the two (2) cotter pins and nuts [3/4 socket] from the bottom of the radius rod ball socket. Remove the two springs, spacers, and caps. Support the radius rod ball end on a 2 X 4 wood block to temporarily hold it in place.

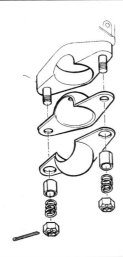

17. Lower the floor jack under the front axle to allow the ends of the leaf spring to rise above the axle. Place a small block of wood under both spring eyes (between the axle and spring eye).
18. Slowly raise the floor jack under the axle, spreading the spring ends on the wood blocks.

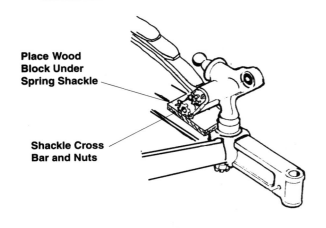

Place Wood Block Under Spring Shackle

Shackle Cross Bar and Nuts

19. Remove the cotter pins and nuts [5/8 socket] from the back side of the spring shackles. Remove the shackle cross bar.

20. Continue raising the axle to spread the spring until most tension is released from the spring shackles. Drive the spring shackles out through the front of the spring eyes and spring perch.
21. Lower the floor jack and remove the axle and radius rod (wishbone).
22. Remove the cotter pin and nut [3/4 socket] on the bottom of each spring perch and drive the spring perch out of the axle and radius rod.

NOTE
Lots of heat and WD-40 may be needed to remove the spring perches from the axle. It's best to have a machine shop press them out.

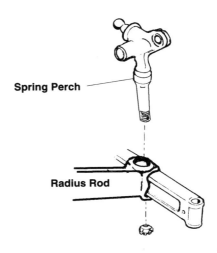

Spring Perch

Radius Rod

23. Knock out the old bushings in the spring perches. Weld around the spring perch bushing hole if excessively worn and insert new bushings. (These should be steel bushings.)
24. Check the axle to ensure that it is straight across the face side, with no bends or twist. Inspect the radius rod for bends and cracks. The axle and radius rod must be absolutely straight before reassembling.

Service and Repair

AXLE-FRONT

Installing Front Axle

1. Attach the radius rod to the axle with the spring perch bolts. Attach nuts (special convex shape) to spring perch bolts. The two spring perches must be very closely aligned or the spring shackles will not line up with the spring eyes when attaching the front leaf spring. To align the two spring perches, clamp a straight edge (angle iron) against the shackle bushing hole on both perches. Then torque the two perch nuts to 100 ft. lbs.

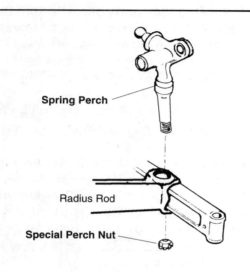

2. Before attaching axle to leaf spring, insert the spring shackle (new or used) through the spring eye bushing and spring perch bushing to ensure correct fit. The fit should be an easy slip through. If the shackle is a tight fit in the bushing, the bushing will need to be reamed. A slightly loose fit is okay.
3. Place the axle on the floor jack and raise far enough to allow a spring shackle to be inserted in one end of the spring and spring perch. Apply the shackle bar and nuts on the back side of the shackle. Do not tighten nuts at this time.
4. Place wood blocks under each end of the spring (spring eyes) and raise the axle until the other spring shackle can be easily inserted through the spring eye and spring perch. Apply the shackle cross bar and nuts [5/8 socket].
5. Tighten the nuts on both shackles just enough to allow the cotter pins to be inserted.

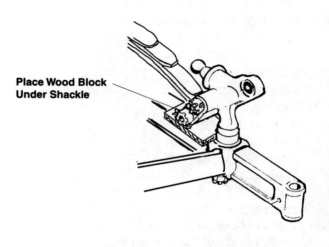

6. Install the radius rod ball on the bottom of the flywheel housing. Place the ball cup with the hole on the top side of the radius ball. Insert the two spacers, springs, and nuts [3/4 wrench] as shown below. Tighten the two castle nuts until they touch the spacers and insert cotter pins.

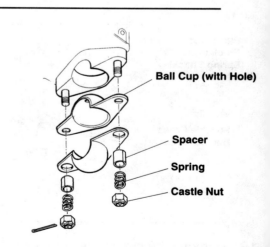

Service and Repair

AXLE-FRONT

7. Place the spindle on the axle. Apply a coat of grease to the king pin shaft and insert the king pin, new thrust bearing (T83) (open side facing down) and shim through the spindle and axle, through the felt washer cup, and into the lower bushing.

NOTE

The new thrust bearings are thinner than the originals. One or two shims will be needed to take up the difference. This will allow the thrust bearings to support the total weight of the car, producing easy and smooth steering. The grooved locking pin securely fastens the king pin to the axle. The weight of the car then creates a downward force on the king pin, placing the car's weight on the thrust bearing, between the king pin upper cup and the top of the spindle. If the thrust bearing is too thin, the weight of the car will be transferred to the bottom of the axle, at the felt washer and cup. This is not a bearing surface and will cause stiff and hard steering. The front end weight of the car should be totally supported on the thrust bearing. Adding a shim or two under the thrust bearing will shift the weight to the bearing.

8. Insert the end of the brake actuating arm into the king pin cup and then rotate the actuating arm bolt into the spring perch. Allow the king pin to rotate to prevent damage to the actuating arm bolt threads when inserting into the spring perch. Apply a nut and lock washer to the actuating arm bolt. Securely tighten.
9. Rotate the king pin to align the king pin locking pin groove with the hole in the axle.
10. Insert the grooved locking pin through the front of the axle to lock the king pin in place. Hammer the locking pin all the way in before applying the lock washer and nut. (This will prevent applying excessive force on the bolt threads.)
11. Apply the locking pin lock washer and nut. Securely tighten. Check the thrust bearing operation as follows before continuing assembly.
    a.) Place a floor jack under the spindle and raise just enough to support the total weight of the car on the jack.
    b.) Try to move (rotate) the thrust bearing on top of the axle and the felt washer cup under the axle. The felt washer cup should rotate freely and the thrust bearing, supporting the car's weight, should not rotate. If the thrust bearing can be moved, add a shim under the thrust bearing.
    c.) Lower the front end back onto the jack stands. Grabbing the spindle axle, rotate the spindle back and forth to ensure free movement.

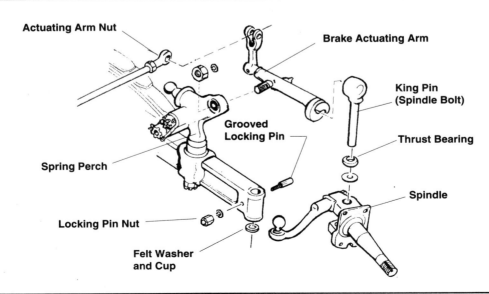

1-9 Service and Repair

AXLE-FRONT

12. Place a metal cap and rubber grease seal over the spindle arm ball stud. (The rubber grease seal usually needs replacing.)

13. Place the end of the tie-rod over the spindle arm ball stud and screw in the end plug. After the end plug contacts the ball, screw in the end plug an additional 1 to 1-1/2 turns. Align the end plug slot with the cotter pin holes in the tie-rod. Insert cotter the pin.

NOTE
The tie-rod ball spring should be compressed 25% for correct tension. Steering is affected if this adjustment is too loose or too tight.

14. Place the backing plate and grease baffle on the spindle and attach with four (4) bolts (3/8-24 X 7/8) and nuts [9/16 socket]. Securely tighten all nuts and insert cotter pins.

15. Push the operating pin up into the center of the king pin. Insert a felt washer over the operating pin and into the backing plate access hole.

16. Hold the operating pin up while attaching the operating wedge with wedge stud, stud washer (spacer), and castle nut (5/8 socket). Securely tighten stud nut and insert cotter pin. Check for free movement (up and down) of the operating wedge.

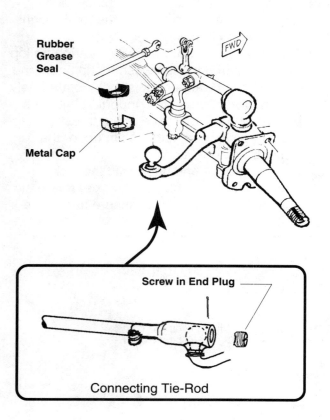

Connecting Tie-Rod

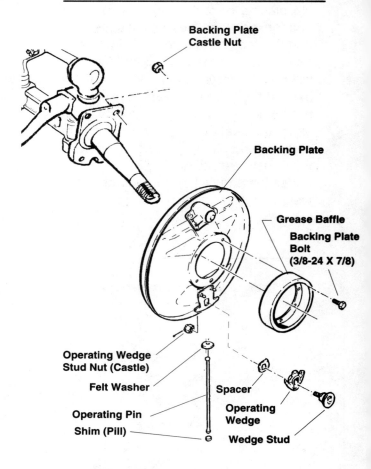

Installing Backing Plate

Service and Repair

AXLE-FRONT

17. Clean all components on the brake shoes before installing them on the backing plates.

18. Place each brake shoe adjusting shaft into the top adjuster housing on the backing plate.

19. Pull the two shoes together to allow the top (long) spring to be easily attached between the two shoes.

20. Pull the bottom of the shoe in and attach the short spring from the shoe to the spring stud. The bottom of the shoe can then be pushed outward and slipped onto the roller track, with the rollers contacting the operating wedge. This can all be done without tools.

21. Pack all wheel bearings with grease. Install the inner wheel bearing, hub, outer wheel bearing, key washer, and axle nut. Tighten the axle nut until a heavy drag is felt on the wheel, then back off the axle nut one castle position from the cotter pin hole. Install cotter pin.

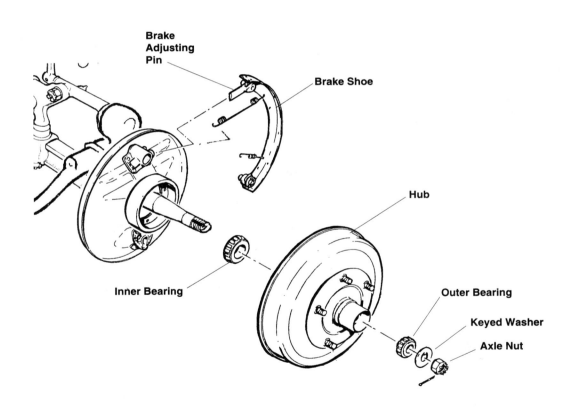

Installing Brake Shoes and Drum

Service and Repair

AXLE-FRONT

22. Assemble and install both front shock links as shown below. Screw in the end plug and insert the cotter pin.

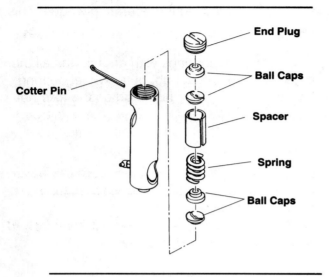

23. Install the drag link on the left spindle. Screw in the drag link end plug and tighten sufficiently to compress the internal spring 25%. (Usually 1 to 1-1/2 turns past contact with the ball stud.) Install the cotter pin.

24. Attach both brake rods to brake actuating arms with clevis pin and cotter pin.

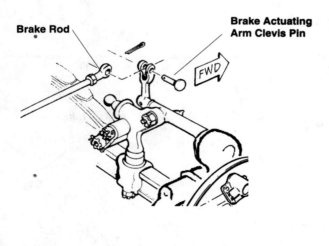

25. Adjust the brakes in accordance with the "Brake Adjusting Procedure". (See Section II.)

26. After completion of front end assembly, readjust the front toe-in. See Section II, Adjustments.

27. Attach the front splash apron with four screws [**28/29 Model** use 1/4-20 X 1-1/4" oval head] [**30/31 Model** use 1/4-20 X 1/2" round head].

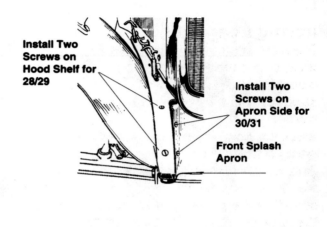

Service and Repair 1-12

AXLE-REAR

Removing and replacing a rear axle can be accomplished without removing the entire rear end and drive line assembly from the car. The axles and differential carrier can be withdrawn from the left side of the rear end housing assembly. A complete overhaul of the rear end assembly, including drive line, ring and pinion gear, bearings, and differential assembly, requires removal of the differential and driveline assembly from the car. For complete overhaul and alignment of the rear end assembly, refer to "Differential/Rear End Assembly ", page 1-87. The following procedure describes only how to remove and replace a broken rear axle.

Removing Rear Axle

1. Drain the differential oil by removing the bottom drain plug on the differential housing (3/8 square hole pipe plug). The drain plug can be removed with the square end of a 3/8 drive ratchet.
2. Block the front wheels and release the emergency brake.
3. Jack up the rear end of the car and place jack stands under the frame, just behind the running board brackets. Remove both rear wheels.
4. Disconnect the service brake rod and emergency brake rod (remove clevis pins) at the left rear wheel.
5. Remove the left-rear shock arm from the shock (remove shock arm bolt [9/16 socket] and pull the arm off the shock shaft).
6. Remove both rear axle nuts [15/16 wrench] and remove both rear wheel drums.

NOTE
A rear wheel hub puller may be needed to remove the drums from the axle.

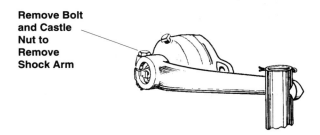

Remove Shock Arm

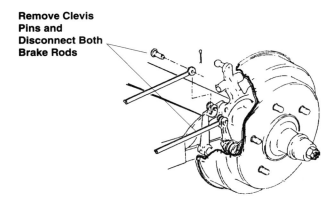

Remove Brake Rods

Remove Drum

Service and Repair

AXLE-REAR

7. Remove the clevis pin from the emergency brake connecting link on the left wheel brake assembly. This will allow access to the four (4) backing plate bolts and nuts.

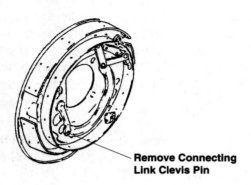

8. Loosen the bolt and nut [7/8 wrench] at the front of the torque tube, attaching the radius rods to the torque tube. Loosen enough to allow the left radius rod to float freely.

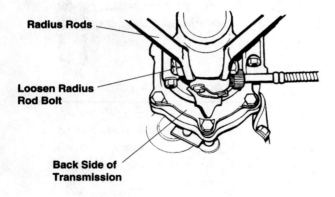

9. Remove the four (4) backing plate bolts and nuts [9/16 socket] (left side only) and remove the backing plate with brake assembly attached. Place the end of the left radius rod on the floor, clear of the axle housing.

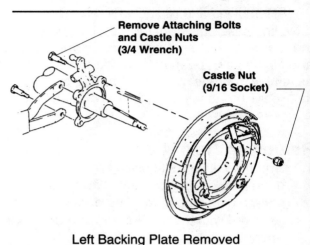

Left Backing Plate Removed

10. Place a floor jack under the differential housing (banjo) for support while removing the left spring shackle.
11. Place a full length Model A spring spreader on the rear spring and adjust sufficiently to allow the left spring shackle to be removed.
12. To remove the spring shackle, remove the two (2) rear shackle nuts [11/16 socket] and remove the shackle cross bar. With spring tension removed, the shackle can be driven out of the spring perch and spring eye.

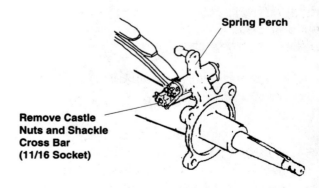

AXLE-REAR

13. Remove the ten (10) bolts [9/16 socket] from the left side of the differential housing (banjo) and slide the left axle housing off the axle. The axles and differential, including ring gear and carrier assembly, can be pulled out of the differential housing from the left side.

2. Remove the nine (9) nuts and bolts [9/16 socket] around the carrier assembly. Separate the two halves and remove the spider shaft and gears.

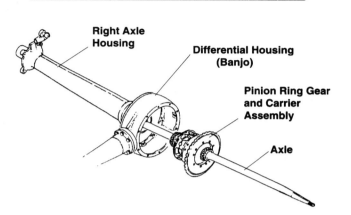

Removing Carrier and Axle Assembly

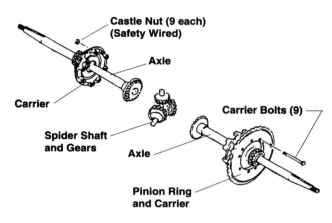

Split Carrier Assembly

Removing/Replacing Axle in Carrier Assembly

The carrier assembly must be separated to remove and replace an axle. The carrier assembly should be reassembled in the same position as disassembled (in reference to the two carrier halves). Before disassembling, check along the separation line of the carrier for punch marks identifying a matching point of the two halves. If no marks are found, punch identifying marks on each carrier half for reassembly alignment.

1. Cut and remove the safety wire around the nine (9) carrier assembly nuts.

NOTE
Before separating the carrier, make note of the position of the spider and spider gears. The spider and gears should be placed in the same position at reassembly.

3. Remove and replace the axle in the carrier half, and reinsert the spider and gears.
4. Assemble the two carrier halves (aligned with punch marks) and reinsert the nine (9) bolts and nuts [9/16 socket]. Torque all nuts to 35 ft/lbs. and safety wire.

NOTE
Before applying safety wire, check the end play of the axles in the carrier assembly (.010-.015"). Excessive end play is caused by worn carrier assembly or worn spider gears.

AXLE-REAR

Installing Rear Axle

1. Place the assembled rear axle assembly through the left side of the differential (banjo) housing, with the ring gear on the left side of the banjo.
2. Replace the banjo gasket with the same thickness as removed. Slip the left axle housing over the axle and bolt to the differential housing with ten (10) 3/8-24 X 5/8 Hx Hd bolts [9/16 socket]. Torque to 35 ft. lbs.
3. Using the floor jack under the differential housing, raise the rear end assembly enough to allow the left shackle to be inserted through the spring perch and spring eye. The left radius rod must be placed into position on the axle housing before the rear spring is attached to the spring perch. The attached spring spreader may need adjusting to allow the spring shackle to be inserted. Apply the shackle cross bar and two (2) castle nuts [11/16 socket]. Tighten only enough to allow the cotter pin to be inserted.
4. Place the backing plate with brake assembly against the axle housing and attach the radius rod and backing plate assembly with four (4) bolts and nuts [3/4 wrench on bolt head and 9/16 socket on castle nut]. Use special shouldered bolts, two long bolts through the radius rods and backing plate, and two short bolts through the rear backing plate holes. Use 7/16-20 castle nuts [9/16 socket] positioned inside the backing plate/brake assembly. Securely tighten and insert cotter pins.
5. Securely tighten front radius rod to torque tube bolt/nut [7/8 socket].

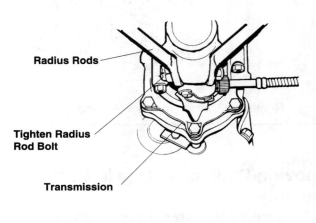

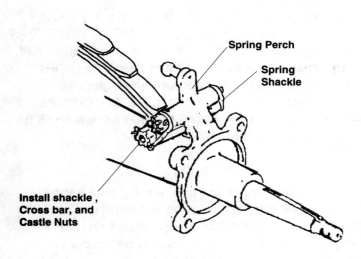

6. Inspect the axle keys before installing them in the axle. The axle key should fit in the axle slot fairly snug. Replace the axle key if it is worn, chipped, or grooved. The tapered end is placed toward the inside of the axle.

AXLE-REAR

7. Install both wheel drums, using fiber axle seal washer, steel washer, and axle nuts. Torque axle nuts to 125 ft/lbs. Insert cotter pin.
8. Install the service brake rod and emergency brake rod clevis pins and cotter pins at the rear wheel.

9. Install the left shock arm and link. Firmly tighten the shock arm bolt to remove all movement between shock arm and shaft. Install the cotter pin in the castle nut [9/16 socket].

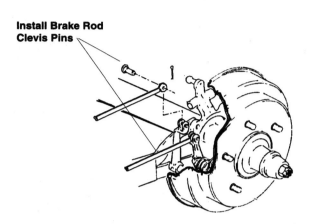

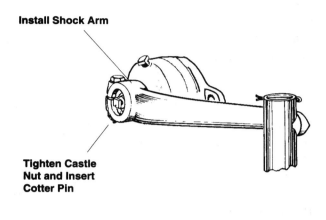

10. Install both rear wheels. Torque the wheel lug nuts to 64 ft. lbs. Remove the jack stands and floor jack.
11. Fill the differential housing with 2-1/4 pints of 600W oil. Insert grease in both rear axle grease fittings.
12. Check for installation of all cotter pins. Test drive and check for rear end oil leaks.

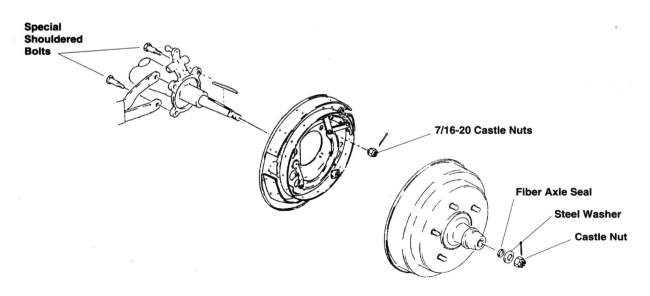

Install Rear Backing Plate and Hub

1-17

Service and Repair

BATTERY

The Model A uses a +6 volt, group 1 battery. A well-charged battery, proper maintenance (water level maintained), and a correctly set charging generator, will maintain most batteries for three years or longer. Each cell should be checked with a hydrometer every three months to determine the charge level of the battery. A fully charged battery has a specific gravity level of 1.28 to 1.3. A fully discharged cell will have a specific gravity reading of 1.1. A battery charger should be applied when the specific gravity of a cell drops below 1.26. Use distilled water when filling the cells. The Model A utilizes a positive (+) ground system.

Removing Battery

1. Remove the front floor mat (or carpet) and shift lever plate.
2. Remove the bottom section of the front floor board [6 flathead screws] for access to the battery terminals.
3. Remove the ground strap from the (+) battery terminal and the battery cable (from the starter switch) from the (-) battery terminal.
4. Remove the nuts and washers securing the battery hold-down clamps (bracket). Attach a battery lifting strap to the two battery posts and lift the battery out of the battery frame.

Installing Battery

1. Set a fully charged battery in the battery frame, positioned so that the (+) battery terminal post is next to the frame cross member for ground strap connection.
2. Attach the battery hold-down clamps with two (2) 3/8-24 nuts and lock washers.
3. Connect the battery cable (from the starter switch) to the (-) battery post. Attach the battery ground strap to the (+) battery post.
4 Install the front floor board and floor mat. Secure the floor board with six (6) flat head screws [12-24 X 1-1/8"] and cup washers.

Battery Hold-Down Bracket

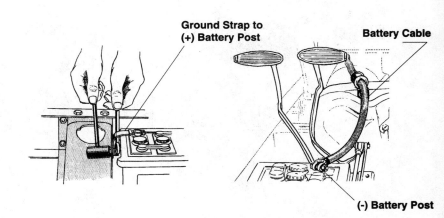

Ground Strap To (+) Post

Battery Cable To (-) Post

Service and Repair 1-18

BATTERY

BATTERY EFFICIENCY

A battery has 100% of rated capacity at 80°F. At 0°F, the same battery has only 40% of the capacity (Amp Hours) it had at 80°F. At 40°F the starter requires over twice as much energy to turn the engine over as it did at 80°F.

This is why weak batteries will fail in extreme cold or hot conditions.

STARTING POWER AVAILABLE FROM BATTERY	Temperature	STARTING POWER REQUIRED BY ENGINE
105%	125°	(UP TO) 250%
100%	80°	100%
65%	32°	155%
40%	0°	210%
18%	-20°	268%

Service and Repair

BENDIX DRIVE

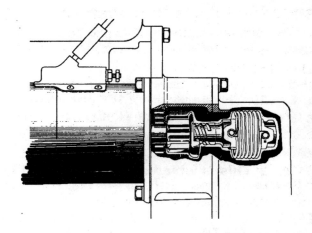

BENDIX DRIVE ASSEMBLY

The bendix drive assembly is used to engage the starter motor with the flywheel ring gear. The bendix spring absorbs the initial torque shock when the bendix drive gear engages with the flywheel ring gear. The high RPM of the starter motor throws the bendix gear into the flywheel ring gear, thereby driving (spinning) the flywheel. Upon release of the starter switch, the starter motor stops, allowing the high RPM of the rotating ring gear (engine running) to spin the bendix drive gear off the flywheel ring gear. If the starter motor does not engage the flywheel, the problem is usually the bendix drive assembly. One or more of the following three (3) faults can occur: (1) broken bendix spring, (2) broken starter drive sleeve, or (3) bendix spring bolts broken or vibrated loose. The starter motor must be removed from the flywheel housing to determine the repairs needed.

Removing Starter Motor

1. Remove the front floor mat (or carpet) and shift lever plate attached to floor board with three (3) clips.
2. Remove the bottom section of the front floor board [6 flathead screws] for access to the battery terminals.
3. Remove the battery ground cable from the (+) battery post.
4. Unscrew the starter push rod from the starter switch and push it all the way up.
5. Remove the oil dip stick.
6. Remove battery cable and harness wire from the starter switch [5/8 box wrench].
7. Remove the three (3) starter motor bolts [9/16 socket]. Remove the top bolt last. It will support the weight of the starter motor while the other two are being removed (starter motor weighs 21 lbs.) Lift the starter up and pull the motor and bendix drive assembly out of the flywheel housing.

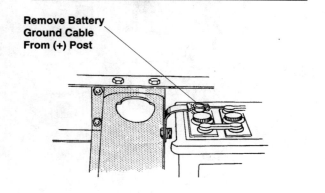

Remove Battery Ground Cable From (+) Post

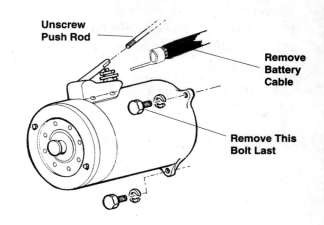

Unscrew Push Rod
Remove Battery Cable
Remove This Bolt Last

Service and Repair

BENDIX DRIVE

Inspection - Parts Replacement

Two different starter motors and bendix drive assemblies were installed on the Model A. <u>The two are not interchangeable.</u> The early starter motor (Abell) was used from beginning of production until Oct. 1, 1928. This starter had a 1/2" motor shaft. The later starter motor (Oct. 1,1928 to end of production) has a 5/8" motor shaft. <u>The early bendix drive has a special form of ten-tooth pinion gear and can only be used with the early flywheel ring gear.</u> The flywheel ring gear changed with the change in starter motor and bendix drive assembly (Oct.1, 1928.) The figure to the right identifies the different bendix drive assembly components. The service sleeve and drive head are not available (new). Always use correct size part to prevent damage to the ring gear and bendix drive assembly.

1. Check for a cracked or broken bendix drive sleeve.

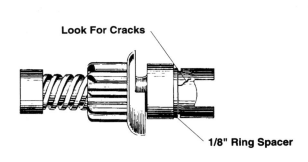

2. The standard bendix sleeve cannot be removed and installed without special equipment, so Ford provided a replacement serviceable sleeve in December 1929. A 1/8" ring spacer between the sleeve and shoulder was used with the standard sleeve. Remove this ring spacer when installing a service sleeve.

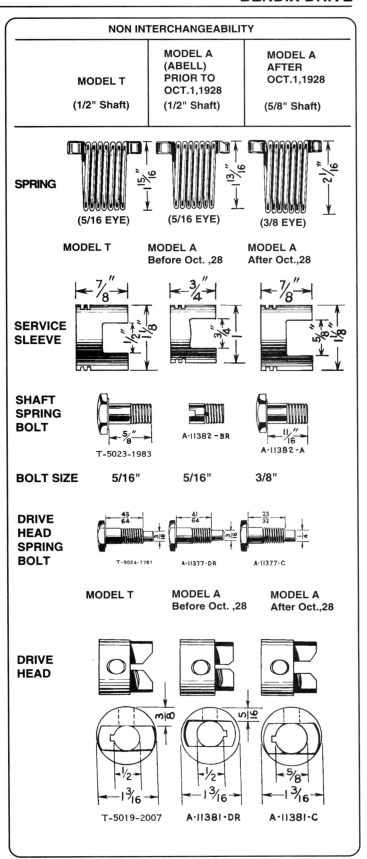

Service and Repair

BENDIX DRIVE

3. To install the new sleeve, place it on the shaft so that tongue "A" in the sleeve is directly over groove "B" on the bendix shaft. With a screw driver or small chisel, press the tongue firmly into the groove.

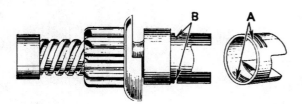

4. **Spring Support Clip.** The spring clip was a service item after June 1931. The purpose of the spring clip is to form a support for the first 1/4 coil on each end of the driving spring and prevent bending of the spring screws. Two clips were used, one snapped over the head and one over the shaft.

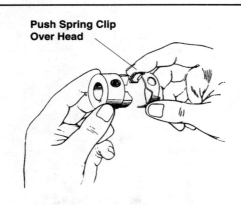

5. When the clip is in place, the hole in the clip should line up with the screw hole in the head or shaft. The bent-under portion should sit over against the shoulder caused by the reduction of the diameter of the head and shaft. This bent-under portion prevents side-ways cocking of the clip. When assembled in this position, the first 1/4 coil of the spring will sit firmly on the reinforced lamination.

6. When assembling springs and bolts with spring support clips, do not tighten the spring bolt to the point where the spring eye cuts the clip enough to break it.

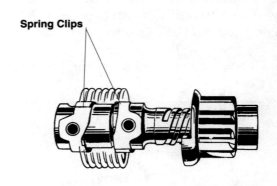

7. Place a tabbed lock washer on both spring bolts. The tab on the lock washer should be bent to lock the bolt in place. The tab on the washer must be bent upward until it presses tightly against a flat side of the bolt head.

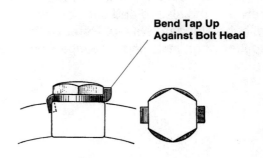

BENDIX DRIVE

Installing Starter Motor

1. Install the starter motor with three (3) bolts and lock washers (3/8-16 X 1") [9/16 socket]. Install the top-outside bolt first. This will hold the starter motor in place while the other two bolts and lock washers are being installed.

2. Connect the battery cable and harness wire to the starter switch. Screw the starter push rod to the starter switch.

3. Connect the battery ground strap to the (+) battery post.

4. Install the front floor board and floor mat. Secure the floor board with six (6) flat head screws [12-24 X 1-1/8"] and cup washers.

5. Slip on the shifting tower boot and emergency handle boot. Screw the knob on top of the shifting tower and screw on the accelerator pedal (top cap).

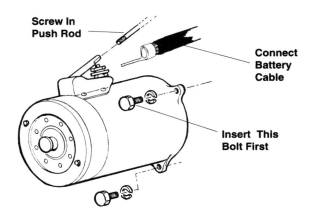

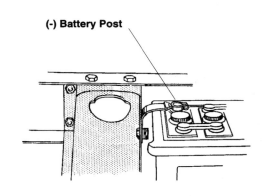

Service and Repair

BODY BLOCKS

Wood body blocks were used to support the body on the frame, providing a non-squeak support and a means to shim various points of the body for door and hood alignment. The blocks were made of a hard wood (oak or alder). Not all body styles used body blocks. All Fordor Sedans (except 1931 slant windshield), Victorias, A 400, Cabriolets, Deliveries, Town Sedans, and Station Wagons utilized wood subframes, and therefore did not require body blocks. Body blocks were specially cut for each position, and were placed in the body U-channel cross members. The front body block (under the cowl) and the rear body block (on the rear cross member ears) are placed parallel with the frame. All other body blocks are positioned in the U-channel cross members and lie perpendicular to the frame. Rubber pads are placed under each body block and serve as a shim for body alignment with doors and the hood. Various thickness pads will need to be added or removed to obtain correct hood and door alignment. The body blocks are most conveniently replaced when the body has been removed for restoration. However, the blocks can be replaced by removing all body bolts and raising the body approximately 4" above the frame and placing 2 X 4's across the frame to support the body while changing the blocks. All body blocks should be treated with a wood preservative and then painted black before installing. As seen in the following diagrams, Block #2 has two holes drilled for mounting (Frame Hole 4). The blocks were made so that the same block would fit on either side of the frame. Therefore, two holes were drilled in block #2 to allow the same block to be used on both sides. The figure to the right shows the correct sequence of frame webbing, splash apron, rubber (shim) pads, and body block placement on the frame. The figures on the following pages identify each body block position and correct orientation according to body style. Body block sets can be purchased from most parts suppliers.

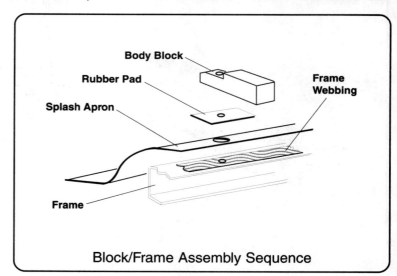

Block/Frame Assembly Sequence

BODY BLOCKS

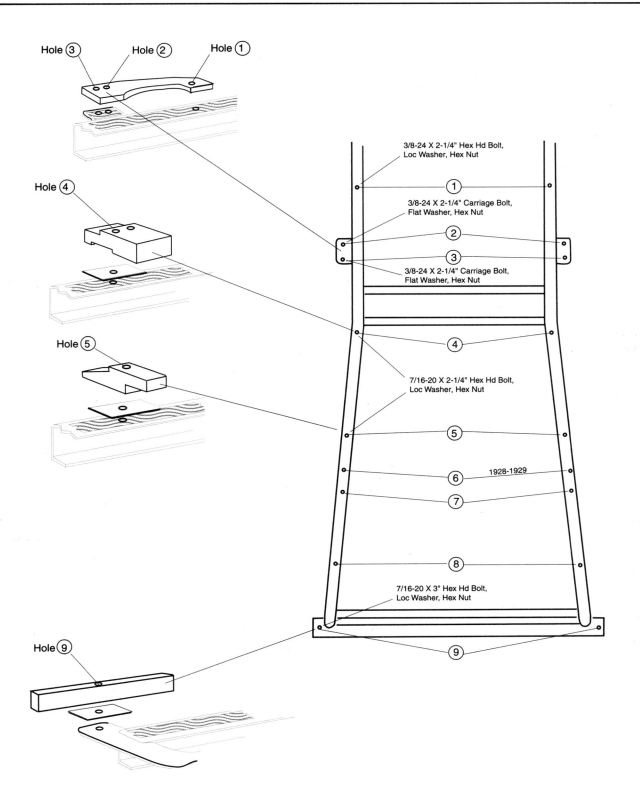

1928/1929 Coupe, Sport Coupe, Bus Coupe

BODY BLOCKS

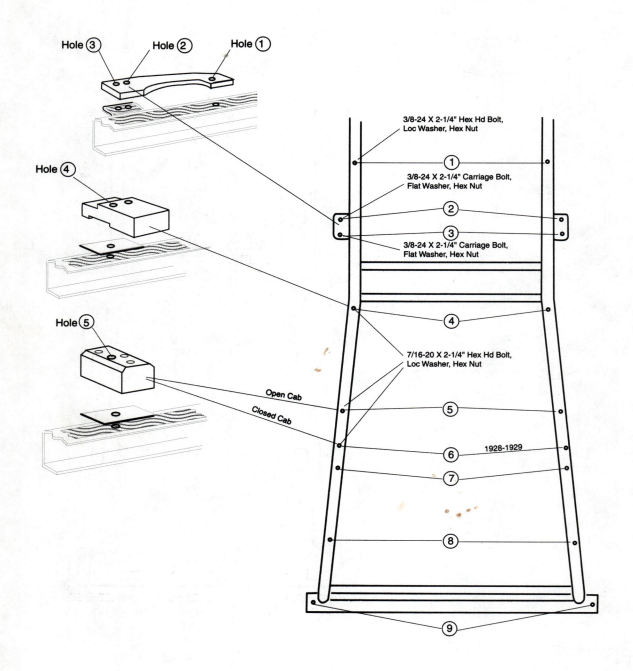

1928/1929 Pickup

BODY BLOCKS

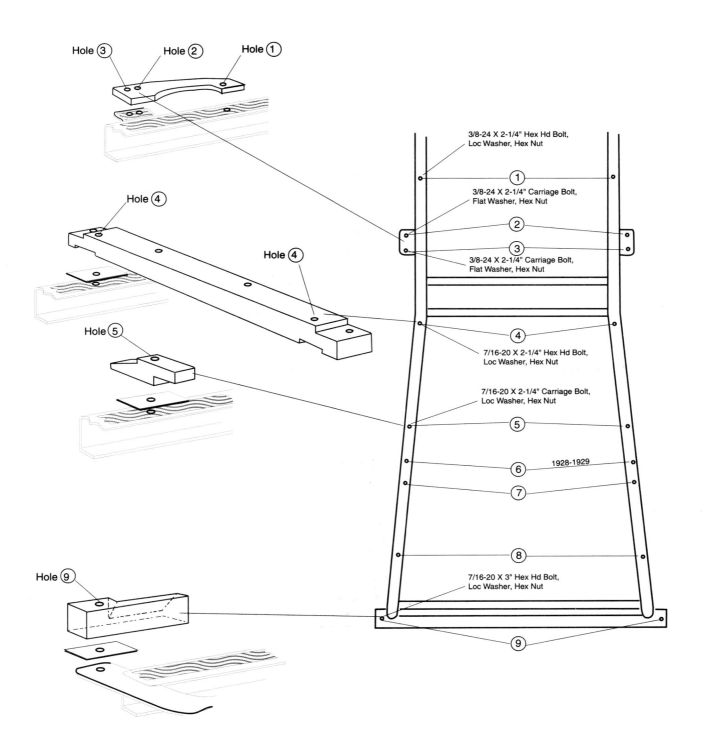

1928/1929 Tudor

Service and Repair

BODY BLOCKS

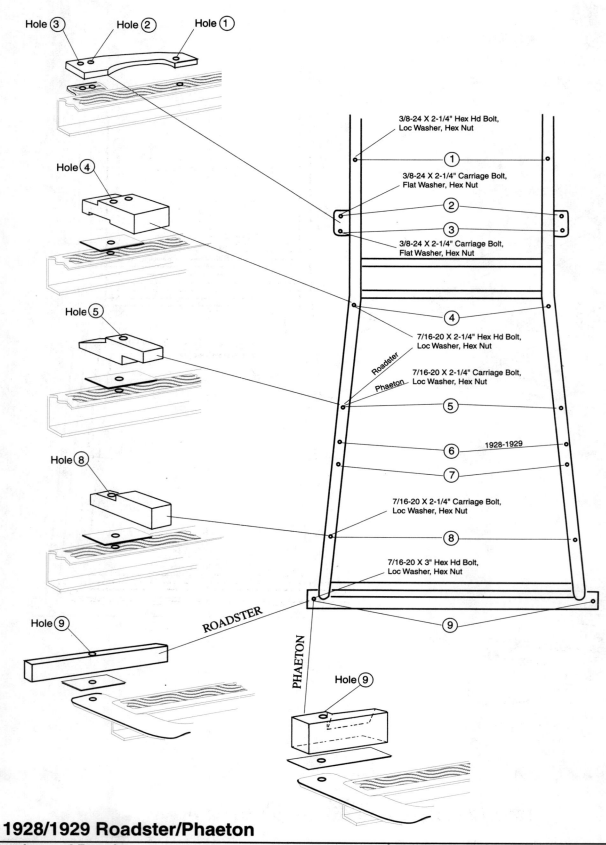

1928/1929 Roadster/Phaeton
Service and Repair
1-28

BODY BLOCKS

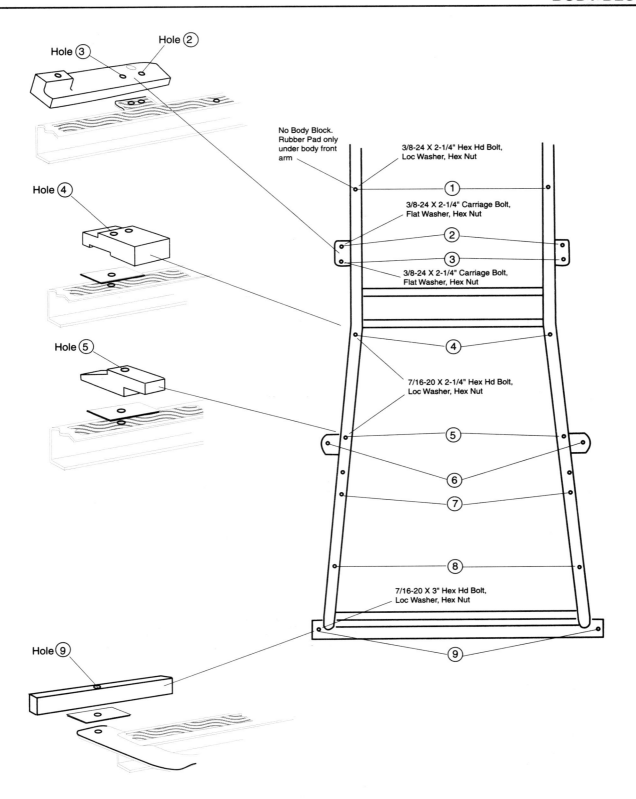

1930/1931 Coupe, Sport Coupe, Bus Coupe

1-29

Service and Repair

BODY BLOCKS

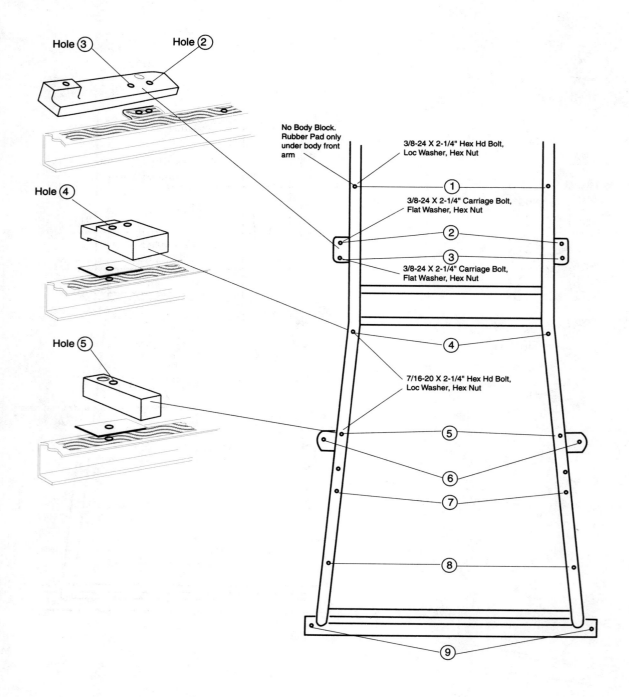

1930/1931 Pickup

BODY BLOCKS

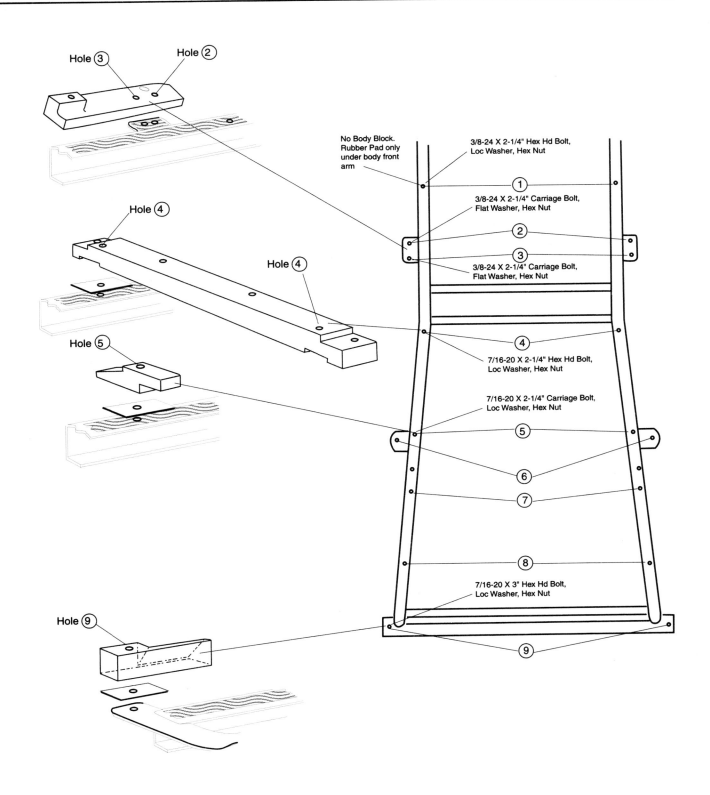

1930/1931 Tudor

Service and Repair

BODY BLOCKS

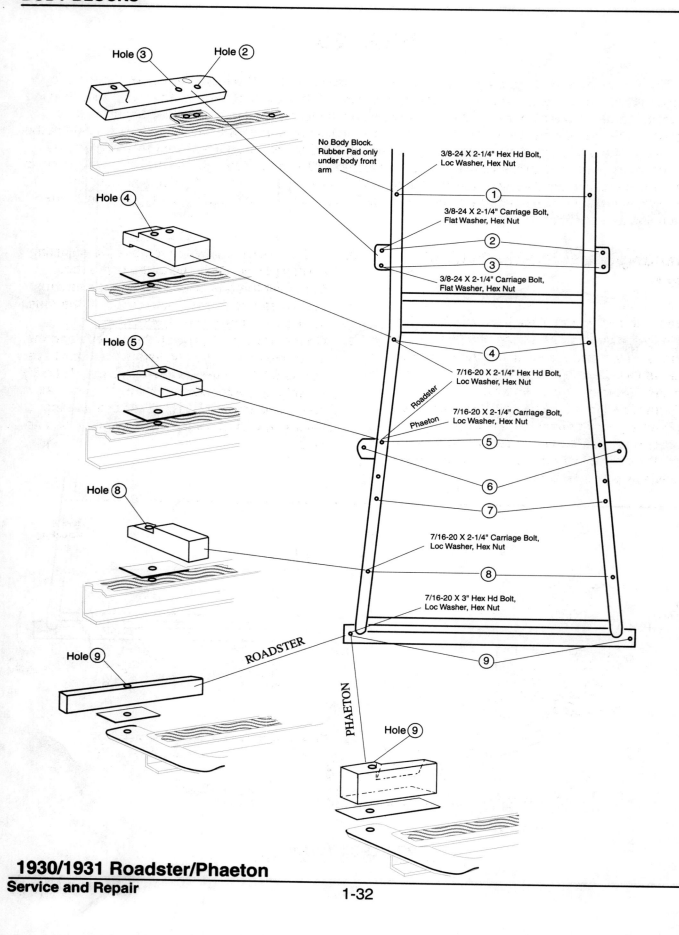

1930/1931 Roadster/Phaeton
Service and Repair

BRAKES

"There must be metal from the pedal to the road." - Henry Ford - The Model A brakes consist of a system of mechanical levers. Henry Ford's statement refers to the fact that there is no room for slack in the "mechanical" brake system on the Model A. Every brake job must start with a complete inspection and correction of the mechanical levers. Wear in the mechanical lever system will cause inefficient action at the brake shoes. The brake shoes themselves represent only 60% of the efficiency of the brake system. Do not expect much from your brakes if the mechanical lever system is overlooked. The braking mechanism in each wheel should be completely disassembled for proper inspection and rework. A close inspection should always be made of each brake drum thickness for safe and reliable usability, as most drums are worn too thin for safe operation.

Inspecting/Repairing Mechanical Levers

1. Jack the car up and place jack stands under the front axle near the spring perches on both sides. Place jack stands under the rear axle about two (2) inches from the wheel on both sides. Remove all four wheels.
2. Remove all four (4) service brake rods, the two (2) emergency brake rods, the brake pedal to cross shaft rod, and emergency handle to cross shaft rod. The eight (8) rods are attached with clevis pins at each end.
3. Loosen locking nuts and remove the adjusting clevis eyes on each end of the brake rods. Clean the threads, check for stripped threads, over-stretched threads, and cracks in the rods. All rods must be perfectly straight.
4. Check clevis pin fit in both the rod eye and the lever eye on all rods and levers. Standard eye size is 5/16". Use oversize clevis pins (11/32") or weld up eyes and re-drill if necessary. All clevis pins must fit both the rod eye and the lever eye with absolute free movement and no slop.

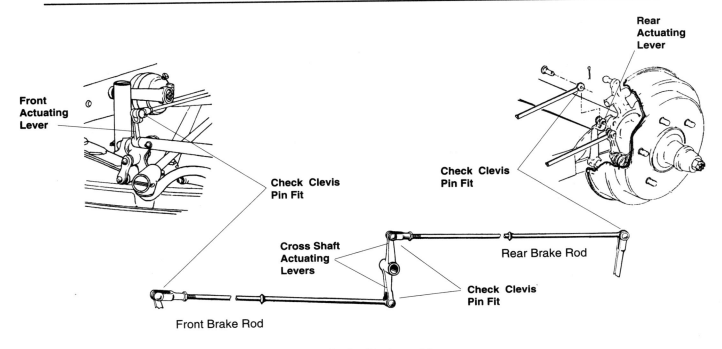

Service Brake Rods and Levers

BRAKES

5. Check clevis pin fit on the brake pedal-to-cross shaft rod, and the clevis pin eyes at the brake pedal arm and cross shaft arm.

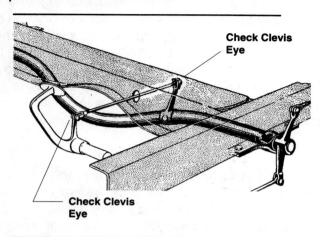

6. Check the service brake cross shaft bushings at both ends of the cross shaft. For complete repairs of the cross shaft, refer to "Section 1 - Cross Shaft." It is important that the ends of the cross shaft and cross shaft bushings maintain a close fit with no slop.

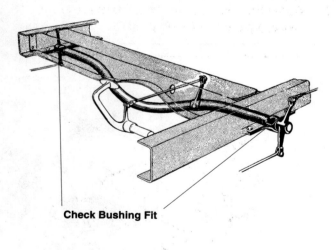

7. Check the front brake actuating arm for side wobble. All side wobble can be removed by installing new bushings in the brake actuating arm.

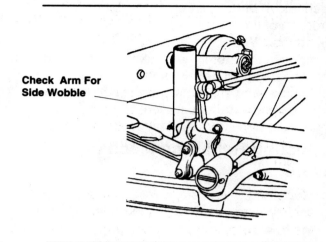

Brake Actuating Arm Repair

1. Remove the spindle locking pin nut [9/16 socket] and lock washer. Reinsert the locking pin nut, screwing in only 1/2 the thread length. The nut is used to knock out the grooved locking pin. With a small hammer, hit the end of the nut to drive out the pin. A drift punch may be needed to completely drive out the locking pin.

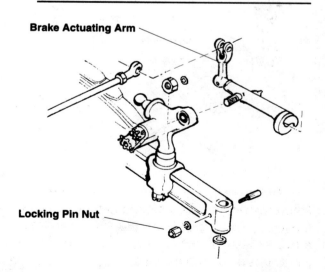

BRAKES

2. Remove the actuating arm nut [9/16 socket] and lock washer from the back side of the spring perch. With large pliers or pipe wrench rotate the king pin cup (top portion of king pin) outward (toward front) enough to release the actuating arm. Remove the actuating arm from the spring perch and king pin cup.

CAUTION
The king pin must be slightly rotated outward to allow the actuating arm bolt to release from the spring perch without damaging the threads on the actuating arm bolt.

3. Grind off the end of the arm rivet and drive it through the arm. The actuating arm shaft can then be pulled out of the housing.
4. Knock out the old bushings and press in new bushings.
5. Insert the shaft back into the housing, place a dust ring on the end of the shaft, and install the clevis arm. Use a 1/4" X 3/8" pin to attach the clevis arm to the shaft. Make sure the small cup on the end of the shaft is pointing down and the clevis arm is in the straight up position before riveting the clevis arm to the shaft.

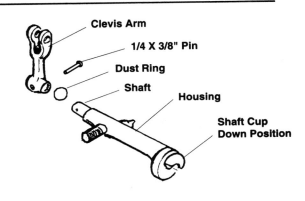

6. Insert the end of the brake actuating arm into the king pin cup and then rotate the actuating arm bolt into the spring perch. Allow the king pin to rotate to prevent damaging the actuating arm bolt threads when inserting into the spring perch. Apply nut and lock washer to the actuating arm bolt. Securely tighten.

7. Rotate the king pin to align the king pin locking pin groove with the hole in the axle.

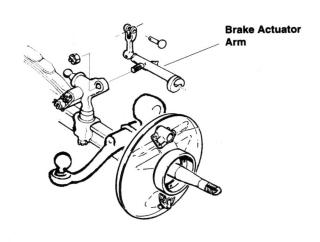

8. Insert the grooved locking pin through the front of the axle to lock the king pin in place. Hammer the locking pin all the way in before applying the lock washer and nut. (This will prevent applying excessive force on the bolt threads.)
9. Apply the locking pin lock washer and nut. Securely tighten [9/16 socket].

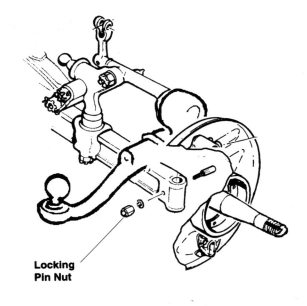

Service and Repair

BRAKES

Disassembling Front Brakes

1. Remove the front wheel axle nut, wheel bearings, and drum.
2. Remove the three brake shoe springs (1 long and 2 short) and remove the brake shoes.

NOTE

The brake shoe can be easily removed by pulling down on the bottom of the shoe, releasing it from the operating wedge. The springs can then be removed by hand and the shoes removed from the backing plate.

3. Remove the operating wedge stud nut [5/8 socket], located on the back side of the backing plate. The operating wedge stud and operating wedge can now be removed. The operating pin will then drop down out of the king pin.

NOTE

Be sure to retain any operating pin shims (pill) that may be in the operating wedge dimple, and the operating pin felt washer.

4. Remove the four (4) backing plate bolts (inside grease baffle) and castle nuts [9/16 socket]. The grease baffle and backing plate can now be removed from the spindle.
5. On the back side of the backing plate, screw the brake adjusting wedge (brake adjuster) all the way in. Then tap the square end, pushing the dust cap off, and removing the adjusting wedge through the front side of the backing plate.

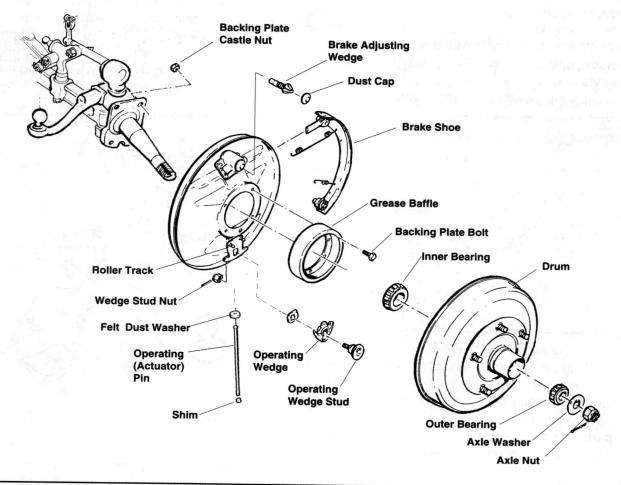

Service and Repair   1-36

BRAKES

6. Re-tap the adjusting wedge threads (5/8-18).
7. Clean all parts thoroughly. (Backing plate, adjusting wedge, wedge stud, operating pin, and shoes.)
8. The roller tracks on the backing plate must be built up (welded) and filed or ground flat. The top edge of the track should be 1-5/16" from the spring stud/rivet. (New replacement roller tracks are available from parts suppliers.)

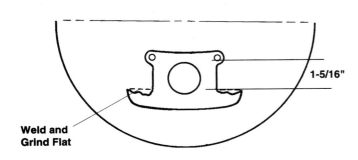

Weld and Grind Flat

9. Remove the roller pins, brake shoe rollers, and brake adjusting shaft from the brake shoes. Inspect the rollers and roller pins for wear. Roller pins and rollers should be replaced if flat spots or wear is detected.

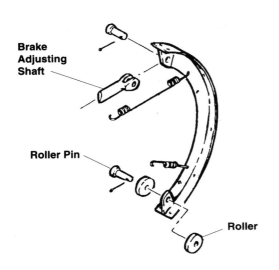

Brake Adjusting Shaft
Roller Pin
Roller

10. The brake adjusting shafts should be checked and reworked as a pair. The length of the shaft is not critical, but both shafts on the shoe <u>must</u> be the same length and have the same bevel. Use a brake adjusting shaft fixture to set the length and bevel of the shafts. See below. Using this fixture, both shafts can be ground to the same length and bevel. Place each shaft in the fixture to check length and bevel.

NOTE

Do not reassemble the pins and rollers on the shoes until the drums have been reworked and the brake shoes arched to the drum diameter.

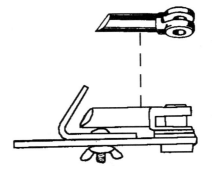

Place Adjusting Shaft on Fixture to Check Length and Bevel

Brake Adjusting Shaft Fixture

Service and Repair

BRAKES

Reworking and Inspecting Drums

1. Inspect (measure) the drums for excessive wear. The original Model A drums are steel and had a wall thickness of .145" thick when new. Most drums have worn too thin (as thin as .070"). The minimum safe wall thickness for steel drums is .120". If the original steel drums are marginally in tolerance and are to be used, it is advisable to install reinforcing bands to the drums. The bands will absorb the heat, keeping the drums from expanding. This will lessen brake fading. The bands are installed by heating them with a torch and pressing them onto the drum.
2. Drums that are out-of-tolerance should be replaced with new cast iron drums made by the Plasmeter Corporation. The cast iron drums are made with a wall thickness of .270". These drums are quality made and offer much more reliability for the Model A braking system. Full instructions are provided with the drums to install your hubs to the new drums.
3. Inspect both inner and outer hub races and bearings. Replace if there are signs of pitting or wear.
4. The drums must always be turned (trued for roundness) on a brake lathe, and the shoes arched to the same diameter as the drum. The drums can be turned and the shoes arched at a qualified brake and clutch shop. Correct brake adjustment can only be obtained when the brake shoes have been arched to the drum diameter. After arching, keep the shoes matched to the correct drum.

NOTE
Both the steel and cast iron drums must always be turned true before assembly. The new cast iron drums will require turning after pressing in hub lug bolts. Any time the drums are turned, the shoes must be arched.

Assembling Front Brakes

1. Install the backing plate and grease baffle to the spindle with four (4) bolts and castle nuts (3/8-24 X 7/8)[9/16 socket]. Apply cotter pins to all four castle nuts.
2. Apply a small amount of grease on both ends of the operating pin and push it up through the king pin. Place a felt dust washer in the backing plate hole for the operating pin.

NOTE
A new operating pin 7-1/4" long should be used.

3. Install the operating wedge stud, operating wedge, and stud washer. Secure on the back side with a castle nut [5/8 socket]. Insert cotter pins.

NOTE
Do not over-tighten the stud castle nut. The operating wedge must move freely on the operating wedge stud.

4. Apply a light coat of grease to the adjusting wedge. Screw the adjusting wedge into the backing plate and tap the adjusting wedge dust cap in place. Back out the adjusting wedge to its stop.
5. Assemble the roller pins, rollers, and adjusting shafts on each brake shoe. The adjusting shafts for each shoe must have been set to equal length and bevel on the brake adjusting shaft fixture.
6. Apply a light coat of grease on the adjusting shafts on both brake shoes. Insert the adjusting shafts into the adjusting wedge bracket and apply the long brake spring between the two brake shoes.

Service and Repair

BRAKES

7. Apply the short brake spring on the shoe and track stud. Pull the bottom of the shoe out and place the shoe roller on the operating wedge with the roller pin head riding on the roller track.

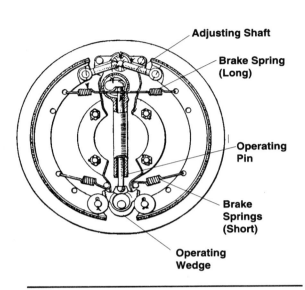

Adjusting Shaft
Brake Spring (Long)
Operating Pin
Brake Springs (Short)
Operating Wedge

8. Check the position of the brake actuating arm. The arm should be tilted forward about 15° from perpendicular. The operating pin length determines the position of the brake actuating arm. Adjust the arm position by grinding the tip of the operating pin or adding a shim (pill) under the operating pin.
9. Pull back on the actuating arm to ensure free movement of the operating wedge and full expansion of the brake shoes. The brake shoes should be fully expanded with the brake actuator arm pulled to the vertical (straight up) position.

Centering Front Brake Shoes

The brake shoes need to be centered to the drum in the vertical plane. This will allow the arch of the shoe to fit the full arch of the drum.

1. Install the front wheel drum with bearings and axle nut. Turn the brake adjusting wedge in until the drum just starts to bind, then remove the drum.
2. Install the front brake centering tool.
3. Check the clearance at the top and bottom of both shoes. Carefully bend the bottom roller tracks up or down to adjust for zero (0) clearance at the top of the shoe and .010"-.015" clearance at the bottom of the shoe. This may require removing and replacing the shoes several times and rechecking before the correct measurement is obtained. After each adjustment of the roller track, repeat steps 1 through 3 until the correct measurement is obtained. When bending the roller tracks, ensure the front face of the roller track remains in a flat plane. The distance from the top of the roller track to the bottom of the spring stud/rivet should be 1-5/16" ± 1/16.
4. Pack both front wheel bearings (inner and outer) with wheel bearing grease. Install bearings and drum on the front axle. Tighten the axle nut until a slight drag is felt and then back off the castle axle nut one castle position, leaving the cotter pin holes aligned to accept the cotter pin. Bend one cotter pin leg up over the castle nut to hold it in position.

Service and Repair

BRAKES

Rear Brake Assembly

1. Remove both rear axle nuts [7/8 wrench] and remove both rear wheel drums.

NOTE
A rear wheel hub puller may be needed to remove the drums from the axle.

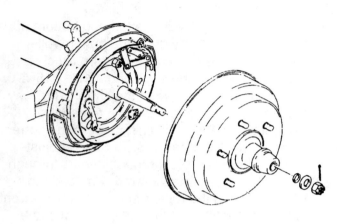

2. Remove both springs from the emergency brake band. Remove the clevis pin at the emergency brake connecting link. The emergency brake band can now be removed.
3. Remove the four (4) castle nuts inside the grease baffle [9/16 socket]. Lift the backing plate with brake shoes off the axle housing and place on work bench for further disassembly.
4. The emergency brake lever must be removed before the emergency brake band carrier plate can be removed.
   a. Remove the brake lever bolt [1/2" wrench] and lock washer. Slide the lever off the toggle shaft. Retain the woodruff key.
   b. Pull the lever toggle shaft out of the backing plate and emergency brake carrier plate.
5. Remove the two (2) front retracting springs (short) and the rear (long) retracting spring and remove the brake shoes.
6. Check the cam shaft bushing inside the backing plate roller track. If the bushing needs replacing, the service brake actuating arm will have to be removed from the end of the cam shaft.
   a. Remove the pin from the service brake actuating arm.
   b. Slide the actuating arm off the cam shaft and remove the cam shaft from the front side of the roller track.
   c. Punch out the two (2) cam shaft bushings inside the roller track and press in new bushings.
7. Check the emergency brake band carrier bushings (for toggle shaft). To replace the toggle shaft bushings, punch out the old bushings and press in new bushings.

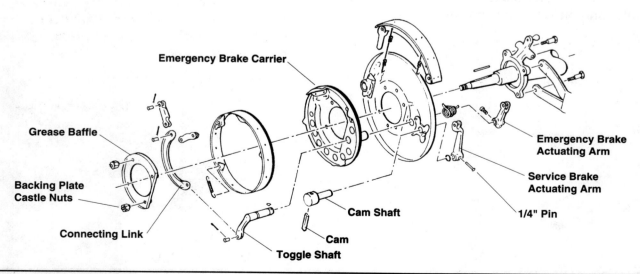

BRAKES

8. On the back side of the backing plate, screw the brake adjusting wedge (brake adjuster) all the way in. Then tap the square end, pushing the dust cap off and removing the adjusting wedge through the front side of the backing plate.
9. Re-tap the adjusting wedge threads (5/8-18).
10. Apply a light coat of grease to the adjusting wedge. Screw the adjusting wedge into the backing plate and tap the adjusting wedge dust cap in place. Back out the adjusting wedge to its stop.

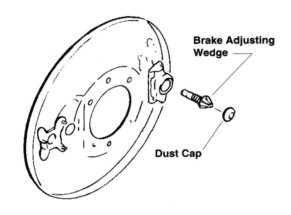

11. Thoroughly clean all rear brake components.
12. The roller tracks on the backing plate must be built up (welded) and filed or ground flat. The top edge of the track should be 1" from the spring stud/rivet.

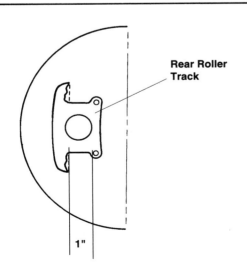

13. Remove the roller pins, brake shoe rollers, and brake adjusting shaft from the brake shoes. Inspect the rollers and roller pins for wear. Roller pins and rollers should be replaced if flat spots or wear is detected.

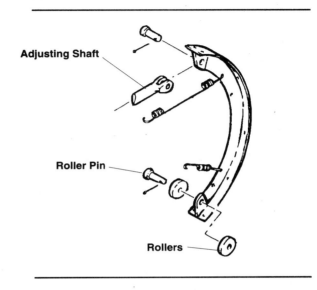

14. The brake adjusting shafts should be checked and reworked as a pair. The length of the shaft is not critical, but both shafts on the shoe <u>must</u> be the same length and have the same bevel. Use a brake adjusting shaft fixture to set the length and bevel of the shafts. Using this fixture, both shafts can be ground to the same length and bevel. Place each shaft in the fixture to check length and bevel.

NOTE
Do not reassemble the pins and rollers on the shoes until the drums have been reworked and the brake shoes arched to the drum diameter.

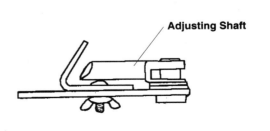

Brake Adjusting Shaft Fixture

Service and Repair

BRAKES

Inspecting and Reworking Rear Drums

1. Inspect (measure) the drums for excessive wear. The original Model A drums are steel and had a wall thickness of .145" thick when new. Most drums have worn too thin (as thin as .070"). The minimum safe wall thickness for steel drums is .120." If the original steel drums are marginally in tolerance and are to be used, it is advisable to install reinforcing bands to the drums. The bands will absorb the heat, keeping the drums from expanding. This will lessen brake fading. The bands are installed by heating them with a torch and pressing them onto the drum.
2. Drums that are out-of-tolerance should be replaced with new cast iron drums made by the Plasmeter Corporation. The cast iron drums are made with a wall thickness of .270". These drums are quality made and offer much more reliability for the Model A braking system. Full instructions are provided with the drums to install your hubs to the new drums.
3. The drums must always be turned (trued for roundness) on a brake lathe, and the shoes arched to the same diameter as the drum. The drums can be turned and the shoes arched at a qualified brake and clutch shop. Correct brake adjustment can only be obtained when the brake shoes have been arched to the drum diameter. After arching, keep the shoes matched to the correct drum.

NOTE
Both the steel and cast iron drums must always be turned true before assembly. The new cast iron drums will require turning after pressing in hub lug bolts. Any time the drums are turned, the shoes must be arched.

4. Inspect the rear wheel bearings and grease seal. Replace the grease seal and bearing if there are signs of pitting or wear.
5. Check the bottom side of the wheel bearing race (on axle housing) for wear (flat spot). The race can be resleeved if badly worn. See "Differential " section for removal of axle housing for repairs.

Assembling Rear Brakes

1. Place the brake cam shaft through the roller track bushings. Place a dust ring over the end of the shaft and attach the service brake actuating arm. Attach the arm to the shaft with a 1/4" pin.

NOTE
The actuating arms are marked **LH** (left side) and **RH** (right side).

Emergency Brake Arms - Left / Right

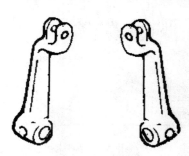

Service Brake Arms - Left / Right

2. Slide the cam into the cam shaft slot. Make sure the cam slides freely in the cam shaft.
3. Assemble the roller pins, rollers, and adjusting shafts on each brake shoe. The adjusting shafts for each shoe must have been set to equal length and bevel on the brake adjusting shaft fixture.
4. Apply a light coat of grease on the adjusting shafts on both brake shoes. Insert the adjusting shafts into the adjusting wedge bracket on the backing plate and apply the long brake spring between the brake shoes.

Service and Repair

BRAKES

5. Apply the short brake spring on the shoe and track stud. Pull the bottom of the shoe out and place the shoe roller on the operating cam with the roller pin head riding on the roller track. Attach the second brake shoe using the same process.

6. Place the emergency band carrier plate on the backing plate. (There is a left hand and right hand carrier plate.) Place the toggle shaft through the carrier plate bushings and slide the emergency brake retracting spring over the end of the shaft. Insert a No. 5 woodruff key on the toggle shaft and slide on the actuating arm (left or right hand). Insert bolt (5/16-24 X 1-1/8) and lock washer and firmly tighten.

7. Place the backing plate assembly (with emergency brake carrier plate and grease baffle) on the rear axle housing and bolt in place with four (4) special shouldered backing plate bolts and castle nuts (7/16-20)[9/16 socket for castle nut, 3/4 wrench for bolt head]. Insert cotter pins in all four castle nuts. Before attaching emergency brake band, adjust centering of brake shoes.

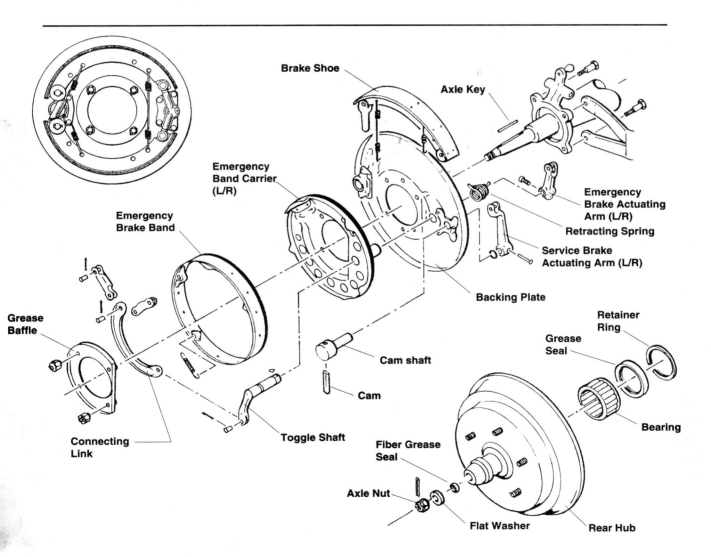

Service and Repair

BRAKES

Centering Rear Brake Shoes

The rear brake shoes need to be centered to the drum in the horizontal plane. This will allow the arch of the shoe to fit the full arch of the drum.

1. Install the rear wheel drum with bearing and axle nut. Turn the brake adjusting wedge in until the drum just starts to bind, then remove the drum.
2. Install a rear brake centering tool.
3. Check the clearance at the rear and front of both shoes. Carefully bend the roller tracks forward or back to adjust for zero (0) clearance at the rear of the shoe and .010"-.015" clearance at the front of the shoe. (The front of the shoe is the end with rollers and operating cam.) This may require removing and replacing the shoes several times and rechecking before correct measurement is obtained. After each adjustment of the roller track, repeat steps 1 through 3 until correct measurement is obtained. When bending the roller tracks, ensure the front face of the roller track remains in a flat plane. The distance from the top of the roller track to the bottom of the spring stud/rivet should be 1"±1/32".
4. Pull forward on the brake actuating arm to check for smooth, nonbinding action and complete expansion of the brake shoes.

Installing Emergency Brake Band

1. Connect the connecting link and actuating links to the emergency brake band as shown below.

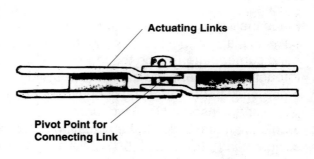

2. Place the emergency brake band over the carrier plate and attach with two (2) springs.
3. Connect the connecting link to the toggle arm with a clevis pin. Double check to see that cotter pins have been installed in all clevis pins.
4. Pull forward on the emergency brake actuating arm and check for smooth, nonbinding action and good expansion of the emergency brake band.
5. Install axle key (must be tight fit) and rear drum. Place an axle seal washer and flat washer over the axle and install the axle (castle) nut. Torque the axle nut to 125 ft/lbs. Apply the cotter pin.

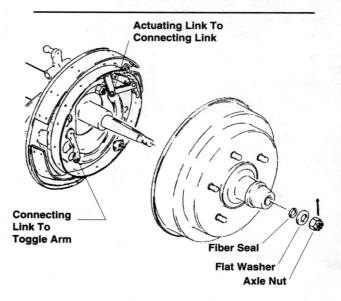

BRAKES

Installing Brake Rods

1. Set all four (4) service brake rods to a length of 51-7/16" to 51-1/2" from eye to eye centers.
2. Check all clevis eyes on the rod ends for no-slop fit, using 5/16" clevis pin or 11/32" (oversize) clevis pin.
3. The rear service brake rods are installed with the adjustable clevis eye attached to the cross shaft arm.
4. The front service brake rods are installed with the adjustable clevis eye attached to the front actuator arm.
5. The emergency brake rods are installed with the adjustable clevis eyes attached to the emergency cross shaft arm.
6. Install the rod connecting the brake pedal to the cross shaft. Check the clevis eyes for correct fit.
7. Install the rod connecting the emergency brake handle to the cross shaft. Check clevis eyes for correct fit.
8. Make sure the brake antirattlers are properly installed. The antirattlers must be applying pressure on the brake rod, away from the cross shaft. The antirattler is necessary to fully retract the brake rods. Weak or broken antirattlers should be replaced.
9. Adjust the brakes and rods in accordance with Section II- Service Adjustments.

   NOTE : Do not set emergency brake when the drums are hot. This can push the drums out of round.

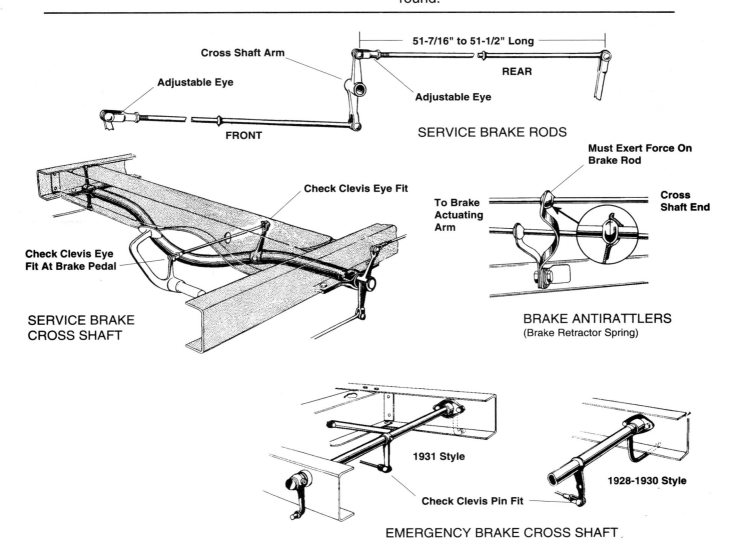

Service and Repair

CAM SHAFT

The cam shaft can be removed from the engine without removing the engine from the car. If removing the cam shaft is part of an engine overhaul, refer to "Section I, Engine Overhaul", for complete instructions. This step-by-step procedure explains how to remove and replace the camshaft without removing the engine, usually for the purpose of replacing the camshaft because of defective lobes or the need for a cam shaft with higher lift lobes. The cam shaft is removed through the front timing gear cover. This procedure describes removing the radiator and other parts necessary to remove and replace the cam shaft through the front timing gear cover.

Removing Cam Shaft

1. Remove front floor mat (or carpet) and shift lever plate.
2. Remove the bottom section of the front floor board [6 flathead screws] for access to the battery terminals.
3. Remove the battery ground strap from the (+) battery post.

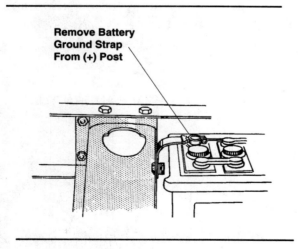

4. Drain radiator water. Drain petcock is located on bottom of the water return pipe, under the generator.

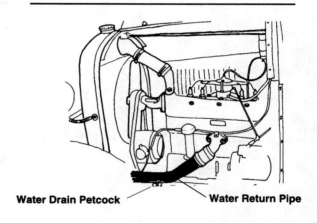

5. Move to the front of the car and remove the horn cover by removing the single round head screw on the back cover [10-32 x 3/4 screw]. Remove the two horn wires from the terminal under the horn motor (pull out type).
6. Remove the headlight conduit connectors (push and twist counterclockwise to release).

CAM SHAFT

NOTE

Some headlight wiring may have been modified by eliminating the connector plug from inside the conduit socket. The wires would then be routed directly from the conduit into the headlight bucket and attached to the bulb sockets with wire nuts. The wires would have to be disconnected from behind the headlight reflector. To access the headlight bucket, release the front lens clip, pull the clip down (spring loaded latch) and lift up on the lens rim to remove. Remove the center bulb and lift the reflector out of headlight bucket.

7. Pull the headlight wires back through the conduit to the inside of the radiator shell, leaving the metal conduit and grommets attached to the radiator shell. Do the same for both headlight harness wires and the horn harness wires.

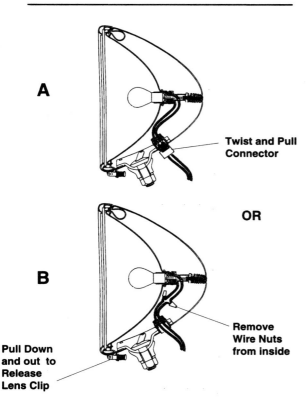

A — Twist and Pull Connector

OR

B — Remove Wire Nuts from inside

Pull Down and out to Release Lens Clip

8. Remove the Radiator cap.

9. Under the hood, remove the two screws and nuts from the hood rear hold down bracket.

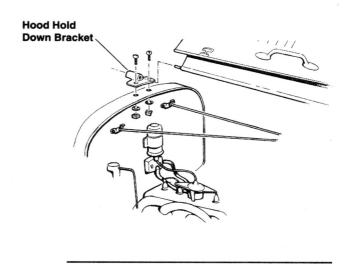

Hood Hold Down Bracket

10. Remove the hood and place it in a safe location on cardboard or carpet to prevent chipping the paint. Do not lay the hood down on the side louver panels. It's best to stand the hood up on the back edge to prevent warping or creasing the top panels.

11. Loosen the two (2) nuts [1/2 inch wrench] on the front end of the two radiator support rods. Pull the rods up out of the radiator bracket.

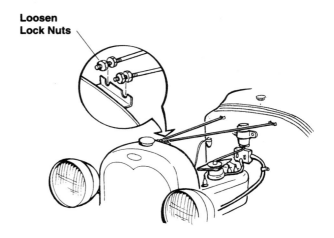

Loosen Lock Nuts

Service and Repair

CAM SHAFT

12. Loosen the hose clamp on the top radiator hose. Pull the radiator forward enough to pull the radiator neck out of the hose.
13. To remove the radiator, first remove the radiator shell by removing the two (2) screws and nuts on each side of the radiator, attaching the shell to the radiator brackets. Then remove the cotter pin from the two radiator mounting bolts. Using a 3/8 ratchet drive with a 6-inch extension and 9/16 inch deep socket, reach under the front cross member and place the 9/16 inch socket on the head of the radiator mounting bolt. Hold the nut on top with a 9/16 inch box wrench and ratchet the bolt from the bottom. Remove the bolt, spring, and nut from each side of the radiator.

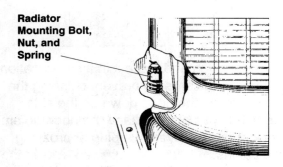

Radiator Mounting Bolt, Nut, and Spring

14. Remove and retain the rubber pads under the radiator mounting brackets (both sides). Move the radiator to one side to clear the fender and lift the radiator and shell off the frame. On the 28 models, a fan shroud may be attached to the radiator. This can be left in place when removing the radiator.
15. Turn OFF the fuel shut-off valve located under the gas tank (or on the firewall under the hood on late 31 model year).
16. Remove the throttle linkage to the carburetor, choke rod, and spring by pushing the sleeve up against the spring, and disconnecting the rod from the carburetor.

17. Remove the carburetor gas line [1/2 or 9/16 open end wrench]. Remove the carburetor [two bolts, 1/2 inch wrench].
18. Disconnect the exhaust pipe clamp from the manifold (two (2) bolts and nuts)[9/16 socket]. Remove the intake and exhaust manifold assembly from the engine block (four (4) manifold nuts and washers) [11/16 socket].

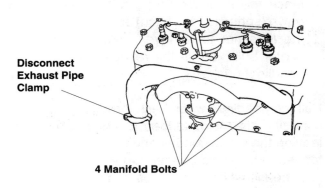

Disconnect Exhaust Pipe Clamp

4 Manifold Bolts

19. Remove the two (2) wires connected to the cutout relay on the generator.
20. Loosen the generator mounting bolt nut [3/4 socket] and push the generator toward the engine to remove the fan belt. Remove the generator mounting bolt and remove the generator.

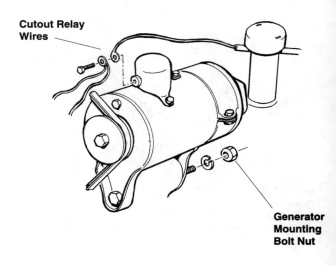

Cutout Relay Wires

Generator Mounting Bolt Nut

Service and Repair

CAM SHAFT

21. Remove the two (2) bolts [1/2 socket] and brass washers attaching the oil return pipe.
22. Remove the ten (10) bolts [1/2 inch socket] and lock washers from around the valve cover and remove the cover plate. When removing the valve cover, there may be a small amount of oil left in the valve chamber. A shop towel may be needed for clean up when removing the cover.

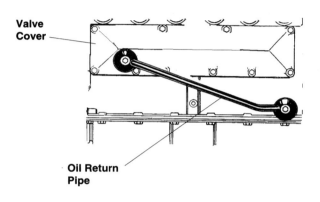

23. Place a floor jack under the engine pan for support. Remove the front two (2) motor mount bolts (3/4 wrench) and lock washers.

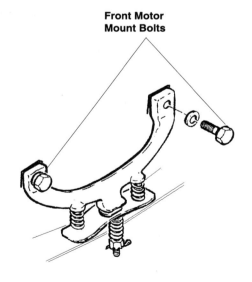

24. Remove the front four (4) pan bolts and the seven (7) bolts [9/16 socket] and lock washers from the front timing gear cover and remove the cover. The front timing gear cover is under slight spring tension. After removing the cover, remove the spring plunger and spring recessed in the back side of the cover.
25. Remove the two (2) bolts [5/8 socket] and lock washers from the side timing gear cover and remove the side cover.

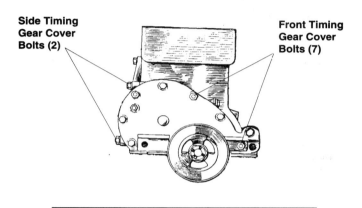

26. Move to the right side of the engine and loosen the distributor shaft locking nut [9/16 box wrench]. Back out the locking screw and lift the distributor and shaft from the block. Unscrew the distributor cable from the distributor body.

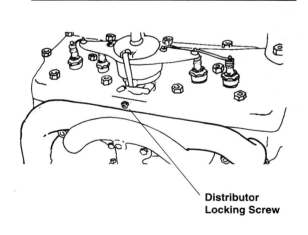

Service and Repair

CAM SHAFT

27. Move to the valve chamber side of the engine and remove the oil pump/distributor drive gear spring. The oil pump/distributor drive gear spring can be removed by pulling down on the spring about 1/2 inch to remove it from the top of the chamber, then lifting it off the drive gear. The drive gear can now be lifted out of the valve chamber.

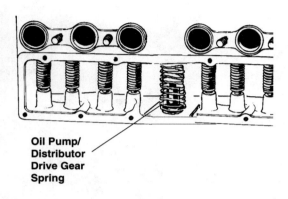

Oil Pump/Distributor Drive Gear Spring

28. Remove all eight (8) valve springs using a valve spring compressor to enable removal of the valve spring keepers from around the bottom mushroom of the valve.

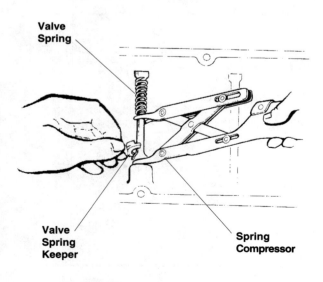

Valve Spring

Valve Spring Keeper

Spring Compressor

29. After all valve springs have been removed, pull all valve lifters up and place a spring loaded clothes pin around the shank of the valve lifters to hold them in the full up position.

30. Before removing the cam shaft and timing gear, rock the cam timing gear to check the amount of back lash between the crank and timing gears (.003-.005"). If there is more than .010" back lash between the two gears, replace the cam timing gear or preferably, both gears. Remove the crank pulley nut [1-3/8 socket], and pull the pulley off the end of the crank shaft. The front of the engine must be raised about 1" to allow removal of the crank gear. If the crank gear is to be replaced, use a gear puller to remove the keyed crank gear from the crank shaft.

NOTE

The crank pulley nut (ratchet) has been found in several sizes. Model A standard size is 1-3/8". Other sizes that exist are 1-1/8, 1-1/4, and 1-5/16, and most likely aftermarket.

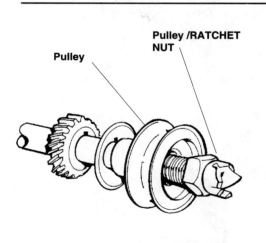

Pulley

Pulley /RATCHET NUT

31. The cam shaft with timing gear can now be pulled straight out of the block.

CAM SHAFT

Installing Cam Shaft

1. Place the timing gear on the end of the cam shaft and push the gear on the two aligning pins. Apply and tighten the timing gear nut. It may be easier to fully tighten the timing gear nut after the cam shaft has been installed in the engine.

CAUTION
The two timing gear alignment pin holes are slightly off center. The timing gear will only align with the two pins one way. If the gear does not align precisely with the pins, rotate the gear 180° and reinsert. Forcing could cause damage.

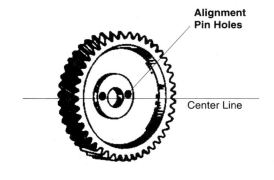

2. Coat the cam shaft lobes and journals with Lubriplate. Insert the cam shaft through the front end of the block, carefully aligning the timing gear mark with the crank gear mark.

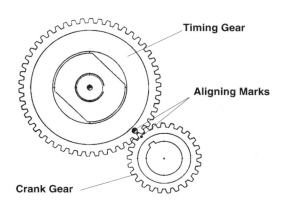

3. Insert the asbestos rope gasket (previously soaked in oil) into the timing gear cover.

4. Insert the thrust spring into the camshaft thrust plunger and place into the timing gear cover recess.

NOTE
Check the thrust spring for correct compression tension of 35 to 38 lbs.

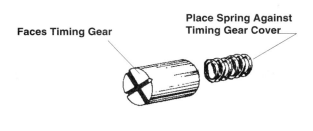

Service and Repair

CAM SHAFT

5. Apply a thin coat of Permatex gasket sealer to the timing gear cover gasket and apply the gasket to the timing gear cover.
6. Place the pulley on the end of the crank shaft and tighten the ratchet nut [1 3/8" socket] on the end of the shaft.

NOTE

Before installing the ratchet nut, make sure the end of the pulley extends slightly beyond the end of the crank shaft. If the crank shaft extends beyond the end of the pulley by the slightest amount, the ratchet nut cannot be tightened against the pulley. The ratchet nut must screw up tight against the pulley. Add another oil slinger washer if necessary to move the pully forward.

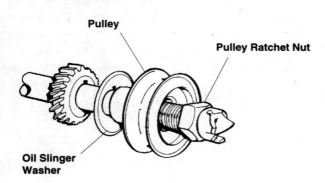

7. Install the side timing gear cover using two (2) 7/16 hex dome head bolts [5/8 socket]. The top bolt is 1-3/8" long and the bottom bolt is 2-1/8" long.
8. Bolt the front timing gear cover in place with seven (7) 3/8-16 X 1-1/8" dome head bolts [9/16 socket] and lock washers.
9. Install the front four (4) pan bolts (5/16-18 X 3/4 Hex Hd bolts)[1/2 socket].
10. Insert the front two (2) motor mount bolts (1/2-13 X 1 3/8") and lock washers [3/4 socket].
11. Remove the floor jack from under the engine pan.

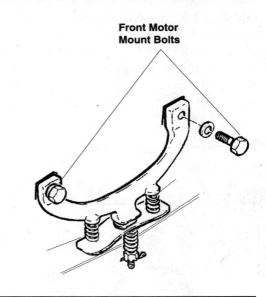

12. Remove the clothes pins from all the valve lifters, allowing them to sit on the cam lobes.
13. Rotate the crank until the valve lifters are seated all the way down. This will make it easier installing the valve spring and keeper on the valve. Use a valve spring compressor to compress the valve spring and install the spring keeper over the valve stem mushroom.

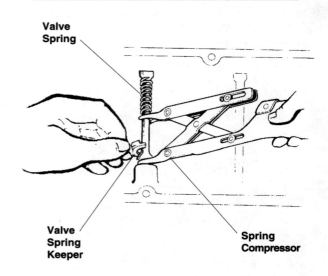

CAM SHAFT

14. The valves will need readjustment after installing a new cam shaft. Refer to Section II, Service Adjustments for valve adjustment procedure.
15. After the valves have been adjusted, insert the distributor /oil pump drive gear into the valve chamber hole. Lightly lubricate before installing. (Replace drive gear if badly worn.) Place the retainer spring on top of the drive gear and then push the spring in against the top of the valve chamber.

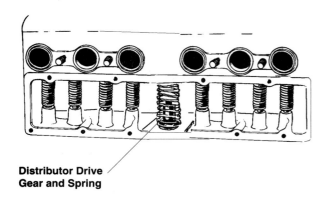

Distributor Drive Gear and Spring

16. Apply a thin coat of Permatex gasket sealer on the new valve cover gasket. Install the valve cover using ten (10) 5/16 X 3/4 hex bolts [1/2 socket] and lock washers. Torque to 20 ft. lbs.
17. Install a cork ring gasket in each end of the oil return pipe and install the pipe using two (2) 5/16 X 1-3/8 bolts [1/2 socket] and two flat copper washers.

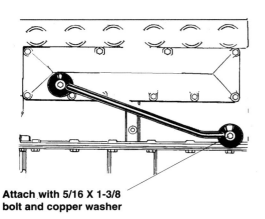

Attach with 5/16 X 1-3/8 bolt and copper washer

18. Insert the distributor shaft into the head, aligning the bottom slot of the shaft with the tab on the cam gear shaft. The slot and tab are offset.

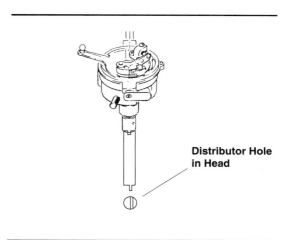

Distributor Hole in Head

19. Screw the ignition cable into the distributor body and then position the distributor in place, seating the distributor locking pin in the hole on the cylinder head. The distributor base should sit flat against the top surface of the cylinder head. Rotate the distributor shaft with the rotor to correctly align the shaft with the slot, allowing the distributor body to fully seat against the block.

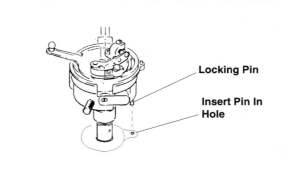

Locking Pin

Insert Pin In Hole

1-53 Service and Repair

CAM SHAFT

20. Insert the distributor locking screw and locking nut. Tighten the locking screw until it seats firmly against the distributor shaft. Tighten the locking nut [9/16 wrench].

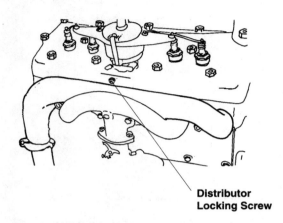

Distributor Locking Screw

21. Install the manifold using two copper/asbestos manifold gaskets.

NOTE

Do not install the gland rings in the exhaust ports unless the port holes have been checked for true alignment with the exhaust ports in the block. Through years of heat and warping, most manifolds have dropped at the rear port and will not match the gland ring insert. The copper clad gaskets will seal without the use of the gland rings. The manifold should be surfaced (milled) before installing.

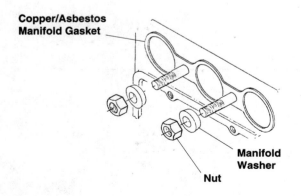

Copper/Asbestos Manifold Gasket
Manifold Washer
Nut

22. Install the special manifold washers and tighten the four (4) manifold nuts (7/16-20) [11/16 socket].

23. Connect the exhaust pipe to the manifold with clamp and two (2) bolts and nuts [9/16 socket].

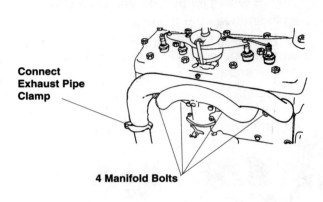

Connect Exhaust Pipe Clamp
4 Manifold Bolts

24. Install the generator using a special shoulder hinge bolt (1/2-20 X 2-7/8"), lock washer, and nut [3/4 socket]. Do not tighten until the fan belt has been installed. Install the fan belt (Dayco No. 22425) and adjust for 1/2" movement. (See Section II, Service Adjustments.)

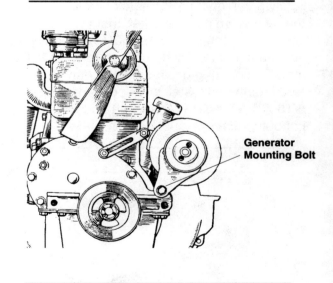

Generator Mounting Bolt

25. From the right side of the engine, install the carburetor with two (2) bolts and lock washers (5/16-18 X 3/4) [1/2" wrench]. Install the throttle linkage to carburetor, choke rod, and spring by pushing the sleeve up against teh spring, and connecting the choke rod to the carburetor. Connect the carburetor gas line [1/2 or 9/16 open end wrench].
26. Set the radiator on the front cross member. Place a rubber pad under both radiator mounting brackets (28/29 use 1/8" pad, 30/31 use 1/16" pad). A piece of old inner tube works fine. Install the radiator mounting bolts, nuts and spring assembly as shown below. Tighten the bolts only enough to install cotter pins in the mounting bolts.

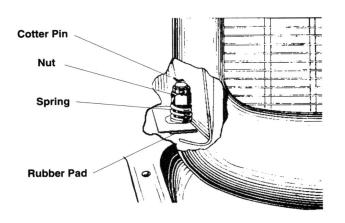

27. Secure the water return pipe hoses to the radiator lower pipe and the water inlet neck on the engine block. Securely tighten all four (4) hose clamps.

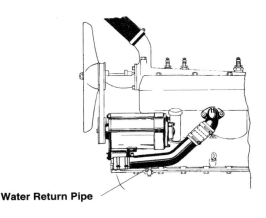

28. Slip the top radiator neck into the top hose and install the hose clamps. Do not tighten these hose clamps until the radiator support rods have been installed and the hood installed and adjusted.
29. Attach the ends of the support rods into the radiator bracket with a nut and lock washer on each side of the bracket [1/2" wrench].

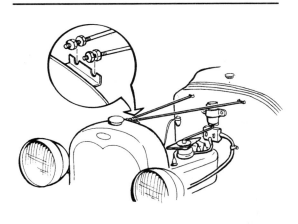

30. If the radiator shell was removed from the radiator, reinstall it at this time, attaching it with four (4) pan head screws (12-24 X 19/32") and square nuts.
31. Set the hood in place and attach it with two (2) screws, lock washers, and nuts [12-24 X 5/8" round head] on the rear hold down bracket.

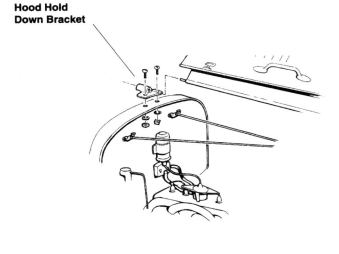

CAM SHAFT

32. After the hood has been installed and properly aligned, securely tighten both front radiator support rod nuts. Securely tighten the two (2) radiator hose clamps on the upper radiator hose (radiator to goose neck). Check all four (4) hose clamps on the water return pipe hoses. Ensure all hose clamps are tight.
33. Route the wiring harness through the radiator shell to the head lights and horn. Connect the horn wires.
34. Connect the headlight conduit connectors (push and twist clockwise to connect).

NOTE

Some headlight wiring may have been modified by eliminating the connector plug from inside the conduit socket. The wires would then be routed directly from the conduit into the headlight bucket and attached to the bulb sockets with wire nuts. The wires would have to be connected from behind the headlight reflector. To access the headlight bucket, release the front lens clip (spring loaded latch) and lift up on the lens rim to remove it. Remove the center bulb and lift the reflector out of the headlight bucket.

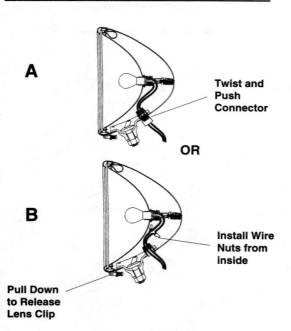

35. Attach three (3) harness wires to the generator cutout terminal (terminal box wire, horn and headlight harness wire).

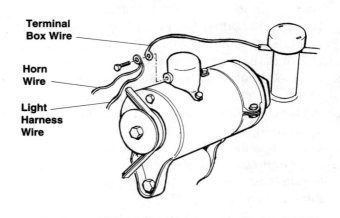

36. Connect the battery ground strap to the (+) battery post.

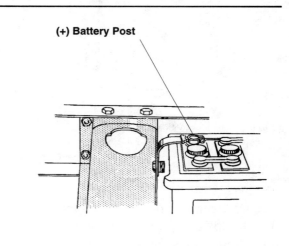

37. Install the front floor board and floor mat. Secure the floor board with six (6) flat head screws [12-24 X 1-1/8"] and cup washers.
38. From under the hood, set the distributor timing in accordance with Timing Procedure, Section II, Service Adjustments.
39. Pour three (3) gallons of water into the radiator. Check the oil dip stick. Add only enough oil to bring the oil level up to the "F" on the dip stick.

Service and Repair

CARBURETOR REPAIRS

The Model A carburetor, most commonly known as the "Zenith" carburetor, was made by three different manufactures. Zenith-1 made by Zenith, Zenith-2 made by Holly, and Zenith-3 made by Ford. For the purpose of maintenance and repair, all three carburetors were basically the same, although at least eleven (11) changes were made during the four years of production. The following procedures describe general maintenance and repair, since all parts are interchangeable and the basic design remained the same.

Most carburetor problems are related to either dirt or rust in the jets and passageways, incorrect float level (relates to fuel level in the jets), or leaking gaskets.

Removing Carburetor

1. Turn OFF the fuel shut-off valve located under the gas tank (or on the firewall under the hood on late 31 model year).

2. Raise the hood on the right side. Remove the throttle linkage to the carburetor, choke rod, and choke spring by pushing the sleeve up against the spring, and disconnecting the rod from the carburetor.

3. Remove the carburetor gas line [1/2 or 9/16 open end wrench]. Remove the carburetor [two bolts, 1/2 inch wrench].

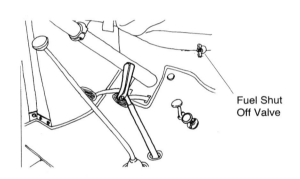

Fuel Shut Off Valve

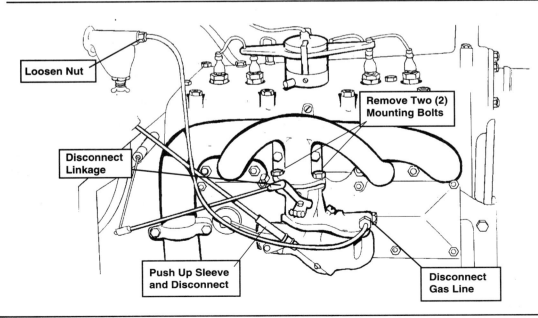

CARBURETOR

Disassembly

1. The upper and lower bodies must first be separated. There are two bolts on the bottom of the carburetor. Remove the steel body bolt [9/16 wrench] toward the front to separate the upper and lower body.

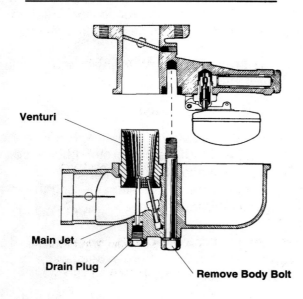

2. Lift the venturi out of the lower body. Heat may be needed to remove the venturi.
3. Unscrew the drain plug and screw out the main jet.
4. Remove the nut on the choke shaft and remove the choke lever and driver.
5. On the lower body, screw out the gas adjusting needle.

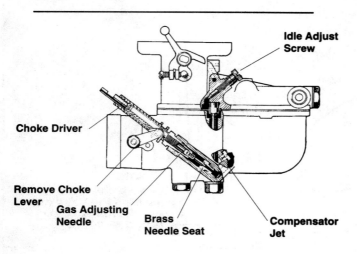

6. Screw out the fuel adjusting needle housing [7/16 or 13/32 socket]. Some carburetors had a screw in brass needle seat for the gas adjust needle. Remove with narrow blade screwdriver.
7. Use a 5/16" hollow nut driver to remove the cap jet inside the throat of the carburetor.
8. Remove the compensator jet (inside the fuel bowl) with a screwdriver.
9. Carefully screw out the secondary well.

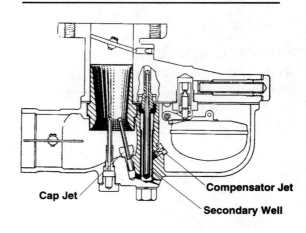

10. On the upper body, screw out the idle adjust screw.
11. Remove the float hinge pin to remove the float.
12. Unscrew the float valve [5/8 wrench].
13. Unscrew the idle jet [9/32 wrench].
14. Unscrew the front strainer bolt [5/8 wrench].
15. Thoroughly rinse the upper and lower body and all parts with a strong solvent (not gasoline). Blow dry air through all passages. Make sure all old gaskets have been removed.

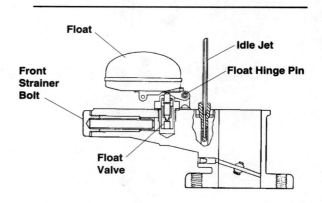

CARBURETOR

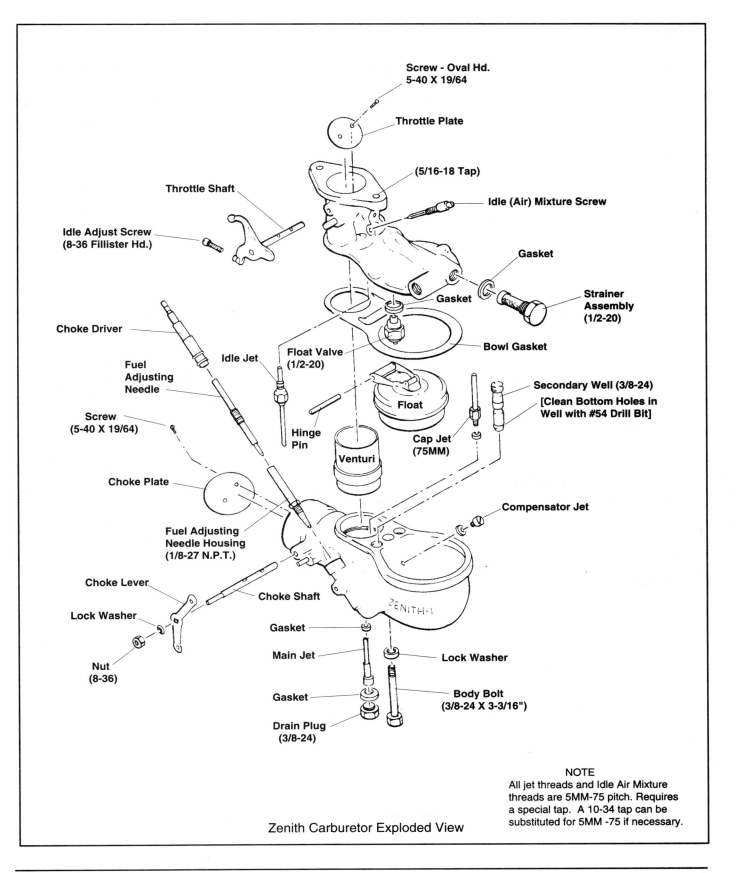

Zenith Carburetor Exploded View

CARBURETOR

Inspection and Repair

1. Re-tap all threads for jets and bolts. See exploded view for tap sizes.
2. Check the fuel inlet seat for smooth rust free surface. This must be a non-pitted surface to provide a proper seal with gas line ferrule. A pitted seat can be cleaned with a 7/16" ball-ended grinding stone in a drill motor. Only a light touch is needed as cast iron grinds easily.
3. Check the throttle shaft bushing fit. A loose fit is due to a worn bushing or a worn throttle shaft. A loose fit will cause air leakage, resulting in poor idle. An oversized shaft can be installed or new bushings installed. To install a new bushing, drill out the old shaft bushing to 5/16" and install 5/16" O.D. thin wall brass tubing (can be obtained from hobby shop).

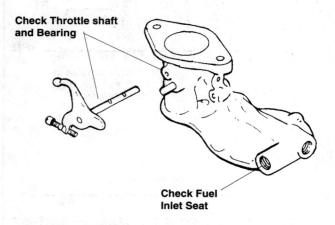

Check Throttle shaft and Bearing

Check Fuel Inlet Seat

4. Check for a good seat for the gas adjusting needle. If the seat is cast into the body, pitting is common. The gas adjusting needle must be smooth and sharply pointed on the end. The shank end of the needle should be flush with the end of the needle housing when the needle is fully seated.

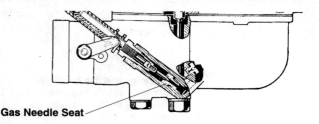

Gas Needle Seat

5. Check for stripped body bolt threads in the upper body. If the threads are stripped, buy a longer bolt and tap the threads deeper into the body.

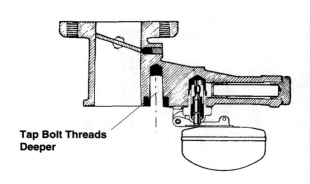

Tap Bolt Threads Deeper

6. If passages are badly plugged, drill out the brass clean out plugs with a 1/8" drill bit and clean passages with a small drill bit (#25) or wire. Tap in new brass plugs (1/8").
7. Zenith built carburetors had a cap pressed in the casting for the end of the throttle shaft. Recap to prevent air leak and poor idle.
8. When threads for bolts on the mounting flange are stripped, insert a helicoil repair kit.

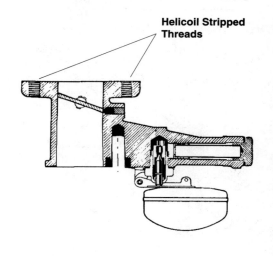

Helicoil Stripped Threads

Paint body castings with Gloss Black No. 903, Orr-Lac label, made by Spray Products Corp, Fresno, Calif.

Service and Repair

CARBURETOR

9. When threads for the drain plug are stripped, file down the casting at the gasket seat area just enough to allow the drain plug to reach good threads.

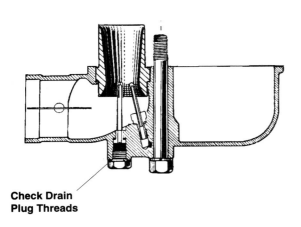

Check Drain Plug Threads

10. A badly varnished and dirty body can be soaked in a container of undiluted household ammonia. Do not let soak for more than two or three days. The brass plugs and other brass parts may start to dissolve after prolonged soaking in ammonia. Rinse in hot water and dry.

11. Check all jets for correct length and orifice size. Do not use jets of incorrect length or orifice size.

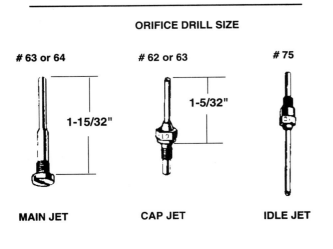

ORIFICE DRILL SIZE

63 or 64 — MAIN JET — 1-15/32"
62 or 63 — CAP JET — 1-5/32"
75 — IDLE JET
65 — COMPENSATOR JET

Assembling Carburetor

Assembling the carburetor components is a simple task. Precise placement of the main jet and cap jet relative to the venturi throat and correct float level adjustment are important for efficient carburetor operation.

The nozzle tips of the main jet and cap jet should be located at the narrowest opening of the venturi. This can be adjusted with gasket thickness of the jets.

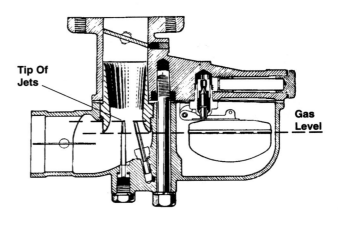

Tip Of Jets — **Gas Level**

When the gas level in the gas bowl is correct, the fuel level inside the main jet and cap jet should be just below the nozzle tips. When the fuel level is too high, the fuel mixture will run too rich, and gas will probably leak out the top of the jets when the motor is not running. When the fuel level is too low, the fuel mixture will run too lean, causing overheating and popping from the carburetor.

Incorrect positioning of the jets in the venturi, incorrect jet nozzle tip size, and incorrect float level will upset the gas-air ratio in the carburetor, resulting in inefficient and poor operation.

Service and Repair

CARBURETOR

Assembly - Lower Body

Before starting assembly, check all jets for correct length and orifice size.

1. Screw in the compensator jet with washer.
2. Screw in the fuel adjust needle seat (if required).
3. Screw in the main jet with thin gasket.
4. Screw in teh cap jet with gasket.
5. Set the venturi in place and check the nozzle tip placement of the main jet and cap jet. Adjust nozzle tip placement with different thickness gaskets for the jets.

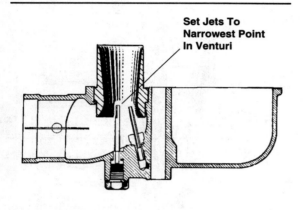

Set Jets To Narrowest Point In Venturi

6. After correct placement of main and cap jets, screw in the drain plug with gasket.
7. Screw in the secondary well.
8. Assemble the choke shaft and choke plate if previously removed.
9. Screw in the fuel adjusting needle housing [7/16 or 13/32 thin wall deep socket].

NOTE

Remove and discard the end ring clip on the tip of the housing before installing a new housing.

10. Screw in the fuel adjusting needle. The shank end of the adjusting needle should be flush with the end of the needle housing when the needle is fully seated. Do not over-tighten the adjusting needle into the seat.
11. Install the choke driver. Place the choke lever on the shaft and attach with an 8-36 nut and lock washer.
12. Place the bowl gasket over the venturi and on top of the lower bowl.

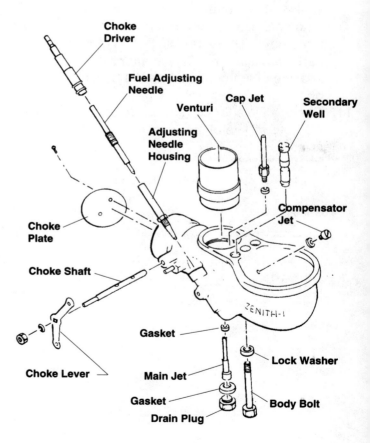

Service and Repair

CARBURETOR

Assembly - Upper Body

1. Install the throttle shaft and throttle plate (two each 5-40 oval hd. screws). Check shaft fit at both bearing ends. Ensure that there is free movement with no play. Install the shaft end cap if required (only on Zenith 1 carburetors).
2. Screw in the idle mixture screw with spring and cap. Back out the screw 1-1/2 turns from full bottom seat position.
3. Screw in the strainer bolt assembly with gasket.
4. Screw in the float valve with thick gasket.
5. Attach the float with the hinge pin. Turn the upper bowl upside down and set float level for 1" measurement from float ring to body surface. Adjust the float level with appropriate gasket thickness under float valve. Float must remain parallel with body.
6. Screw in the Idle jet (no gasket)[9/32 wrench].
7. Place the upper body on the lower body and bolt the two halves together with the body bolt (3/8-24 X 3-3/16)[9/16 socket].
8. Rock the carburetor back and forth and listen for free movement of the float in the fuel bowl.

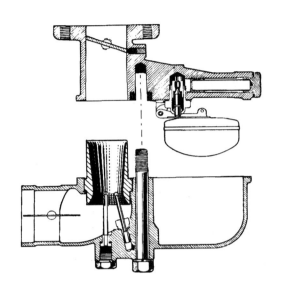

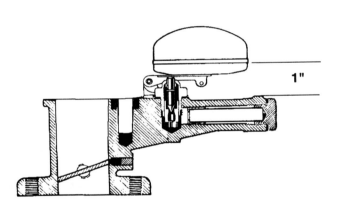

Float Level Adjustment

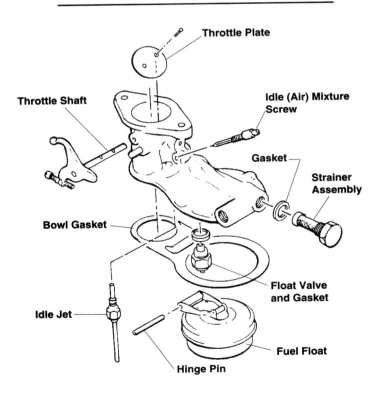

Service and Repair

CARBURETOR

Installing Carburetor

1. Attach the carburetor to the manifold (with new gasket) using two (2) bolts and lock washers (5/16-18 X 3/4)[1/2" wrench].
2. Connect the throttle linkage to the carburetor, choke rod, and choke spring by pushing the sleeve up against the spring, and connecting the rod to the carburetor.

NOTE

Before connecting the gas line, check the ferrule for damage and replace it if necessary (1/8" from end of fuel line). A damaged ferrule is a common cause of gas leaks.

3. Connect carburetor gas line [1/2 or 9/16 open end wrench].
4. Turn ON the fuel shut-off valve located under the gas tank (or on the firewall under the hood on late 31 model year).
5. Turn the gas adjusting knob (from inside car) to 3/4 turn open. Start the engine and let it run until it reaches normal operating temperature.
6. Close the gas adjusting knob between 1/4 to 1/8 turn open.
7. Fully retard the spark. For best performance, set the idle air mixture needle screw on the carburetor about 1-1/2 turns open.
8. Advance the spark setting and set the idle adjust screw on the throttle shaft for desired idle speed.
9. Test drive for performance.

CLUTCH

Clutch chatter and a slipping clutch can be caused by a worn or defective clutch disk, grease and oil on the clutch disk, glazed or burned pressure plate, warpage within the clutch system, or a defective clutch throwout bearing. All of the mentioned defects can only be corrected by removing the clutch and pressure plate assembly. Either the engine or the transmission and rear end assembly must be removed for access to the clutch and pressure plate assembly. If the engine is being removed for overhaul, the clutch assembly can be accessed and overhauled during that process. The following procedure describes removing the rear end assembly and transmission for access to the clutch assembly, and repair/replacement procedures for the clutch assembly.

Clutch Removal

1. Remove the transmission drain plug (bottom of transmission) and drain all oil. Replace drain plug.
2. Remove front floor mat (or carpet) and shift lever plate, attached to floor board with three (3) clips.
3. Remove both sections of the front floor boards [12 flathead screws].
4. Remove the clevis pin attaching the rod at the bottom of the emergency brake handle.

5. Remove the six (6) bolts [1/2" socket] and lock washers on top of the shifting tower and lift the tower off the transmission housing. Cover the top so nothing falls into the transmission.

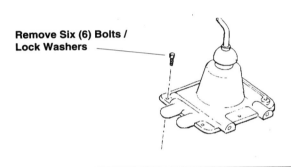

Remove Six (6) Bolts / Lock Washers

6. Remove the brake pedal clevis pin, disconnecting the brake actuating rod and stop light switch on 28/29 models.
7. Remove the clutch pedal clevis pin, disconnecting the clutch arm.
8. Tap out the pedal shaft collar pin and remove the pedal shaft collar. Slide the clutch and brake pedals and spring washer off the shaft.

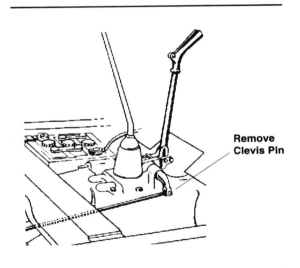

Remove Clevis Pin

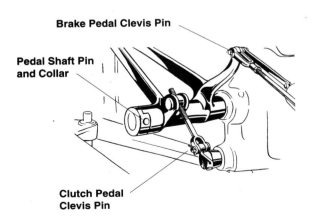

Brake Pedal Clevis Pin

Pedal Shaft Pin and Collar

Clutch Pedal Clevis Pin

CLUTCH

9. Place a floor jack under the transmission for support.
10. Remove the rear end assembly, following the procedures for "Rear End Assembly Removal," page 1-88, steps 2 through 12A.
11. Disconnect the radius ball from the bottom of the bell housing. Remove cotter pins, castle nuts [3/4 wrench], springs, sleeves, and ball cups.

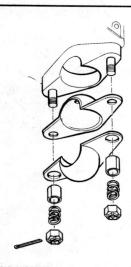

12. After the rear end assembly has been removed, remove the eleven (11) bell housing to flywheel housing bolts [9/16 socket] and separate the bell housing from the flywheel housing. The splined transmission drive shaft will separate from the clutch assembly. The complete transmission assembly with bell housing can be rolled out from under the car on a floor jack.

13. Remove the twelve (12) bolts [1/2 socket] and lock washers from around the clutch pressure plate. The pressure plate weighs 15 pounds and is bolted to the flywheel under heavy spring pressure (1100 lbs). Loosen all bolts evenly. The clutch disk floats behind the pressure plate. After removing the pressure plate the clutch disk can be lifted out.

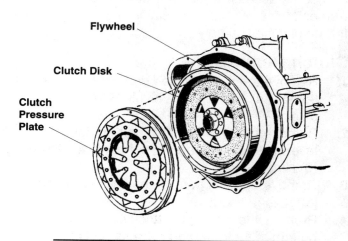

Inspection and Repairs

1. **Clutch Disk** Inspect for excessive wear, glazed surface, loose rivets, broken springs, grease or oil on disk surface.
   - Standard thickness = .340"
   - Replace if thickness is less than .300"
   - Minimum acceptable thickness = .250"

2. **Pressure Plate** Inspect for glazed surface, heat cracks, warped surface, or weak springs. Send to clutch shop for rebuilding if defective. Finger adjustment - (with clutch disk and pressure plate bolted to flywheel)
   - Top of collar to top of finger = .625"
   - Equal finger adjustment ±.002" difference

3. **Throw Out Bearing and Slider** Clean slider, replace weak spring, and replace bearing.

4. **Pilot Bearing** Check for damage. Check end of transmission drive shaft for wear on pilot bearing surface. Transmission drive shaft and flywheel pilot bearing must be replaced if shaft is badly worn.

CLUTCH

Clutch and Pressure Plate Installation

Before installing the clutch disk, measure the clutch disk thickness. Replace the clutch disk if less than .300" thick or if the disk shows signs of glazing (minimum thickness - .250").

1. Place the clutch disk on the flywheel with the thicker side of the hub facing out.
2. If the flywheel and pressure plate were statically balanced together, an alignment mark was made on the edge of the flywheel and the pressure plate bolt flange. Place the pressure plate on the flywheel in alignment with the balancing mark. Insert all twelve (12) 5/16-18 X 3/4" hex head bolts (grade 5) [1/2" socket] and lock washers. DO NOT TIGHTEN pressure plate bolts at this time.

3. Using a splined clutch centering tool, center the clutch disk in the pressure plate by inserting the centering tool into the pilot bearing.

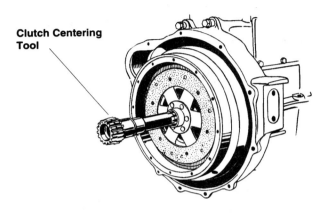

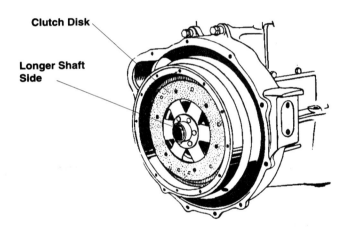

4. After the clutch disk has been centered, tighten all twelve (12) mounting bolts evenly. Torque to 20 ft. lbs. Remove the clutch disk centering tool.
5. Check the fingers on the pressure plate for correct depth adjustment. Readjust the fingers to 5/8" below the top of the pressure plate collar.

Service and Repair

CLUTCH

Installing Transmission - *With Rear End Assembly Removed*

1. Place the two (2) sliding gears in neutral position. Place the transmission on a floor jack and slide it under the car.
2. Raise the transmission level with the flywheel housing.
3. Remove the bell housing cover plate so the splined transmission drive shaft can be viewed.
4. Viewing through the bell housing top cover plate, align the transmission drive shaft spline with the clutch spline. Push the transmission drive shaft into the clutch spline.
5. Install the eleven (11) bell housing to flywheel bolts (3/8-16 X 1")[9/16 socket] and lock washers.
6. Install the radius rod ball on the bottom of the flywheel housing. Place the ball cup with the hole on the top side of the radius ball. Insert the spacers, springs, and nuts [3/4 wrench] as shown below. Tighten the two (2) castle nuts until they touch the spacers and insert cotter pins.

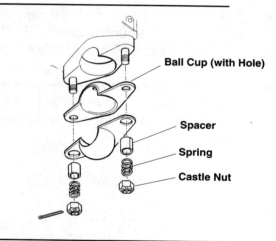

7. Install the rear end assembly by following step-by-step instructions under "Installing Rear End Assembly" beginning on page 1-97, steps 1 through 8.
8. Remove the temporary cover from the top of the transmission and pour in 1-1/2 pints of 600W gear oil. Do not fill above the oil fill hole.
9. Place a transmission cover gasket on top of the transmission. Install shifting tower, using six (6) bolts and lock washers (4 each 5/16-18 X 3/4, 2 each 5/16-18 X 1-3/8")[1/2" socket]. Watch to make sure the shifting forks seat correctly in the two sliding gear collars.

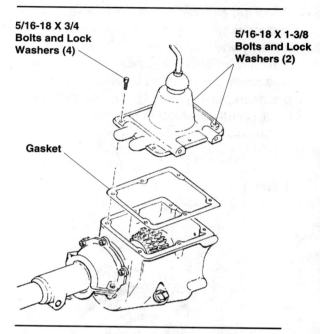

10. Attach the emergency brake actuating rod to the emergency brake handle with a clevis pin. Lock the clevis pin with cotter pin.

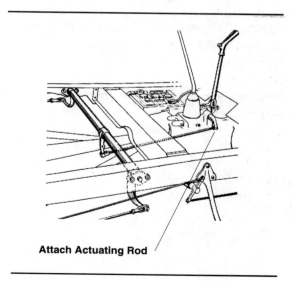

Service and Repair

CLUTCH

11. Slide the brake and clutch pedals on the pedal shaft, inserting a thin spring washer between the two pedals (after May 1929).
12. Install the pedal shaft collar on the end of the shaft and insert the collar pin. Insert a cotter pin through the end of the collar pin.
13. Attach the clutch arm to the clutch pedal adjusting yoke with a clevis pin. Lock with cotter pin.

NOTE
Adjust the clutch pedal with pedal adjusting yoke for 1" free pedal travel before the clutch engages.

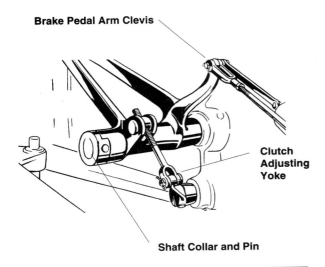

14. Attach the brake actuating rod and stop light linkage to the brake pedal arm with a clevis pin. Lock clevis pin with cotter pin.
15. Attach the brake rod anti-rattler springs to the rear radius rods (5/16-24 X11/16")[1/2 wrench].
16. Attach all four (4) rear brake rods with clevis pins and cotter pins.

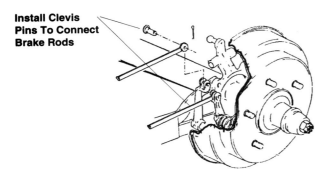

17. Assemble and install both rear shock links as shown below. Screw in end plug and insert cotter pin.

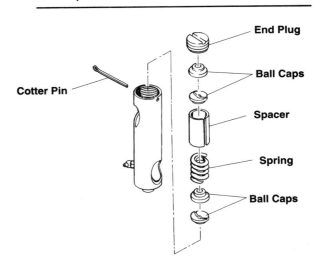

18. From inside the car apply a small amount of grease to the clutch throwout bearing slider shaft. This grease fitting is accessible under the inspection plate located in front of the emergency brake handle (on top of the bell housing). Install inspection plate (two screws, 5/16-18 X 3/8).

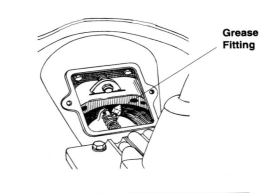

19. Install the front floor boards, shift lever plate, and floor mat. Secure the floor board with twelve (12) flat head screws (12-24 X 1-1/8") and cup washers.
20. Slip on the shifting tower boot and emergency handle boot. Screw the knob on top of the shifting tower.

CRANK PULLEY

The Crank Pulley is a one piece casting, as made by Ford for the Model A. Removing and replacing a broken crank pulley requires removing the radiator to provide enough room to remove the pulley from the end of the crank shaft. The pulley and shaft is 3-1/2" long. There is just a little over 2" clearance between the pulley and radiator. After market pulleys have been made in two pieces, the pulley as one piece and the shaft as a separate piece. The pulley itself is only 2" long, and can be removed from the end of the crank without removing the radiator. The ratchet nut can be screwed out using a special socket wrench to allow removal of the pulley. The following procedure describes how to remove and replace the standard one piece pulley assembly.

Removing Crank Pulley

1. Remove the front floor mat (or carpet) and shift lever plate, attached to floor board with three (3) clips.
2. Remove the bottom section of the front floor board [6 flathead screws] for access to the battery terminals.
3. Remove the battery ground strap from the (+) battery post.

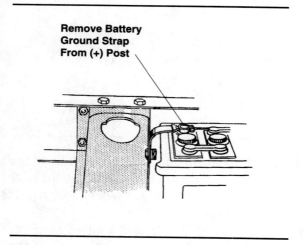

4. Drain the radiator water. The drain petcock is located on the bottom of the water return pipe, under the generator.

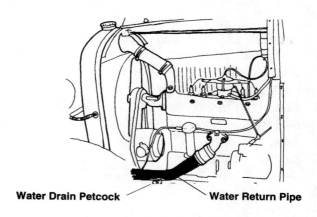

5. Move to the front of the car and remove the horn cover by removing the single round head screw on the back cover [10-32 x 3/4 screw]. Remove the two horn wires from the terminal under the horn motor (pull out type).
6. Remove the headlight conduit connectors (push and twist counterclockwise to release).

CRANK PULLEY

NOTE
Some headlight wiring may have been modified by eliminating the connector plug from inside the conduit socket. The wires would then be routed directly from the conduit into the headlight bucket and attached to the bulb sockets with wire nuts. The wires would have to be disconnected from behind the headlight reflector. To access the headlight bucket, release the front lens clip, pull the clip down (spring loaded latch) and lift up on the lens rim to remove. Remove the center bulb and lift the reflector out of the headlight bucket.

7. Pull the headlight wires back through the conduit to the inside of the radiator shell, leaving the metal conduit and grommets attached to the radiator shell. Do the same for both headlight harness wires and the horn harness wires.
8. Remove the radiator cap.

9. Under the hood, remove the two (2) screws and nuts from the hood rear hold down bracket.

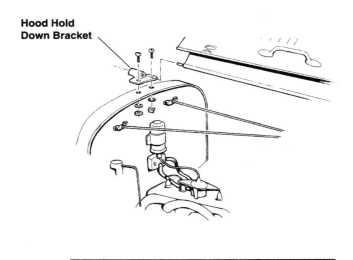

10. Remove the hood and place it in a safe location on cardboard or carpet to prevent chipping the paint. Do not lay the hood down on the side louver panels. It's best to stand the hood up on the back edge to prevent warping or creasing the top panels.

11. Loosen the two (2) nuts [1/2 wrench] on the front end of the radiator support rods. Pull the rods up out of the radiator bracket.

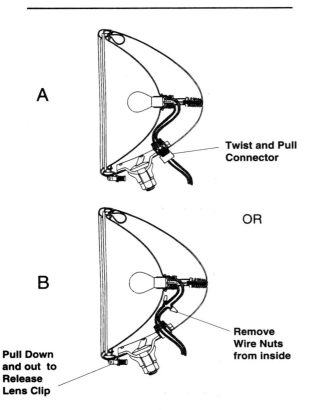

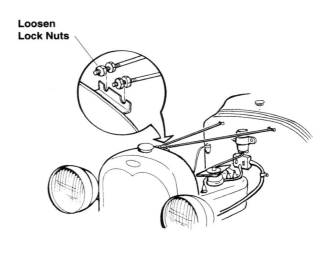

Service and Repair

CRANK PULLEY

12. Loosen the hose clamp on the top radiator hose. Pull the radiator forward enough to pull the radiator neck out of the hose.

13. To remove the radiator, first remove the radiator shell by removing the two (2) screws and nuts on each side of the radiator, attaching the shell to the radiator brackets. Then remove the cotter pin from the two radiator mounting bolts. Using a 3/8 ratchet drive with a 6-inch extension and 9/16 inch deep socket, reach under the front cross member and place the 9/16 inch socket on the head of the radiator mounting bolt. Hold the nut on top with a 9/16 inch box wrench and ratchet the bolt from the bottom. Remove the bolt, spring, and nut from each side of the radiator.

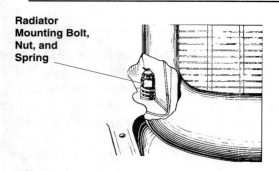

14. Remove and retain the rubber pads under the radiator mounting brackets (both sides). Move the radiator to one side to clear the fender and lift the radiator and shell off the frame. On the 28 models, a fan shroud may be attached to the radiator. This can be left in place when removing the radiator.

15. Loosen the generator mounting bolt, push the generator toward the engine block, and remove the fan belt.

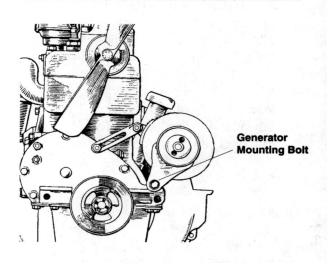

16. Place a floor jack under the engine pan and raise the engine about an inch to allow removal of the pulley.
17. Remove the crank pulley nut [1-3/8 socket], and pull the pulley off the end of the crank shaft.

NOTE
The crank pulley nut (ratchet) has been found in several sizes. Model A standard size is 1-3/8". Other sizes that exist are 1-1/8, 1-1/4, and 1-5/16, which are most likely aftermarket.

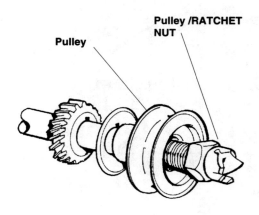

CRANK PULLEY

Installing Crank Pulley

1. Install the new crank pulley and tighten the ratchet nut.

   NOTE

   Before installing the ratchet nut, make sure the end of the pulley extends slightly beyond the end of the crank shaft. If the crank shaft extends beyond the end of the pulley by the slightest amount, the ratchet nut cannot be tightened against the pulley, allowing the pulley to move against the woodruff key. The ratchet nut must screw up tight against the pulley.

2. Lower the engine and remove the floor jack.
3. Set the radiator on the front cross member. Place a rubber pad under both radiator mounting brackets (28/29 use 1/8" pad, 30/31 use 1/16" pad). A piece of old inner tube works fine. Install the radiator mounting bolts, nuts and spring assembly as shown below. Tighten the bolts only enough to install cotter pins in the mounting bolts.

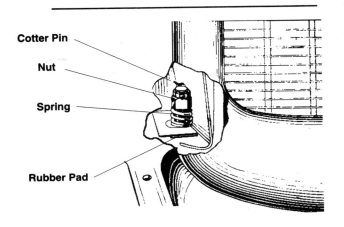

4. Place a short radiator hose over each end of the water return pipe with two (2) hose clamps on each hose section. Secure the water return pipe hoses to the radiator lower pipe and the water inlet neck on the engine block. Securely tighten all four (4) hose clamps.

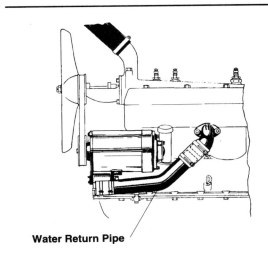

Water Return Pipe

5. Slip the top radiator neck into the top hose and install the hose clamps. Do not tighten these hose clamps until the radiator support rods have been installed and the hood installed and adjusted.

Service and Repair

CRANK PULLEY

6. Attach the ends of the support rods to the radiator bracket with nut and lock washer on each side of the bracket [1/2" wrench].

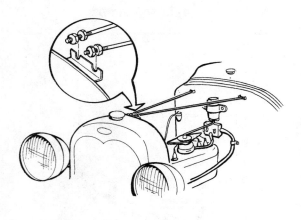

7. If the radiator shell was removed from the radiator, reinstall it at this time, using with four (4) pan head screws (12-24 X 19/32") and square nuts.
8. Install the fan belt (Dayco No. 22425) and adjust it for 1/2" movement. (See Section II, Service Adjustments.)

9. Set the hood in place and attach it with two (2) screws, lock washers, and nuts [12-24 X 5/8" round head] on the rear hold down bracket.

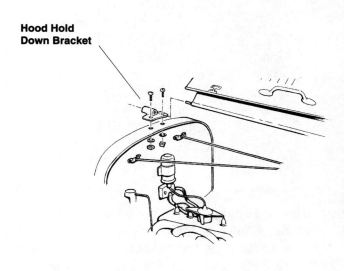

Hood Hold Down Bracket

10. After the hood has been installed and properly aligned, securely tighten both front radiator support rod nuts. Securely tighten the two (2) radiator hose clamps on the upper radiator hose (radiator to goose neck). Check all four (4) hose clamps on the water return pipe hoses. Ensure all hose clamps are tight.
11. Route the wiring harness through the radiator shell to the head lights and horn. Connect the horn wires.
12. Connect the headlight conduit connectors (push and twist clockwise to connect).

CRANK PULLEY

NOTE

Some headlight wiring may have been modified by eliminating the connector plug from inside the conduit socket. The wires would then be routed directly from the conduit into the headlight bucket and attached to the bulb sockets with wire nuts. The wires would have to be disconnected from behind the headlight reflector. To access the headlight bucket, release the front lens clip (spring loaded latch) and lift up on the lens rim to remove it. Remove the center bulb and lift the reflector out of the headlight bucket.

13. Connect the battery ground strap to the (+) battery post.

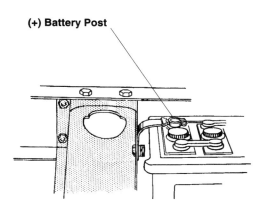

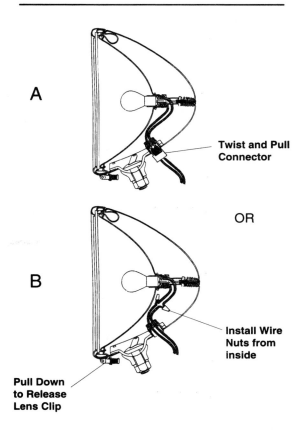

14. Install the front floor board and floor mat. Secure the floor board with six (6) flat head screws [12-24 X 1-1/8"] and cup washers.
15. Pour three (3) gallons of water into the radiator.
16. Start the engine, and let it run for approximately 15 minutes or until operating temperature is reached. Check all water connections for leaks. Tighten connections as needed.

Service and Repair

CROSS SHAFT

The service brake cross shaft must operate with no slop in the end bushings and the clevis eyes for correct brake operation and adjustment. Slop in the cross shaft is due to worn end shaft bushings and worn clevis eyes in the operating levers. The emergency cross shaft is not so critical in free play movement. Service and maintenance of the emergency cross shaft includes repairing the clevis eye for the emergency handle rod, disassembling and cleaning the end bracket assemblies (possibly replacing the end shaft springs), and replacing the end shaft felt grease seals. The service brake cross shaft and emergency brake cross shaft can both be easily removed for repairs.

Service Brake Cross Shaft Repairs

1. Remove the brake rod clevis pins to disconnect the brake pedal to cross shaft rod and the four (4) service brake rods.
2. Remove the two (2) castle nuts and bolts from the cross shaft bracket on each end of the cross shaft [1/2" socket]. The complete cross shaft and brackets can now be removed from the car.
3. Check all five (5) clevis eyes for wear and clevis pin fit. The clevis pin and eye should be 5/16" with no slop in the fit. If wear is not excessive, use an oversize clevis pin (11/32"). If necessary, weld up the clevis eye and re-drill it for a 5/16" clevis pin.
4. Check the end shaft bushings for wear. The bushing needs to be replaced if any slop exists.

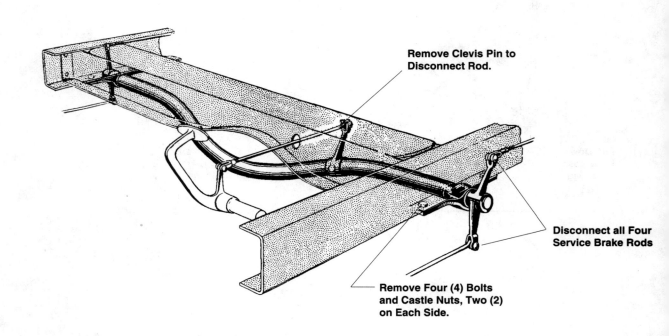

CROSS SHAFT

5. To replace the bushings, cut the old bushings off with a "Zizz Wheel" or hacksaw.

NOTE

Split bushings are available that will allow new bushing installation without removal of the end levers.

6. Replacing a solid one-piece end shaft bushing requires removal of the end operating levers. Place a small punch mark on the cross shaft and on the lever to indicate the side on which the rivet head is located. The rivet head needs to be on the same side when reinstalling.

NOTE

Do not attempt to grind off the rivet heads and drive the rivets out of the levers and cross shaft ends. They will not drive out. The rivets must be drilled and removed as described.

7. Use a center drill and drill a pilot hole in the center of the head at both ends of the rivet.

8. Use a 17/64" drill bit and drill through each end of the rivet, through the thickness of the levers and into the shaft a little. Do not attempt to drill all the way through from one side to the other. Be careful not to enlarge the rivet holes in the lever.

9. After drilling, place the cross shaft in a press and push the shaft out through the lever, shearing off the drilled out rivets.

10. Use a drift punch and drive out the remains of the rivet in the cross shaft.

11. On one end of the shaft the distance is greater between the end of the shaft and the shoulder. This allows a little lateral play for minor differences in frame width and length of cross shaft.

12. Slip the new bushing on the cross shaft (add a little axle grease to the shaft) and then slip on the operating lever. Position the lever according to the punch marks made during disassembly. The bent end of each lever goes UP. The slight angle is toward the rear brakes. The front brake rod comes off the bottom lever and runs straight with the frame.

13. After the operating lever is in place, insert a 5/16" X 1-1/2" iron rivet, as was originally installed, and peen it over.

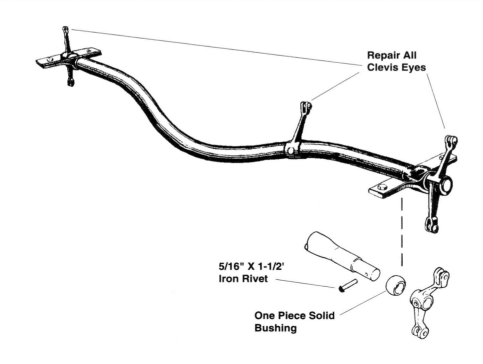

Repair All Clevis Eyes

5/16" X 1-1/2" Iron Rivet

One Piece Solid Bushing

Service and Repair

CROSS SHAFT

14. Mount the cross shaft under the frame with four (4) bolts [5/16-24 X 3/4"] and castle nuts. The two (2) mounting brackets on each end of the shaft must clamp tight on the bushing, holding the bushing and brackets tight against the frame.

15. Attach the brake pedal to cross shaft rod and all brake rods with clevis pins. Check the placement of all cotter pins at the end mounting brackets and on the brake rod clevis pins.

16. Readjust the brakes in accordance with Section II, Service Adjustments.

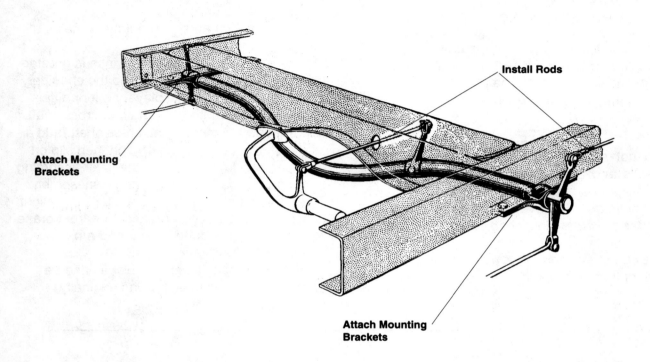

Service Brake Cross Shaft

CROSS SHAFT

Emergency Brake Cross Shaft Repairs

The emergency brake cross shaft is not as critical as the service brake cross shaft when correcting for wear. If the end of the lever arm clevis shaft is excessively worn, fill the worn grooves with weld and dress down with a file. The clevis eye on the brake rod may also be welded and a smaller eye drilled. The center lever arm clevis eye may also need repairing the same way. The cross shaft will need to be removed to inspect and make repairs to the end bracket assembly.

1. Remove the grease fittings on the outside of the frame on both ends of the cross shaft (1928 - 1930).
2. Remove the two (2) bolts, nuts, and lock washers [1/2" socket] from each end bracket.

NOTE
The cross shaft is spring loaded at the end brackets on each end of the cross shaft.

3. After removing the cross shaft, clean all grease from inside the brass end cups. Replace the spring and the felt grease seal.
4. Place a new spring inside the mounting brackets.
5. Slide the felt grease seal over the ball end of the cross shaft, grease the ball end, and place the brass cup over the ball. Reassemble on the car frame, using two (2) bolts, lock washers, and nuts (5/16-24 X 11/16")[1/2" wrench].
6. Attach both brake rods and the brake handle to cross shaft connecting rod with clevis and cotter pins.
7. Insert grease fittings on the outside of the frame. This completes repairs to the emergency brake cross shaft.

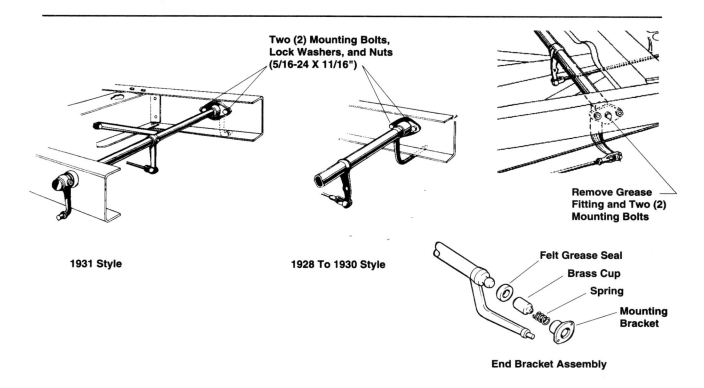

Emergency Brake Cross Shaft

Service and Repair

CYLINDER HEAD AND GASKET

This procedure explains how the engine cylinder head is removed when replacing the head gasket, replacing the cylinder head, or removing the head for milling. This process starts by using engine compression to pop the head loose before disassembly. To remove the cylinder head, the following items must be removed: hood, radiator support rods, top radiator water hose, distributor, spark plugs, and fan belt.

Removing Head and Gasket

1. Drain the radiator.
2. Loosen the generator mounting bolt to allow removal of the fan belt. This releases stress on the front of the head.
3. Loosen every head stud nut [11/16 socket] at least 1/2 the thread length of the nut. This should raise the nuts at least 1/8" above the head on each stud. The front two (2) nuts can be removed.
4. Squirt WD-40 or Liquid Wrench (liberally) around every stud and let soak for one or two days. This will soften any rust formed around the studs in the head.
5. Start the engine. After about the second revolution, the head will pop loose. With loss of compression, the engine will immediately stop. You can now start disassembly with a loose head.
6. Disconnect the battery ground strap from the (+) battery terminal.

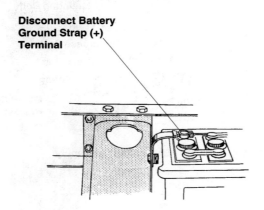

7. Under the hood, remove the two (2) screws and nuts from the hood rear hold down bracket.

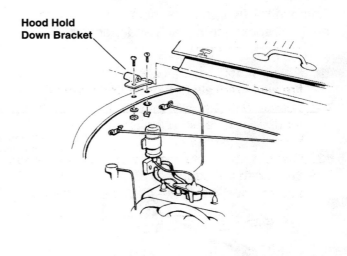

8. Remove the hood and place it in a safe location on cardboard or carpet to prevent chipping the paint. Do not lay the hood down on the side louver panels. It's best to stand the hood up on the back edge to prevent warping or creasing the top panels.

CYLINDER HEAD AND GASKET

9. Loosen the two (2) nuts [1/2 inch wrench] on the front end of the two radiator support rods. Pull the rods up out of the radiator bracket.

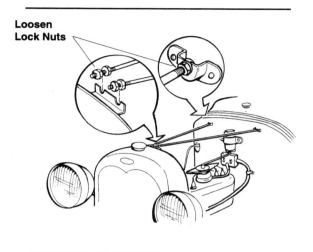

Loosen Lock Nuts

10. Remove both radiator support rods from the fire wall brackets [5/8 open end wrench].
11. Loosen both hose clamps on the top radiator hose and remove the top radiator hose from the goose neck.
12. Remove the center head stud nut that holds the distributor cable clamp [11/16 socket] and remove the clamp from the head stud.

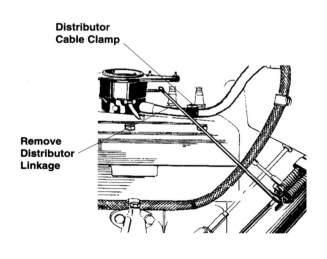

Distributor Cable Clamp

Remove Distributor Linkage

13. Remove the spark control linkage from the steering column to distributor.

14. Move to the right side of the engine and loosen the distributor shaft locking nut [9/16 box wrench]. Back out the locking screw and lift the distributor and shaft from the block. Unscrew the distributor cable from the distributor body. Wrap the distributor cable behind the coil body.

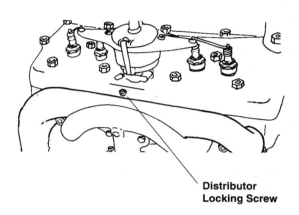

Distributor Locking Screw

15. Remove all four (4) spark plugs [1-1/8" open end wrench for standard Model A spark plug].
16. Remove the front two stud nuts holding the water outlet casting (goose neck). Remove the water outlet casting and double nut the two front studs (7/16-20 nuts). This will allow removal of the front two studs.

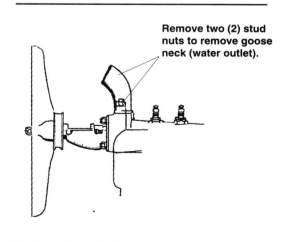

Remove two (2) stud nuts to remove goose neck (water outlet).

1-81 Service and Repair

CYLINDER HEAD AND GASKET

17. Remove the front two head studs [11/16 socket]. Removing these long studs will make it easier to remove the head.
18. Remove the remaining twelve (12) stud nuts [11/16 socket].
19. The head must be lifted straight up for removal. This can be done easiest by screwing a 3/8 lifting eye into spark plug hole number 4. Lift the head from the water pump and the lifting eye.

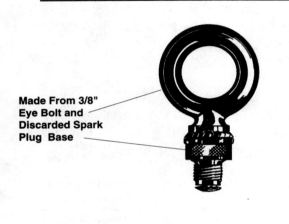

Made From 3/8" Eye Bolt and Discarded Spark Plug Base

20. If the head will not release and pull up, a little prying may be needed.

CAUTION
Do not pry on either side of the head near the center. The head will crack when pried on either side. The head can only be pried from the block at the four corners.

21. Excessive prying between the block and head should not be necessary. If the head will not release with gentle prying at the four corners, it is usually because of rust build up around some of the head studs. Further applications of Liquid Wrench or WD-40 around the head studs may be necessary.
22. Thoroughly clean all gasket material from the block.
23. Remove the four (4) nuts [9/16 inch box wrench] and lock washers that attach the water pump to the front of the cylinder head. Remove the water pump.

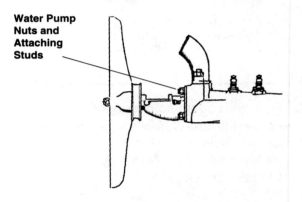

Water Pump Nuts and Attaching Studs

Head Preparation
1. Before installing a new head gasket, check to see if the pistons extend beyond the top of the block. If they do, a .100" oversize gasket should be used.
2. The cylinder head must be properly prepared before installing.
   a. The head must be magnafluxed to check for cracks.
   b. The bottom side should be surfaced on a mill to remove any warping.
   c. Mill flat the raised boss for the water outlet goose neck, on the top side of the head.
3. Remove and inspect all head studs for excessive rust pits and damaged threads. Replace all damaged head studs.

Service and Repair

CYLINDER HEAD AND GASKET

Installing Cylinder Head

1. Apply anti-seize compound to the bottom threads on all fourteen (14) head studs. Insert the studs in the block until they bottom. If any of the studs fit loosely in the threaded hole, remove the stud and insert a Helicoil.

Thread Repair with Helicoil

Repairing damaged threads involves drilling out stripped threads, retapping the hole, and installing a prewound insert.
Typical thread repair kits contain a prewound threaded insert, a tap (corresponding to the outside diameter threads of the insert), and an installation tool.

1. Drill out the damaged threads with the specified drill.
2. With the tap supplied, tap the hole to receive the prewound threaded insert. Keep the tap well oiled and back out frequently to avoid clogging the threads.
3. Screw the threaded insert into the installation tool until the tang engages the slot.
4. Screw the insert into the tapped hole until it is 1/4-1/2 turns below the top surface of the block.
5. After installation break off the tang with a hammer and punch. Remove the tang from hole.

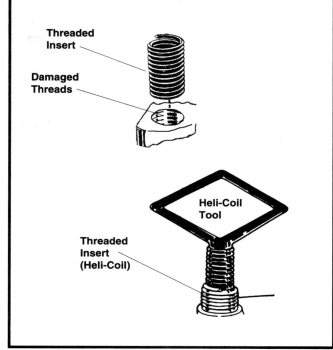

---

2. All studs except no. 8, 11, and 13 should extend 2-3/4 inches above the block. The two front studs (no. 11 and 13) for the water outlet casting should extend 5 inches above the block. The no. 8 stud (for ignition cable hold down bracket) should extend 2-29/32 inches above the block.

3. Spray a thin even coat of Permatex High Tack (in a spray can) head gasket sealant on both sides of the copper head gasket. Place the head gasket over the head studs so the rolled edge around the cylinder opening is face down (rolled seam bottom down).

NOTE
Check to see if pistons extend above top of block surface. If they do, you must use a .100 (oversized) head gasket.

4. Install the four (4) water pump studs (3/8-16 X 1-1/4") in the head. Apply the water pump gasket with a small amount of Permatex gasket sealer on both sides. Mount the water pump with four (4) nuts (3/8-24) and lock washers [9/16 socket].

5. Set the head down evenly over all head studs. Make sure no harness wiring or other matter has slipped under the head while lowering it in place.

6. Apply a thin coat of gasket sealant on both sides of a <u>thin</u> water outlet gasket and set in place over the front two head studs.

CYLINDER HEAD AND GASKET

NOTE

There are two different size water outlet castings (goose neck). The short casting is used on the 28/29 models and the tall casting is used on the 30/31 models. The correct casting must be used to ensure proper radiator hose connection.

CAUTION

Mill or file the bottom surface of the water outlet casting (goose neck) flat before installing it, and use a <u>paper thin</u> gasket. This will allow the front two nuts to be torqued to 55 lbs. without cracking the stud flanges.

7. Install all fourteen (14) head stud nuts and hand tighten.

8. Torque all head nuts to 35 ft. lbs., in correct sequence. Torque all nuts again to 45 ft. lbs. and then a final torque to 55 ft. lbs.

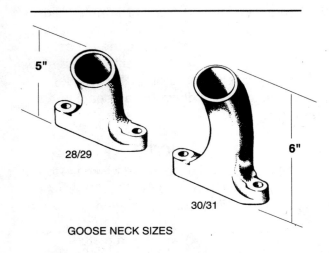

GOOSE NECK SIZES

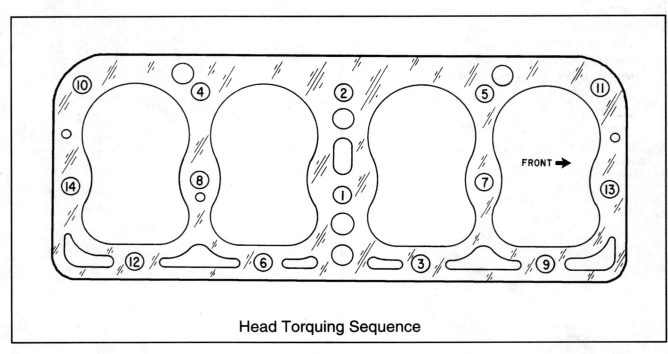

Head Torquing Sequence

Service and Repair

CYLINDER HEAD AND GASKET

9. Install all four (4) spark plugs. Torque to 25 ft. lbs.
10. Insert the distributor shaft into the shaft hole, aligning the slot on the shaft with the tab on the cam drive gear. The slot and tab are offset so the shaft can only be aligned one way.

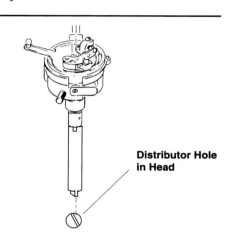
Distributor Hole in Head

11. Screw the ignition cable into the distributor body and then position the distributor in place, seating the distributor locking pin in the hole on the cylinder head. The distributor base should sit flat against the top surface of the cylinder head. Rotate the distributor shaft with the rotor to correctly align the shaft with the slot, allowing the distributor body to fully seat against the block.

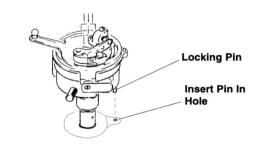
Locking Pin

Insert Pin In Hole

12. Insert the distributor locking screw and locking nut. Tighten the locking screw until it seats firmly against the distributor body. Tighten the locking nut [9/16 wrench].

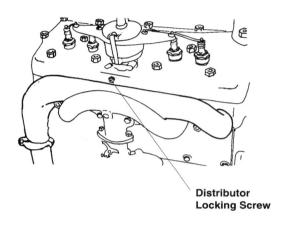
Distributor Locking Screw

13. Slip two (2) hose clamps over the long radiator hose and install the hose from the top radiator neck to the goose neck. Do not tighten these hose clamps until the radiator support rods have been installed and the hood installed and adjusted.
14. Install the two (2) radiator support rods in the firewall brackets. Tighten the locking nuts with a 5/8 open end wrench. Attach the other ends of the support rods in the radiator bracket with nut and lock washer on each side of the bracket [1/2 wrench].

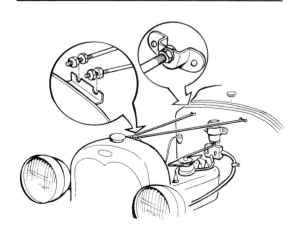

CYLINDER HEAD AND GASKET

15. Attach the distributor advance control rod (17-5/16" long) from the distributor plate to the steering column.

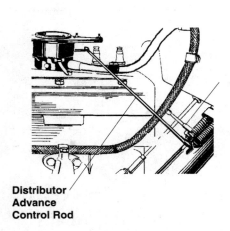

Distributor Advance Control Rod

16. Install the fan belt (Dayco No. 22425) and adjust for 1/2" movement. (See Section II, Service Adjustments.)

17. Set the hood in place and attach with two (2) screws, lock washers, and nuts [12-24 X 5/8" round head] on the rear hold down bracket.

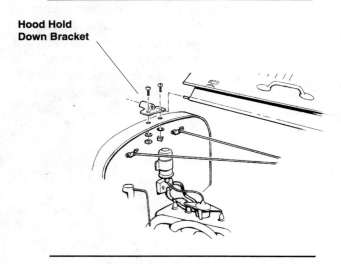

Hood Hold Down Bracket

18. After the hood has been installed and properly aligned, securely tighten both front radiator support rod nuts. Securely tighten the two radiator hose clamps on the upper radiator hose (radiator to goose neck).

19. Connect the battery ground strap to the (+) battery terminal.

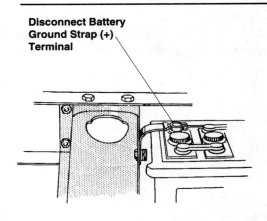

Disconnect Battery Ground Strap (+) Terminal

20. Install the front floor board and floor mat. Secure the floor board with Twelve (12) flat head screws [12-24 X 1-1/8"] and cup washers.

21. Slip on the shifting tower boot and emergency handle boot. Screw the knob on top of the shifting tower.

22. From under the hood, set the distributor timing in accordance with Timing Procedure, Section II.

23. Pour three (3) gallons of water into the radiator.

24. Turn the gas shut off valve ON, start the engine, and let it run for approximately 15 minutes or until operating temperature is reached. Check all water connections for leaks (water pump and hose connection). Tighten connections as needed.

25. Take a five to ten mile test drive and then retorque the head bolts to 55 ft.lbs. The head should be retorqued again after 300 miles.

Service and Repair

DIFFERENTIAL/REAR END ASSEMBLY

The differential/rear end assembly consists of the torque tube and drive shaft, differential gears, ring and pinion gear, rear axles, axle housings, and rear radius rods. The rear end assembly must be removed from the car when making repairs to the speedometer drive gear, ring and pinion gears and bearings, or the differential assembly, including axle housing races and bearings.

Transmission and engine noises are sometimes confused with rear end noises. There are four types of rear end noises which may indicate the necessity for a rear end overhaul: (1) drive noise, (2) coast noise, (3) float noise, and (4) bearing noise. The <u>Drive Noise</u> is heard on constant acceleration through the speed range of 15 m.p.h. through 60 m.p.h. The <u>Coast Noise</u> is noticeable as the car decelerates, opposite of Drive Noise. <u>Float Noise</u> is noticeable at a constant level speed between 15 m.p.h. to 60 m.p.h. The ring and pinion gear is usually at fault for the above three noise conditions. <u>Bearing Noise</u> is caused by loose, worn, or rough bearings and will add greatly to the above three noises. Bad bearings cause a heavy irregular noise on acceleration and a little less noticeable at deceleration. <u>Ring Gear Noise</u> is a whine, while <u>Bearing Noise</u> is more like a growl or rumble. A worn U-joint can cause a clunking or scraping noise and can be mistaken for rear end noise.

Depending on the severity, many times the problem can be corrected by completely disassembling the rear end, performing a thorough cleaning of gears and housings, replacing bearings and races, and reassembling the rear end while making correct preload adjustments on bearings and adjusting clearances with proper shimming and gaskets.

Parts For Overhaul	
Grease Seals (Axle Housings and Torque Tube)	3 ea.
Bearings (Pinion and Carrier) Timken 28156	4 ea.
Bearing Cups (Axle Housings) Timken 28317	2 ea.
Bearing Cup Shims (Assorted Thickness)	.005-.010"
Bearing Cup (Double Cone/Pinion) Timken	1 ea.
Drive Shaft Bearing Race (Cylinder)	1 ea.
Drive Shaft Roller Bearing	1 ea.
Spring Shackle Bushings (Steel)	4 ea.
Differential Hsng Gaskets (Assorted Thickness)	.002-.010"
Torque Tube Gasket	1 ea.

Specifications and Clearances		
Drive Shaft (front) Roller Bearing Surface		1.085" Min.
Pinion Bearing Torque -	20 in. lbs. (New Bearing)	
	12-15 in. lbs. (Used Bearing).	
Pinion Gear Backlash	.005-.010"	
Axle Backlash	.010-.015"	
Axle End Play	.015-.020"	
Carrier Assy Bolts	35 lbs Torque (Safety Wire)	
Axle Housing Bolts	35 lbs Torque	
Torque Tube Bolts	35 lbs Torque (Safety Wire)	
Bolts		
Axle Housing	3/8-24 X 5/8"	20 ea.
Torque Tube	3/8-24 X 3/4"	6 ea.

DIFFERENTIAL/REAR END

Removing Rear End Assembly

1. Drain differential oil by removing the bottom drain plug on the differential housing (3/8 square hole pipe plug). The drain plug can be removed with the square end of a 3/8 drive ratchet.
2. Block the front wheels and release the emergency brake.
3. Jack up the rear end of the car and place jack stands under the frame, just behind the running board brackets. Remove both rear wheels.
4. Disconnect the service brake rod and emergency brake rod (remove clevis pins) at both rear wheels.

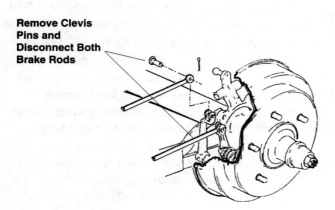

Remove Brake Rods

5. Disconnect the brake rod anti-rattlers from the radius rods (bolt and lock washer, 1/2 socket).

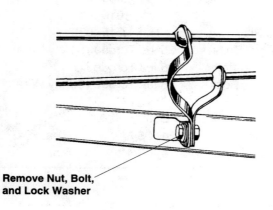

6. Remove the cotter pin from the top of the shock link and screw out the end plug for removal of the shock link from the shock arm and the axle housing.

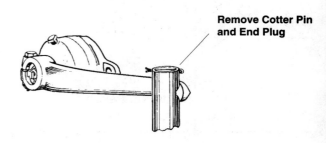

Remove Shock Link

7. If the rear end is being removed for differiential disassembly and repairs, remove both rear axle nuts [15/16 wrench] and remove both rear wheel drums. Otherwise the drums can be left on the axle.

NOTE
A rear wheel hub puller may be needed to remove the drums from the axle.

Remove Drum

Service and Repair 1-88

DIFFERENTIAL/REAR END

8. Disconnect the speedometer cable (screw out the cap) from under the torque tube.

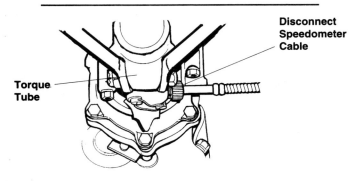

9. Remove the two (2) bolts [9/16 socket] and nuts on each side of the U-joint outer cover.
10. Remove the six (6) bolts and nuts [9/16 socket] from around the U-joint outer cover. Remove both halves of the outer cover.

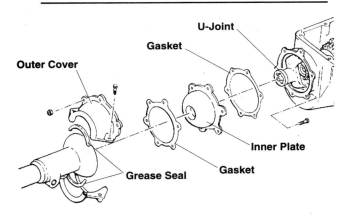

11. Place a floor jack under the differential housing.

12A. **For Transmission or Clutch Repairs Only**
When the rear end assembly is to be removed for transmission or clutch repairs, the rear end assembly should be removed with the rear leaf spring left on the rear end assembly. Remove the four (4) nuts (7/8 wrench) from the rear spring hanger U-bolts. Remove the hanger bars and lower the rear end assembly until the spring is out of the rear cross member channel. Slide the rear end assembly with spring out from under the car.

12B. **For Differiential Repairs** Place a full length Model A spring spreader on the rear spring and adjust sufficiently to allow the left spring shackle to be removed.

CAUTION
For safety purposes use only a full length spring spreader that has end spades that lock around the bottom spring leaf.

13. To remove the spring shackle, remove the two (2) rear shackle nuts [11/16 socket] and remove the shackle cross bar. With spring tension removed from the shackle, the shackle can be driven out of the spring perch and spring eye. Remove the spring shackle from the other side and lower the rear end assembly. Slide the rear end assembly out from under the car.

NOTE
When removing the rear end assembly from under the car, do not allow the front end of the torque tube to fall off the cross shaft. Carefully remove the torque tube from the cross shaft as the rear end is pulled out from under the car.

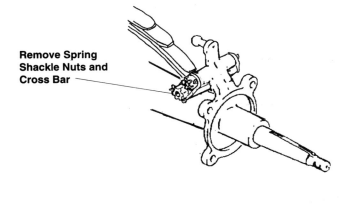

Service and Repair

DIFFERENTIAL/REAR END

Rear End Disassembly

1. Remove the clevis pin from the emergency brake connecting link on the wheel brake assembly. This will allow access to the four (4) backing plate nuts.

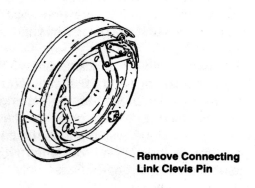

2. Remove the four (4) backing plate bolts and nuts [9/16 socket] and remove both backing plates with brake assembly attached.

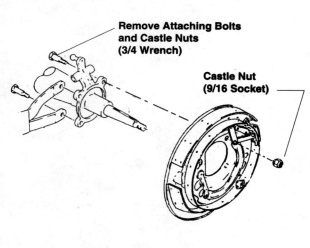

Backing Plate Removed

3. Remove the radius rod bolt and nut (7/8 wrench) at the front of the torque tube. Set both radius rods aside.

4. Remove the two (2) bolts and lock washers (7/16 socket) from the speedometer gear cap. Remove the gear cap and set it aside.

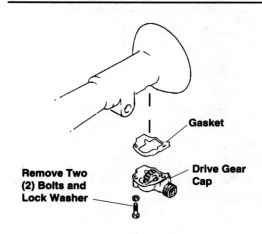

5. Remove the retaining clip ring from the front of the drive shaft, just in back of the spline. Slide the speedometer drive gear, thrust washer, and roller bearing off the end of the drive shaft.

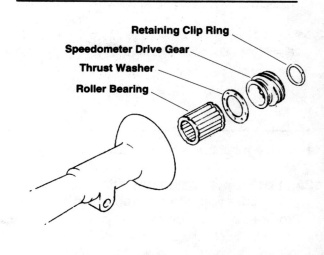

Service and Repair   1-90

DIFFERENTIAL/REAR END

6. Cut the safety wire from the torque tube-to-differential housing bolts. Remove all six (6) bolts [9/16 socket] and slide the torque tube off the drive shaft.
7. Remove the ten (10) bolts [9/16 socket] from the left side of the differential housing (banjo) and slide the left axle housing off the axle. The axles and differential, including ring gear and carrier assembly, can be pulled out of the differential housing from the left side.

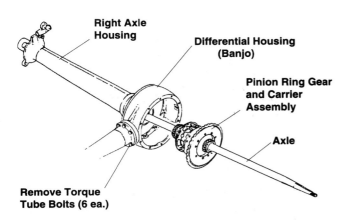

Removing Carrier and Axle Assembly

8. Remove the ten (10) bolts [9/16 socket] from the right side of the differential housing and set the axle housing aside.

9. Before separating the carrier assembly, check axle end play by moving the axle in and out in the carrier assembly. End play should be .015 - .020". Cut and remove the safety wire around the nine (9) carrier assembly nuts.

NOTE

Before disassembling the carrier assembly, check along the separation line of the carrier for punch marks identifying a matching point of the two halves. If no marks are found, punch identifying marks on each carrier half for reassembly alignment. Before separating the carrier, make note of the position of the spider yoke and gears. They should be placed in the same position at reassembly.

10. Remove the nine (9) nuts and bolts [9/16 socket] around the carrier assembly. Separate the two halves and remove the spider yoke and gears. Remove both axles from the carrier halves.

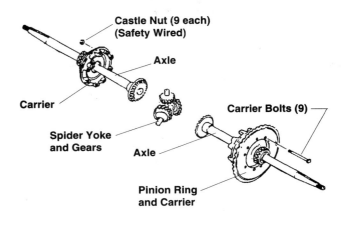

Split Carrier Assembly

Service and Repair

DIFFERENTIAL/REAR END

11. The drive shaft and pinion gear is removed through the side of the differential (banjo) housing. Remove the large locking nut on the drive shaft side of the pinion bearing (bend locking tabs off nut).
12. Remove the locking nut, locking washer, bearing torque nut, thrust washer, and bearing from the drive shaft. Pull the pinion gear, bearing, and drive shaft out through the side of the differential housing.

Differential Inspection

1. **Axle Housing** Inspect spring perches at both ends of the axle housings. If badly worn, weld up the casting if necessary and press in new bushings (steel bushings). Check the bottom side of the bearing race for a flat wear spot. If badly worn, new sleeves are available and can be pressed on. The race surface will need to be turned down and a new sleeve pressed on by a qualified machine shop.

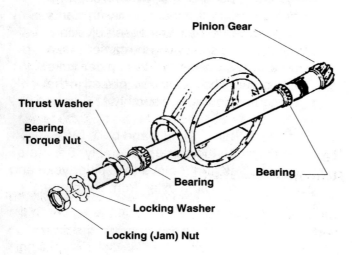

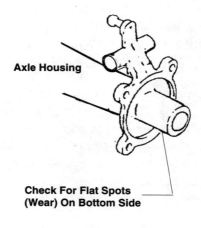

13. Clean and thoroughly inspect all parts for defects. Replace all defective parts.

2. **Radius Rods** Check both radius rods for straightness. If bent they must be replaced. When radius rods are straightened, they will lengthen and not align correctly with the torque tube front bolt hole.
3. **Axles** Check the back side of the gear end. If badly worn or gouged, replace the axle. Too much wear in this area will cause excessive axle end play. Check the groove for the axle key. The axle key should fit tightly into the groove. Check the tapered end of axle for uneven wear. If unevenly or excessively worn, the hub will not fit on the axle properly. This can cause the emergency brake bands to rub on the drum, damaging the hub. Check the axle nut threads for badly stretched or damaged threads.

DIFFERENTIAL/REAR END

4. **Drive Shaft** Check the spline on the end of the drive shaft for excessive wear. Measure the front bearing surface on the drive shaft. Maximum bearing wear on the drive shaft is .005". If the bearing surface is less than 1.085 inches, the drive shaft should be replaced. Check the pinion gear for pits and excessive wear on the teeth. To replace the pinion gear, remove the castle nut and press the gear off the shaft.

5. **Spider Yoke and Gears** Check gears and yoke closely for hairline cracks. Check for damaged, worn, or pitted gears. Replace defective spider gears and yoke.

6. **Pinion Ring** Check pinion and ring gear for broken, worn, or pitted teeth. Replace if defective.

7. **Carrier Housing** Check for excessive wear and gouging on the inner surface, where the back side of the axle gear and spider gears contact the inside of the carrier. Excessive wear will cause too much axle end play. Check the tapered bearing pressed on the outside of each carrier half. Replace bearings during overhaul.

8. **Axle Housing Bearing Races (Cups)** Check the bearing cups for excessive wear or pitting. The cups should always be replaced when new carrier bearings are installed.

NOTE

When removing axle housing bearing cups, look for shims under each cup. These shims are used to set carrier bearing preload. Take note of the number of shims under each cup and replace same number when installing new cups.

9. **Pinion Bearing and Race** Check the pinion bearing cup (double cone race) in the differential (banjo) housing. This race can be pressed out with a small hydraulic jack placed inside the banjo housing. Replace both bearings and race.

10. **Grease Seals** Replace the grease seals in the outer ends of both axle housings and the grease seal in the front end of the torque tube. The two (2) axle grease seals are installed with the seal's rubber lip facing the differential housing. The drive shaft seal rubber lip faces the bell end of the torque tube. The axle housing seals can be removed by using a seal removal tool screwed to the end of a 1/2" X 4' length of pipe. The axle seals are driven out toward the differential banjo. The torque tube seal is driven out toward the front of the tube.

Rear End Assembly and Bearing Preload

The following procedures describe in detail the process for preload adjustments of the carrier and pinion bearings. This can be a long and tedious process, but the results are rewarding. Completing this procedure can mean the difference between a quiet and smooth running rear end or an annoying noisy rear end. Allow 4 to 6 hours to complete this process. It is not difficult but can be time consuming.

1. Insure all parts have been thoroughly cleaned. Bolt both halves of the carrier together without axles and spider gears, using the nine (9) carrier bolts and nuts. Ensure the two carrier halves have been assembled according to the alignment punch marks on each half of the housing. Torque nuts to 30 ft. lbs.

2. Install the carrier (with tapered bearings installed) in the banjo housing (with no drive shaft and pinion gear) with the ring gear on the left side of the banjo. Bolt on both axle housings (with bearing cups installed) without gaskets. [ten (10) bolts on each side of banjo, (3/8-24 X 5/8") [9/16 socket]. Torque each attaching bolt to 35 ft. lbs.

Service and Repair

DIFFERENTIAL/REAR END

3. Reach through the pinion hole and try to turn the ring gear. It should not turn. If the ring gear turns snug, remove the axle housings and add a .005" shim under the bearing race (cup) on each axle housing. If the ring gear turns easily, add a .010" shim under each bearing race. Repeat steps 2 and 3 above until the ring gear cannot be turned.

Carrier Bearing Preload

4. Remove both axle housings and insert a .022 to .025" banjo gasket on both sides of the banjo (do not use sealant). Reinstall axle housings and torque attaching bolts to 35 ft. lbs. (Left axle housing has a weld seam toward front.)
5. Reach through the pinion hole and turn the ring gear. The ring gear should turn freely with no side movement. Reduce the gaskets on each side of the banjo by .007 to .008", or until the ring gear can be turned snugly with a little drag. Make sure an equal number of gaskets are on both sides at this time. The ring gear should turn snugly with .010 to .012" gaskets on each side. After obtaining correct adjustment, remove axle housings and carrier assembly from banjo housing. Be sure to retain the same axle housing-to-banjo gaskets for each side.

Pinion Bearing Preload

6. Press the double coned bearing race into the banjo housing.
7. Install the drive shaft with pinion gear and bearing through the side of the banjo and through the double coned race.
8. From the drive shaft end, slide on the outside tapered bearing, thrust washer, and adjusting nut. Tighten the adjusting nut to eliminate all end play, with free rotation.

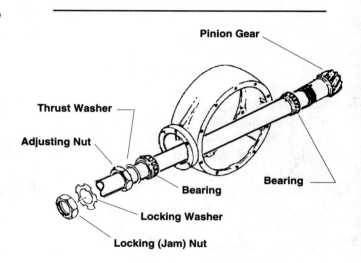

9. Attach a torque wrench to the end of the drive shaft spline, using a 1-1/16 six point socket. Tighten the pinion bearing adjusting nut for 20 inch lbs. of drag on the drive shaft while tightening the pinion bearing adjusting nut.

NOTE
If the same (used) bearing is being used, adjust for 12-15 inch lbs. of drag.

10. Install the pinion locking plate and locking (jam) nut. Recheck the drive shaft for 20 inch lbs. drag. Bend a locking plate tab over the side of both nuts.

Service and Repair

DIFFERENTIAL/REAR END

Ring Gear Pattern and Backlash

11. Apply bluing or white lead to the ring gear to check gear tooth pattern. Reassemble the banjo with carrier and no axles (install carrier in banjo with ring gear on left side). Install both axle housings with the preestablished banjo gaskets. Torque the axle housing bolts to 35 ft. lbs. (Left axle housing has weld seam to front.)

12. Rotate the drive shaft so that the pinion gear pattern will be left on the ring gear. Reach into the oil filler plug hole to check gear backlash. Backlash should be .008 to .010". Adjust backlash and gear pattern by moving the ring gear closer to or further away from the pinion gear. This adjustment is made by moving the proper gasket thickness from one side of the banjo to the other side. This maintains the carrier bearing preload while moving the position of the ring gear relative to the pinion. Remove the left axle housing and check gear tooth pattern on the ring gear. Move banjo gaskets from the left side (driver's side) to the right side to move the ring gear closer to the pinion (for closer gear mesh and less backlash), and vice versa. After moving the gasket, apply bluing, reassemble and recheck backlash and gear pattern. The correct gear pattern is shown below. Note the gasket thickness or number of gaskets on each side of the banjo.

13. After obtaining correct backlash and gear pattern, completely disassemble differential housing and carrier assembly. Maintain the previously set gasket thickness on each side of the differential housing. Do not remove drive shaft and pinion from banjo.

Assembling Differential

1. Disassemble the carrier halves and reassemble with axles and spider yoke and gears. Place the spider yoke in the same location as disassembled. Be sure to align carrier halves to the previous punch marks on each half. Torque all nine (9) bolts to 35 ft. lbs. Check end play at both axles (.015 - .020"). If end play does not exceed limits, safety wire the carrier bolts. If end play exceeds limits, disassemble the carrier and check for worn carrier housing or worn spider gears.

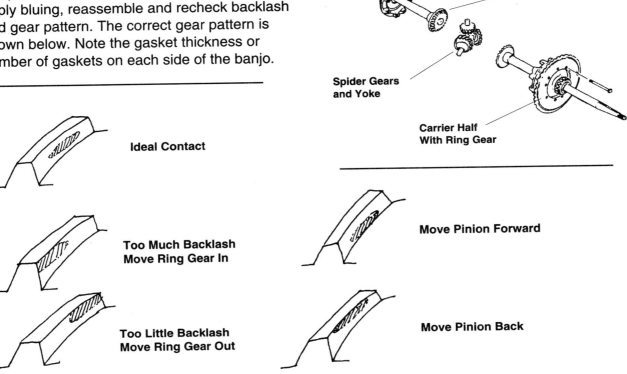

Gear Mesh Patterns

Ideal Contact

Too Much Backlash Move Ring Gear In

Too Little Backlash Move Ring Gear Out

Move Pinion Forward

Move Pinion Back

Service and Repair

DIFFERENTIAL/REAR END

2. Make sure new grease seals have been installed in both axle housings and the front end of the torque tube. Place the carrier with axles in the differential housing, placing the ring gear on the left (driver) side. Install both axle housings with preset gasket thickness on each side. <u>Do not use any sealant</u>. Ensure that the left axle housing weld seam faces toward the front. Torque all twenty (20) axle housing bolts (3/8-24 X 5/8')[9/16 socket] to 35 ft.lbs. Check axle end play (.015 - .020").

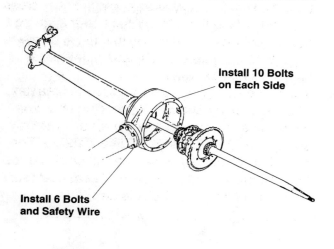

Install 10 Bolts on Each Side

Install 6 Bolts and Safety Wire

3. Place a new drive shaft bearing race (cylinder) in the end of the torque tube. The split in the bearing race faces up. Make sure the race dimple seats properly in the torque tube.

4. Slide the torque tube gasket and torque tube over the drive shaft and bolt to the differential with six (6) drilled head bolts (3/8-24 X 3/4" drilled head)[9/16 socket]. <u>Safety wire all six bolt heads together.</u>

5. Install drive shaft roller bearing sleeve, roller bearing, thrust washer, splined speedometer drive gear, and retaining ring. Install the speedometer drive gear with the gear end facing the front retaining ring as shown.

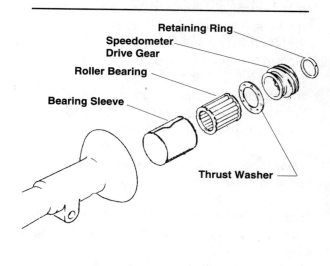

Retaining Ring
Speedometer Drive Gear
Roller Bearing
Bearing Sleeve
Thrust Washer

6. Place the radius rods on the end of the axle housings and attach with two (2) long-shouldered backing plate bolts.

7. Install the front radius rod bolt through the radius rods and torque tube (9/16-18 X 3-1/8")[7/8 wrench]. Tighten castle nut and insert cotter pin.

DIFFERENTIAL/REAR END

Installing Rear End Assembly

1. Check the U-joint at this time for excessive end and side play. The U-joint should be replaced if the joints are loose, showing signs of wear. (Refer to Section I, U-Joint.)

2. Pack a liberal amount of grease around the U-joint.

3. Place gaskets and inner cover over the U-joint on the back side of the transmission as shown below.

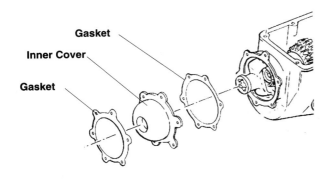

4. Place the differential housing on a floor jack and raise the assembly until the end of the drive shaft can be inserted into the U-joint. The drive shaft is a splined fit into the U-joint. Rotating the rear axles will cause the drive shaft to turn, allowing the drive shaft spline to align with the U-joint.

5A. **After Rear End Overhaul** After the drive shaft and U-joint have been mated, raise the differential to allow the spring shackles to be installed. Attach the right spring shackle first. (Shackle grease fittings face the outside, rear of car.) Apply cross bar and two (2) castle nuts but do not tighten nuts at this time.

5B. **After Transmission or Clutch Removal**
If the rear end assembly has been removed for transmission or clutch repairs, the rear leaf spring should still be in place on the rear end. Place the differiential on a floor jack and raise until the spring is fully seated into the rear cross member. Place the retainer bars on the spring hanger U-bolts and attach with four (4) castle nuts (9/16-18) [7/8 wrench] and install cotter pins. Proceed to step 7.

6. Adjust the spring spreader to allow installation of the left spring shackle. Apply cross bar and castle nuts. Tighten all four (4) castle nuts only enough to allow cotter pins to be inserted. The shackles will not flex if the shackle bolts are too tight. Remove spring spreader. Grease all four (4) grease fittings on the shackles.

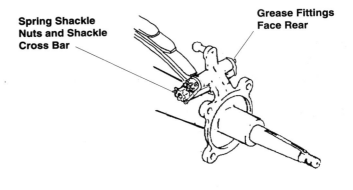

Service and Repair

DIFFERENTIAL/REAR END

7. Place new grease seals (felt or cork) in the U-joint outer cover. Clamp the two halves around the torque tube and install the two (2) side bolts, lock washers, and nuts [3/8-24 X 1", 9/16 socket]. Do not tighten at this time.

8. Install the six (6) bolts, nuts, and lock washers around the U-joint cover [3/8-24 X 1-1/4", 9/16 socket]. Now firmly tighten all eight (8) bolts and nuts. Pump a liberal amount of grease into the bottom grease fitting for the U-joint.

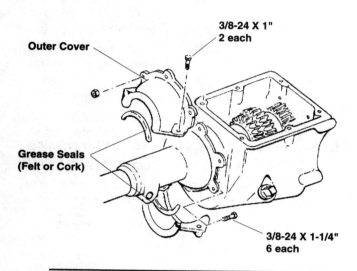

9. Install the speedometer gear cap and gasket with two (2) bolts and lock washers [1/4-28 X 1", 7/16" wrench]. Safety wire the two bolt heads.

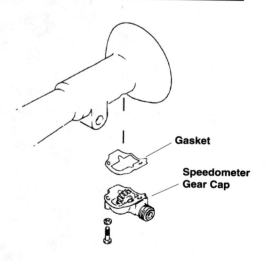

10. Connect the speedometer cable to the speedometer gear cap.

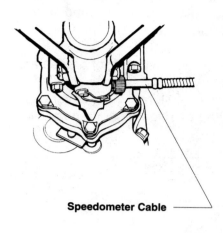

11. Install both backing plates with special shouldered backing plate bolts and castle nuts [7/16-20, 9/16 socket]. Firmly tighten and install cotter pins in all four (4) castle nuts on each backing plate assembly.

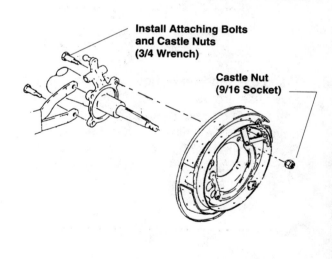

Service and Repair

DIFFERENTIAL/REAR END

12. Connect the emergency brake connecting link with clevis pin.

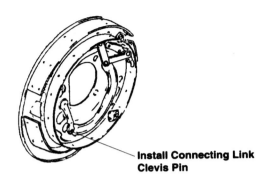

Install Connecting Link Clevis Pin

14. Attach all four (4) rear brake rods with clevis pins and cotter pins.

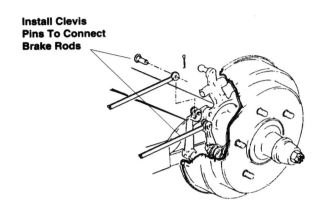

Install Clevis Pins To Connect Brake Rods

13. Attach the brake rod anti-rattler springs to the rear radius rods (5/16-24 X11/16")[1/2 wrench].

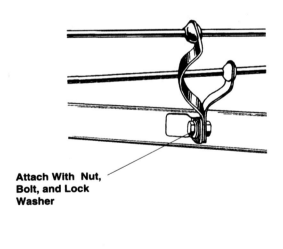

Attach With Nut, Bolt, and Lock Washer

15. Assemble and install both rear shock links as shown below. Screw in the end plug and insert a cotter pin.

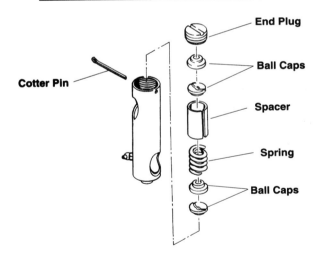

End Plug, Ball Caps, Cotter Pin, Spacer, Spring, Ball Caps

Service and Repair

DIFFERENTIAL/REAR END

16. Inspect the axle key for wear. The axle key should be replaced if it does not fit tight in the axle groove. Install the axle key with the beveled end toward the inside of the axle.
17. Install the rear drum with fiber axle seal, flat washer, and castle nut (5/8-18)[15/16 wrench]. Torque the axle nut to 125 ft/lbs. and install cotter pin.
18. Install both rear wheels and torque the lug nuts to 64 ft. lbs.
19. Check rear brake adjustment (See Section II, Service Adjustments).
20. Remove all jacks and blocks from under the car. Apply grease to all rear grease fittings.
21. Tighten the differential drain plug and add 2-1/4 pints of 600W gear oil to the differential. Install fill plug.
22. Check tire pressure and test drive.

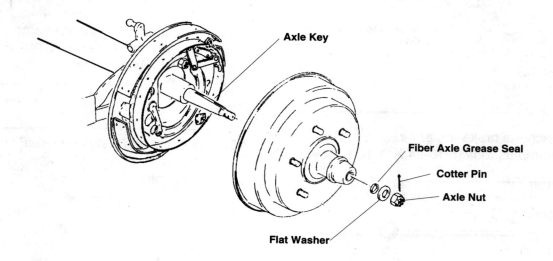

Service and Repair

DISTRIBUTOR

The distributor is the heart beat of the engine. It was originally designed and built with precise tolerances. These tolerances must be checked and maintained if the engine is expected to run smoothly and efficiently.

Repair or overhaul of the distributor is fairly simple. Most distributor problems can be traced to a worn distributor shaft and/or bushings, shorted lower plate, defective condenser, defective points, worn cam lobes, or upper body cracks. A defective ignition switch and/or cable can appear to be a distributor problem. Refer to Section IV - Troubleshooting for testing of the ignition circuit.

Distributor Specifications	
Main Shaft	.4985" Dia.
Main Shaft Bushing	.500" I.D.
Main Shaft Side Play	.001" max.
Main Shaft End Play	.003" max.
Cam Lobe Differences	.0005" max.
Point Gap	.018"
Rotor-to-Body Terminal Gap	.025"
Spark Control Advance	20 Degrees

Removing Distributor

1. Remove spark plug straps, distributor cap, rotor, and upper distributor body.
2. Disconnect advance control rod from distributor upper plate arm.
3. Remove the center head stud nut to allow removal of the ignition cable clamp. Replace the stud nut and firmly tighten.

NOTE

The original ignition cable is a 9/16" round armored cable. The distributor body and shaft must be removed from the engine and the distributor unscrewed from the ignition cable. Aftermarket replacement type ignition cables (non-pop out switch) use a small 3/16" cable. The connector into the distributor for this type cable can be screwed out of the distributor body before the distributor is removed from the engine.

4. Loosen the distributor locking screw jam nut (9/16 wrench) located on the side of the cylinder head. Screw out the locking screw far enough to allow the distributor and shaft to be lifted out of the head.

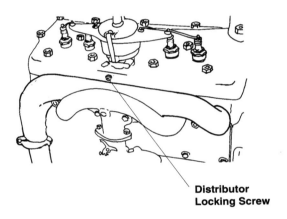

Distributor Locking Screw

5. Unscrew the distributor body off the ignition cable (for original pop-out type ignition switch and cable).

DISTRIBUTOR

Disassembly and Overhaul

1. Place the end of the distributor shaft in a vise and remove the cam screw and washer. Do not misplace the thin flat washer under the cam screw. Remove the cam from the shaft.
2. Rotate the upper plate counterclockwise to release the upper plate from the lower body (casting). Remove the tension spring.
3. Remove the nut and lock washer from the bottom point stud to remove the lower plate pigtail wire. Set the upper plate aside for further inspection and repairs later.

NOTE
The pigtail wire connects directly to the side of the points for a modern point upper plate.

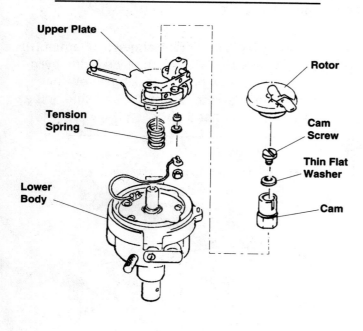

Original Type Upper Plate

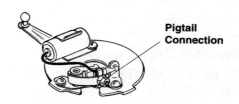

Modified Modern Point Upper Plate

4. Remove condenser mounting screws from each side of the body and pull the condenser out of the lower body casting. The condenser must be removed before the lower plate can be removed.

DISTRIBUTOR

5. Remove the two (2) screws and lock washers securing the lower plate in the body. Lift the lower plate from the body.

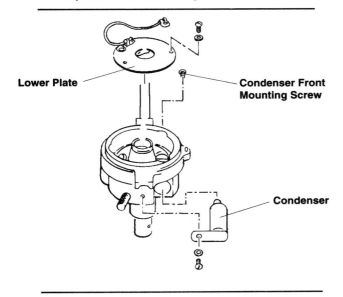

6. Check the distributor shaft end play and side play. If the shaft shows evidence of side play, the shaft bushing and possibly the shaft should be replaced.

7. To replace the bushings and shaft, grind off one peened end of the shaft sleeve pin and drive out the pin with a small drift punch. Pull the sleeve off the end of the shaft and pull the shaft out through the top of the body. Retain the thin flat washer between the shaft collar and distributor body.

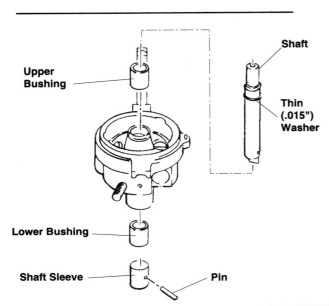

8. Measure the distributor shaft diameter. If less than .498", replace the shaft. Remove the two (2) shaft bushings in the body. Press in two (2) new bushings and ream or hone for a free but not loose fit of the shaft. (No greater than .500" inside diameter.)

Inspection and Assembly

1. Place a thin washer (.015" thick) on the distributor shaft, under the collar, and place the shaft in the lower body casting. Make sure the shaft bushings have been reamed for a free, no slop fit (shaft - .4985", bushing - .500").

NOTE
The distributor shaft and cam screw should be drilled for upper bushing oiling. Drill a 3/16" hole down the center of the shaft, 1.5" deep, and 3/32" hole through side.

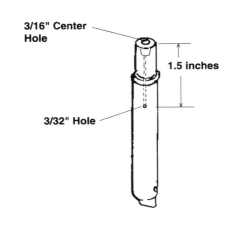

2. Pin the sleeve to the bottom of the shaft. Check for shaft end play. If end play exceeds .003", remove the pin and sleeve and add a fiber (spacer) washer above the sleeve to take up the end play. Reinstall sleeve and pin. After correct end play adjustment, peen both ends of the sleeve pin.

DISTRIBUTOR

3. Inspect the lower plate rivets for tight fit. With an ohmmeter, test for no continuity between the lower contact bracket and the plate. If there is continuity, the rivets are probably shorted to the plate. The lower plate should be replaced rather than attempting to repair it.
4. Check the lower plate pigtail wire for frayed strands. If broken or frayed strands or insulation, replace the pigtail wire with 60 or 80 strand, 16 gauge insulated wire. (This wire must be flexible.)
5. Attach the lower plate assembly inside the lower body with two (2) 8-32 X 1/4" round head screws.

6. **Upper Plate Inspection** Either of two upper plates can be used for mounting of the points. The original upper plate uses a separate point block that screws to the plate. It is sometimes difficult to maintain a true alignment between the point block and the points. This can cause poor firing and arcing of the points, resulting in premature failure. The cam contact block on the original type points also tend to wear prematurely, resulting in the need to readjust the points every 100 miles or so. Use of the original upper plate also requires the condenser to be placed in the lower distributor body. This is a heat trap for the condenser and will usually cause premature failure of the condenser.

The best solution for reliability of a driven Model A is to install a modified upper distributor plate that provides mounting of modern points (1970 Ford V8 points) and condenser mounted on top of the plate. The advantages are:

a). The cam contact block is nylon and offers little or no wear. Readjustment of point gap is nearly eliminated (every 5,000 miles).

b). Point block and points are one unit, precisely aligned, providing accurate firing and long life.

c). Condenser mounted on top of the upper plate, eliminates condenser heat problems. Ford made two different thicknesses of upper plates. Therefore, the groove in the cast body that the upper plate rides in was also made in two different widths. A Teflon washer (spacer) is available and should be used when a thinner plate is used with a cast body with a wider groove.

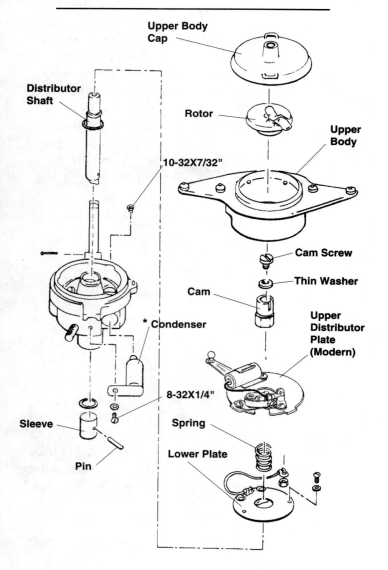

* Do not install this condenser if modern upper plate is installed with mounted condenser

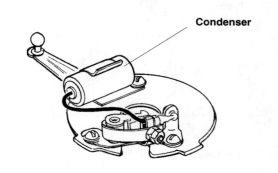

Modern Upper Plate

DISTRIBUTOR

7. Attach the lower plate pigtail to the upper plate point stud. The original plate point stud is on the bottom side of the upper plate. The modern point stud is on the top side of the plate. A longer pigtail may be needed when using a modern point upper plate.
8. Place the tension spring over the center shaft. Push the upper plate down on the spring, inserting the three (3) tabs in the cast body groove and twisting clockwise. The upper plate control arm must be toward the back of the engine.
9. Place the cam on the shaft and lock down with cam screw and thin thrust washer. The point gap and timing placement can be set after the distributor is placed in the engine.
10. **(For original plate and points only.)** Place a new condenser in the lower cast body opening. Secure with an 8/32 X 1/4" screw (and lock washer) at the ground tab end and a 10/32 X 7/32" screw at the condenser end. Do not install this condenser in the body if a small condenser is mounted on top of the upper plate.

11. Screw the distributor body onto the end of the ignition cable.

NOTE
If the ignition cable is screwed in too far, the cable housing will sometimes short out against the bottom bracket on the lower plate. Screw in the ignition cable only far enough to allow the spring loaded end to make good contact with the lower plate bracket.

12. Place the distributor with shaft into the cylinder head, carefully aligning the shaft slot with the tab on the distributor drive gear. When correctly positioned, the small pin on the bottom of the distributor housing must fully seat in the pin hole in the top of the cylinder head. The bottom of the distributor body must sit down fully on the cylinder head. Some reproduction distributor shafts are too long and will not allow the distributor body to fully seat on the cylinder head. The shaft must be shortened (ground off) to allow the distributor body to sit flat against the cylinder head.

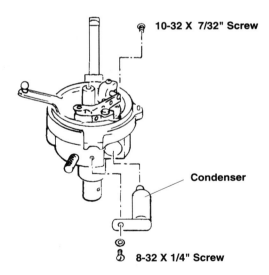

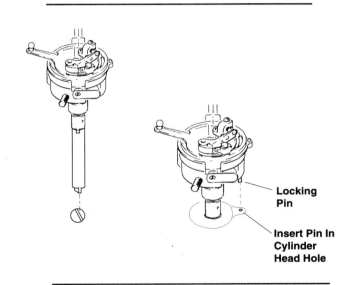

Service and Repair

DISTRIBUTOR

13. Install the distributor locking screw and jam nut into the side of the head. Screw in the locking screw only far enough to lock the distributor in place with no movement. Adjusting the lock screw too tight can cause binding on the distributor shaft, damaging the shaft and bushing. Lock the screw in place with the jam nut.

NOTE

The distributor hole in the cylinder head is not always precisely aligned with the lower drive gear. The two-piece distributor shaft allows for slight variation in this alignment (U-joint effect). The connecting slots in the shaft may need to be opened (filed) slightly to eliminate binding on the shaft. If a knocking noise (similar to a timing gear knock) is heard after installing a rebuilt distributor, try loosening the side locking screw to eliminate binding on the shaft.

14. After the distributor has been locked in place, place a small piece of paper between the point contacts (insulator). With an ohmmeter check continuity from the point arm to the upper plate (or any ground point). There should be no continuity (open circuit).

15. Turn ON the ignition key and check for 6 volts from the point arm to a ground point. This verifies that the ignition circuit, except for the condenser and coil, is electrically okay. With the ignition key ON, open and close the points and look for a spark each time the points open. This verifies the condenser is good. (No spark at this point indicates a bad condenser or very poor point contact.) If any of the above tests fail, a short or open circuit exists in the ignition circuit. See Section IV - Troubleshooting for further troubleshooting of the ignition circuit.

16. Attach the ignition cable clamp to the center head stud and torque the stud nut to 55 ft. lbs.

17. Connect the advance control rod to the distributor upper plate arm.

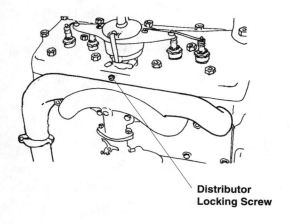

Distributor Locking Screw

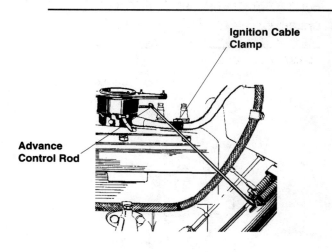

Ignition Cable Clamp

Advance Control Rod

DISTRIBUTOR

18. Set the point gap to .018" and adjust timing in accordance with Section II, Service Adjustments.
19. After timing adjustment, install upper distributor body and rotor. Check rotor-to-body terminal gap. Bend or file the rotor tab for .025 gap.

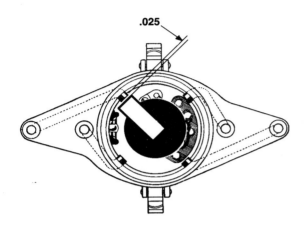

20. Install body cap (with high tension lead from coil) and the spark plug straps to the upper body terminals.

DOOR HANDLES

Door handles varied in design and construction and were made by eight (8) different companies. Handles have no manufacturing identification marks. Early type door handles were not made to be repaired or the lock cylinders to be replaced. The 1928-1929 handles and most 1930 handles have an "A" number on the shaft that matches the locking cylinder number. Beginning in 1929, door handles with crowned locking cylinders were the first to have removable cylinders. Some cylinders require a special locking key to remove the cylinder. In most cases it is best to replace a defective door handle rather than try to repair it. A lock smith can some times re-key a lock cylinder.

Removing Door Handles

1. To remove an outside door handle on closed cars, remove the two mounting screws and turn the handle 1/4 turn to the left and pull the handle out.
2. To remove the outside handle on open cars, remove the center screw from the inside door handle and remove the handle. Remove the two mounting screws from the outside door handle and pull the handle straight out. On open cars the inside door handle attaches to the shank of the outside door handle.

Door Handle Cleaning and Repair

It is usually best to replace a defective door handle rather than attempting repairs. Most handles must be disassembled for thorough cleaning or for re-keying. The disassembly and repair of all handles is basically the same for all outside handles with a few exceptions. Before disassembling, try spraying the lock cylinder with WD-40 and then rinse well with lacquer thinner and blow dry. After drying, lubricate the cylinder with dry graphite.

Not all handles have the same parts, so pay special attention when disassembling. Make note of each part and the order of disassembly. Most handles contain the following components.

1. End retainer
2. Spring and its retainer
3. Escutcheon Retainer Lock
4. Escutcheon
5. Slide Lock
6. Sleeve
7. Cylinder Holding Spring
8. Cylinder w/Tumblers
9. Cylinder Face

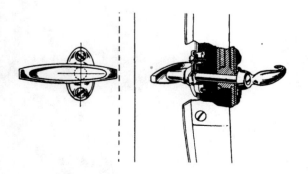

DOOR HANDLES

Disassembly

1. Drill a small hole in the shaft against the retainer for a small cotter pin after reassembly.
2. File the four raised corners on the shaft flush and remove all parts including the escutcheon. (Make note of disassembly sequence for all parts.) It may be necessary to turn the key while tipping the escutcheon for removal. Some slide locks are wider than the sleeve.
3. In an unlocked position, file the small end of the slide lock down so that the sleeve can be removed. In some cases the slide lock may still be used by beveling the corners that have been filed.
4. With the key in place, depress the internal retainer spring and remove the cylinder. With the key in place all tumblers should be flush with the body. File smooth if necessary. If the cylinder turns tight in the handle, sand with fine wet/dry paper and clean.
5. When replacing the cylinder, install the retainer spring on the cylinder, install the sleeve, the slide lock, and with the key in place, push the cylinder into the handle while depressing the spring.
6. Replace all other parts as removed. Try the handle for working ability before installing. Original locking handles take a Briggs & Stratton groove 3 or groove 5 key.

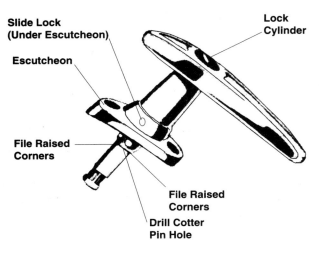

LOCKING HANDLE

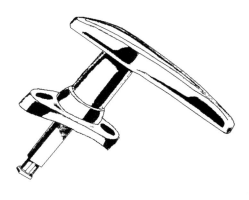

NON-LOCKING HANDLE

INSIDE DOOR HANDLE

DRAG LINK/TIE-ROD

The drag link and tie rod should be inspected for wear on the left side of the car at the point where the tie-rod crosses over the top of the drag link. A sagging and weak front spring will cause the drag link and tie-rod to make contact at the cross over point when the wheels are turned. The tie-rod is a hollow tube and should not be allowed to rub on the drag link. This condition can be corrected by replacing the front leaf spring. To remove and replace the tie-rod requires removing both front wheel backing plates. This will allow the end plugs to be removed from the end of the tie-rod.

Installing Drag Link

1. Position the drag link so that the pitman arm ball fits in the wide end of the drag link.

2. Assemble the pitman arm end with two ball caps, spring, and end plug. Screw in the end plug far enough to allow 25% compression of the spring. This is important to maintain stable steering motion.

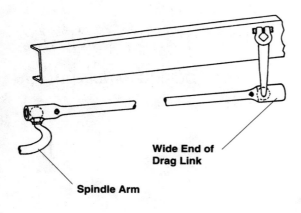

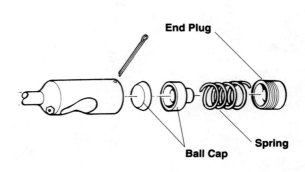

DRAG LINK/TIE-ROD

3. Assemble the spindle end with spring, ball cap, and end plug. The end plug on this end serves as the end ball cap. Screw end plug in far enough for 25% spring compression. Install cotter pin at both ends.

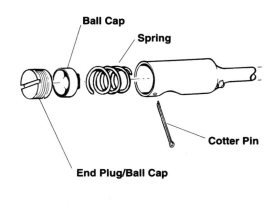

Tie-Rod Assembly

1. Assemble the tie-rod ends with spring, ball cap, and end plug. The end plug serves as the end ball cap.

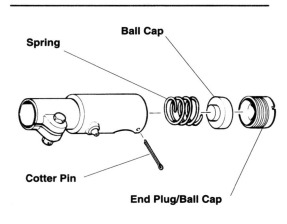

2. Screw end plug in far enough for 25% spring compression. Install cotter pin at both ends. To remove and replace the tie-rod requires removing both front wheel backing plates. To remove the front backing plates, refer to the KING PIN section, pages 1-209 and 1-210.

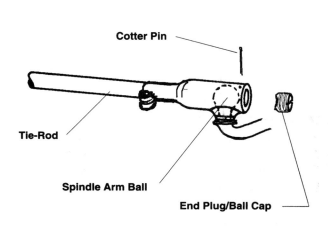

3. Anytime the tie-rod has been removed or readjusted, recheck the front wheel toe-in measurement. Adjust to specification. (See Adjustment section.)

NOTE

The spindle arm balls for the tie-rod and pitman arm ball for the drag link must be round to enable proper spring compression adjustment. The balls can be replaced if excessively worn.

EMERGENCY BRAKE HANDLE

The emergency brake handle went through four (4) design changes during Model A production. The very early emergency brake handle was located on the left side of the driver's compartment, next to the cowl panel and had a squeeze grip handle release. In June 1928 the emergency brake system was changed and the emergency brake handle was moved in front of the gear shift lever, and remained a squeeze grip handle. From December 1928 until July 1929 the handle remained in front of the shift lever but was changed to a pushbutton release. From July 1929 to the end of production, the emergency brake handle was moved to the right of the shift lever, and mounted to the side of the transmission case. This handle remained a pushbutton release.

A spring loaded pawl rod through the middle of the brake handle operates a pawl at the bottom of the handle to set and lock the emergency brake. Squeezing the grip on the early handles or pressing the button on the later handles will release the pawl and allow the handle to move forward to release the emergency brake. The return spring in the handle can be replaced if it becomes weak or broken. The bottom pawl can be replaced when worn, and the pawl rod and button can be removed for re-plating of the handle.

EMERGENCY BRAKE HANDLE

Removing and Disassembling Squeeze Grip Handle

The squeeze grip handle is bolted to the toggle lever in front of the shift lever.

1. Remove the front floor boards for access to the toggle lever.

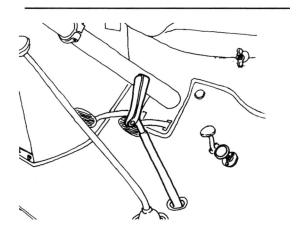

Squeeze Grip Handle
June 1928 to Dec 1928

2. Remove the cotter pin and castle nut on the bottom of the brake handle. Slip the brake handle off the end of the toggle lever shaft (left side).

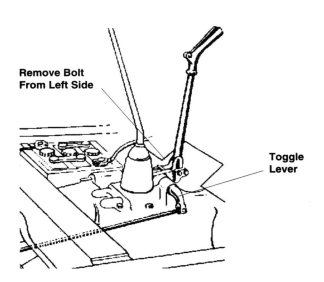

3. The squeeze grip is riveted to the handle. To remove the pawl rod and spring, the squeeze handle hinge rivet must be removed. Be sure to locate a new rivet (special thin head aluminum rivet) before disassembling.

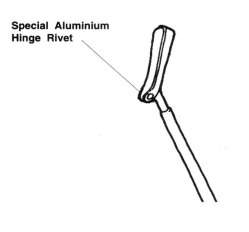

4. Remove the two cotter pins attaching the pawl to the lower end of the handle. Remove the pawl from the pawl rod.
5. Push the pawl rod up far enough to access the attaching rivet at the grip handle. Remove the small rivet from the grip handle to release the pawl rod. The pawl rod can now be removed from the bottom of the handle and the spring pulled out through the top of the handle.

Used On Squeeze Handle June 1928 to Dec 1928

Used On Front Mounted Push Button Handle Dec 1928 to July 1929

Used On Side Mounted Push Handle. 1/4" Thick From July 1929 Till Late 1930. 5/16" Thick From Late 1930 to End Of Production

Emergency Brake Handle Pawls

EMERGENCY BRAKE HANDLE

Removing and Disassembling Pushbutton Handle

The pushbutton handle was used for both the front-mounted handle and the side-mounted handle. Although the lower pawl end was configured differently, the two are disassembled in the same way.

1. Remove the front floor boards for access to the mounting bolts.
2. To remove the front-mounted handle, remove the cotter pin and castle nut on the bottom of the brake handle. Slip the brake handle off the end of the toggle lever shaft (left side).
3. To remove the side-mounted handle, you must first remove the two (2) bolts (3/8-16 X 13/16) and lock washers that attach the brake handle assembly to the side of the transmission. Then you can remove the clevis pin that attaches the emergency brake rod (short) to the cross shaft.

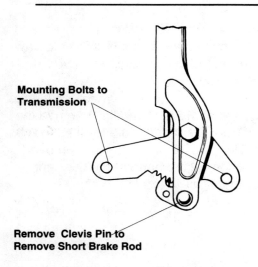

4. To remove the pawl rod and spring, disconnect the small pawl from the pawl rod on the bottom of the handle. Push the rod up far enough to access the pushbutton pin.
5. Remove the small pin from the pushbutton to release the pawl rod.
6. Pull the pawl rod out the bottom of the handle. Lift the spring out the top end.

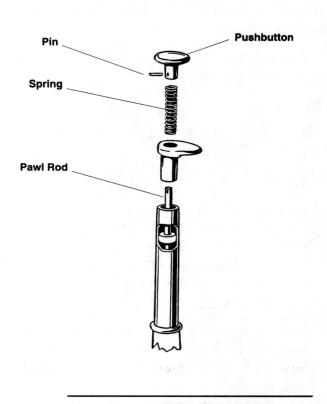

7. Reassemble as shown above. Before bolting the emergency brake handle to the transmission, attach the short brake rod to the bottom of the handle with a clevis pin. (Insert the clevis pin from the outside.) It is much easier to attach the rod with clevis pin and cotter pin before mounting to the transmission due to close proximity to the transmission case.

ENGINE OVERHAUL

This procedure includes step-by-step instructions to remove the engine from the car, engine overhaul requirements, engine disassembly and reassembly, and step-by-step procedures to reinstall the engine. Before removing the engine from the car, a complete analysis should be made to help determine the repairs needed. A compression check of each cylinder will help determine piston ring and valve condition. Identifying engine noises (Section IV, Troubleshooting) will also help identify engine condition and possible repairs needed.

The engine needs to be removed from the car for the following repairs:

- Replace Main Bearings (poured babbitt)
- Replace Crank Shaft
- Replace Valve Lifters
- Rebore Cylinders
- Complete Engine Overhaul
- Replace Clutch or Pressure Plate
- Replace Flywheel or Ring Gear
- Replace Clutch Throwout Bearing
- Remove Transmission (optional)

The following individual repairs can be made without removing the engine from the car:

- Replace Head or Head Gasket
- Replace Pan Gasket
- Replace Crank Pulley
- Replace Cam Shaft
- Replace Timing Gear
- Replace Oil Pump
- Replace Valves and/or Guides
- Replace Piston Ring(s)
- Replace Connecting Rod
- Adjust Rod Bearing Clearance
- Adjust Main Bearing Clearance

Engine Removal

1. Remove the oil pan drain plug and drain the motor oil. Replace the drain plug.
2. Drain the radiator water. The drain petcock is located on the bottom of the water return pipe, under the generator.
3. Remove or cover the front seat. Remove (unscrew) the gear shift knob. Slip off the emergency brake handle boot and shifter boot. Remove (unscrew) the accelerator pedal (top cap).
4. Remove the front floor mat (or carpet) and shift lever plate, attached to floor board with three clips.
5. Remove both sections of the front floor boards [12 flathead screws].
6. Disconnect the battery ground strap from the (+) battery terminal.

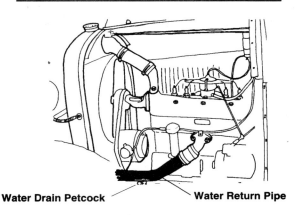
Water Drain Petcock — Water Return Pipe

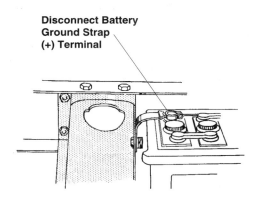
Disconnect Battery Ground Strap (+) Terminal

ENGINE

7. Turn OFF the fuel shut-off valve located under the gas tank (or on the firewall under the hood on late 31 model year).

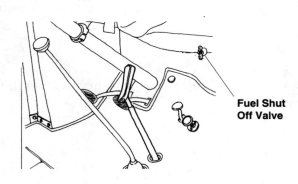

Fuel Shut Off Valve

8. Move to the front of the car and remove four screws holding the front splash apron and remove the front apron. This will allow easier access to the radiator mounting bolts later.

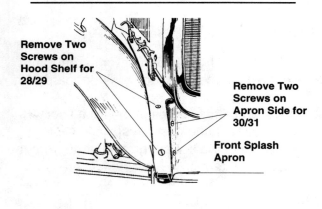

Remove Two Screws on Hood Shelf for 28/29

Remove Two Screws on Apron Side for 30/31

Front Splash Apron

9. Raise hood on left side of engine. Remove short hand throttle linkage and spark control linkage from steering column to distributor.

10. From underneath the car, remove the engine side pans. The engine pans are attached to the frame with three 1/4-28 X 1/2" Hex Hd bolts [7/16 wrench], lock washer and nuts, and two attaching ears under two oil pan bolts [1/2" socket].

11. Loosen all four (4) hose clamps on the two lower water hoses. Remove the two lower water hoses and water return pipe.

12. Remove the oil filler tube and oil dip stick. The oil filler tube is a press-in fit and can be removed by slightly tapping each side with a rubber mallet.

13. Unscrew the starter push rod from the starter switch.

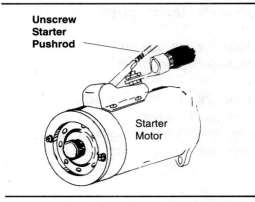

Unscrew Starter Pushrod

Starter Motor

14. Raise the hood on the right side. Remove the throttle linkage to the carburetor, choke rod, and spring by pushing sleeve up against the spring, and disconnecting the rod from the carburetor.

15. Remove the carburetor gas line [1/2 or 9/16 open end wrench]. Remove the carburetor [two bolts, 1/2 inch wrench].

16. Disconnect the exhaust pipe clamp from the manifold (two (2) bolts and nuts)[9/16 socket]. Remove the intake and exhaust manifold assembly from the engine block (four (4) manifold nuts and washers) [11/16 socket].

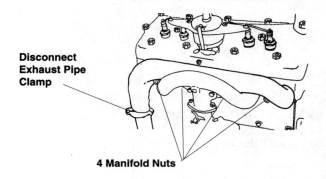

Disconnect Exhaust Pipe Clamp

4 Manifold Nuts

Service and Repair

ENGINE

17. From inside the car remove the choke rod and starter push rod.

18. Remove the accelerator linkage bracket from the rear of the engine [two bolts, 5/8 socket]. The two bolts for the accelerator bracket are located in front of the emergency brake handle, on top of the flywheel housing. It may be necessary to fully depress the gas pedal to allow access to the two mounting bolts. The bracket is then removed by pulling it down from inside the car.

19. Remove the top five (5) bell housing bolts [9/16 socket] from inside the car.

20. Move to the front of the car and remove the horn cover by removing the single round head screw on the back cover [10-32 x 3/4 screw]. Remove the two horn wires from the terminal under the horn motor (pull out type).

21. Remove the headlight conduit connectors [push and twist counterclockwise to release].

NOTE
Some headlight wiring may have been modified by eliminating the connector plug from inside the conduit socket. The wires would then be routed directly from the conduit into the headlight bucket and attached to the bulb sockets with wire nuts. The wires would have to be disconnected from behind the headlight reflector. To access the headlight bucket, release the front lens clip, pull the clip down (spring loaded latch) and lift up on the lens rim to remove it. Remove the center bulb and lift the reflector out of the headlight bucket.

22. Pull the headlight wires back through the conduit to the inside of the radiator shell, leaving the metal conduit and grommets attached to the radiator shell. Do the same for both headlight harness wires and the horn harness wires.

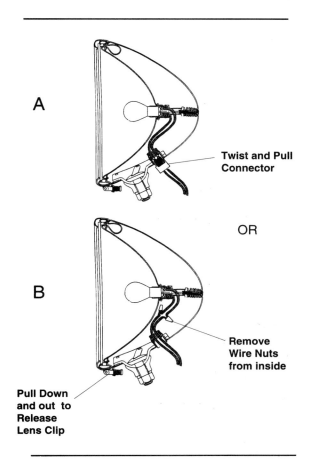

A — Twist and Pull Connector

OR

B — Pull Down and out to Release Lens Clip; Remove Wire Nuts from inside

23. Remove the radiator cap.

24. Under the hood, remove the two (2) screws and nuts from the hood rear hold down bracket.

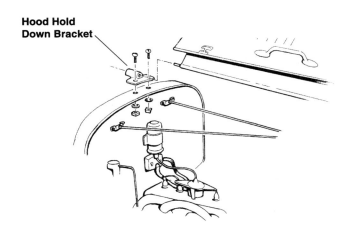

Hood Hold Down Bracket

ENGINE

25. Remove the hood and place it in a safe location on cardboard or carpet to prevent chipping the paint. Do not lay the hood down on the side louver panels. It's best to stand the hood up on the back edge to prevent warping or creasing the top panels.

26. Loosen the two (2) nuts [1/2 inch wrench] on the front end of the two radiator support rods. Pull the rods up out of the radiator bracket.

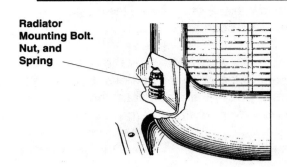
Radiator Mounting Bolt. Nut, and Spring

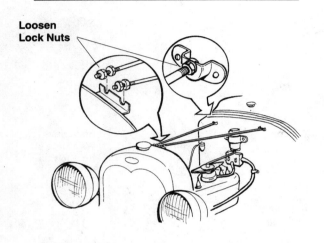
Loosen Lock Nuts

27. Remove both radiator support rods from the fire wall brackets [5/8 open end wrench].

28. Loosen both hose clamps on the top radiator hose and remove the top radiator hose from the goose neck.

29. To remove the radiator, first remove the radiator shell by removing the two (2) screws and nuts on each side of the radiator, attaching the shell to the radiator brackets. Then remove the cotter pin from the two radiator mounting bolts. Using a 3/8 ratchet drive with a 6-inch extension and 9/16 inch deep socket, reach under the front cross member and place the 9/16 socket on the head of the radiator mounting bolt. Hold the nut on top with a 9/16 box wrench and ratchet the bolt from the bottom. Remove the bolt, spring, and nut from each side of the radiator.

30. Remove and retain the rubber pads under the radiator mounting brackets (both sides). Move the radiator to one side to clear the fender and lift the radiator and shell off the frame. On the 28 models, a fan shroud may be attached to the radiator. This can be left in place when removing the radiator.

31. Remove the headlight bar with headlights and horn attached. Four (4) carriage bolts, lock washers, and nuts attach the headlight bar to the fender braces [5/8 deep socket], [Early 28 11/16 socket].

32. Remove the battery cable and harness wire from the starter switch [5/8 box wrench].

33. Remove the starter motor [three bolts, 9/16 socket].

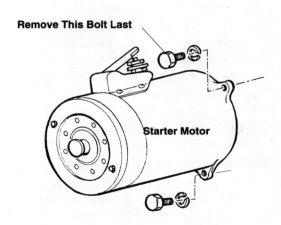
Remove This Bolt Last
Starter Motor

Service and Repair 1-118

ENGINE

34. Remove the two (2) wires connected to the cutout relay on the generator.

35. Loosen the generator mounting bolt nut [3/4 socket] and push the generator toward the engine to remove the fan belt. Remove the generator mounting bolt and remove the generator.

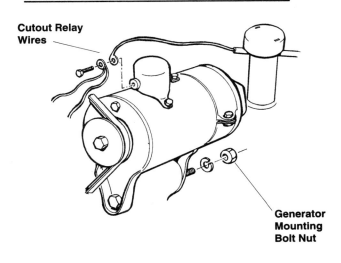

Cutout Relay Wires

Generator Mounting Bolt Nut

36. *(28/29 Models)* Remove the two (2) brass wing nuts on the firewall terminal box and remove the cover. Remove the nuts on both terminal posts and remove the two (2) wires in the metal harness (yellow and yellow w/ black strip) to the generator and starter. Remove the harness clip on the firewall and on the water outlet casting to remove the metal harness from the engine compartment.

(30/31 Models) Loosen the harness clip on the firewall and on the water inlet casting to release the fabric covered harness. Because this is a fabric covered harness, it is not necessary to remove the harness wires from the terminal box. Fold the harness wires around behind the coil.

37. Remove the side water inlet neck [two bolts, 5/8 socket].

38. Release the bail wire from the light switch (push bail down) on the lower end of the steering column. Pull the light switch from the end of the steering column.

39. Pull the harness wires to the left side of the engine, folding the harness back onto the fender apron, clear of the engine.

40. Remove the center head stud nut that holds the distributor cable clamp [11/16 socket] and remove the clamp from the head stud.

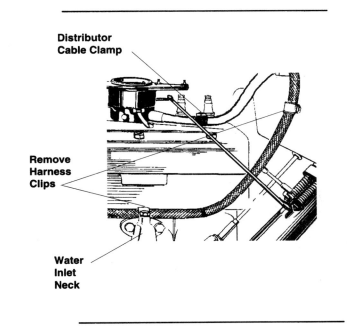

Distributor Cable Clamp

Remove Harness Clips

Water Inlet Neck

1-119 Service and Repair

ENGINE

41. Move to the right side of the engine and loosen the distributor shaft locking nut [9/16 box wrench]. Back out the locking screw and lift the distributor and shaft from the block. Unscrew the distributor cable from the distributor body. Wrap the distributor cable behind the coil body.

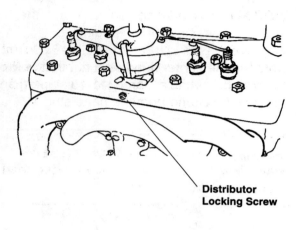

Distributor Locking Screw

42. Place a floor jack under the transmission and raise slightly for support. Remove the safety wire from the four (4) rear engine mounting bolts and remove the bolts [3/4 inch short thin-wall socket] inside the rear engine mounts, two (2) on each side of the flywheel housing.

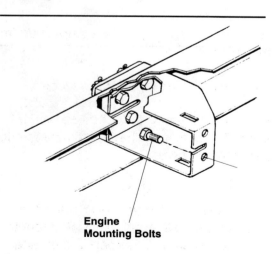

Engine Mounting Bolts

NOTE

If the rear engine motor mount brackets have been replaced with Float-A-Motor brackets, remove the single bolt and nut from the center of the bracket. Do not remove the brackets from the car frame or the flywheel housing. The engine will remain stable until it is lifted from the motor mounts.

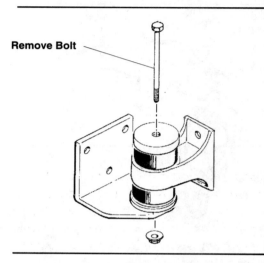

Remove Bolt

43. Position the car under an engine hoist. The hoist must be capable of lifting 500 lbs. To safely lift the engine, attach a lifting bracket to the top of the engine head, using spark plug holes for attachment. Attach the chain hook above the number three spark plug hole and remove slack from the chain.

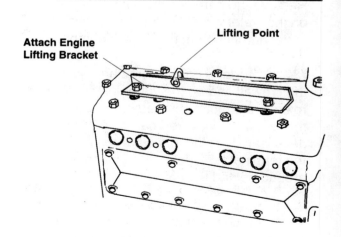

Attach Engine Lifting Bracket **Lifting Point**

Service and Repair

ENGINE

44. Move to the front of the car and remove the two (2) front motor mount bolts [3/4 socket].

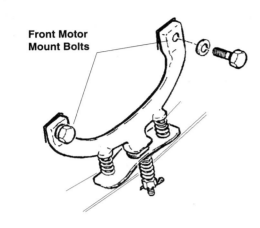

Front Motor Mount Bolts

45. From underneath the car, remove the remaining bell housing bolts [9/16 socket] except the bottom two. The bottom two bolts (behind the wishbone ball socket) can be backed out until they hit the wishbone. As the engine is separated from the bell housing, the bottom two bolts can be backed out.

46. Raise the engine approximately one (1) inch, or until a slight gap appears between the clutch and flywheel housing. Be careful not to raise the engine too much or the clutch disk hub can be bent out of alignment. Raise the floor jack under the transmission as the front of the engine is raised. The transmission and clutch housing should be raised only until the flywheel housing contacts the firewall. Continue to back out the two bottom bell housing bolts as the flywheel housing separates from the bell housing.

47. The engine can now be carefully raised until the oil pan clears the front motor mount bracket. As the engine is being raised, continue to pull forward on the engine to separate the flywheel from the splined transmission shaft. Be careful not to allow the flywheel housing to touch the terminal box or coil.

48. Lower and remove the floor jack from under the transmission. Roll the car back from the engine and lower the chain hoist. Place the engine on an engine stand. When attaching the engine to the engine stand, maintain the engine in its normal horizontal position until after the oil pan has been removed. There will still be oil in the oil pan baffles.

Engine Disassembly

1. Remove the cotter pin and nut [9/16 socket] from the front of the fan blade to remove the fan and pulley from the keyed and tapered shaft on the water pump.

2. Remove the four (4) nuts [9/16 inch box wrench] and lock washers that attach the water pump to the front of the cylinder head. Remove the water pump.

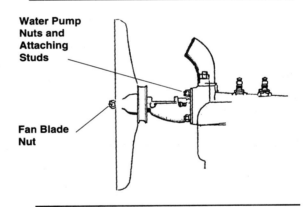

Water Pump Nuts and Attaching Studs

Fan Blade Nut

3. Remove the four (4) water pump studs from the cylinder head.

4. Remove the four (4) manifold studs.

5. Remove all twenty (20) oil pan bolts [1/2 socket] and lock washers. Remove the oil pan and oil pump.

NOTE
Do not rotate the engine upside down to remove the oil pan. A small amount of oil remains in the pan baffles and valve chamber.

Service and Repair

ENGINE

6. Remove the twelve (12) bolts [1/2 inch socket] and lock washers from around the clutch pressure plate. The pressure plate weighs 15 pounds and is bolted to the flywheel under heavy spring pressure (1100 lbs). Loosen all bolts evenly. The clutch disk floats behind the pressure plate. After removing the pressure plate the clutch disk can be lifted out.

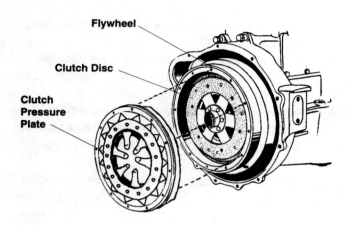

7. Cut the safety wire around the four (4) bolt heads in the center of the flywheel. Remove the four (4) bolts [5/8 socket] and retaining plate.

CAUTION
The flywheel weighs 63 pounds. Exercise caution when removing.

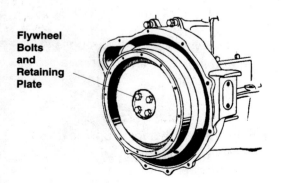

8. The flywheel aligns to the end of the crank shaft flange with two 1/4 inch pins. The pins have a slight taper in the flywheel flange and therefore cannot be driven back toward the engine. The flange of the crank sits into a 1/8 inch recess on the back side of the flywheel.

9. After removing the four (4) flywheel bolts, the flywheel may or may not release easily. To remove it, first insert two short manifold studs in two of the flywheel to flange bolt holes to support the flywheel during removal. Insert a 3/8-16 X 2" bolt in the upper inside starter mounting bolt hole on the front side of the flywheel housing. Screw the bolt in to push the flywheel off the crank flange. Loosen the push bolt periodically and rotate the flywheel 90° and again tighten down the push bolt. DO NOT OVER TIGHTEN PUSH BOLT. Continue rotating the flywheel and using the push bolt to remove the flywheel from the flange.

CAUTION
Do not allow the flywheel to drop from the flywheel housing. The flywheel weighs 63 pounds. Exercise caution when removing.

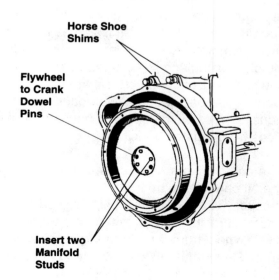

Service and Repair

ENGINE

10. After the flywheel has been removed from the end of the crank flange, remove the push bolt from the starter mounting hole and the two (2) support studs inserted in the crank flange. Cut the safety wire around all four (4) bolts attaching the flywheel housing to the engine block. Remove all four (4) bolts [5/8 socket]. The flywheel housing can now be separated from the engine.

NOTE

When removing the bell housing, two (2) horseshoe shaped shims should be found between the block and the two ears on top of the bell housing. Retain these shims for reassembly.

11. Remove the two (2) bolts [1/2 socket] and brass washers attaching the oil return pipe.

12. Remove the ten (10) bolts [1/2 inch socket] and lock washers from around the valve cover and remove the cover plate. When removing the valve cover, there may be a small amount of oil left in the valve chamber. A shop towel may be needed for clean up when removing the cover.

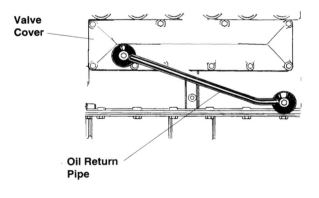

13. Remove the fourteen (14) head stud nuts [11/16 socket] to remove the head from the block.

NOTE

After all nuts have been removed from the head studs, the head must be raised up evenly from the studs to remove it. Due to water leakage, rust may have formed around some of the studs in the head, causing difficulty in raising the head. Apply WD-40 or Liquid Wrench around each head stud to help dissolve any rust. It may be necessary to remove all of the studs from the block to allow head removal.

14. After removing the head, remove all head studs if not already removed. Studs should be removed using a stud removal tool, or can be easily removed by double nutting the stud (locking the two nuts together). Then use the lower nut to unscrew the stud.

15. Remove the seven (7) bolts [9/16 socket] and lock washers from the front timing gear cover and remove the cover. The front timing gear cover is under slight spring tension. After removing the cover, remove the spring plunger and spring recessed in the back side of the cover.

16. Remove the two (2) bolts [5/8 socket] and lock washers from the side timing gear cover and remove the cover.

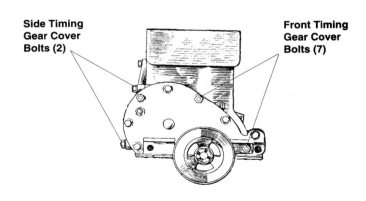

1-123 Service and Repair

ENGINE

17. Move to the valve chamber side of the engine and remove the oil pump/distributor drive gear spring. The oil pump/distributor drive gear spring can be removed by pulling down on the spring about 1/2 inch to remove it from the top of the chamber. Then lift it off the drive gear. The drive gear can now be lifted out of the valve chamber.

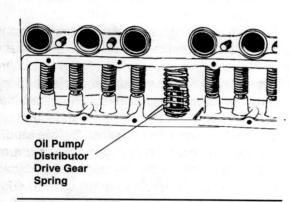

Oil Pump/Distributor Drive Gear Spring

18. Remove all eight (8) valve springs using a valve spring compressor to enable removal of the valve spring keepers from around the bottom mushroom of the valve.

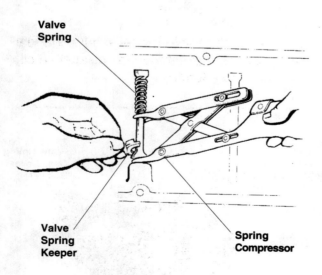

Valve Spring
Valve Spring Keeper
Spring Compressor

19. With the valve springs and keepers removed, pull up on each valve and insert a valve guide removing tool to drive out the split valve guides.

NOTE
Keep the valve guides and matching valves together as pairs.

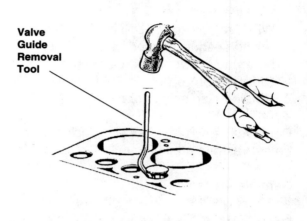

Valve Guide Removal Tool

20. Check the top edge of each cylinder for a ridge. This can be detected by pulling your fingernail up the inside surface of the cylinder to the top edge. If a ridge is felt at the top edge of the cylinder, a ridge reamer will be needed to remove the ridge before the pistons can be removed.

ENGINE

21. To remove the pistons rotate the engine upside down for access to the rod bearing cap nuts. Remove cotter pin and nuts [17mm or 19/32 socket] and push each rod and piston out the top of the cylinder.

    NOTE
    Keep the mating rod bearing cap and shims with each rod and piston if the existing rods are going to be reused. Be sure to mark each piston and rod with the cylinder number from which it was removed.

22. Before removing the cam timing and crank gears, rock the cam timing gear to check the amount of play between the two gears. If there is an excessive amount of movement between the two gears (.008 max.), replace the cam timing gear or preferably, both gears. Remove the crank pulley nut [1-3/8 socket], oil slinger washer, and pull the pulley off the end of the crank shaft. Using a gear puller, remove the keyed crank gear from the crank shaft.

    NOTE
    The crank pulley nut (ratchet) has been found in several sizes. Ford standard size is 1-3/8". Other sizes that exist are 1-1/8, 1-1/4, and 1-5/16. These are most likely after-market.

23. With the engine upside down, all of the valve lifters are seated down, allowing the cam shaft to be pulled out of the block. After removing the cam shaft, remove all eight (8) valve lifters.

    NOTE
    If the same valve lifters and camshaft are to be reused, mark each valve lifter with its location number for reassembly.

24. With the engine upside down, remove the rear main bearing cap.

    NOTE
    Check the bearing clearance with Plastigage (.001-.0015). The bearing clearance can be adjusted by removing equal number of shims from each side of the journal.

25. Remove the cotter pins and two main bearing cap nuts [3/4 socket], (5/8, 12 point socket will fit the square bolt head). Push the two bolts out of the block. Turn the bearing cap up to view the flat mating surface. Check that the entire mating surface to the block is flat across the entire bearing cap. Before repouring the rear main bearing cap, carefully run a flat mill file across the flat surface of the cap to remove any rounding on the outside edges of the cap. Then hone perfectly flat using emery paper on a flat piece of glass.

    CAUTION
    Attempt to hone surface before using a mill file. A file could cause more damage if not familiar with correct machinists filing procedures.

Any rounding on the outside edge of the rear main bearing cap can be the cause of an oil leak after reassembly.

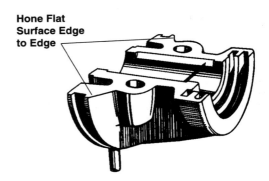

Hone Flat Surface Edge to Edge

Service and Repair

ENGINE

26. Remove the front and center main bearing caps [3/4 socket]. Check the bearing clearance (.001 - .0015) with Plastigage before removing the crank shaft. The front main bolt nuts are accessible from the front of the engine. The right side center main bolt nut is located inside the valve chamber. The left side center main nut is located between the 2nd and 3rd cylinder castings on the left side of the engine (outside).

27. With all three main bearing caps removed, lift the crank out of the engine. The crank should never be laid on its side. Laying a crank on its side can cause it to warp out of tolerance. Reattach the crank pulley with the front pulley nut and hang the crank in a vertical position from the pulley. All engine components can now be inspected for wear tolerance.

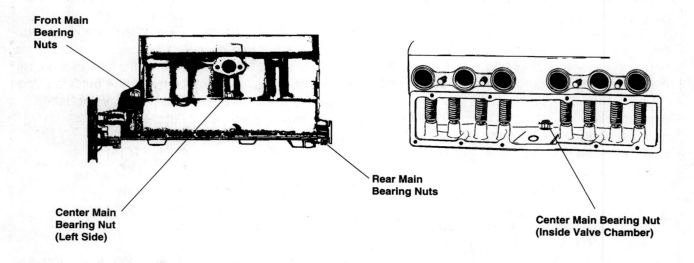

Engine Overhaul

All components of the engine should be fully inspected before beginning engine overhaul. A complete overhaul may not be necessary and can only be determined after inspection and a check of clearances and tolerances. Refer to Table 1-1, Engine Inspection, as an aid in determining engine condition and overhaul requirements. Table 1-2 is a list of requirements for a complete engine overhaul. Table 1-3 lists tap (thread) sizes for all threaded holes that need to be cleaned (chased) in the process of engine overhaul. Table 1-4 lists all hardware sizes (bolts, nuts, washers, and studs) used in engine assembly. Table 1-5 lists the torque values required for engine assembly.

ENGINE

Table 1-1. Engine Inspection

Component	Specification	Inspection
1. Engine Block	---	a. Check for cracks in the block, around the valve seats, valve seats to cylinders, cylinder to water jacket and freeze crack at front of block. Magnaflux block. b. Inspect all bolt threads. (See Table 1-3.) c. Top of block surfaced flat.
2. Cylinders (Cylinder-to-piston measurement made at bottom 1/3 of cylinder)	Run out - .003 in. max. Std. Bore - 3.875 in. Cyl-to-Piston .002 in. .005 in. Max. Taper - .007 in. Max.	Cracks, out of round, excessive taper, glazing, piston-to-cylinder out of tolerance.
3. Valve Ports	---	Burned valve seats, carbon deposit.
4. Valves	Stem-to-Guide - .001 in.	Burnt or warped seats, stem wear, bent stem, recessed seats.
5. Valve Guides	Stem-to-Guide - .001 in.	Excessive wear, carbon deposits.

6. Valve Springs	Length - 2-15/16 in.
	Compression @ 2.50 in.
	  60 ±3 lbs.
	Compression @ 2.75 in.
	  36 ±2 lbs.
		Check for correct compression.

7. Threaded Studs	---	Rusted, pitted, damaged threads. Clean and replace as needed.
8. Head	---	Cracks, carbon deposits, surfaced flat (milled). Magnaflux head.
9. Main Bearings	Clearance - .001 - .0015	Cracks or broken babbitt, excessive babbitt wear.
10. Rod Bearings	Clearance - .001 - .0015	Cracks or broken babbitt, excessive babbitt wear.
11. Crank Shaft	Run out - .002 in. Max. Straightness to .001 in.	a. True straight, no bend, all journals checked for egg shape and taper (out-of-round), all journals shiny smooth, no pits.

Service and Repair

ENGINE

Table 1-1. Engine Inspection (continued)

Component	Specification	Inspection

12. Pistons	Piston-to-cylinder - .002 .005 in. Max
	Ring Gap -
	  Top .012 - .015
	  Mdl .010 - .012
	  Btm .008 - .010
		a. No carbon deposits, cylinder clearance (.002 - .007 in. Max). Ring grooves cleaned.
		b. Ring gap in spec.
		c. Ring groove wear.

13. Wrist Pin	Push Fit .0005	Wrist pin-to-piston fit to spec.

14. Rods	Bearing Clearance -
	  .001 - .0015 in. max.
	Wrist Pin Fit - .0003 in.
	Balanced rod-to-rod
	  2 grams max difference.
		a. Check bearings for cracks and broken pieces.
		b. Worn wrist pin bushing, check for loose fit.
		c. Straight shaft, no twist.
		d. Piston/Rod balanced.

15. Cam Shaft	Straight to .001 in.	Lobe wear, cam drive gear wear, rust pits. Bearing Journals a min. of 1.557" dia. (new 1.560" dia.)

16. Cam Timing Gear	Back Lash Play between
	  gears -- .003 in. Min.
	               .008 in. Max.
		Excessive wear and back lash, center hub tight, no wobble, no broken teeth.

17. Valve Lifters	---	Excessive wear. No cup on bottom. Replace with adjustables.
18. Crank Pulley	---	Cracks in spokes, wobble fit, worn keyway, excessive shaft wear from front oil seal.

Service and Repair

ENGINE

Table 1-1. Engine Inspection (continued)

Component	Specification	Inspection
19. Distributor/Oil Pump Drive Gear	---	Worn teeth, worn tab and slot for distributor shaft and oil pump shaft. Replace if worn.
20. Cam Spring and Plunger (inside Timing Gear Cover).	Spring Tension 35 lbs. min.	Weak spring tension.
21. Oil Pump	---	Worn shaft bushings, worn gears, (See Oil Pump Repair.)
22. Flywheel	Pressure Plate Mount Surface to Clutch Disc Surface - Maintain 1.123 in if resurfacing.	a. Worn ring gear, burned or heat cracks in clutch disc surface, stripped threads (pressure plate mounting bolts). b. Dynamically balance with pressure plate.
23. Clutch Disc	Thickness - .340 in. .250 in min	Excessive wear, glazed surface, loose rivets, or broken springs.
24. Pressure Plate	Finger Adjustments - Top of Collar to top of finger .625 inches. Equal finger adjustment ± .002 Max. difference (Adjust with clutch disk and pressure plate bolted to flywheel.)	a. Burns or heat cracks on plate surface, glazed surface. b. Insufficient or unequal finger adjustment. c. Dynamically balance with flywheel.

Service and Repair

ENGINE

Table 1-2. Complete Engine Overhaul Considerations

BLOCK

1. Block hot tanked, magnafluxed, and bead blasted.
2. Piston cylinders bored to size or sleeved to standard.

NOTE
Pistons must be purchased before cylinder boring. The last .002 inches of cylinder bore are honed for piston fit.

Piston Sizes
Std Size (3.875)
.020   oversize
.030   oversize
.040   oversize
.060   oversize
.080   oversize
.100   oversize
.125   oversize

3. Block surfaced and checked for maximum .003 in. run out.
4. Hardened valve seats installed in exhaust ports (for unleaded fuel).
5. Intake valve seats ground to specification.
6. New stainless steel valves and keepers. (Seal Power V1558 and VK115)
7. New one-piece valve guides for above. (Seal Power VG361)
8. New Valve Springs. (Seal Power VS71)
9. Spring Retainers (Chevrolet # 3279363 - small block Chevy)
10. Chase all threaded holes. (Refer to Table 1-3 for tap sizes) Insert Helicoils if necessary.
11. New pistons and rings fitted. (.002 in. cylinder-to-piston clearance)
    Ring Gap set : Top - .012 - .015
                    Mid - .010 - .012
                    Bot - .008 - .010
    Wrist pin fit in piston: .0003 in.
    Pistons balanced -
    Variance in Piston weight: ± 2 grams max.

12. Connecting Rods balanced ± 1 gram
    Wrist Pin bushing fit : .0003 in.
    Rod bearing clearance : .001 - .0015 in.
    Rods staightened in fixture.
13. Adjustable valve lifters installed.
    Valve clearance set : Exh - .015 in.
                          Intk - .013 in.
14. Head Magnafluxed for Cracks and Milled Flat.
15. Rebuild Oil Pump
16. Inspect Cam Drive Gear. Replace if gears are worn.

CRANKSHAFT

1. Checked for straightness: .0005 - .001 in.
2. Journals checked for roundness: .0005 in.
3. Journals polished.
4. Shaft dynamically balanced.
5. Crank gear and front oil slinger installed. (Crank gear matched to timing gear)
6. End Play: .003 maximum

CAMSHAFT

1. Checked for straightness: .0005 - .001 in.
2. Lobes checked for wear.
3. New timing gear matched to crank gear.
4. End play spring tension: 35 lbs.

FLYWHEEL/CLUTCH

1. Replace flywheel ring gear if worn.
2. Replace pilot bearing. (p/n GMN6203DV)
3. Resurface face if needed. Must maintain 1.123 inches between clutch disc surface and pressure plate mounting flange. Mill equal amounts from each surface to maintain 1.123 inch dimension.
4. Replace clutch disc if less than .300 inch thickness.
* 5. Pressure plate adjustment: .625 inches from top of collar to finger surface.
6. Flywheel/pressure plate dynamically balanced to 0.15 inch/oz.

*   Adjustment made with pressure plate bolted to flywheel.

ENGINE

Table 1-3. Engine Thread (Tap) Sizes

Threaded Hole	Location	Qty	Tap Size
Manifold Studs	Block	4	7/16 - 14
Water Pump Studs	Block	4	3/8 - 16
Head Studs	Block	14	7/16 - 14
Front Timing Gear Cover	Block	7	3/8 - 16
Side Timing Gear Cover	Block	2	7/16 - 14
Accelerator Bracket	Block	2	7/16 - 14
Pan Bolts	Block	20	5/16-18
Side Water Inlet	Block	2	7/16-14
Flywheel Housing to Block	Block	4	7/16-14
Oil Return Pipe	Block	1	5/16-18
Oil Pump Plug	Block	1	1/8 pipe
Distributor Locking Screw	Head	1	3/8-24
Flywheel Housing Inspection Plate	Flywheel Hsng	3	1/4-28
Crank Flange	Crank	4	7/16-20
Valve Cover	Block	10	5/16-18
Pressure Plate Mounting	Flywheel	12	5/16-18
Flywheel Housing to Bell Housing	Bell Housing	11	3/8-16
Front Motor Mount	Timing Cover	2	1/2-13
Rear Motor Mount	Flywheel Hsng	4	1/2-13
Floor Boards	Body	12	12-24
Coil Bracket	Firewall	2	1/4-20
Starter Pushrod Grommet	Firewall	2	12-24
Clip - Generator Harness	Firewall	1	12-24
Clip - Speedometer Cable	Firewall	1	12-24
Clip - Generator Harness	Water Inlet	1	1/4-28
Starter Mounting	Flywheel Hsng	3	3/8-16

Service and Repair

ENGINE

Table 1-4. Engine Assembly Hardware

Hardware (Bolts, Washers, Nuts, Studs)	Qty	Size (Wrench)
Head Studs	14 Total	7/16-14 [Block end] 7/16-20 [Top end]
Short	11	3-1/2 in. long
Med. (between 3 and 4 spark plug for ignition cable)	1	3-11/16 in. long
Tall (for goose neck - water outlet)	2	5-23/32 in. long
Manifold Studs	4	7/16-14 [Block end] 7/16-20 [Manifold Nut] 2-3/16 in. long
Manifold Nuts	4	7/16-20 Hex (11/16)
Water Pump Studs	4	3/8-16 [Block end] 3/8-24 X 1-1/4 in. long
Washer - Lock	4	3/8 Lock
Nut	4	3/8-24 Hex (9/16)
Front Timing Gear Cover Bolts (Dome Head)	7	3/8-16 X 1-1/8 (9/16)
Washer - Lock	7	3/8 Lock
Side Timing Gear Cover Bolts (Dome Head)	1 (top)	7/16-14 X 1 3/8 (5/8)
	1 (botm)	7/16-14 X 2 1/8 (5/8)
Washers - Lock	2	7/16 Lock
Accelerator Bracket Bolts	2	7/16-14 X 1 3/4 (5/8)
Washers - Lock	2	7/16 Lock
Pan Bolts	20	5/16-18 X 3/4 (1/2)
Washers - Lock	20	5/16 Lock
Water Inlet (left side) Bolts	2	7/16-14 X 1 3/8 (5/8)
Washers - Lock	2	7/16 Lock
Flywheel Housing to Block Bolts	4	7/16-14X 1 1/16 (5/8) drilled head
Oil Return Pipe Bolts	2	5/16-18 X 1 3/8 (1/2)
Washer - Flat - Copper	2	5/16 Flat Copper
Starter Motor Mounting Bolts	3	3/8-16 X 1 (9/16)
Washer - Lock	3	3/8 Lock
Flywheel Housing Insp Plate Bolts	3	1/4-28 X 1/2 (7/16)
Washer - Lock	3	1/4 Lock
Throw Out Bearing Insp Plate Screw (Round Head)	2	5/16-18 X 3/8 Screw
Flywheel-to-Crank Flange Bolts	4	7/16-20 X 13/16 (5/8) drilled head
Pressure Plate-to-Flywheel Bolts (grade 5)	12	5/16-18 X 3/4 (1/2)
Washers - Lock	12	5/16 Lock

Service and Repair

ENGINE

Table 1-4. Engine Assembly Hardware

Hardware	Qty	Size (Wrench)
Distributor Shaft Lock Screw	1	3/8-24 X 11/16 Slotted
Lock Nut	1	3/8- 24 (9/16)
Crank Shaft Main Bearing Bolts	6	Special Square Head
Main Bearing Nuts	6	1/2-20 Castle (3/4)
Rod Bearing Nuts	8	7/16-20 Castle (21/32)
Starter Switch Screws	4	10-32 X 5/16 Screw
Washer - Lock	4	5/16 Lock
Starter Switch Battery Cable Nut	1	3/8-16 thin (5/8)
Washer - Lock	1	3/8 Lock
Washer - Flat	1	3/8 Flat
Flywheel Housing-to-Bell Housing Bolts	11	3/8-16 X 1 in (9/16)
Washer - Lock	11	3/8 Lock
Front Motor Mount-to-Timing Gear Cover Bolts	2	1/2-13 X 1-1/16 (3/4)
Washer - Lock	2	1/2 Lock
Rear Motor Mount-to-Flywheel Housing Bolts	4	1/2-13 X 1-3/8 (3/4) Drilled Head
Rear Motor Mount-to-Frame Bolts	6	5/16-24 X 1-3/8 (1/2) with cotter hole
Nut - Castellated	6	5/16 Castle
Generator Mounting Bolt	1	1/2-20 X 2-7/8 (3/4)
Washer - Lock	1	1/2 Lock
Nut	1	1/2-20 (3/4)
Carburetor Mounting Bolts	2	5/16-18 X 3/4 (1/2)
Floor Board Screws	12	12-24 X 1-1/8 Screw
Washer - Cup	12	Special Cup Washer
Coil Clamp Screws	2	1/4-20 X 1/2 Rd Hd
Washer - Lock	2	1/4 Lock
Terminal Box Screws-Firewall Mounting	4	10-32 X 3/8 Screw
Washer - Lock	4	#10 Lock
Starter Push Rod Grommet Screws	2	12-24 X 1/2 Rd Hd
Clip - Generator Harness - Firewall Clip Screw	1	12-24 X 1/2 Rd Hd
Washer - Lock	1	#12 Lock
Clip - Generator Harness - Water Inlet Clip Bolt	1	1/4-28 X 1/2 (7/16)
Washer - Lock	1	1/4 Lock
Clip - Speedometer Cable - Firewall Clip Screw	1	12-24 X 1/2 Rd Hd
Washer - Lock	1	#12 Lock
Engine Side Pans-to-Frame (3 each side)	6	1/4-28 X 1/2 Hex Hd
Washer - Lock	6	1/4 Lock
Nut	6	1/4-28 Square

Service and Repair

ENGINE

Table 1-4. Engine Assembly Hardware (continued)

Hardware (Bolts, Washers, Nuts, Studs)	Qty	Size (Wrench)
Valve Cover Bolts	10	5/16-18 X 3/4 (1/2)
Washer - Lock	10	5/16 Lock
Radiator Mounting Bolts	2	3/8-24 X 2 (9/16) with cotter hole
Nut - Castle	2	3/8-24 Castle (9/16)
Headlight Bar Bolts (Carriage)	4	3/8-16 X 1-9/16 carriage bolt
Washer - Lock	4	3/8 Lock
Nut	4	3/8-16 (5/8) Early 28 only - (11/16)
Fan Blade Nut - Castle	1	7/16-20 Castle (5/8)
Generator Cutout Mounting Screws	2	10-32 X 5/16 Screws
Washer - Lock	2	# 10 Lock
Oil Pump Plug	1	1/8 X 5/16 pipe thread

Table 1-5. Engine Assembly Torque Values

Bolt / Nut	* Torque (ft. lbs.)
Cylinder Head Nuts	55 ft. lbs.
Manifold Nuts	45 ft. lbs.
Flywheel Housing-to-Cylinder Block Bolts	55 ft. lbs. (Grade 8 Bolts)
Flywheel-to-Crank Bolts	65 ft. lbs. (Grade 8 Bolts)
Pressure Plate-to-Flywheel Bolts	20 ft. lbs (Grade 5 or better Bolts)
Camshaft Nut	100 ft. lbs.
Crankshaft Pulley Nut	80 ft. lbs.
Main Bearing Cap Bolts	80 ft. lbs.
Rod Bearing Nuts	35 ft. lbs.
Valve Chamber Cover Bolts	20 ft. lbs
Spark Plugs	25 ft. lbs

* All torque values expressed as Dry Torque values. See Appendix for additional torque information.

Service and Repair

ENGINE

Engine Assembly

Before engine assembly is started, all machining work must have been completed on the cylinder block and babbitt bearings poured. If new bearings have been poured, the machine shop that poured and line-bored the new bearings should install and properly fit the crank. New poured main bearings will include a shim pack on each side of the bearing cap. This will allow for adjustment as the bearings wear. The recommended clearance for the main and rod bearings is .001" to .0015". If you install the crank, do one bearing at a time and finish it completely before moving to the next. Check the rotation of the crank, noting the drag after each bearing cap has been tightened. The amount of drag you feel while turning the engine over indicates the clearance between the bearings and crankshaft. Assembly of the engine components should be completed in the order given.

Before starting engine assembly, have the following items on hand:

- Tube of Lubriplate to pre-lube the bearings.
- Two strips of .001" to .003" Plastigage.
- Tube of #2 Permatex gasket sealant.
- A complete engine gasket set.
- A variety of main and rod bearing shims.

Remove the two asbestos rope gaskets (half moon shaped) from the engine gasket set and soak in oil for two or three days before starting engine reassembly. Place the rear main cork gasket (3/8" wide X 1/4" thick X 8" long) in a pan of water and allow to soak for 24 hours before using.

Before starting engine assembly paint the following items Ford Engine Green:
- Engine Block
- Front Timing Gear Cover
- Side Timing Gear Cover
- Valve Cover
- Flywheel Housing
- Cylinder Head
- Top Water Outlet Casting (Goose Neck)
- Side Water Inlet Casting

Install Crankshaft

1. Align the oil slinger washer and crank gear with the keyed end on the crank shaft. Press the gear and oil slinger on the shaft. The cup opening faces the front. Place the pulley on the end of the crank shaft and tighten the ratchet nut [1 3/8" socket] on the end of the shaft.

NOTE

Before installing the ratchet nut, make sure the end of the pulley extends slightly beyond the end of the crank shaft. If the crank shaft extends beyond the end of the pulley by the slightest amount, the ratchet nut cannot be tightened against the pulley, allowing the pulley to move against the woodruff key. The ratchet nut must screw up tight against the pulley. Add an extra oil slinger washer if necessary to push the pulley forward.

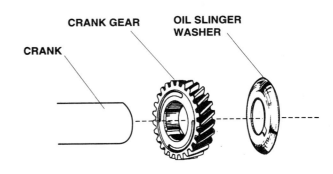

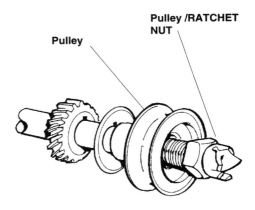

ENGINE

2. With the engine upside down on the engine stand, check the rear main bearing oil seal to make sure it does not extend above the block surface. The block surface at the rear main needs to be perfectly flat from the oil seal to the front of the bearing. This is necessary for correct oil seal at the rear main. If necessary, use a flat mill file to remove any protrusion of the rear main seal above the block surface.

NOTE
Some replacement rear oil seals are too long and must be filed down after installation.

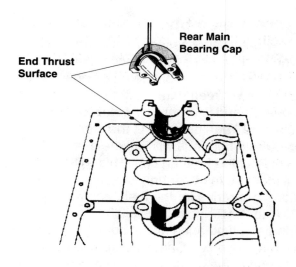

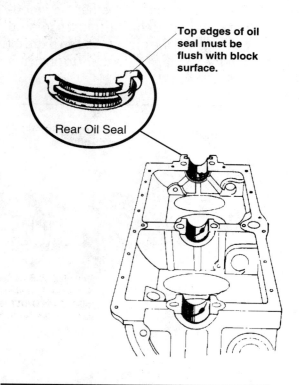

3. Set the crank in the main bearings. The rear main bearing establishes the thrust clearance of the crankshaft. There is a thrust surface cut on the front and back portion of the rear main bearing. Check the thrust clearance for a maximum of .003" clearance.

4. Set the center and front main bearing caps in place, with the correct shim pack placed on each side of the bearing cap. Install the two center and two front main bearing bolts and firmly tighten (approximately 50 ft. lbs. torque for testing) with the socket wrench. (Use a 5/8 socket on the square head of the main bearing bolt and a 3/4 socket on the nut.) Rotate the crank and check for a slight drag on the crank. Add or remove shims until a slight drag is felt on the rotation of the crank.

5. Remove the two (2) center main bearing cap bolts and bearing cap (installed in previous step), being careful not to disturb the shim pack on each side of the cap. Thoroughly clean all oil and lubricant from the main bearing cap and crank journal. Place a 1 inch strip of Plastigage on top of the crank journal. Replace the bearing cap, being careful to replace the same shim pack on each side of the bearing cap. Firmly tighten the two main bolts (approximately 50 ft. lbs. torque). DO NOT ROTATE THE CRANK WHEN USING PLASTIGAGE TO CHECK BEARING CLEARANCE.

Service and Repair

ENGINE

6. Remove the bearing cap and measure the width of the Plastigage on the crank journal, using the printed gage on the outside of the Plastigage package. The main bearing clearance should be set at .001 to .0015 inches. Add or remove shims on each side of the bearing to obtain correct clearance. Thoroughly clean all Plastigage material from the bearing cap and crank journal before making a second measurement.

NOTE

A shim pack is a laminated pack of shims usually consisting of four or five shims, measuring .001 to .003 " each. Shims can be peeled from the pack using a knife blade to separate the shims.

7. After correct clearance has been made, clean the bearing cap and crank journal and apply a thin coat of Lubriplate on the bearing surface. Torque the center main bolts to 80 ft. lbs. Check the rotation of the crank for a slight drag before adjusting the front main. The crank should rotate with 25 ft.lbs. or less torque applied. Readjust shims if necessary. Install cotter pins in each bolt end.

8. Remove the two (2) front main bearing cap bolts and bearing cap, being careful not to disturb the shim pack on each side of the cap. Thoroughly clean all oil and lubricant from the main bearing cap and crank journal. Place a 1/2 inch strip of Plastigage along the crank journal. Replace the bearing cap, being careful to replace the same shim pack on each side of the bearing cap. Firmly tighten the two main bolts.

9. Remove the bearing cap and measure the width of the Plastigage on the crank journal, using the printed gage on the outside of the Plastigage package. The main bearing clearance should be set at .001 to .0015 inches. Add or remove shims on each side of the bearing to obtain correct clearance. After correct clearance has been made, clean the bearing cap and crank journal and apply a thin coat of Lubriplate on the bearing surface. Torque the front main bolts to 80 ft. lbs. Always finish the adjustment by rotating the crank to check for proper drag. (25 ft. lbs. or less.) Install cotter pins in each bolt end.

10. Check the rear main bearing cap to make sure the mating surface is perfectly flat across the entire cap. Check the oil return passage and oil return tube to make sure there are no obstructions. Check the oil return tube and make sure it fits tight in the cap. Make sure the threads are not long enough to allow the tube to be screwed in too far, causing the oil passage to be blocked. Maximum thread length 3/16".

11. Check the rear main bolts for correct length. The steel forging has 9/16" bolt bosses and the cast iron cap has 1-1/8" bosses. Use 4-3/16" long bolts on the cast iron bearing and 3-5/8" bolts for the steel forged bearing.

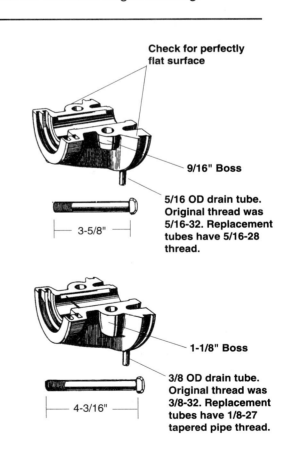

Check for perfectly flat surface

9/16" Boss

5/16 OD drain tube. Original thread was 5/16-32. Replacement tubes have 5/16-28 thread.

3-5/8"

1-1/8" Boss

3/8 OD drain tube. Original thread was 3/8-32. Replacement tubes have 1/8-27 tapered pipe thread.

4-3/16"

Service and Repair

ENGINE

12. Now set the rear main bearing cap in place, with the correct shim pack placed on each side of the bearing cap. Install the two (2) rear main bearing bolts and firmly tighten with the socket wrench. (Do not use sealants on or around the rear main shims.) Rotate the crank and check for a slight drag on the crank. Add or remove shims until a slight drag is felt on the rotation of the crank. Check the clearance with Plastigage for .001" clearance. After correct clearance has been made, clean the bearing cap and crank journal and apply a thin coat of Lubriplate on the bearing surface. Make sure the shims have been pushed against the crank bearing surface (Elongate shim bolt holes if necessary). Torque the main bolts to 80 ft. lbs. Finish the adjustment by rotating the crank to check for proper drag (25 ft. lbs. or less). Install cotter pins in each bolt end.

Install Valve Lifters and Cam Shaft

1. Rotate the engine bottom side up on the engine stand.

2. Remove the crankshaft pulley nut [1-1/8" socket] and remove the pulley to allow clearance for cam shaft and timing gear installation.

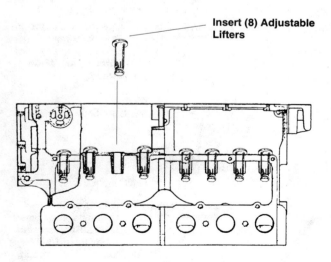

Insert (8) Adjustable Lifters

3. Insert all eight (8) adjustable valve lifters.
4. Place the timing gear on the end of the cam shaft and push the gear on the two aligning pins. Apply and tighten the timing gear nut.

CAUTION

There is a slight off center of the two timing gear aligning pins. The timing gear will only align with the two pins one way. If the gear does not align precisely with the pins, rotate the gear 180° and reinsert. Forcing could cause damage.

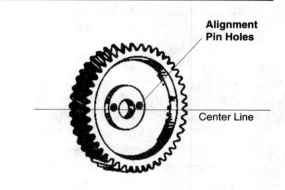

5. Coat the cam shaft lobes and journals with Lubriplate. Insert the cam shaft through the front end of the block, carefully aligning the timing gear mark with the crank gear mark. Check back lash between timing gear and crank gear (.003-.005").

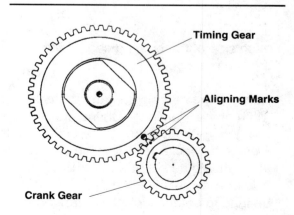

ENGINE

6. Insert the asbestos rope gasket (previously soaked in oil) in the timing gear cover.

7. Insert the thrust spring into the camshaft thrust plunger and place into the timing gear cover recess.

NOTE

Check the thrust spring for correct compression tension. (35 - 38 lbs.)

8. Apply a thin coat of Permatex gasket sealer to the timing gear cover gasket and place gasket on the timing gear cover.

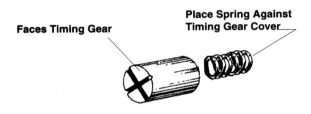

9. Bolt the front timing gear cover in place with seven (7) 3/8 inch dome head bolts [9/16 socket] and lock washers. The engine can now be rotated right side up on the engine stand. Install the crankshaft pulley and pulley nut [1-1/8 socket]. Tighten the nut firmly against the pulley.

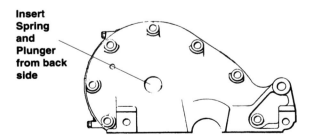

10. Install the side timing gear cover using two (2) 7/16 hex dome head bolts [5/8 socket]. The top bolt is 1-3/8" long and the bottom bolt is 2-1/8" long.

Assemble Pistons and Rods

It is important that the pistons and rods be installed and rod bearing clearance be set before valves and valve springs are installed. The proper drag on the crank for rod bearing clearance can be better detected without valve spring pressure. Piston and rod specifications are as follows:

<u>Ring Gap</u>
    Top Ring   .012 to .015"
    Middle Ring   .010 to .012"
    Bottom Ring   .008 to .010"
<u>Weight Balance</u>
    Differential between pistons : ± 1 gram
    Differential between rods : ± 1 gram
<u>Wrist Pin Fit</u>
    In Piston :   .0003"
    In Rod Bushing   .0005"
<u>Rod Bearing Clearance</u>   .001 to .0015
<u>Piston to Cylinder Clearance</u> .002"

Wrist Pin Bushings

Wrist pin bushings should be checked for proper fit. If wrist pin bushings need replacing, have a qualified auto machine shop install and ream/hone the bushings for correct fit to your wrist pins. The wrist pin should fit the rod bushing and the piston for a "push" fit with the palm of your hand. No clearance movement should be detected.

1. Test the fit of the wrist pin in each rod and piston before starting assembly.

2. Remove the clip rings on each side of the piston to remove the wrist pin.

3. Assemble each piston and rod with wrist pin. Replace the ring clip on each end of the wrist pin.

Service and Repair

ENGINE

Piston Ring Gap

Ring gap must be checked and set before the rings are installed on the pistons. The ring gap allows for heat expansion in the cylinder. Too little gap can cause damage to the cylinder walls. Separate the piston rings into sets and arrange them in the order in which they will be installed on the pistons.

1. Place the top ring in the cylinder, approximately 1" down from the top. Measure the gap in the ring. If the gap is less than .012" clearance, remove the ring and very carefully file the ends until a gap clearance of .012 to .015" clearance is achieved.

NOTE
Use the top end of a piston to squarely push the ring into the cylinder for measurement.

2. Check the ring gap for the middle ring. (All rings can be measured 1" to 2" down from the top of the block.) Very carefully file the ring ends until a clearance of .010 to .012" is achieved.

3. Check ring gap for the bottom ring (oil ring). File the ends for a clearance of .008 to .010".

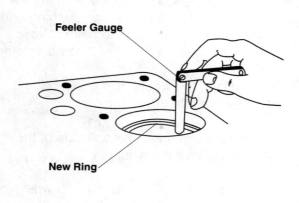

4. Measure and set the ring gap for the other cylinders. Always measure the ring gap in the cylinder where the rings will be installed.

Ring Installation

Install the rings on the corresponding piston, for the corresponding cylinder. Start with the bottom oil ring, then middle ring, and then the top compression ring. Make sure each ring is installed in the correct piston groove and with the correct side down. Stagger the ring gaps (about 120° apart) so that none are in line.

Top Ring   - Inside bevel up
Middle Ring - Step groove down
Bottom Ring - Do Not overlap Expander

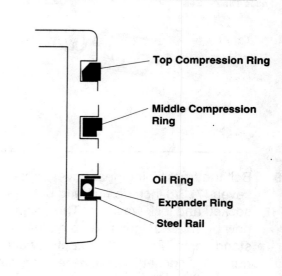

Service and Repair — 1-140

ENGINE

1. Install the oil ring expander-spacer in the cleaned oil ring groove with the gap directly above wrist pin hole. The ends of the expander-spacer are to be butted with two different colors visible.

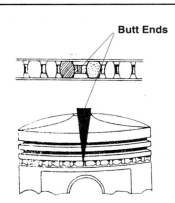

2. Install a steel rail on the top side of the Expander-Spacer, making sure Expander-Spacer ends are not overlapped. The steel rail gap should be 2" to the left of the Expander-Spacer gap.

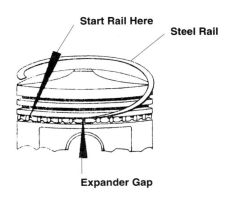

3. Install the remaining steel rail below the Expander-Spacer. The gap of the steel rail should be 2" to the right of the Expander-Spacer gap.

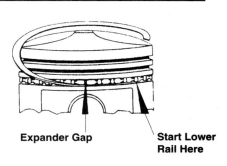

4. Make sure the Expander-Spacer ends have not overlapped and are still in the butted position.
5. Install the two compression rings on each piston.

Pistons Installed

Before installing the piston and rod assemblies in each cylinder, rotate the crank so that the journal for the installed piston is at its longest stroke position (furthest point away from the cylinder). Fully complete the connection of each piston and rod assembly to the crank before installing the next piston. The new manufactured pistons have no slit in the piston skirt. It therefore makes no difference in positioning the piston in the cylinder. The bearing cap on each rod must remain in the same position as when the bearing was line bored. The rod and cap must be clearly marked for correct positioning before the cap is removed for installation. When removing the bearing cap from the rod, keep the shims separated and identified so they can be reinstalled on the same side as removed. As the rods are being lowered into the crankcase, care should be taken that the rod bolts do not strike the crank journal (or slip a short piece of 7/16 I.D. thin wall clear plastic tubing over rod bolts). Torque the rod bearing nuts to 35 ft.lbs.

Service and Repair

ENGINE

1. Check the piston diameter measurement at the skirt. Then measure the cylinder diameter near the bottom of the cylinder. If lthe difference measured is less than .002 inches, the cylinder must be honed for .002 inches fit. If the clearance is greater than .007 inches, the cylinders should be rebored and new pistons fitted.

2. Ensure the rod and bearing cap are clearly marked for orientation before separating them. Carefully remove the rod bearing caps and shims. Keep the bearing cap and shim packs together.

3. Apply engine oil over #1 piston and rings. Apply a ring compressor over the rings so that the bottom of the ring compressor is approximately 1/2 inch below the bottom ring. Tighten the compressor firmly with a square wrench. Make sure rings are fully compressed.

4. Insert the piston in #1 cylinder until the bottom of the ring compressor rests on the top of the block. Turn the rod for correct alignment with the crank. (The cap oil slinger opening must face the camshaft.) Hold the ring compressor in place while tapping the piston down into the cylinder with a large wooden dowel. Once the bottom ring enters the top of the cylinder, do not stop. Continue firmly tapping the piston down until the top of the piston is even with the top of the cylinder.

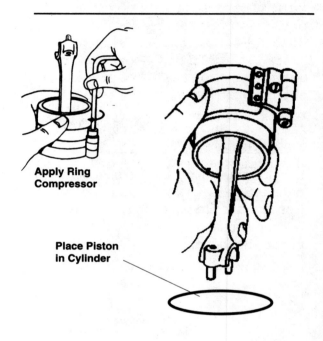

Apply Ring Compressor

Place Piston in Cylinder

ENGINE

5. Carefully place the rod bearing, shims and bearing cap on the crank journal. Ensure the rod is correctly positioned on the crank so that the open end of the bearing cap oil slinger is facing the camshaft. Torque the rod nuts to 35 ft.lbs. [19/32 or 5/8 socket] Rotate the crank to check for proper drag. The crank should rotate with 35 ft.lbs. torque or less. If needed, adjust rod bearing clearance to .001 to .0015".

6. Install rings on each of the other three (3) pistons and install the pistons in the cylinders using the ring compressor. Complete the installation of #2 piston before starting #3 piston, etc., being sure to rotate the crank after each rod is torqued.

7. After all pistons have been installed the crank should easily rotate with 35 ft. lbs. torque (or less) applied. If cylinder clearance is too tight or rod-to-crank clearance is too tight, causing excessive drag, damage to the bearing surfaces or cylinders can occur.

Valves and Valve Guides Installed

All valve seats in the block should have been ground to specification and hardened seats installed in the exhaust ports. If modern stainless steel valves are being installed (SealPower V1558), use one-piece valve guides (SealPower VG361). Approximately 1/4"(0.25") must be cut from the end of each valve to allow for proper adjustment. The cut must be made square with the stem, preferably cut on a lathe.

Installing Original Mushroom Valves w/ Split Guides

1. Drop the valve into the guide hole and wrap the split guide around the valve stem from inside the valve chamber. Push the valve guide up into the valve guide hole. The guide should fit tight enough to stay in place.

2. Rotate the crank until the valve push rod is seated all the way down. This will make it easier to install the valve spring and keeper on the valve. Use a valve spring compressor to compress the valve spring and install the spring keeper over the valve stem mushroom.

3. Repeat steps 1 and 2 for each valve and guide. Refer to Section II, Service Adjustments, for valve adjustment procedure.

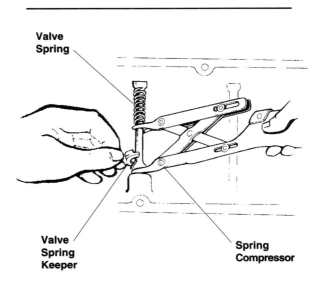

Service and Repair

ENGINE

Installing Modern Stainless Steel Valves W/ One Piece Guides

1. Insert the one-piece guide (SealPower VG 361).

2. Insert the modern valve (SealPower V1558) into the guide. (Cut the valve stem 1/16" below the retainer before installing. See figure below.) Install the spring (Seal Power VS71), keepers (Seal Power VK115), and spring retainers (GM 14003974 or small block Chevy).

3. Rotate the crank until the valve lifter is seated all the way down. This will make it easier to install the valve spring and keeper on the valve stem. Use a little grease to stick the split keepers in the groove on the end of the valve shaft. Use a valve spring compressor to compress the valve spring and install the spring retainers over the valve stem keepers. Repeat the above three (3) steps for each valve and guide. Refer to Section II, Service Adjustments, for valve adjustment procedure.

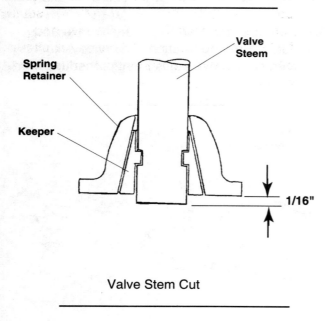

Valve Stem Cut

Distributor/Oil Pump Drive Gear and Valve Cover Installed

1. After the valves have been adjusted, insert the distributor/oil pump drive gear into the valve chamber hole. Lightly lubricate the gear before installing it. (Replace the drive gear if badly worn.) Place the retainer spring on top of the drive gear and then push the spring in against the top of the valve chamber.

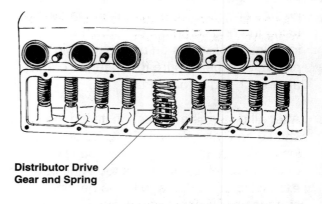

Distributor Drive Gear and Spring

2. Apply a thin coat of Permatex gasket sealer on the new valve cover gasket. Install the valve cover using ten (10) 5/16 X 3/4 hex bolts [1/2 socket] and lock washers. Torque to 20 ft. lbs.

3. Install a cork ring gasket in each end of the oil return pipe and install the pipe using two (2) 5/16 X 1-3/8 bolts [1/2 socket] and two (2) flat copper washers.

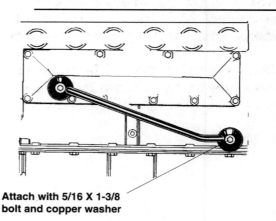

Attach with 5/16 X 1-3/8 bolt and copper washer

ENGINE

Oil Pump and Oil Pan Installed

1. Inspect and overhaul the oil pump according to section titled "Oil Pump".

2. Rotate the engine upside down on the engine stand.

3. Make sure the oil pump spring is attached to the bottom of the inspected and overhauled oil pump.

4. Place the pump shaft into the block in alignment with the locating pin.

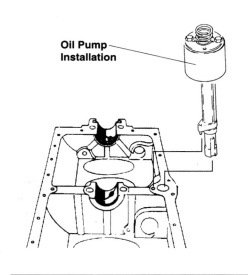

Installing Pan Gaskets

Take extreme care when installing the following pan gaskets. Correct installation of the pan gaskets is essential to prevent oil pan leaks.

1. Check the mating flange of the oil pan to make sure it is not bent and that surface around the entire flange is clean and flat.

2. Insert the half-round asbestos gasket from the gasket set (oil soaked) in the front recess of the oil pan. (New neoprene seal may be available.)

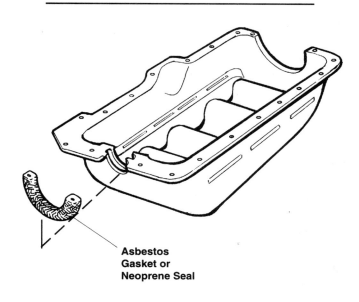

3. Put a thin coat of Permatex gasket sealer on both sides of the two pan gaskets and set the two gaskets in place <u>on the block surface</u>. Make sure the end tabs on each gasket half fit all the way into the rear main bearing gasket groove.

Service and Repair

ENGINE

4. Place the soaked rear main cork gasket around the rear main bearing cap. Make sure that both ends of the cork sit on top of the pan gasket tabs. Place a little gasket sealer in the area where the rear main cork gasket meets the pan gasket.

5. Carefully set the pan in place on the gaskets, placing one pan bolt and lock washer on each side of the pan and finger tighten. Now install the remaining 5/16-18 X 3/4 hex head bolts [1/2" socket] and 5/16 lock washers. Tighten all bolts evenly. Torque to 20 ft. lbs.

Installing Flywheel Housing and Flywheel

1. Install the inspection plate to the flywheel housing with three (3) 1/4-28 X 1/2 hex head bolts [3/8 " socket] and lock washers.

2. Insert the two (2) locating dowel pins into the rear of the block.

3. Place the flywheel housing gasket on the two (2) locating pins. No sealant is needed. This gasket prevents oil from leaking out the rear cam shaft bearing hole.

4. Place the flywheel housing on the two (2) locating dowel pins and bolt the housing to the block using four (4) 1/2-13 X 1-3/8" special hex head bolts w/drilled head [5/8 socket]. Before tightening the four (4) mounting bolts, insert two (2) accelerator bracket mounting bolts in the two mounting holes on top of the housing.

5. Position the two (2) horseshoe shaped shims (.010") between the block and flywheel housing over each accelerator bracket bolt.

Horseshoe Shims

ENGINE

6. Torque the four (4) flywheel housing mounting bolts to 55 ft. lbs. and safety wire them.

NOTE

Before installing the flywheel, the flywheel housing must be checked for correct alignment. Bolt a crank-to-flywheel housing gauge to the crank flange and check the flywheel housing variation according to the procedure in Section II, titled "Flywheel Housing Variation Measurement." (See Service Adjustments.) This is an important measurement to ensure correct engine to transmission and driveline alignment. Incorrect alignment at this point can result in damage to the clutch assembly and can cause the transmission to chatter or drop out of gear under load.

7. Before installing the flywheel, inspect the ring gear for excessive wear. Replace if necessary. The ring gear can be removed from the flywheel by heating the gear with an acetylene torch and knocking it off with a hammer. To install a new ring gear, heat the gear to at least 300° F (with an acetylene torch) and tap it onto the flywheel. The bevel side of the ring gear faces the pilot bearing side of the flywheel.

8. Replace the pilot bearing in the flywheel (p/n GMN 6203 DV).

9. Install the two (2) locating dowel pins in the crank flange. Then temporarily screw two short manifold studs into two adjacent bolt holes in the crank flange. Apply a little grease to the stud threads before installing to assist in easy removal. The studs will assist in aligning the flywheel to the crank flange.

CAUTION

The stock flywheel weighs 63 lbs. 4 oz. Do not drop it. Keep feet clear when lifting the flywheel into place. Feet do not mesh well with the flywheel ring gear.

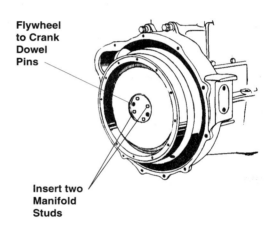

Flywheel to Crank Dowel Pins

Insert two Manifold Studs

10. Lift the flywheel onto the crank flange, using the locating dowel pins and the two studs to assist in positioning. Fully seat the flywheel against the crank flange.

NOTE

Flywheel mounting bolt length is critical to prevent damage to the rear main oil seal. The flywheel bolt spacer plate must be used and the mounting bolt length checked before installing.

ENGINE

11. Insert the spacer plate and two (2) 7/16-20 X 13/16" bolts w/drilled hex head [5/8" socket] in the two open mounting holes. Remove the two previously inserted studs and insert the two remaining mounting bolts. Torque all four mounting bolts to 65 ft. lbs. and safety wire.

12. Install a Flywheel-to-Housing gauge and again check flywheel housing variation (see Addendum).

Clutch and Pressure Plate Installation

Before installing the clutch disk, measure the clutch disk thickness. Replace the clutch disk if it is less than .300" thick or if the disk shows signs of glazing. (Minimum thickness - .250".)

Check the fingers on the pressure plate for correct depth adjustment. If the flywheel and pressure plate were statically balanced at the machine shop, the pressure plate fingers were probably fully adjusted out to allow the plate to be installed on the balancing fixture. Readjust the fingers to 5/8" below the top of the pressure plate collar.

1. Place the clutch disk on the flywheel with the thicker side of the hub facing out.

2. If the flywheel and pressure plate were statically balanced together, an alignment mark was made on the edge of the flywheel and the pressure plate bolt flange. Place the pressure plate on the flywheel in alignment with the balancing mark. Insert all twelve (12) 5/16-18 X 3/4" hex head bolts (grade 5) [1/2" socket] and lock washers. DO NOT TIGHTEN the pressure plate bolts at this time.

3. Using a splined clutch centering tool, center the clutch disk in the pressure plate by inserting the centering tool into the pilot bearing.

4. After the clutch disk has been centered, tighten all twelve (12) mounting bolts evenly. Torque to 20 ft. lbs. Remove the clutch disk centering tool.

5. Check the fingers on the pressure plate for correct depth adjustment. Readjust the fingers to 5/8" below the top o the pressure plate collar. The top of each pressure finger should be adjusted to within .002" or less of each other. All fingers should be equal adjustments.

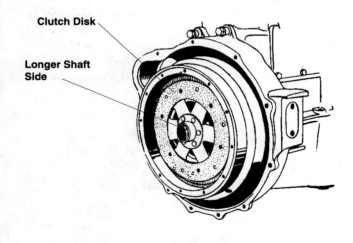

Clutch Disk
Longer Shaft Side

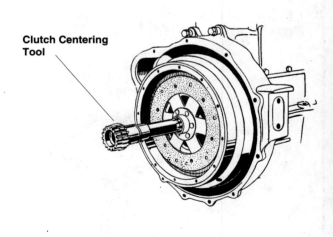

Clutch Centering Tool

Service and Repair

ENGINE

Installing Cylinder Head

1. Apply anti-seize compound to the bottom threads on all fourteen (14) head studs. Insert the studs into the block until they bottom. If any of the studs fit loosely in the threaded hole, remove the stud and insert a Helicoil.

Thread Repair with Helicoil

Repairing damaged threads involves drilling out stripped threads, retapping the hole, and installing a prewound insert.

Typical thread repair kits contain a prewound threaded insert, a tap (corresponding to the outside diameter threads of the insert), and an installation tool.

1. Drill out the damaged threads with the specified drill.
2. With the tap supplied, tap the hole to receive the prewound threaded insert. Keep the tap well oiled and back it out frequently to avoid clogging the threads.
3. Screw the threaded insert into the installation tool until the tang engages the slot.
4. Screw the insert into the tapped hole until it is 1/4-1/2 turns below the top surface of the block.
5. After installation, break off the tang with a hammer and punch. Remove the tang from the hole.

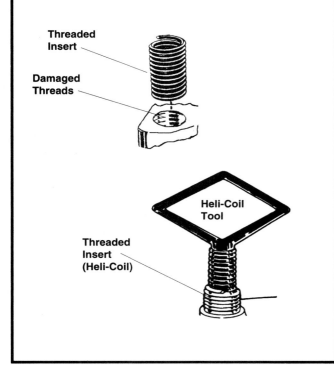

---

2. All studs except no. 8, 11, and 13 should extend 2-3/4 inches above the block. The two front studs (no. 11 and 13) for the water outlet casting should extend 5 inches above the block. The no. 8 stud (for the ignition cable hold down bracket) should extend 2-29/32 inches above the block.

3. Spray a thin even coat of Permatex High Tack (in a spray can) head gasket sealant on both sides of the copper head gasket. Place the head gasket over the head studs so the rolled edge around the cylinder opening is face down (rolled seam bottom down).

NOTE
Check to see if the pistons extend above the top of block surface. If they do, you must use a .100 (oversized) head gasket.

4. Set the head down evenly over all head studs. Make sure no harness wiring or other matter has slipped under the head while lowering it into place.

5. Apply a thin coat of gasket sealant on both sides of a thin water outlet gasket and set the gasket in place over the front two (2) head studs.

NOTE
There are two different size water outlet castings (Goose Neck). The short casting is used on the 28/29 models and the tall casting is used on the 30/31 models. The correct casting must be used to ensure proper radiator hose connection.

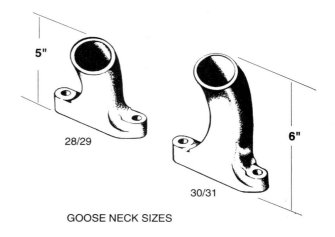

GOOSE NECK SIZES

ENGINE

6. Install all fourteen (14) head stud nuts and hand tighten them.

CAUTION
Take extreme care when torquing the front two nuts for the water outlet casting. Place a paper match stick under both corners to help prevent breaking the mounting flanges when using a standard thick gasket. The best fix is to mill the bottom surface flat before installing and use a <u>thin</u> paper gasket. This will allow the front two nuts to be torqued to 55 ft.lbs.

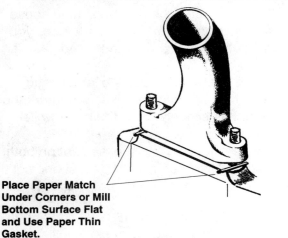

Place Paper Match Under Corners or Mill Bottom Surface Flat and Use Paper Thin Gasket.

7. Torque all head nuts to 35 ft. lbs., in correct sequence. Torque all nuts again to 45 ft. lbs, and then give them a final torque to 55 ft. lbs.

8. Install the four (4) short manifold studs on the manifold side of the block.

Preparing to Install Engine

Before installing the engine in the car, the throwout bearing should be cleaned and inspected. The front motor mount and the two (2) rear motor mounts should also be inspected and defective components replaced.

Throwout Bearing Maintenance Check

1. Remove the throwout bearing spring and slide the throwout bearing assembly off the transmission shaft. (Located inside the transmission bell housing.)

2. Thoroughly clean the sliding shaft for the throwout bearing and the bearing housing assembly. Replace the throwout bearing if necessary. (p/n Bower 2065)

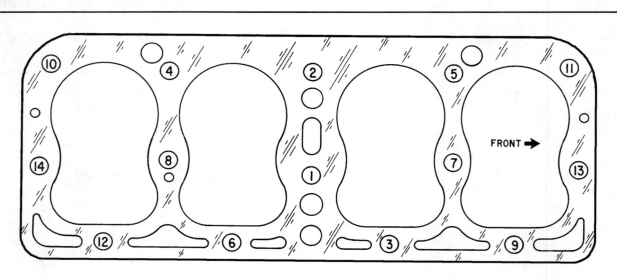

Head Torquing Sequence

Service and Repair

ENGINE

3. Lightly grease the transmission shaft and reinsert the throwout bearing and slider assembly. Attach the retaining spring. Make sure the slider assembly slides smoothly on the shaft.

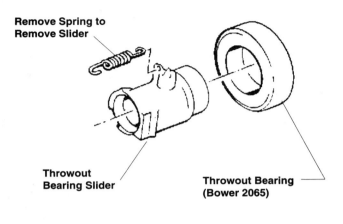

Front Motor Mount Inspection

1. Remove the cotter pin and nut on the bottom of the front motor mount assembly to remove the assembly.
2. Clean and inspect all parts and reassemble in accordance with the figure below. Look for excessive wear around the lower stud where it goes through the frame cross member. Repair or replace if needed.

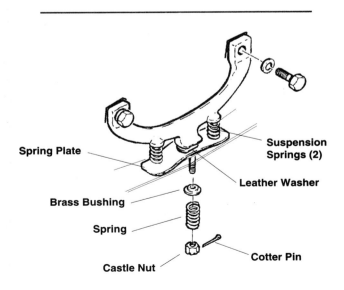

Rear Motor Mount Inspection

Properly functioning rear motor mounts will help reduce engine vibration. If the rubber pads on the rear motor mounts (between bracket and frame) are hard and cracked, they should be replaced. Replace both rubber pads and the mounting bolt sleeves. Refer to Figure A for standard motor mount assembly or Figure B for Float-A-Motor brackets.

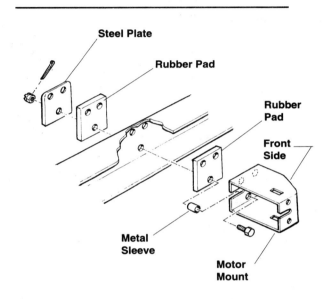

Figure A (Left Side Shown)

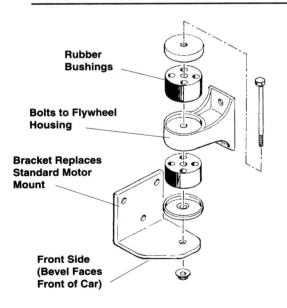

Figure B (Right Side Shown)

1-151   Service and Repair

ENGINE

Engine Installation

1. To safely lift the engine, attach a lifting bracket to the top of the engine head, using spark plug holes 1 and 4 for attachment. Attach the chain hook above the number three spark plug and remove slack from the chain.

2. Use a chain hoist capable of lifting 500 pounds and place the engine over the engine compartment. Slowly lower the engine to align with the transmission splined shaft.

3. Place a floor jack under the transmission and raise slightly if necessary to align the transmission splined shaft with the clutch. Place the transmission in neutral position. The transmission shaft and clutch spline can be visually aligned from inside the driver's compartment, viewing through the throwout bearing inspection plate.

4. With the transmission shaft spline aligned with the clutch spline, push the engine onto the shaft.

5. Insert the top four (4) flywheel housing to bell housing attaching bolts (3/8-16 X 1") and lock washers [9/16 socket].

6. Slowly lower the engine onto the front motor mount while screwing in the bottom two (2) bell housing bolts located behind the wishbone. If the radius ball was previously disconnected, reattach at this time.

7. Insert all remaining bell housing bolts and lock washers and firmly tighten.

8. Move to the front of the car and insert the front two (2) motor mount bolts (1/2-13 X 1 3/8") and lock washers [3/4 socket].

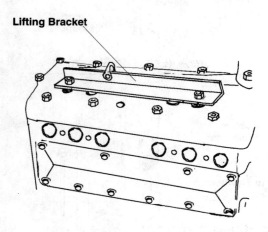

Lifting Bracket

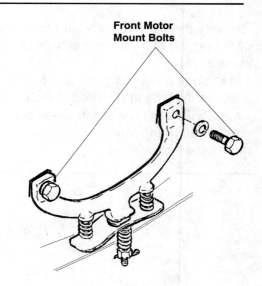

Front Motor Mount Bolts

ENGINE

9. From under the car, insert the two (2) rear motor mount bolts (1/2-13 X 1-3/8" drilled) on each side of the flywheel housing [3/4 socket]. Tighten firmly and safety wire.

NOTE

If the rear engine motor mount brackets have been replaced with Float-A-Motor brackets, insert the single bolt and nut through the center of the bracket. Install the rubber bushings.

10. Remove the engine lifting bracket from the engine.

11. Check the position of the engine relative to the front crank hole. The crank should be easily inserted through the front crank bracket and in straight alignment with the crank pulley nut. The front motor mount nut can be tightened down to position the front of the engine with the crank hole. If there are rubber bushings inside the front motor mount springs, remove them or replace the spring assembly. This type of front motor mount spring assembly is after-market and will usually not allow correct positioning of the engine. See the figure below for correct front motor mount spring assembly.

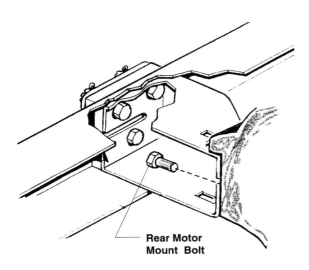

Original Rear Motor Mounts (Left Side Shown)

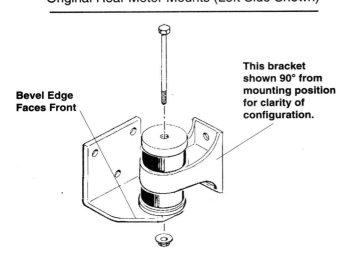

Float-A-Motor Rear Motor Mounts (Right Side Shown)

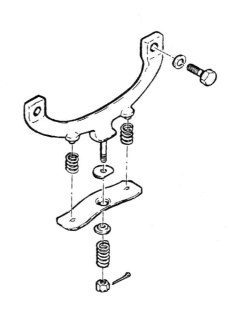

Correct Motor Mount Assembly

Service and Repair

ENGINE

12. Remove the two (2) accelerator bracket mounting bolts [5/8 socket] from the back side of the engine. These bolts can be accessed from inside the car. Make sure the two (2) horseshoe shims remain in place between the engine block and flywheel housing.

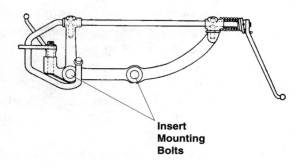

Insert Mounting Bolts

(Viewed From Inside car)

13. From inside the car, slide the accelerator linkage bracket up between the firewall and engine block. Insert the two (2) mounting bolts and lock washers (7/16-14 X 1-3/4") and firmly tighten [5/8 socket]. Check clearance between the firewall and the right end of the accelerator bracket (1/8 to 1/4" clearance). If the accelerator bracket contacts the firewall, readjust (lower) the front motor mount by tightening the center motor mount nut on the bottom of the assembly.

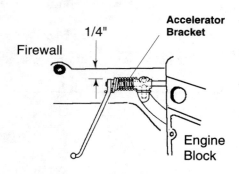

(Viewed From Right Side Engine Compartment)

14. Install all four (4) spark plugs. Torque to 25 ft. lbs.

15. Pour two (2) quarts of oil through the distributor shaft hole. This will lubricate the top end of the engine and lubricate the crank main bearings before the engine is started.

16. Insert the distributor shaft into the shaft hole, aligning the slot on the shaft with the tab on the cam drive gear. The slot and tab are offset so the shaft can only be aligned one way.

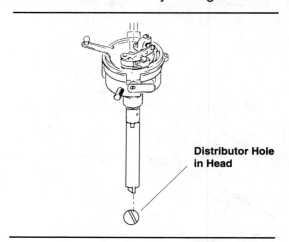

Distributor Hole in Head

17. Screw the ignition cable into the distributor body and then position the distributor in place, seating the distributor locking pin in the hole on the cylinder head. The distributor base should sit flat against the top surface of the cylinder head. Rotate the distributor shaft with the rotor to correctly align the shaft with the slot, allowing the distributor body to fully seat against the block.

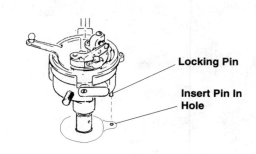

Locking Pin

Insert Pin In Hole

Service and Repair

ENGINE

18. Insert the distributor locking screw and locking nut. Tighten the locking screw until it seats firmly against the distributor body. Tighten the locking nut [9/16 wrench].

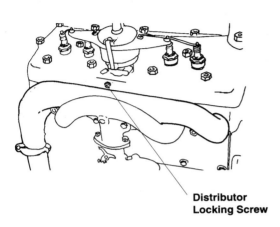

Distributor Locking Screw

19. Install the four (4) manifold studs on the right side of the engine (7/16-14 x 2-3/16"). Install the manifold using two (2) copper/asbestos manifold gaskets.

NOTE

Do not install the gland rings in the exhaust ports unless the port holes have been checked for true alignment with the exhaust ports in the block. Through years of heat and warping, most manifolds have dropped at the rear port and will not match the gland ring insert. The copper clad gaskets will seal without the use of the gland rings. The manifold should be surfaced (milled) before installing.

20. Install the special manifold washers and tighten the four (4) manifold nuts (7/16-20) [11/16 socket].

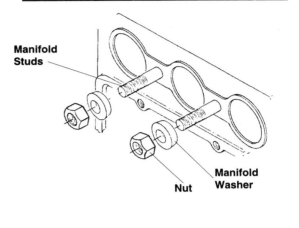

Manifold Studs
Nut
Manifold Washer

21. Install the four (4) water pump studs (3/8-16 X 1-1/4"). Apply the water pump gasket with a small amount of Permatex gasket sealer on both sides. Mount the water pump with four (4) nuts (3/8-24) and lock washers [9/16 socket].

22. Mount the fan/pulley on the end of the water pump shaft with a castle nut (7/16-20) and cotter pin.

CAUTION

Fully inspect the fan blade for cracks before installing.

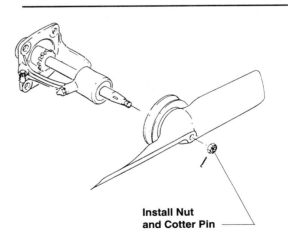

Install Nut and Cotter Pin

Service and Repair

ENGINE

23. Install the generator using a special shoulder hinge bolt (1/2-20 X 2-7/8"), lock washer, and nut [3/4 socket]. Do not tighten until the fan belt has been installed. Install the fan belt (Dayco No. 22425) and adjust for 1/2" movement. (See Section II, Service Adjustments.)

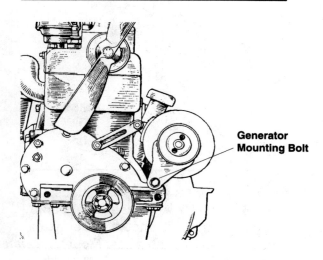

Generator Mounting Bolt

24. Install the water inlet neck casting with gasket and two (2) mounting bolts and lock washers (Dome hd, 7/16-14 X 1-3/8") [5/8 socket].

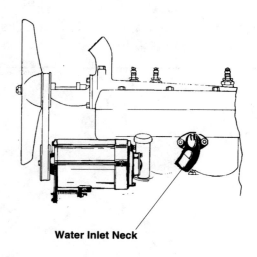

Water Inlet Neck

25. Install the starter motor with three (3) bolts and lock washers (3/8-16 X 1") [9/16 socket]. Install the top-outside bolt first. This will hold the starter motor in place while the other two bolts and lock washers are being installed.

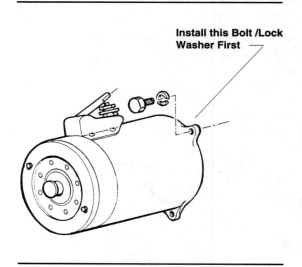

Install this Bolt /Lock Washer First

26. From the right side of the engine, install the carburetor with two (2) bolts and lock washers (5/16-18 X 3/4) [1/2" wrench].

27. Set the radiator on the front cross member. Place a rubber pad under both radiator mounting brackets (28/29 use 1/8" pad, 30/31 use 1/16" pad). A piece of old innertube works fine. Install the radiator mounting bolts, nuts and spring assembly as shown below. Tighten the bolts only enough to install cotter pins in the mounting bolts.

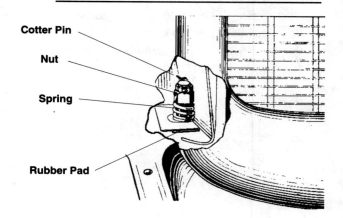

Cotter Pin

Nut

Spring

Rubber Pad

ENGINE

28. Clean the water return pipe and the drain petcock to make sure it is not plugged. Place a short radiator hose over each end of the water return pipe, with two (2) hose clamps on each hose section. Secure the water return pipe hoses to the radiator lower pipe and the water inlet neck on the engine block. Securely tighten all four (4) hose clamps.

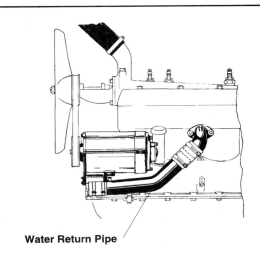

Water Return Pipe

29. Slip two (2) hose clamps over the long radiator hose and install the hose from the top radiator neck to the goose neck. Do not tighten these hose clamps until the radiator support rods have been installed and the hood installed and adjusted.

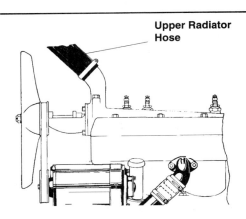

Upper Radiator Hose

30. Install the two (2) radiator support rods in the firewall brackets. Tighten the locking nuts with a 5/8 open end wrench. Attach the other ends of the support rods in the radiator bracket with nut and lock washer on each side of the bracket [1/2" wrench].

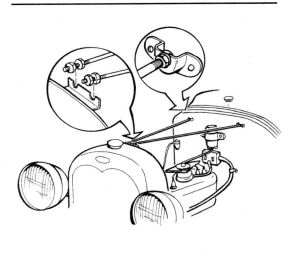

31. The radiator shell and fan shroud may not have been removed from the radiator during disassembly. If the shell was removed from the radiator, reinstall it at this time, attaching it with four (4) pan head screws (12-24 X 19/32") and square nuts.

Service and Repair

ENGINE

32. Attach the accelerator control rod (10-3/4" long) from the carburetor to the accelerator linkage arm, the short throttle control rod (6" long) from the steering column to the accelerator linkage, and the distributor advance control rod (17-5/16") from the distributor plate to the steering column. Attach the harness clips to the firewall and water inlet neck. Route the harness under the clips.

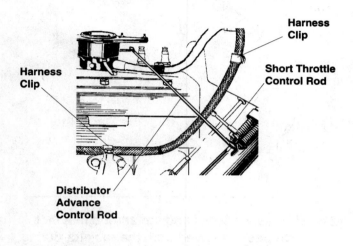

33. Attach the fuel line from the firewall sediment bowl to the carburetor [1/2 " or 9/16 " open end wrench fittings]. Turn the gas shut-off valve ON and check the fittings for leaks. Tighten gas line fittings as needed. Turn OFF the gas shut-off valve after leak test.

34. Attach the vacuum line to the intake manifold if the car is equipped with vacuum wipers.

35. Connect the battery cable to the starter switch. Screw the starter push rod to the starter switch.

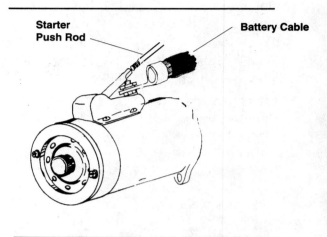

36. Insert the oil filler tube and cap. Insert the oil dip stick.

37. Attach the headlight bar to the fenders with two (2) carriage bolts, lock washers, and nuts on each side [3/8-16 X 1-3/4" carriage bolt] [5/8 deep socket for nuts].

38. Attach the front splash apron with four screws [*28/29 Model* use1/4-20 X 1-1/4" oval head] [*30/31 Model* use 1/4-20 X 1/2" round head].

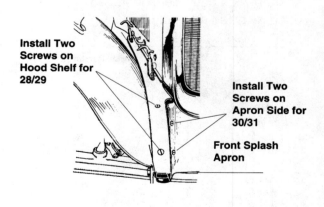

39. Route the wiring harness through the radiator shell to the head lights and horn. Connect the horn wires.

ENGINE

40. Connect the Headlight conduit connectors [push and twist clockwise to connect].

   NOTE
   Some headlight wiring may have been modified by eliminating the connector plug from inside the conduit socket. The wires would then be routed directly from the conduit into the headlight bucket and attached to the bulb sockets with wire nuts. The wires would have to be disconnected from behind the headlight reflector. To access the headlight bucket, release the front lens clip (spring loaded latch) and lift up on the lens rim to remove it. Remove the center bulb and lift the reflector out of headlight bucket.

41. Attach three (3) harness wires to the generator cutout terminals (terminal box wire, horn and head light harness wire).

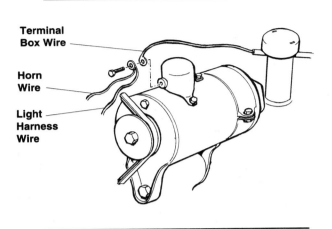

42. Install the light switch on the end of the steering column. Make sure the key slot is on the bottom side.

   NOTE
   Many reproduction light switch assemblies do not fit correctly. An old original will usually fit and operate better.

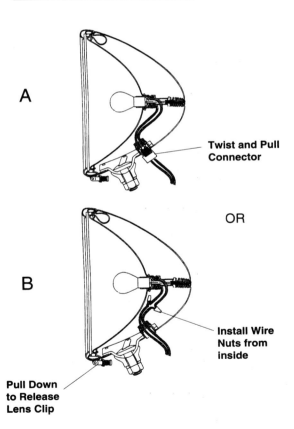

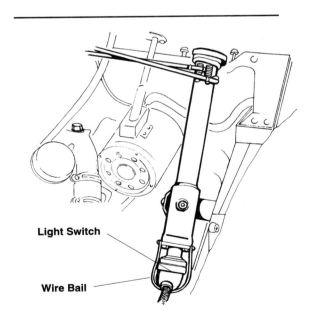

Service and Repair

ENGINE

43. Set the hood in place and attach it with two (2) screws, lock washers, and nuts [12-24 X 5/8" round head] on the rear hold down bracket.

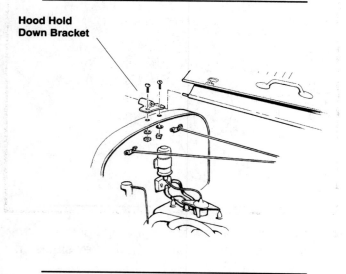

Hood Hold Down Bracket

44. After the hood has been installed and properly aligned, securely tighten both front radiator support rod nuts. Securely tighten the two (2) radiator hose clamps on the upper radiator hose (radiator to goose neck). Check all four (4) hose clamps on the water return pipe hoses. Ensure all hose clamps are tight.

45. Install both engine dust pans from under the car. Attach the two dust pan tabs under two of the oil pan bolts, and attach the other side to the frame with three 1/4-28 X 1/2" hex head bolts, lock washers and square nuts. Make sure the engine pan bolts have been securely tightened after inserting the dust pan tabs.

46. Install the battery and connect both battery cables.
    - Connect the ground strap to the (+) 6 volt battery terminal.
    - Connect the starter cable to the (-) battery terminal.

47. From inside the car apply a small amount of grease to the clutch throw out bearing. This grease fitting is accessible under the inspection plate located in front of the emergency brake handle (on top of the bell housing).

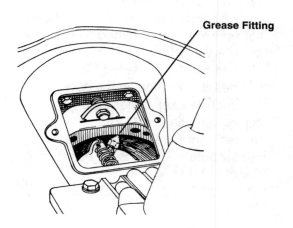

Grease Fitting

48. Install the front floor board and floor mat. Secure the floor board with twelve (12) flat head screws [12-24 X 1-1/8"] and cup washers.

49. Slip on the shifting tower boot and emergency handle boot. Screw the knob on top of the shifting tower.

50. From under the hood, set the distributor timing in accordance with Timing Procedure, Section II, Service Adjustments.

51. Pour three (3) gallons of water into the radiator and two (2) quarts of oil through the oil filler tube. Check the oil dip stick. Add only enough oil to bring the oil level up to the "F" on the dip stick. DO NOT OVER FILL.

52. Turn the gas shut off valve ON, start the engine, and let it run for approximately 15 minutes or until operating temperature is reached. Check all water connections for leaks (water pump and hose connection). Tighten connections as needed.

NOTE

There may be a slight amount of smoke and odor from the engine when first started after an overhaul, due to the heating of the newly painted block. All indications of smoke and odor should quickly dissipate as the engine heats up.

53. Take a five to ten mile test drive and then retorque the head bolts to 55 ft. pounds. The head should be retorqued again after 300 miles.

ENGINE INSTALLATION FINAL CHECK LIST

1. Lubricate water pump.
2. Check all hose connections.
3. Check fuel line connections.
4. Check horn and lights operation.
5. Check crank case oil level.
6. Check radiator water level.
7. Check for oil leaks.

FAN BELT

Replace the Model A fan belt with a Dayco No. 22425. This is a replacement for the original Gates 700 belt.

Replacing Fan Belt

1. Loosen the generator mounting bolt and nut [3/4 socket].

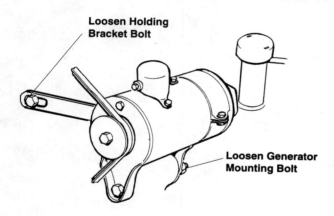

2. If a generator holding bracket is installed, loosen the holding bracket bolt [9/16 socket] on the timing gear cover and swing the bracket away from the generator. Push the generator toward the engine to release belt tension.
3. Slip the belt off the generator pulley and then off the crank pulley. The belt can now be removed from the fan pulley.
4. Place a new belt over the fan pulley, and then under the crank pulley. With the generator pushed up against the engine block, slip the belt over the generator pulley.
5. Pull the generator away from the block to apply tension on the belt. Set the generator holding bracket against the generator and tighten the holding bracket bolt on the timing cover [9/16 socket].
6. Pull hard on the generator while tightening the generator mounting bolt [3/4 socket]. Push on the belt at a point half way between the fan pulley and the generator pulley. Correct tension will allow the belt to be pushed in 1/2" to 1".
7. After correct belt tension is set, push the generator holding bracket tight against the generator and tighten the bracket bolt on the timing gear cover. Retighten the generator mounting bolt.

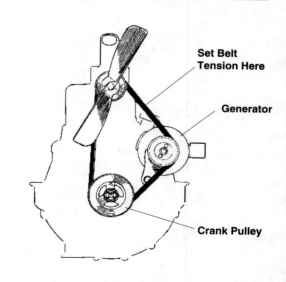

Belt Routing

Service and Repair 1-162

FAN BLADE

The Model A was originally equipped with a 2-blade fan. The most common defect of a 2-blade fan is cracks that are usually found on the blade near the hub. These cracks can be repaired by TIG welding. After welding, the blade must be balanced. The 2-blade fan should be inspected often, as it is susceptible to cracks due to rust, metal fatigue, and vibration. Paint the fan blades a high gloss black for better visibility of cracks. Many 2-blade fans have been replaced with a 4-blade fan. Tests have shown that the 4-blade fan does not provide any better cooling capacity but can be purchased new. The original 2- blade fan can be removed and replaced with very little disassembly. To remove a 2-blade fan requires removal of the hood and top radiator hose, allowing the radiator to be pulled far enough forward to remove the fan from the water pump shaft. To either remove or install a 4-blade fan requires removal of the radiator to allow sufficient room for removal or installation of the fan. The following procedure describes how to remove and install both a 2-blade and a 4-blade fan.

Removing Fan Blade

1. Drain the radiator.
2. Loosen the generator mounting bolt [3/4 socket] to allow removal of the fan belt.
3. If a generator holding bracket is installed, loosen the holding bracket bolt [9/16 socket] on the timing gear cover and swing the bracket away from the generator. Push the generator toward the engine to release belt tension.

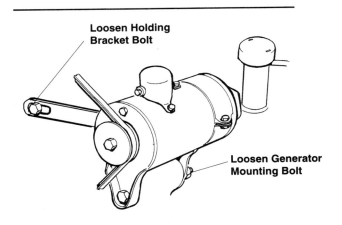

4. Slip the belt off the generator pulley and then off the crank pulley. The belt can now be removed from the fan pulley.

5. Under the hood, remove the two (2) screws and nuts from the hood rear hold down bracket.

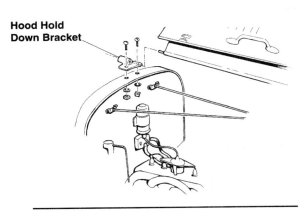

6. Remove the hood and place it in a safe location on cardboard or carpet to prevent chipping the paint. Do not lay the hood down on the side louver panels. It's best to stand the hood up on the back edge to prevent warping or creasing the top panels.

FAN BLADE

7. Loosen the two (2) nuts [1/2 inch wrench] on the front end of the two radiator support rods. Pull the two rods up out of the radiator bracket.

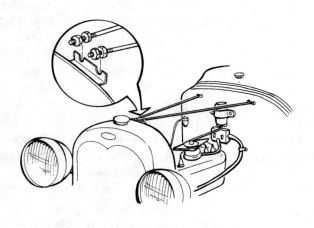

8. Loosen both hose clamps on the top radiator hose and remove the top radiator hose from the goose neck.

9. **(2-Blade Fan)**
Remove the cotter pin and nut [9/16 socket] from the front of the fan to remove the fan and pulley from the keyed and tapered shaft of the water pump. Tap lightly on the back side of the pulley to remove the fan from the tapered and keyed shaft. Pull the radiator forward against the light bar to allow room to remove the fan from the water pump shaft. (May have to loosen the light bar to provide more room.)

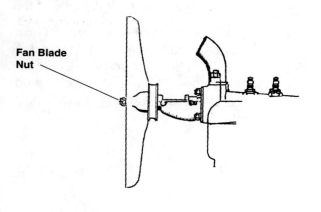

(4-Blade Fan)
Removing a 4-blade fan requires removal of the radiator. Wiring harnesses must be disconnected, and therefore the battery should be disconnected before starting disassembly. Complete the following steps to remove the radiator and the 4-blade fan.

10. Disconnect the battery ground strap from the (+) battery terminal.

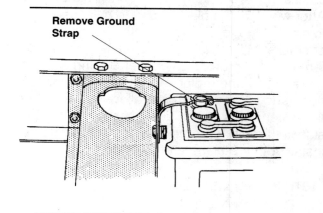

11. Move to the front of the car and remove the four (4) screws holding the front splash apron and remove the front apron. This will allow easier access to the radiator mounting bolts.

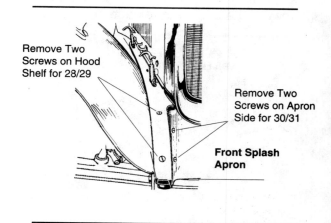

12. Loosen the two (2) hose clamps on the lower water hose.

13. Remove the horn cover by removing the single round head screw on the back cover [10-32 x 3/4 screw]. Remove the two (2) horn wires from the terminal under the horn motor (pull out type).

Service and Repair 1-164

FAN BLADE

14. Remove the headlight conduit connectors [push and twist counterclockwise to release].

NOTE

Some headlight wiring may have been modified by eliminating the connector plug from inside the conduit socket. The wires would then be routed directly from the conduit into the headlight bucket and attached to the bulb sockets with wire nuts. The wires would have to be disconnected from behind the headlight reflector. To access the headlight bucket, release the front lens clip, pull the clip down (spring loaded latch) and lift up on the lens rim to remove it. Remove the center bulb and lift the reflector out of the headlight bucket.

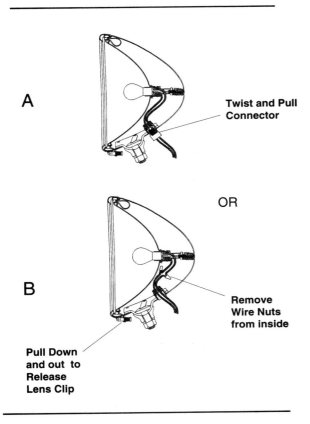

16. To remove the radiator, first remove the cotter pin from the two (2) radiator mounting bolts. Using a 3/8 ratchet drive with a 6-inch extension and 9/16 deep socket, reach under the front cross member and place the 9/16 socket on the head of the radiator mounting bolt. Hold the nut on top with a 9/16 box wrench and ratchet the bolt from the bottom. Remove the bolt, spring, and nut from each side of the radiator.

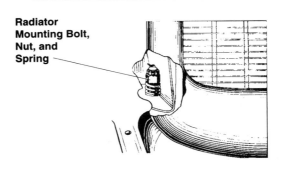

17. Remove and retain the rubber pads under the radiator mounting brackets (both sides). Move the radiator to one side to clear the fender and lift the radiator off the frame. On the 1928 models, a fan shroud may be attached to the radiator. This can be left in place when removing the radiator.

18. Remove the cotter pin and nut [9/16 socket] from the front of the fan to remove the fan and pulley from the keyed and tapered shaft of the water pump. Tap lightly on the back side of the pulley to remove the fan from the tapered and keyed shaft.

15. Pull the headlight wires back through the conduit to the inside of the radiator shell, leaving the metal conduit and grommets attached to the radiator shell. Do the same for both headlight harness wires and the horn harness wires.

Service and Repair

FAN BLADE

Installing 2-Blade Fan

1. Place a woodruff key (No. 3) on the end of the water pump shaft and slide the fan blade onto the shaft.
2. Put a castle nut (7/16-20)[9/16 socket] and cotter pin on the end of the shaft.
3. Pull the radiator back in place and install the top radiator hose. (Do not tighten the top hose clamps at this time.) Tighten the two (2) hose clamps on the bottom radiator hose.
4. Attach the two (2) radiator support rods. Tighten the two (2) front nuts only enough to hold the rods in place.

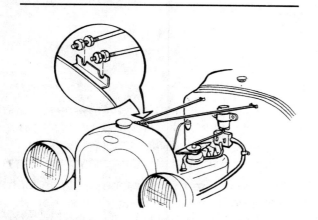

5. Set the hood in place and attach it with two (2) screws, lock washers, and nuts [12-24 X 5/8" round head] on the rear hold down bracket.

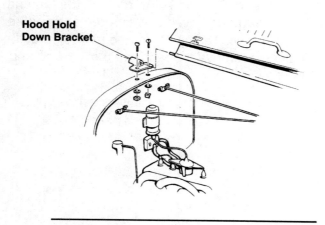

6. After the hood has been installed and properly aligned, securely tighten both front radiator support rod nuts. Securely tighten the two (2) radiator hose clamps on the upper radiator hose (radiator to goose neck).
7. Place the fan belt over the fan pulley, and then under the crank pulley. With the generator pushed up against the engine block, slip the belt over the generator pulley.
8. Pull the generator away from the block to put tension on the belt. Set the generator holding bracket against the generator and tighten the holding bracket bolt on the timing cover [9/16 socket].
9. Pull hard on the generator while tightening the generator mounting bolt [3/4 socket]. Push on the belt at a point half way between the fan pulley and the generator pulley. Correct tension will allow the belt to be pushed in 1/2" to 1".
10. After correct belt tension is set, push the generator holding bracket tight against the generator and tighten the bracket bolt on the timing gear cover. Retighten the generator mounting bolt.

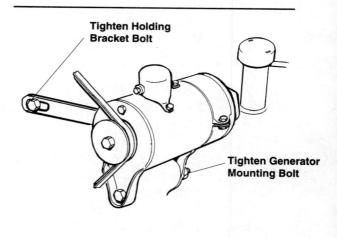

11. Pour three (3) gallons of water into the radiator. Start the engine, and let it run for approximately 15 minutes or until operating temperature is reached. Check all hose connections for leaks. Tighten connections as needed.

FAN BLADE

Installing 4-Blade Fan

1. Place a woodruff key (No. 3) on the end of the water pump shaft and slide the fan blade onto the shaft.
2. Put a castle nut (7/16-20)[9/16 socket] and cotter pin on the end of the shaft.
3. Set the radiator on the front cross member. Place a rubber pad under both radiator mounting brackets (28/29 use 1/8" pad, 30/31 use 1/16" pad). A piece of old inner tube works fine. Install the radiator mounting bolts, nuts and spring assembly as shown below. Tighten the bolts only enough to install cotter pins in the mounting bolts.

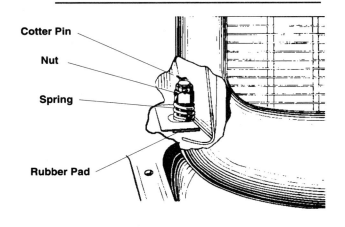

4. Place a short radiator hose over the end of the water return pipe and lower radiator hose pipe and attach with two (2) hose clamps.

5. Slip two (2) hose clamps over the long radiator hose and install the hose from the top radiator neck to the goose neck. Do not tighten these hose clamps until the radiator support rods have been installed and the hood installed and adjusted.

6. Attach the two (2) radiator support rods. Tighten the two front nuts only enough to hold the two rods in place [1/2" wrench].

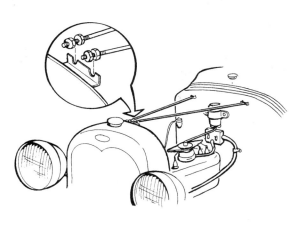

7. The radiator shell and fan shroud may not have been removed from the radiator during disassembly. If the shell was removed from the radiator, reinstall at this time, attaching it with four (4) pan head screws (12-24 X 19/32") and square nuts.
8. Route the wiring harness through the radiator shell to the head lights and horn. Connect the horn wires.
9. Connect the headlight conduit connectors [push and twist clockwise to connect].

NOTE
Some headlight wiring may have been modified by eliminating the connector plug from inside the conduit socket. The wires would then be routed directly from the conduit into the headlight bucket and attached to the bulb sockets with wire nuts. The wires would have to be disconnected from behind the headlight reflector. To access the headlight bucket, release the front lens clip (spring loaded latch) and lift up on the lens rim to remove it. Remove the center bulb and lift the reflector out of the headlight bucket.

Service and Repair

FAN BLADE

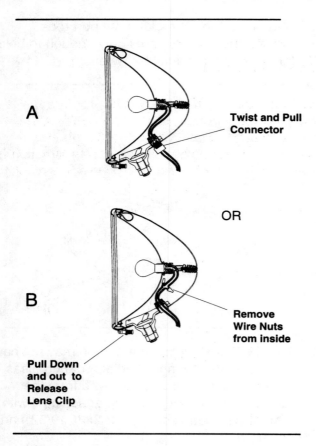

10. Set the hood in place and attach it with two (2) screws, lock washers, and nuts [12-24 X 5/8" round head] on the rear hold down bracket.

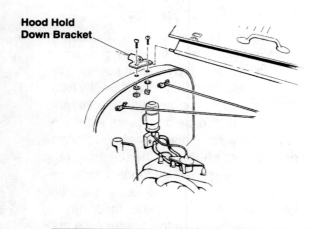

11. After the hood has been installed and properly aligned, securely tighten both front radiator support rod nuts. Securely tighten the two (2) radiator hose clamps on the upper radiator hose (radiator to goose neck).
12. Place the fan belt over the fan pulley, and then under the crank pulley. With the generator pushed up against the engine block, slip the belt over the generator pulley.
13. Pull the generator away from the block to put tension on the belt. Set the generator holding bracket against the generator and tighten the holding bracket bolt on the timing cover [9/16 socket].
14. Pull hard on the generator while tightening the generator mounting bolt [3/4 socket]. Push on the belt at a point half way between the fan pulley and the generator pulley. Correct tension would allow the belt to be pushed in 1/2".
15. After correct belt tension is set, push the generator holding bracket tight against the generator and tighten the bracket bolt on the timing gear cover. Retighten the generator mounting bolt.

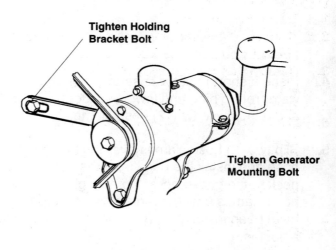

16. Reconnect the battery cable and then pour three (3) gallons of water into the radiator. Start the engine and let it run for approximately 15 minutes or until operating temperature is reached. Check all hose connections for leaks. Tighten connections as needed.

Service and Repair

FUEL SEDIMENT BOWL

The sediment bowl serves as a fuel filter to collect any rust and dirt from the gas tank before fuel is fed to the carburetor. The Model A used a cast iron sediment bowl throughout production (1928-1931). The sediment bowl was located on the firewall from beginning of production until April 1931, and then moved to the side of the carburetor. The carburetor side bowl was cast iron but of different construction for mounting to the side of the carburetor. A glass type sediment bowl was a production option and was used from mid-1929 to early 1931.

Flushing Cast Iron Sediment Bowl

The cast iron sediment bowl can be flushed or drained by opening the spring-loaded petcock (screw counterclockwise 1/4 turn) on the bottom of the bowl.
1. Turn ON the gas shut off valve.
2. Place a container under the sediment bowl and open the spring-oaded petcock (screw counterclockwise 1/4 turn) on the bottom of the bowl.
3. After flushing, turn the petcock clockwise and firmly tighten.

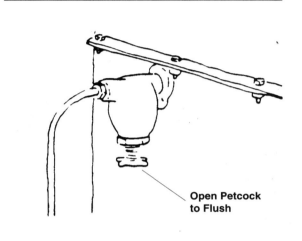

Open Petcock to Flush

Disassembly and Cleaning (Cast Iron Bowl)

1. Turn OFF the gas shut off valve.
2. Unscrew the lower drain petcock. Remove the petcock valve and spring.
3. Remove the large brass nut [7/8 wrench] and lead washer from the bottom of the bowl.
4. Remove and clean or replace the filter screen.
5. Clean rust from the inside of the bowl with a small wire brush.
6. Check the petcock seat in the large brass nut. If the petcock seat is damaged, the brass nut and petcock may need to be honed or replaced to obtain a tight seal.
7. Attach a clean or new filter screen to the large brass nut.
8. Place a lead washer on the nut and screw it into the bottom of the bowl. Tighten only enough to obtain a seal around the lead washer.
9. Screw the petcock with spring into the bottom of the bowl. Tighten the petcock.

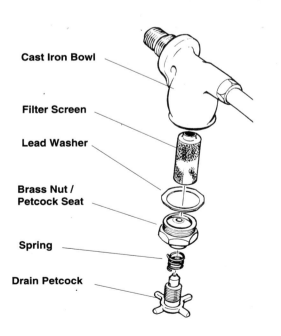

Cast Iron Bowl
Filter Screen
Lead Washer
Brass Nut / Petcock Seat
Spring
Drain Petcock

Service and Repair

FUEL SEDIMENT BOWL

Disassembly and Cleaning Glass Bowl

The glass type sediment bowl can be cleaned by removing the glass bowl.

1. Turn OFF gas shut off valve.
2. Turn the wheel under the glass bowl counter-clockwise 3 or 4 turns and release the bail wire. The bowl can then be removed for cleaning.
3. Clean or replace the filter screen. The screen must set fully into the recess in the top of the bowl. A new screen may have to be trimmed to fit below the top edge of the bowl.
4. Install a new cork gasket on the top edge of the bowl.
5. Place the bowl in the casting and slip the wire bail under the bowl and tighten the wheel.

Removing and Replacing Sediment Bowl

The cast iron and glass sediment bowls are both removed the same way. They are attached to the firewall with a large nut and lock washer on the inside of the firewall.

1. Turn OFF the gas shut off valve.
2. Open the drain petcock on the cast iron sediment bowl and drain all fuel. Remove the bowl from the glass sediment bowl.
3. Disconnect the gas line from the front of the sediment bowl (9/16 wrench).
4. Disconnect the inside gas line from the gas shut off valve to the firewall connection (5/8 wrench).
5. Remove the large nut and lock washer (1-1/4 wrench) that attaches the sediment bowl to the firewall. The nut is accessible from the inside firewall.

NOTE
A second person will be needed to hold the sediment bowl while removing the nut from the inside.

Loosen Wheel to Release Bail Wire

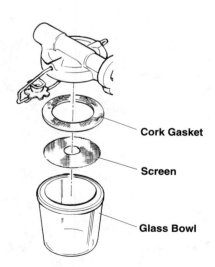
Cork Gasket
Screen
Glass Bowl

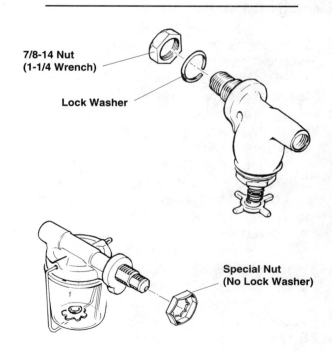
7/8-14 Nut (1-1/4 Wrench)
Lock Washer
Special Nut (No Lock Washer)

Service and Repair

FUEL SEDIMENT BOWL

6. Attach the cleaned and reassembled sediment bowl to the firewall with the large nut [7/8-14] [1-1/4" wrench] and lock washer. Do not over-tighten the large nut when attaching the glass type sediment bowl assembly. The glass sediment bowl housing is made of pot metal. The threads can be stripped if overtightened.
7. Replace the inside gas line, from the gas shut off valve to the firewall (sediment bowl fitting). When installing the gas line, tighten the nuts on each end only finger tight to ensure correct alignment. (The shut-off valve may need to be rotated slightly to obtain correct alignment.)
8. Tighten each end of the gas line until the line is a snug fit against the fittings on the shut-off valve and the sediment bowl fitting (5/8 wrench).

CAUTION
Do not over-tighten the nuts on the gas line. The nuts are brass and will develop hairline cracks (causing a leak) when over-tightened. Tighten each end of the gas line until the gas line is a snug fit against the male fitting.

9. Connect the gas line from the sediment bowl to the carburetor (9/16 wrench).

NOTE
Before attaching the outside gas line, check the end ferrules to see that they are placed no farther than 1/8" from the end of the gas line. Fuel flow will be restricted if the ferrule is placed too far from the end of the line. Check the ferrule for damage. Replace if necessary to ensure a leak-free connection.

10. Close the drain valve on the bottom of the cast iron sediment bowl. If using a glass sediment bowl, check to see that the glass bowl is tight against the upper gasket.
11. Open the gas shut-off valve and check all connections for leaks. Tighten connections as needed.

GAS GAUGE

The Model A gas gauge is a mechanical float indicator. A cork float is attached to the end of a 14" wire, with an indicator dial at the other end. The gauge float assembly pivots up and down similar to a teeter totter, with the cork float at one end and the indicator dial at the other end. The fuel level indicator can be adjusted by bending the float wire up or down to change the level indicator reading.

Two special tools are required to remove the gauge assembly from the gas tank. One is a special ten sided box wrench to remove the outer ring (nut) of the gauge. The other tool is a small inside star or square tool to remove the inside star ring (nut) from the gauge. These tool sets are made in two different configurations. Either set will work. One set is made of cast aluminum and the other set is made of cut steel. The steel tools are far superior, do a better job, and are easier to use.

Most problems encountered with the gas gauge are gasket deterioration, resulting in leaks, and saturated float cork, preventing accurate or no indicator reading. With the proper tools, the gas gauge can be removed, repaired, and reinstalled in about 30 minutes. Anytime repairs are made to the gas gauge assembly, disconnect the battery for safety reasons.

Before removing the gas gauge assembly, ensure there is no more than 1/4 tank of gas in the tank.

Removing Gas Gauge

1. Disconnect the battery ground strap from the (+) battery terminal.

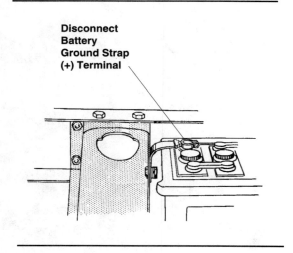

2. Drain enough gas from the gas tank to drop the level to 1/4 tank or less. The gas level must be well below the gauge level before continuing.

NOTE

Place the car in a well ventilated area before draining fuel. Remain 50 feet from flame or spark generating devices when draining fuel. To drain fuel from the gas tank, turn off the gas shut-off valve, disconnect the fuel line from the carburetor, and slip a 3-foot section of 1/4" neoprene hose over the end of the steel gas line removed from the carburetor. Turn on the shut-off valve and drain fuel into a suitable container.

3. Loosen the speedometer cable clamp on the firewall to allow free movement of the cable.

GAS GAUGE

4. Remove the four (4) mounting screws on the instrument panel.

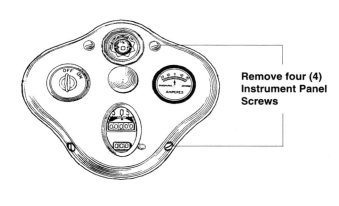

Remove four (4) Instrument Panel Screws

5. Pull the instrument panel and speedometer cable far enough out to allow easy access to the gas gauge. With care the instrument panel can hang by the harness wires.
6. Use the large steel 10-sided box wrench to unscrew the gas gauge outer ring nut from the tank. The entire inner assembly may rotate with the outer ring. This is not a problem.

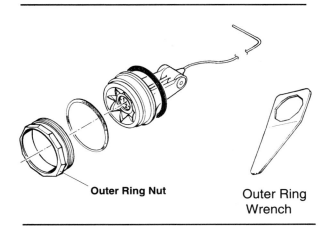

Outer Ring Nut   Outer Ring Wrench

7. With the outer ring removed from the tank, the entire gas gauge assembly can be lifted out of the tank. Move the gauge assembly to the work bench for further disassembly and repairs.

8. Remove the float assembly pin to allow removal of the float and dial assembly from the housing.

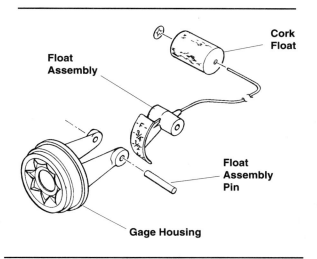

9. Carefully clamp the gauge housing in a vise so the center star ring (nut) can be removed. Place the square block tool inside the inner star ring and screw out the center ring.

Inner Star Ring Tool

NOTE
The inner ring and glass may be difficult to remove because of gasoline varnish build up around the glass and ring. If necessary, soak the assembly in lacquer thinner or carburetor cleaner to soften the varnish around the center ring, gaskets and glass.

Service and Repair

GAS GAUGE

10. After the inner ring has been removed, the metal indicator plate and glass can be removed from the gauge housing.

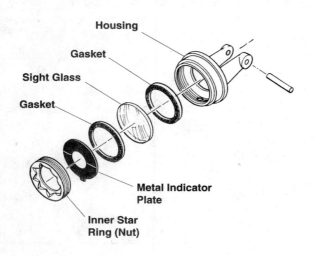

11. Thoroughly clean all gasket material from the back side of the housing and from the inside ring. Soak the parts in lacquer thinner or carburetor cleaner to remove gasoline residue.

Gauge Repair and Assembly

Some gas gauge kits include neoprene gaskets for the center glass seals. The neoprene gaskets are usually too thick and do not fit properly. Use cork gaskets, or some suppliers have a thinner composition cork gasket which works best.

1. After cleaning, assemble the housing with a gasket on each side of the sight glass, the metal indicator plate, and the inner star ring nut, as shown in the above illustration. Do not use sealant on either of the sight glass gaskets. The tab on the metal indicator plate sits in a small dimple in the housing. This prevents the indicator plate from moving when the star ring is screwed down.
2. Using the center star ring tool, tighten the star ring nut to provide good compression of the two sight glass gaskets. This must be tight to provide a good seal around the glass.
3. To replace the float cork, remove the retaining washer at the end of the wire and slide the old cork off the wire.
4. A new cork must be thoroughly coated with shellac to seal the cork. Gasoline will not penetrate shellac.

NOTE
The float can be replaced with either a cork float or a Tilitson carburetor float. A Tilitson carburetor float should be clamped to the wire and then soldered.

5. If a new cork float is installed, place a retaining washer on the end of the wire and attach with a small drop of solder. Originally, the wire end was crimped to spread the wire and retain the washer. It may be easier to solder it in place.

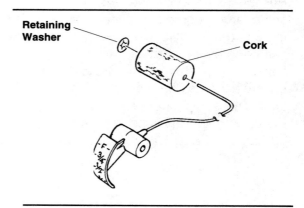

6. Attach the float assembly with dial to the housing with attaching pin as shown. The gauge is now ready to install in the gas tank.

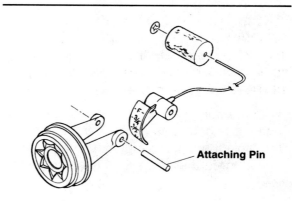

GAS GAUGE

Installing Gas Gauge

1. Thoroughly clean all old gasket material from inside the gas tank gauge hole.
2. Apply a <u>small</u> amount of gas resistant sealant on both sides of the large cork gasket in the gasket kit. Place this gasket in the gas tank gauge hole, fully seated on the inside flange.
3. Insert the gauge assembly in the tank, placed against the cork gasket.
4. Two thin brass washers are used as thrust slip washers for the outer ring nut. Place a light coat of oil on the two (2) brass washers and place them over the gauge assembly and against the back flange of the gauge housing. These washers will prevent the gauge assembly from turning when the outer ring nut is tightened.

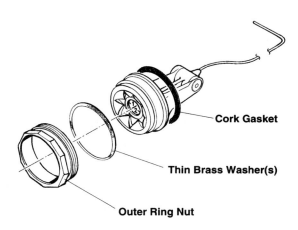

5. With the brass washers in place, screw the outer ring into the tank, pushing the gauge assembly against the inside cork gasket. Do not tighten this outer ring until the float level calibration has been checked.

6. Gas gauges were calibrated so that they register "F" when the cork float just touches the top of the tank. With this setting there will still be a reserve of approximately one gallon in the tank when the gauge registers "0". If the float gauge does not register as above, the float wire should be readjusted by slightly bending the wire until the gauge registers accurately.
7. To check the gauge reading, remove the gas cap and screen and insert a hook wire through the filler opening and lift up the float wire until the cork float just touches the top of the tank. If properly adjusted, the gauge should read full "F". To adjust, remove the gauge from the tank and bend the float wire. There should be only one bend in the wire, 1-1/2" back from the pivot pin. The 1928/1929 gas tank float wire should be nearly straight. The 1930/1931 gas tank float wire required a 1-5/8" drop bend to accommodate the 1930 style gas tank.
8. After the float has been checked and adjusted, screw the outer ring down tight using the ten 10-sided box wrench, pushing the gauge assembly tight against the inside cork gasket. If needed, use the square inner star ring tool to hold the inner gauge assembly level while using the outer ring wrench to firmly tighten the outer ring nut.
9. Attach the instrument panel to the dash with four (4) screws (10-32 X 1/2" oval head.)
10. Tighten the speedometer cable clamp on the firewall.
11. Reconnect the fuel line to the carburetor (if previously disconnected).
12. Reconnect the battery ground strap to the (+) battery terminal

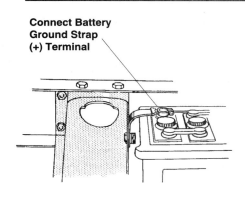

Service and Repair

GAS SHUT-OFF VALVE

The gas shut-off valve was located under the gas tank from 1928 until April 1931. From April 1931 to the end of production it was moved to the firewall on the engine side, in the location of the sediment bowl, as the sediment bowl was moved to the side of the carburetor. The shut-off valve was made in three configurations, although all three have the same basic construction for disassembly and repairs. Before any repairs can be made to the gas shut-off valve, all fuel must be drained from the gas tank.

Removing Gas Shut-off Valve

1. Disconnect the ground cable from the battery (+) terminal post.

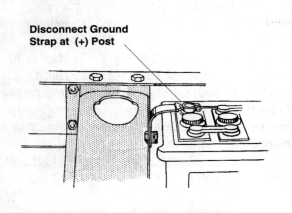

Disconnect Ground Strap at (+) Post

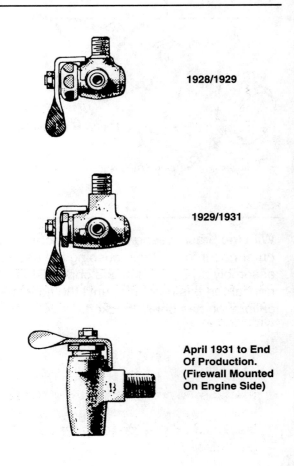

1928/1929

1929/1931

April 1931 to End Of Production. (Firewall Mounted On Engine Side)

2. Turn OFF the gas shut-off valve, located under the gas tank.
3. Disconnect the gas line at the carburetor (9/16 wrench) and drain all gasoline from the tank into a suitable container.
4. Remove the inside gas line from the gas shut-off valve to the firewall connection (sediment bowl connection)[5/8 wrench].

GAS SHUT-OFF VALVE

5. Remove (screw out) the gas shut-off valve from under the tank. Use a 3/4 crows foot wrench.

NOTE
The gas shut-off valve may be difficult to remove without breaking it off at the threads. The shut-off valves are made of brass. Use an "easy out" and 1/2" pipe tap to clean the threads in the tank.

Disassembly and Repair

1. Remove the nut (1/4-28), and lock washer from the end of the valve handle (some are 3/8 wrench and some are 7/16 wrench). Remove the handle.
2. Remove the packing nut (11/16 wrench) and remove the old packing. The old packing will have to be dug out with a pick.
3. Remove the valve cone. Use valve grinding compound to reestablish the cone seat in the valve body.

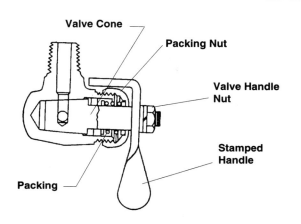

4. After re-seating the cone, flush all grinding compound out of the valve. Rinse thoroughly with lacquer thinner.

NOTE
If the cone and seat are badly scored, the valve will not completely shut off fuel flow. If the scoring cannot be completely burnished out, the valve assembly should be replaced.

5. Install the valve cone and new packing into the valve body. Screw in the packing nut only enough to seal the packing (11/16 wrench).
6. Install the valve handle. The gas valve handle was changed from a forging to a stamping in mid-1929. The length of the shoulder on the valve cone was reduced from 11/64" to 7/64". Both the forging and stamped design handles can be used with the later valve having 7/64" shoulder. When replacing a forged type handle with the stamped handle on a valve having a 11/64" shoulder, it will be necessary to use a flat washer to take up the extra length of the shoulder.

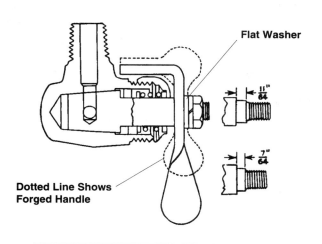

7. Insert a special gas tank filter screen into the top hole of the valve before screwing the valve into the tank. Make sure the end of the filter is a tight fit into the valve.

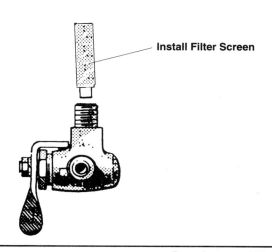

GAS SHUT-OFF VALVE

8. Screw the shut-off valve into the gas tank using a 3/4 crows foot wrench.
9. Replace the inside gas line from the gas shut off valve to the firewall (sediment bowl fitting). When installing the gas line, tighten the nuts on each end only finger tight to ensure correct alignment. (The shut-off valve may need to be rotated slightly to obtain correct alignment.)
10. Tighten each end of the gas line until the line is a snug fit against the fittings on the shut-off valve and the sediment bowl fitting (5/8 wrench).

CAUTION
Do not over tighten the nuts on the gas line. The nuts are brass and will develop hairline cracks (causing a leak) when over tightened. Tighten each end of the gas line until the gas line is a snug fit against the male fitting.

11. Connect the gas line from the sediment bowl to the carburetor (9/16 wrench).

NOTE
Before attaching the outside gas line, check the end ferrules to see that they are placed no farther than 1/4" from the end of the gas line. Fuel flow will be restricted if the ferrule is placed too far from the end of the line. Check the ferrule for damage. Replace if necessary to ensure a leak free connection.

12. Pour one gallon of gasoline into the tank. Open the gas shut-off valve and check all connections for leaks. Tighten connections as needed. After the leak test, connect the battery ground strap and fill the gas tank.

GAS TANK

Four different gas tanks were made for the Model A. The 1928/1929 gas tank is a ten (10) gallon tank with a screw-on (threaded) type gas cap. The 1928/1929 style gas tank also includes the top portion of the firewall as part of the tank structure. The 1930/1931 gas tank is an eleven (11) gallon gas tank with a twist lock type (not threaded) gas cap. The 1930/1931 style gas tank sits behind the firewall and therefore does not include a portion of the firewall. Some of the early 1930 tanks used the 1929 style instrument panel (smooth finish). These 1930 gas tanks had a screw on type gas cap. The fourth style gas tank was used with the late 1931 indented firewall. It was the same style as the 1930/1931 tank except there was no shut off valve hole on the bottom of the tank. The fuel outlet was on the right side and a pipe from the tank connected directlly to the indented firewall shut off valve.

When the tank becomes rusted internally and continues to clog the carburetor jets, it must be removed from the car for proper cleaning and treatment. The 1928/1929 gas tank will sometimes develop a leak around the steering column bracket, where the bracket is riveted and soldered to the tank. This repair can be made only with the tank removed from the car. NEVER ATTEMPT TO WELD A MODEL A GAS TANK. The tanks were specially hardened and will develop many hairline cracks when heated by a welding torch, compounding the problem. The tank should first be boiled out by a radiator shop. The riveted bracket can be re-soldered at the radiator shop. The inside of the tank can then be sealed with a good grade of gas tank sealer.

Removing Gas Tank

1. Disconnect the ground cable from the battery (+) terminal post.

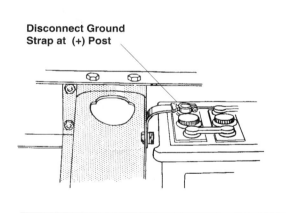

2. Turn OFF the gas shut-off valve, located under the gas tank.
3. Disconnect the gas line at the carburetor (9/16 wrench) and drain all gasoline from the tank into a suitable container.
4. Remove the inside gas line from the gas shut-off valve to the firewall connection (sediment bowl connection)[5/8 wrench].

5. Under the hood, remove the two screws and nuts from the hood rear hold down bracket.

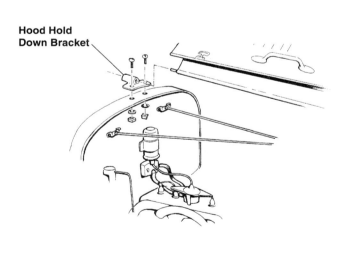

6. Remove the hood and place it in a safe location on cardboard or carpet to prevent chipping the paint. Do not lay hood down on the side louver panels. It's best to stand the hood up on the back edge to prevent warping or creasing the top panels.

GAS TANK

7. Loosen the two (2) nuts [1/2 inch wrench] on the front end of the two radiator support rods. Pull the two rods up out of the radiator bracket.

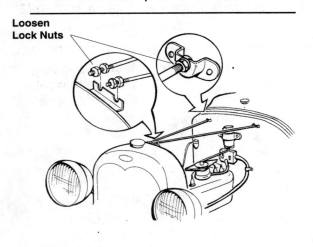

Loosen Lock Nuts

8. Remove both radiator support rods from the fire wall brackets [5/8 open end wrench].
9. <u>1928/1929 ONLY</u>
Remove the ignition coil and bracket from the firewall (2 screws).

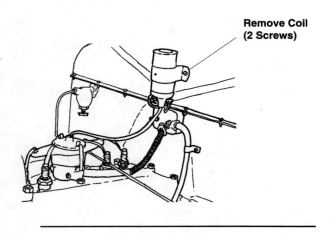

Remove Coil (2 Screws)

10. <u>1928 through 1931</u> - Remove the speedometer cable hold-down clip, located on the firewall next to the choke rod. This will allow the speedometer cable to be pulled up when the instrument panel is released.
11. Remove four (4) 10-32 X 1/2 oval head screws from the instrument panel. Carefully pull the instrument panel away from the dash (gas tank) and unscrew the speedometer cable connector from behind the speedometer.

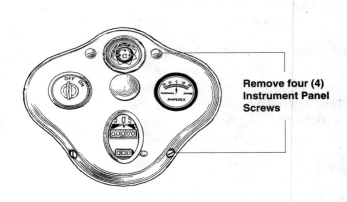

Remove four (4) Instrument Panel Screws

12. Pull the instrument panel out far enough for access to the ammeter terminals on the back side of the panel. Remove the two 8/32 nuts from the ammeter terminals and remove the yellow, yellow/black, and instrument light wires from the ammeter terminals.
13. Remove three (3) screws from around the original pop-out ignition switch to release the entire switch from the instrument panel.

NOTE

If a replacement type ignition switch has been installed, only the two wires (red and black) need to be removed from the switch, leaving the switch attached to the panel.

14. Move the instrument panel to the work bench.

GAS TANK

15. Pull the speedometer cable from the gas tank trough.
16. Remove the two instrument panel harness wires from the terminal box posts. Pull the harness out of the gas tank trough (3 wire harness).
17. Remove the dash rail (1928/1929 has 6 screws, 1930/1931 has 7 screws).

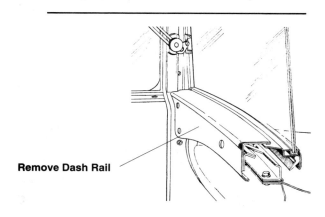

Remove Dash Rail

18. Disconnect the choke rod from the carburetor and remove the rod from the gas tank support bracket.
19. **Open Cars** - Remove the windshield and windshield stanchion post (2 screws on each stanchion).
20. **Closed Cars** - Remove the windshield (8 wood screws in the header, under the top hinge) and windshield post brackets (2 screws on each side).

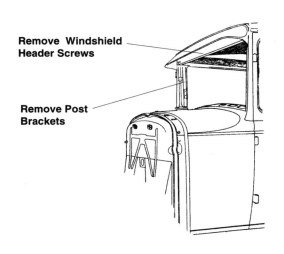

Remove Windshield Header Screws

Remove Post Brackets

21. **All Years and Models** - Remove the steering column support bracket (2 fillister head screws).
22. **All Years and Models** - Remove the two (2) cardboard (padded) cowl panels.

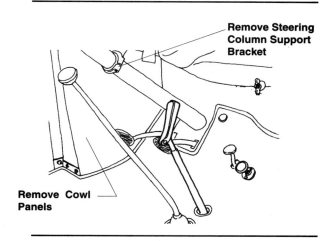

Remove Steering Column Support Bracket

Remove Cowl Panels

23. Remove the "C" shaped clamps that hold the bottom flange of the tank to the cowl panel flange (1928/1929 used 5 clamps each side, 1930/1931 used 2 clamps each side).

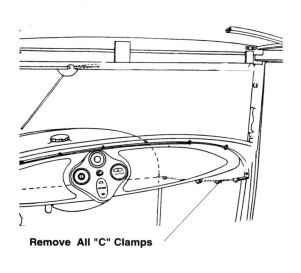

Remove All "C" Clamps

Service and Repair

GAS TANK

24. Remove the twelve (12) bolts, nuts, and lock washers that secure the back edge of the tank to the dash rail support (7/16 wrench).

NOTE

In mid-1930 the bolts changed to 5/16-24. Use 1/2" wrench. From late 1930 to the end of production the nuts were captive.

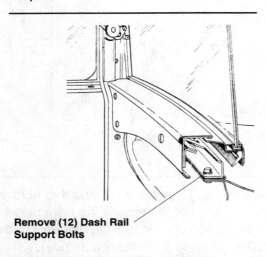

Remove (12) Dash Rail Support Bolts

25. **1928/1929 Only** - Remove the eight gas tank to firewall bolts, nuts, and lock washers (7/16 wrench). On all Fordor Sedans and Cabriolets, the 4" center panel of the firewall will need to be removed (8 additional bolts, nuts, and lock washers).

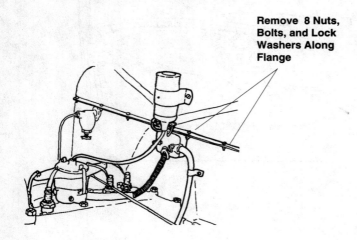

Remove 8 Nuts, Bolts, and Lock Washers Along Flange

26. **1930/1931 Only** - Remove the front cowl band. The cowl band is attached to the body at both ends with a nut and lock washer, accessible from inside the lower cowling. During 1930 some cowl bands had additional clips in the band with bolt shank and nut to hold the sides of the cowl band in. Look for these nuts on the inside cowling.

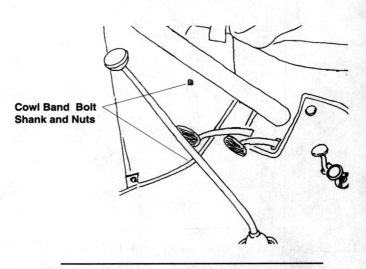

Cowl Band Bolt Shank and Nuts

27. **1930/1931 Only** - Remove the ten (10) pan head screws and lock washers from around the front edge of the gas tank.

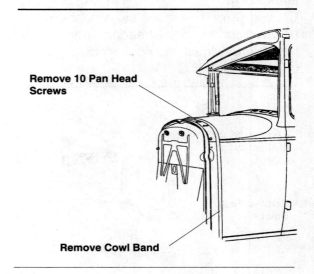

Remove 10 Pan Head Screws

Remove Cowl Band

28. Remove the bottom windshield belt rail, secured by a screw at each end.

GAS TANK

29. Tip the tank slightly up at the front edge and lift it off the dash rail support. Move the tank to a clean work area for further disassembly.
30. Remove (screw out) the gas shut-off valve from under the tank.

NOTE
The gas shut-off valve may be difficult to remove without breaking it off at the threads. The shut-off valves are made of brass. Use an "easy out" and 1/2" pipe tap to clean the threads in the tank.

31. To remove the gas gauge use a special ten (10) sided outer ring box wrench to unscrew the gas gauge outer ring nut from the tank. The entire inner assembly may rotate with the outer ring. This is not a problem.

Outer Ring Wrench

32. With the outer ring removed from the tank, the entire gas gauge assembly can now be lifted out of the tank.

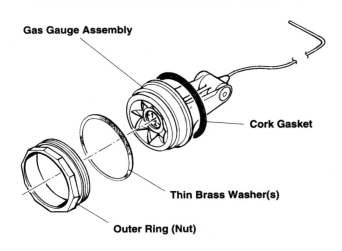

The gas tank should be thoroughly cleaned on the inside (boiled out) by a radiator shop. After cleaning, the steering column bracket should be re-soldered (must use heavy tin solder as used in body work). Apply a good gas tank sealer on all surfaces inside the tank. The tank can then be painted and ready for installation back in the car.

GAS TANK

Installing Gas Tank

1. **1928/1929** - Lay a strip of anti-squeak tape (cloth electrical tape) on the firewall flange where the tank sits, and along the side cowl flange.

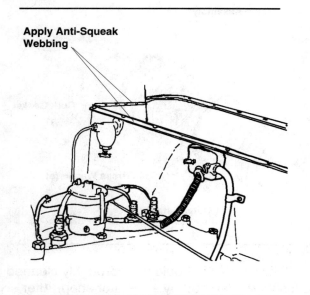

2. **1930/1931** - Lay a strip of anti-squeak tape across the top edge of the firewall and along the dash rail support.
3. Punch out all hole locations in the anti-squeak tape.
4. Lay a 3/16" bead welt across the back edge of the gas tank and down the sides of the cowl for 1928/1929 cars, and around the back edge of the tank and across the side for 1930/1931 cars.
5. To fit the welt to the tank, lay the welt on top of the rear flange of the tank. Hold the welt in place with spring-type clothes pins. Make cuts in the flat part of the welt, about one inch apart, for a smooth bend around the corners.
6. Mark all bolt holes on the welt and remove them for punching holes.
7. After all holes are punched, staple 1" X 8" strips of cloth to the ends of the one inch cuts in the welt at the corners. This will provide a means of pulling the welt into position in the corners during final installation.
8. Carefully lay the tank in the cowl, allowing the stapled cloth strips in the corners to fall to the inward side of the cowl. Use the cloth strips to pull the welt up snugly into position.
9. Place the windshield belt rail across the back edge of the tank and attach with a screw at each end (12-24 X 19/32).
10. Attach the back edge of the gas tank from under the belt rail support with twelve (12) bolts, nuts, and lock washers. (1928 to early 1930 used 1/4-20 X 3/4 bolts. Mid-30 to end of production used 5/16-24 X 25/32 bolts and the nuts were captive in the belt rail.)

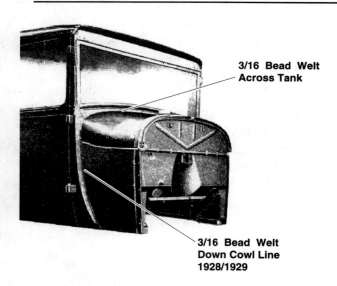

1928/1929 Bead Welt

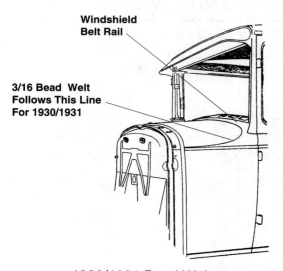

1930/1931 Bead Welt

GAS TANK

11. **1930/1931** - Install the ten (10) pan head screws along the front edge of the gas tank.

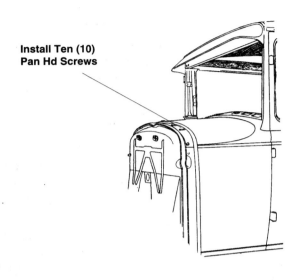

Install Ten (10) Pan Hd Screws

12. Install two (2) "C" clamps on each side along the cowl flange.

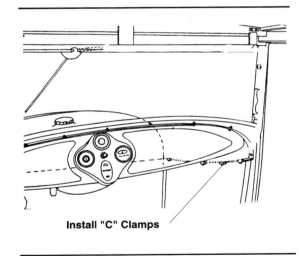

Install "C" Clamps

13. Install the stainless steel cowl band. Secure at both ends with nut and lock washer.
14. Install the inside cardboard cowl panels.

15. **1928/1929** - Install the eight (8) special bolts, nuts, and lock washers along the front edge of the gas tank to the firewall flange.

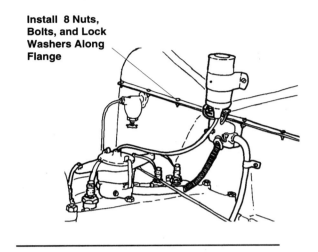

Install 8 Nuts, Bolts, and Lock Washers Along Flange

16. Install five (5) "C" clamps on each side along the cowl flange.

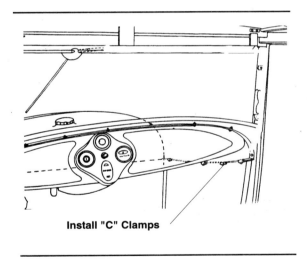

Install "C" Clamps

17. Install the inside cardboard cowl panels.
18. Wrap the steering column rubber bushing around the column and attach the lower bracket with two (2) screws (5/16-24 X 1" Fillister head).

GAS TANK

19. **Open Cars Only** - Attach the two windshield stanchions and install the windshield.
20. Install the dash rail (1928/1929 six (6) screws, 1930/1931 five (5) screws).

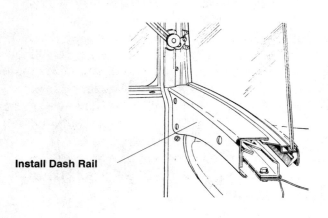

Install Dash Rail

21. Route the instrument panel harness through the gas tank trough. At the terminal box, attach the yellow wire to the passenger side terminal post. Attach the yellow wire from the starter to the same terminal post.
22. Attach the yellow/black wire from the instrument panel and the yellow/black wire from the generator to the terminal box driver side post.

23. **1928/1929** - Attach the coil and bracket to the firewall (2 each 1/4-20 X 1/2 screws)
24. Attach the coil black wire (-) side to the terminal box driver side post.
25. Connect the instrument panel harness red wire to the coil (+) terminal.

Installing Gas Gauge

1. Thoroughly clean all old gasket material from inside the gas tank gauge hole.
2. Place the cork gasket in the gas tank gauge hole, fully seated on the inside flange.
3. Insert the gauge assembly into the tank, placed against the cork gasket.
4. Two thin brass washers are used as thrust slip washers for the outer ring nut. Place a light coat of oil on the two brass washers and place them over the gauge assembly and against the back flange of the gauge housing. These washers will prevent the gauge assembly from turning when the outer ring nut is tightened down.
5. With the brass washers in place, screw the outer ring into the tank, pushing the gauge assembly against the inside cork gasket. Do not tighten this outer ring until the float level calibration has been checked.

Instrument Panel Harness

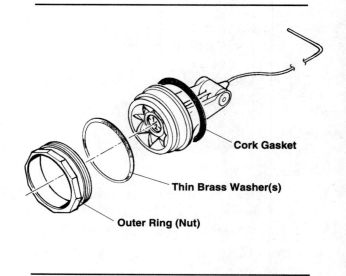

GAS TANK

6. Gas gauges were calibrated so that they register "F" when the cork float just touches the top of the tank. With this setting there will still be a reserve of approximately one gallon in the tank when the gauge registers "0". If the float gauge does not register as above, the float wire should be readjusted by slightly bending the wire until the gauge registers accurately.

7. To check the gauge reading, remove the gas cap and screen and insert a hook wire through the filler opening and lift up the float wire until the cork float just touches the top of the tank. If properly adjusted, the gauge should read full "F". To adjust, remove the gauge from the tank and bend the float wire. There should be only one (1) bend in the wire, 1-1/2" back from the pivot pin. The 1928/1929 gas tank float wire should be nearly straight. The 1930/1931 gas tank float wire required a 1-5/8" drop bend to accommodate the 1930 style gas tank.

8. After the float has been checked and adjusted, screw the outer ring down tight using the ten (10) sided box wrench, pushing the gauge assembly tight against the inside cork gasket. If needed, use the square inner star ring tool to hold the inner gauge assembly level while using the outer ring wrench to firmly tighten the outer ring nut.

Installing Instrument Panel

1. Connect the Yellow/Black Wire round connector to the ammeter (+) post.
2. Connect the Yellow Wire round connector to the ammeter (-) post.
3. Connect the Red Wire round connector to the ignition switch.
4. Screw the speedometer cable into the backside of the speedometer.
5. Place the instrument panel against the dash and attach it with four (4) 10-32 X 1/2" oval Hd screws.
6. Attach the speedometer cable hold-down clip on the firewall (12-24 X 1/2" Rd Hd screw and lock washer).

Installing Gas Shut-Off Valve and Gas Line

1. Screw the gas shut-off valve into the bottom of the tank. This is a 1/2" pipe thread. Tighten the valve into the tank for correct fuel line alignment.
2. Replace the inside gas line from the gas shut off valve to the firewall (sediment bowl fitting). When installing the gas line, tighten the nuts on each end only finger tight to ensure correct alignment. (The shut-off valve may need to be rotated slightly to obtain correct alignment.)
3. Tighten each end of the gas line until the line is a snug fit against the fittings on the shut-off valve and the sediment bowl fitting (5/8 wrench).

CAUTION
Do not over-tighten the nuts on the gas line. The nuts are brass and will develop hairline cracks (causing a leak) when over-tightened. Tighten each end of the gas line until the gas line is a snug fit against the male fitting.

4. Connect the gas line from the sediment bowl to the carburetor (9/16 wrench).

NOTE
Before attaching the outside gas line, check the end ferrules to see that they are placed no farther than 1/8" from the end of the gas line. Fuel flow will be restricted if the ferrule is placed too far from the end of the line. Check the ferrule for damage. Replace if necessary to ensure a leak free connection.

5. Close the drain valve on the bottom of the cast iron sediment bowl. If using a glass sediment bowl, check to see that the glass bowl is tight against the upper gasket.

GAS TANK

Final Assembly

1. Install the two (2) radiator support rods in the firewall brackets. Tighten the locking nuts with a 5/8 open end wrench. Attach the other ends of the support rods in the radiator bracket with a nut and lock washer on each side of the bracket [1/2" wrench].

3. Close the gas shut-off valve and pour one gallon of gas into the tank.
4. Open the gas shut-off valve and check all connections for leaks from the gas tank to the carburetor. Tighten connections as needed.
5. Connect the ground cable to the battery (+) terminal post.

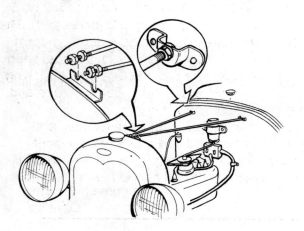

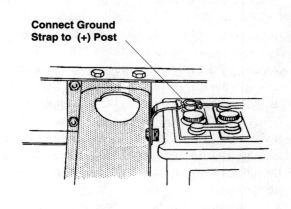

Connect Ground Strap to (+) Post

2. Set the hood in place and attach it with two (2) screws, lock washers, and nuts [12-24 X 5/8" Round Head] on the rear hold down bracket.

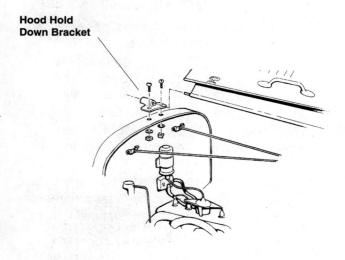

Hood Hold Down Bracket

GENERATOR

Four different generators were used on the Model A, two versions of the Power House generator and two versions of the cylinder style generator. The Power House generator was used from 1928 to mid-1929. The cylinder style was used from mid-1929 through 1931. This section will discuss only the two versions of the cylinder style generator.

The earlier style generator, used from mid-1929 through mid-1930 has a short broad boss on the back end plate to house a ball bearing at the brush end of the armature (in addition to the pulley end). The later style (mid-1930 through 1931) has a narrow boss and an oil cap and wick housing extending down from the bronze bushing housing. The armature, end plates, and pulley are not interchangeable between the two styles, as the armature shafts are different lengths to accommodate either the bearing or bushing on the rear end plate. The front armature shaft is also a different size and length at the cone shaped end for the pulley. Therefore, the pulleys are not interchangeable between the two styles.

The following procedures describe removing the generator from the car, basic disassembly and cleaning procedures, and brush replacement. If it is determined that cleaning and brush replacement (basic maintenance) does not correct generator operation, the generator should then be taken to a qualified generator shop for further testing and repairs. Specialized equipment will be needed for testing and further repairs.

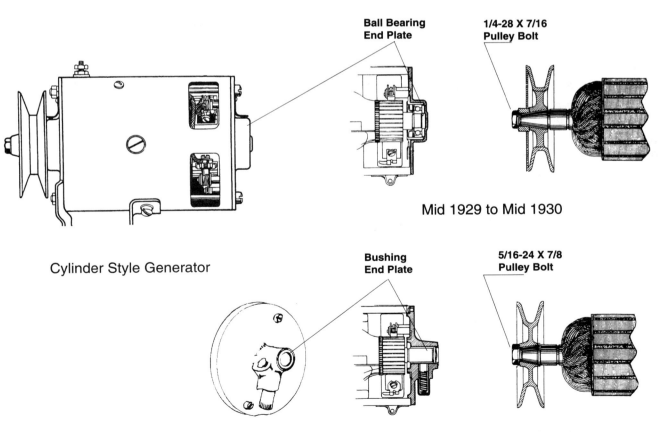

Cylinder Style Generator

Mid 1929 to Mid 1930

Mid 1930 through 1931

Service and Repair

GENERATOR

Removing Generator

1. Disconnect the battery ground strap or remove the fuse if installed.
2. Remove the two (2) wires connected to the cutout relay on the generator. The single yellow/black wire from the terminal box is always hot (6 volts). Tape the end of this wire after removing it from the cutout relay.

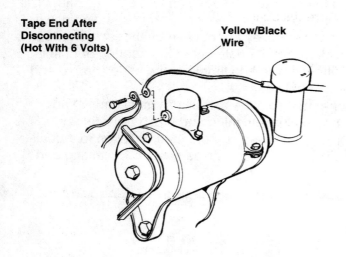

3. Loosen the generator mounting bolt nut [3/4 socket] and push the generator toward the engine to remove the fan belt. Remove the generator mounting bolt and remove generator.

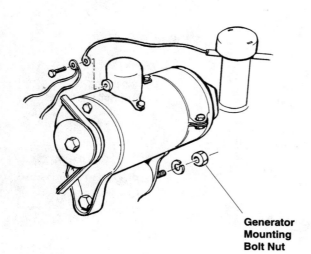

Disassembly, Inspection and Cleaning

1. Remove the two 10-32 X 5/16 screws attaching the cutout to the top of the generator.
2. Loosen the screw on the side of the cover band and slide it back to remove it.
3. Inspect the inside armature and commutator. If the windings of the field coils and armature appear black, and the commutator plates are blue-black, the generator may be damaged by excessive heat.
4. Remove the front pulley bolt and lock washer (1929 until April 1930, 1/4-28 X 7/16 Hex Hd, 7/16 wrench) (After April 1930, 5/16-24 X 7/8 Hex Hd., 1/2 wrench). Pull the pulley off the end of the shaft.

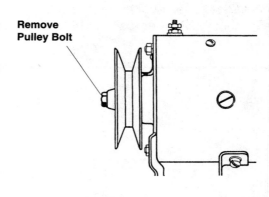

5. Remove the two long bolts (1/4-20 X 6" Fillister Hd.) that hold the generator together.
6. Slide the armature with front plate out of the generator case.
7. Remove the rear brush end plate. Remove the screws attaching the two field coil wires to the brushes. Remove all three (3) brushes.
8. Use a soft brush and compressed air to clean armature, end plates and bushings. A solvent can be used on all components except the armature windings. Some insulating coatings may break down with solvent.
9. Clean and smooth the copper armature with 300 grit sandpaper (Do not use emery cloth). Blow or brush away all sanding residue.

Service and Repair

GENERATOR

10. Undercut the mica separators (between the commutator bars) about 1/32" below the copper. The under cutting can be done using an old hacksaw blade ground to the proper thickness.
11. Inspect the insulation on the field brush leads. Repair breaks or thin spots in the insulation by wrapping with cotton string and then coating with a glue that is resistant to both oil and temperatures up to 400 ° F. Do not use electrician's tape. The high temperatures and oily atmosphere will loosen the tape adhesive, causing the tape to separate and end up under a brush.
12. Check the bushings in the rear end plate (mid-1930 through 1931). Replace bushings if there is more than .002 inches clearance between shaft and bushing. End Plate bushing used I.D. .626, O.D. .752, .965 inches long. (P/N 4278X)
13. Using an ohmmeter, check continuity of the brush holders to the end plate. Only the movable (adjusting) brush holder should be grounded. If either of the other brush holders is grounded to the end plate, check the small insulator that separates the end of the spring from the stop post beside the pivot post.
14. Spin the armature to check the smoothness of the front bearing. Spin the rear bearing to check for smoothness. The bearings should be replaced if not silky smooth when rotated.
    Front Ball Bearing - 6203ZZ
    Rear Ball Bearing - 6202Z
15. Install new brushes in the brush holders. The brushes are slotted to easily fit into the brush holder. They are chamfered on the side that goes toward the brush holder.

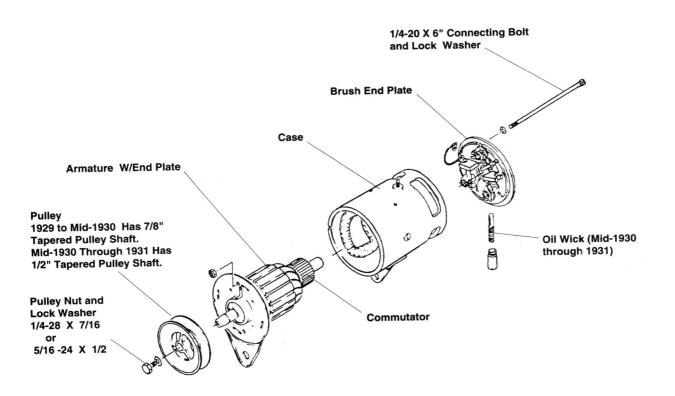

Service and Repair

GENERATOR

Generator Assembly

1. Install the three brushes in the rear end plate. Place the brush holder end plate close to the case so the two field wires can be connected to the two field brushes. The adjustable brush holder is grounded to the end plate.
2. Carefully lift the armature with front end plate into the case from the front end. Align the end plate tab with the slot in the case.

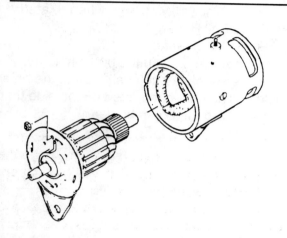

3. Place the brush holder end plate on the rear commutator shaft, while lifting the three brushes onto the commutator, and push the plate against the case.
4. Align the end plate tab with the slot in the case and insert the two long bolts through the rear end plate (1/4-20 X 6"). Tighten both bolts, nuts, and lock washer.

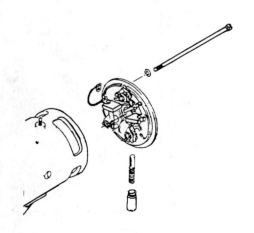

5. With a light and a mechanic's mirror, make sure the brush leads are positioned so as not to rub on the spinning armature.
6. Spin the armature shaft by hand. It should turn smoothly with no rubbing or gritty feeling.
7. Connect a fully charged battery to the terminal post on top of the generator. (Positive (+) lead to the case and negative (-) lead to the terminal post.) The generator should begin to "motor" (turns like an electric motor). This is an indication the generator is in working order.
8. Install the cutout relay on top of the generator with two 10-32 X 5/16 screws.

Installing Generator

1. Install the generator using a special shoulder hinge bolt (1/2-20 X 2-7/8"), lock washer, and nut [3/4 socket]. Do not tighten until the fan belt has been installed.

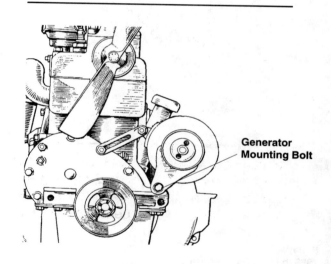

Generator Mounting Bolt

4. Place the belt over the fan pulley, and then under the crank pulley. With the generator pushed up against the engine block, slip the belt over the generator pulley.

GENERATOR

5. Pull the generator away from the block to apply tension on the belt. Set the generator holding bracket against the generator and tighten the holding bracket bolt on the timing cover [9/16 socket].
6. Pull hard on the generator while tightening the generator mounting bolt [3/4 socket]. Push on the belt at a point half way between the fan pulley and the generator pulley. Correct tension would allow the belt to be pushed in 1/2".

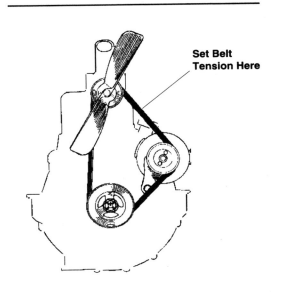

7. After correct belt tension is set, push the generator holding bracket tight against the generator and tighten the bracket bolt on the timing gear cover. Retighten the generator mounting bolt.
8. Attach three harness wires to the generator cutout terminal (terminal box wire, horn and head light harness wire). Connect the battery ground strap.

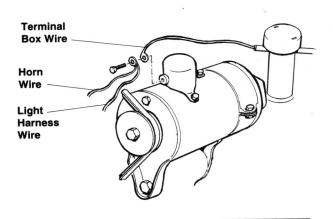

9. To adjust the output charging rate, move the center brush to the top of its travel and then back down about 1/3 of its travel.
10. Start the engine and check the ammeter reading with the engine running at a fast idle. Adjust the generator brush for a 10 amp charge rate on the ammeter. Move the brush up to decrease the amperage and down to increase amperage.
11. Slip the band cover over the case open slots and tighten the side screw (10-32 X 1-1/4 rd hd).
12. Apply a few drops of oil to the front and rear bearing oilers. Slide the clip to one side for access to the oil hole. Move the clip back after oiling.

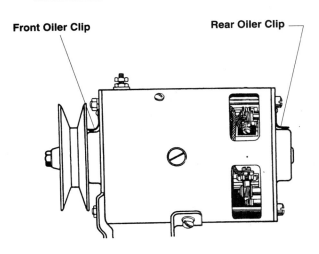

Service and Repair

HORN

The Model A horn was made by five (5) different manufacturers during production.

AMES MFG., E.A. LABORATORIES, STEWART WARNER,
GENERAL INDUSTRIES MFG. (G.I.M.) and SPARTON.

All were very similar in construction with very minor differences. The G.I.M. horn is the only one that has bushings on both ends of the armature shaft. The AMES and G.I.M. horns have 5/16" diameter armature shafts. All others have 1/4" armature shafts. The motor frame varies in width between manufacturers. The STEWART WARNER and AMES have 1-1/8" wide frames. E.A. and SPARTON has a 3/4" wide frame. G.I.M. has a 1" wide frame.

Most problems with the horn can be corrected with a complete disassembly and thorough cleaning. All solder connections should be re-soldered. The field coils can be rewound with no. 20 copper wire that has been coated (insulated) for coil windings. The coils are wound in opposite directions, with 48 turns of wire on each coil. The beginning end of the coil wire is soldered to the connector clip, and the ending end is connected to the brush holder. The motor frame must be removed from the base to re-wind the field coils.

All Model A horns are DC motor driven. As the armature is rotated, a ratchet wheel on the bottom end of the armature shaft makes contact with a beveled stud in the center of the diaphragm, thereby creating a vibration of the diaphragm. The increasing and decreasing RPM of the DC motor creates the distinctive tone of the Model A Horn. A free rotation of the motor armature at a high RPM is the key to proper operation and tone quality.

HORN

Horn Disassembly

1. Remove the cover screw and remove the rear cover.
2. Remove the six (6) nuts and bolts from around the horn bell and separate the bell, diaphragm, and gaskets from the motor base.

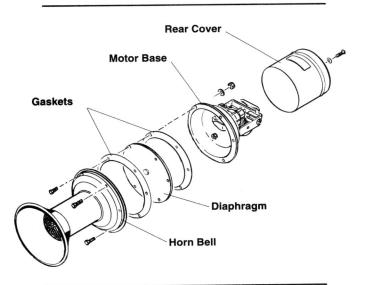

3. Remove the connector block screw, nut, and washers and lift the connector block from the mounting base.

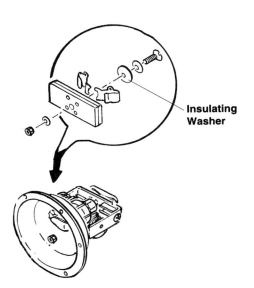

4. On the bottom of the motor base, remove the right side frame nut that holds the ratchet tension clip. Remove the clip and replace the nut.
5. Carefully place the end of a steel rule into one of the slots in the iron core of the rotor. [Take extreme **CAUTION** not to damage any of the fine armature wire windings.] Now turn the rotor until the steel rule is up against the left field housing. This will allow the rotor to be held stationary while removing the ratchet nut.
6. Hold the steel rule and rotor in place while removing the ratchet nut and ratchet wheel.
7. Remove the screw and insulating washers from each side of the motor frame that attach the brush assembly. Remove both brush holders, spring and brushes.
8. On the bottom side of the motor base, remove the two (2) nuts and lock washers that attach the motor frame to the base. Carefully separate the rotor and motor frame from the base.
9. Remove the top adjusting screw, bridge and spring from the motor frame.

Cleaning

1. Soak both brushes in solvent. (The original brushes were woven brass and trapped dirt and oil.) Clean thoroughly and blow dry with compressed air.
2. Spray oiler felt pads on the base and motor frame with WD40 to clean them. Rinse with clean solvent and dry with a paper towel.

HORN

3. Place the rotor shaft (either end) into a variable speed drill motor. Rotate the rotor at a slow RPM while holding a scotch pad on the opposite shaft end for cleaning. Rotate the rotor in the drill motor and clean the shaft on the other end.
4. Chuck the bottom rotor shaft (ratchet end) in the drill motor and rotate slowly while holding a piece of # 320 emery paper on the commutator. Polish the commutator with #400 emery. Remove the rotor from the drill motor.
5. Clean each groove on the commutator with a wooden groove cleaner. DO NOT USE A METAL SHARP OBJECT TO CLEAN COMMUTATOR GROOVES.
6. Clean the field windings with light compressed air. Brush on a light coat of shellac for insulation on the field windings and the rotor windings.
7. Clean all other parts with solvent.

Horn Assembly

1. Place the rotor in the motor frame and mount to the motor base with two nuts and lock washers.
2. Carefully place the end of a steel rule into one of the slots in the iron core of the rotor. [Take extreme **CAUTION** not to damage any of the fine armature wire windings.] Now turn the rotor until the steel rule is up against the right side field housing. This will allow the rotor to be held stationary while tightening the ratchet nut.
3. Hold the steel rule and rotor in place while installing the ratchet nut and ratchet wheel. The depressed side of the ratchet wheel faces the diaphragm.
4. Assemble the brush and spring in the brush holders and attach the screw and insulating washers on each side of the motor frame. An insulating washer is placed on both sides of the frame. The motor field wires are placed between the brush holder and the inside insulating washer. After installation of the brush assembly, check continuity between the brush holder and motor frame. The brush holder must be insulated from the motor frame.

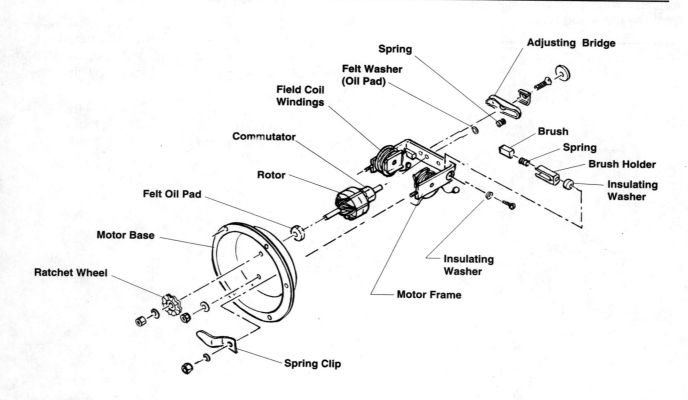

HORN

5. Attach the connector assembly to the motor base with screw, washers and nut.

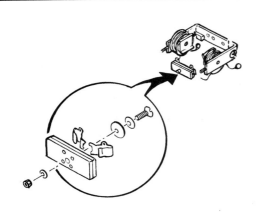

6. On the bottom of the motor base, remove the right side frame nut that holds the ratchet tension clip. Install the clip and replace the nut and lock washer.
7. Install the top adjusting screw, bridge and spring.

8. Position gaskets on both sides of the diaphragm and position in the horn bell with the diaphragm stud pointing up (toward the motor base). Place the motor base assembly on top of the bell assembly and attach with six (6) attaching bolts and nuts.
9. Rotate the rotor with your hand and turn the top adjusting screw until the ratchet just makes contact with the diaphragm stud.
10. Apply two (2) drops of 3-1 oil to each felt oiler pad. DO NOT OVER OIL.
11. Apply 6 volts to the connector block and test for rotation. Adjust for proper **Ahaooooogh !**

HORN MOTOR ASSY

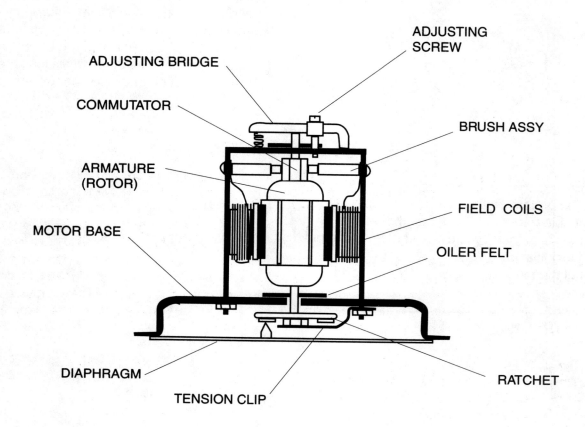

HORN ROD

The horn rod actually serves two functions. (1) It contains the horn button, wire, and contact to complete the electrical circuit for the horn motor, and (2) it is mechanically used to actuate the light switch located at the bottom of the steering column. The horn rod must be removed from the steering column before repairs can be made to the electrical wire inside the rod. If the horn does not operate when the horn button is pressed, the problem may be with the main harness terminal base located inside the light switch at the bottom of the steering column. To test the electrical circuit of the horn rod, remove the light switch at the bottom end of the steering column and check continuity (with an ohmmeter) from the bottom end of the horn rod to a ground point. There should be no continuity reading. When the horn button is pressed, there should be continuity from the tip of the horn rod to any ground point (zero resistance). If this test fails, the horn rod should either be replaced or repaired.

Removing Horn Rod

To remove the horn rod from a coupe or pickup requires removing the entire steering column from the car. There is not sufficient room to pull the horn rod from the steering column. See "Steering " section for removal of steering column. The steering column can be loosened as described below and pulled down enough to allow room to remove the horn rod in sedans. The top can be lowered on all open cars (Roadsters, Phaetons, A400, Cabriolets, and Roadster Pickups) to allow the horn rod to be removed.

1. Release the bail wire from the light switch (push bail wire down) at the end of the steering column. Pull the light switch bulb from the end of the steering column.

2. Push up slightly on the switch spider to remove the retaining clip, spider, and spring from the end of the horn rod.

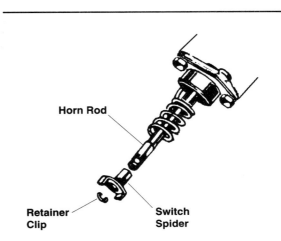

HORN ROD

(All Sedans)

3. Loosen the steering-to-frame bolts/nuts [9/16 wrench].

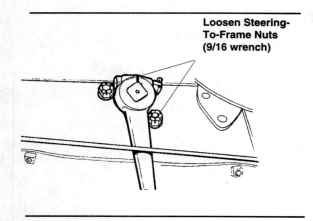

4. Remove the clamp under the steering column [2 Fillister head screws].

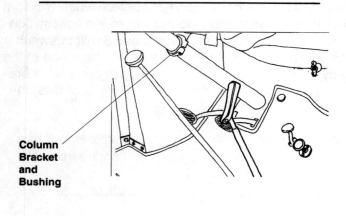

5. Lower the column far enough to pull the horn rod from the center of the steering wheel. A clearance of 46-1/2 to 47-1/2 inches is required to allow removal of the rod.

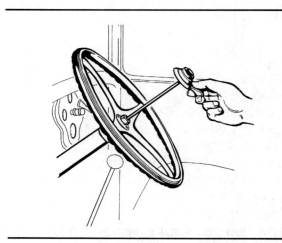

Horn Rod Replacement Deminsions

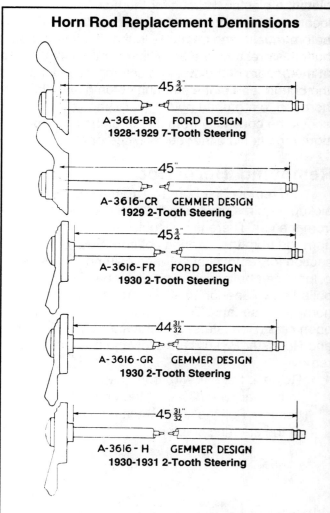

IGNITION SWITCH (POP-OUT)

The pop-out ignition switch was made by Electrolock in two different configurations. The components are not interchangeable between the two. The first style was made from 1928 to mid-1930. This is the simplest of the two and probably the easiest to repair. This switch assembly was used with the 1928/1929 style instrument panel (smooth) and the oval speedometer. The switch body is one solid smooth casting. The armored cable on this unit is a hand tight press fit into the body of the switch. If the armored cable moves out of the body of the switch 1/8", the connection is broken and the engine stops. This is why it is important to keep the cable bolted to the head stud. Most problems encountered with the pop-out switch are usually related to the wire in the armored cable. Heat from the engine breaks down the wire insulation inside the armored cable, causing the ignition wire to short out against the steel armor. The armor cable in this early style switch is fairly easy to remove, therefore replacing the wire in the armor cable is not too difficult.

From mid-1930 through 1931 the second style pop-out ignition switch was used. This style was used with the round speedometer and ribbed instrument panel. The body of this switch has a removable steel back cover plate. The body also has four ribs around the outside of the body. The ignition wire for this unit is crimped and soldered to a terminal board inside the back cover of the switch body. Repairing this later style switch and cable is much more involved.

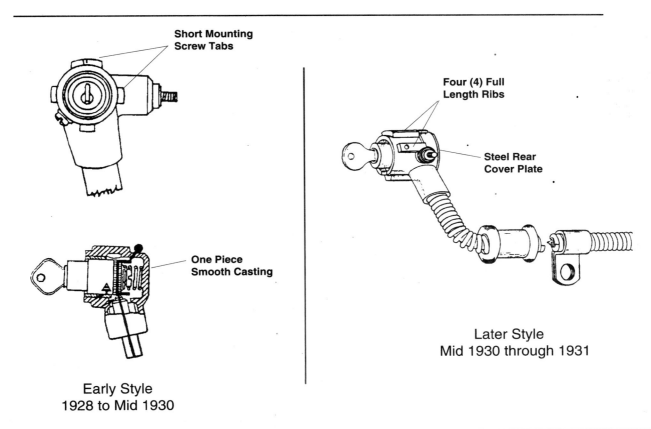

Early Style
1928 to Mid 1930

Later Style
Mid 1930 through 1931

IGNITION SWITCH (POP-OUT)

Removing Ignition Switch and Cable

1. Remove the head stud nut securing the cable to the head. After lifting the cable clamp off the stud, replace the nut immediately and torque it down (50 lbs.) to prevent water seepage from around the head gasket.

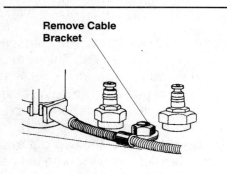
Remove Cable Bracket

2. Loosen the distributor set screw on the side of the head and lift the distributor out of the head. Unscrew the distributor from the cable.

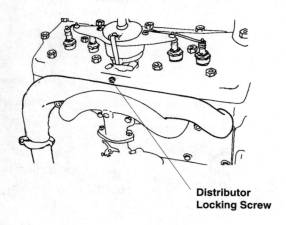
Distributor Locking Screw

3. Remove the two wing nuts from the terminal box and remove the cover.
4. Remove the ignition cable clip from the inside firewall.

5. Remove the instrument panel [four (4) screws].

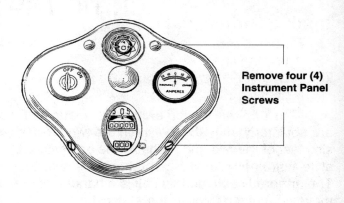
Remove four (4) Instrument Panel Screws

6. Disconnect the red wire from the ignition switch terminal.

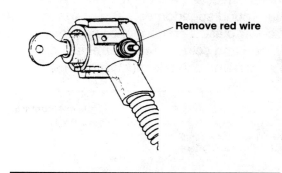
Remove red wire

7. Remove the three screws on the side of the switch body and remove the entire switch assembly from the instrument panel.

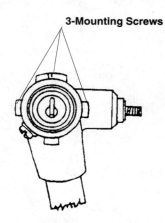
3-Mounting Screws

Service and Repair

IGNITION SWITCH (POP-OUT)

8. Pull the ignition switch and cable out of the gas tank trough for testing and repairs.

Testing Switch and Cable

1. Place the lock cylinder in the OFF position (Push the lock cylinder in until it locks.)
2. With an ohmmeter check continuity from the distributor end tip to the switch lock cylinder. In the OFF position, the ignition wire inside the armor cable is grounded to the lock cylinder. If the circuit tests open, the ignition wire in the cable is broken or the armor cable is not pushed far enough into the switch body to allow the plunger to make contact with the lock cylinder. Try forcing the armor cable farther into the switch body and retest.

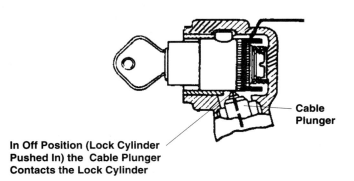

In Off Position (Lock Cylinder Pushed In) the Cable Plunger Contacts the Lock Cylinder

3. With the lock cylinder in the OFF position, test continuity from the screw terminal (red wire terminal) to the distributor end tip. The circuit should test open. If it tests closed (shorted), either the lock cylinder is not locked in, or there is an internal short.
4. Test continuity from the distributor end tip to the armor cable. The circuit should test closed. If it tests open, the internal wire is either broken or the plunger is not making contact at the lock cylinder end. Try pushing the armor cable farther into the lock case. In the OFF position, the cable plunger at the lock cylinder end should contact the lock cylinder to ground the ignition wire.

5. Place the ignition in the ON position (lock cylinder popped out). Test continuity from the red wire terminal on the switch body to the distributor end tip. The circuit should test closed (short circuit). If the circuit tests open, the ignition wire in the cable is broken or the armor cable is not pushed far enough into the switch body to allow the plunger to make contact with the lock cylinder.
6. Test continuity from the red wire terminal to the case (or armor cable). It should test open. If it tests shorted, the ignition wire is shorted inside the armor cable.

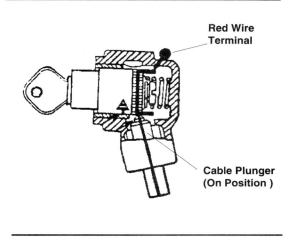

Disassembly and Repair (1928 Through Mid-1930)

1. To remove the lock cylinder place the switch in the locked (OFF) position. Remove the screw and lock washer on the side of the body.

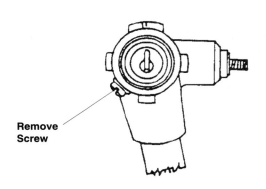

Remove Screw

IGNITION SWITCH (POP-OUT)

2. Insert the key and turn it to the unlocked (ON) position. With the key in the ON position the lock cylinder should pop all the way out of the housing. Holding the key in the ON position depresses the internal plunger to release the cylinder. If needed, spray around the cylinder with WD40 and work the cylinder out with the key held in the ON position.

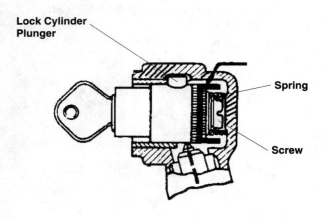

3. With the lock cylinder removed, remove the screw and spring on the back of the lock cylinder. Keep track of the insulating washers under the screw and behind the brass contactor. The insulating washers, brass contactor, and spring must be reassembled in the same order.
4. Clean the brass contactor and spray inside the lock cylinder while operating the key. After cleaning, rinse the lock cylinder with lacquer thinner and blow dry.
5. After thorough drying, lubricate the lock tumblers with dry graphite lock lubrication.
6. Reassemble the lock cylinder with the brass contactor, insulators, and rear spring. When reassembling, rotate the brass contactor so the cable plunger makes contact on a different spot.
7. After reassembly, check continuity from the brass contactor to the lock cylinder body. The reading on the ohmmeter should show OPEN. (No continuity). If the contactor is shorted to the cylinder body, the insulating washers were incorrectly assembled.

8. Insert the lock cylinder into the switch case. To insert the lock cylinder, insert the key and hold it in the ON position to depress the plunger. Line up the locking set screw groove and push the cylinder in place. Turn the key to the OFF position and push the cylinder in until the plunger snaps into the detent.
9. Insert the side locking screw. Turn the key to the ON position to ensure the cylinder functions properly in both the ON and OFF positions.

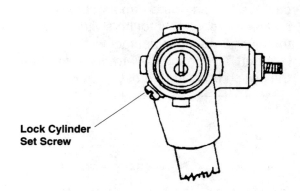

10. After the cable has been tested, the plunger end of the cable can now be twisted into the ignition switch housing. The plunger end must seat all the way into the switch.
11. Test the switch and cable with the testing procedure on page 1-203.

IGNITION SWITCH (POP-OUT)

Disassembly and Repair (Mid-1930 through 1931)

1. To remove the lock cylinder place the switch in the locked (OFF) position. Remove the screw and lock washer on the side of the body.

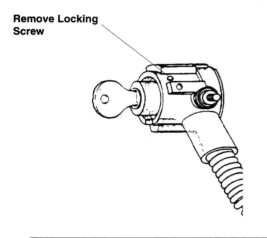

Remove Locking Screw

2. Insert the key and turn it to the unlocked (ON) position. With the key in the ON position the lock cylinder should pop all the way out of the housing. Holding the key in the ON position depresses the internal plunger to release the cylinder. If needed, spray around the cylinder with WD40 and work the cylinder out with the key held in the ON position.

3. The back steel cover must be removed to disconnect the ignition wire inside the armor cable. Pry the back cover off. Uncrimp and unsolder the exposed wire.

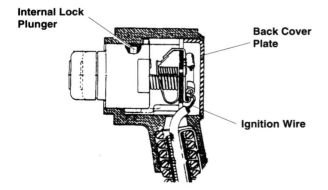

Internal Lock Plunger
Back Cover Plate
Ignition Wire

4. Remove the armor cable by twisting it out of the switch body.
5. Remove the slotted terminal nut, lock washer, fiber washers, and then remove the fiber terminal board with care.

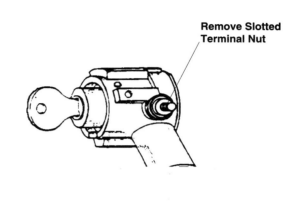

Remove Slotted Terminal Nut

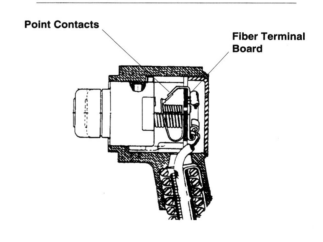

Point Contacts
Fiber Terminal Board

6. File, clean, and adjust the contact points.
7. Insert fiber terminal board, fiber insulating washers, and slotted terminal nut. Ensure all insulating washers are in place.

Service and Repair

IGNITION SWITCH (POP-OUT)

8. After the armor cable wire has been repaired and tested, twist the armor cable into the switch body. Pull the wire snug.
9. Crimp and solder the cable ignition wire to the fiber terminal board. Install the back cover.
10. Insert the lock cylinder into the switch case. To insert the lock cylinder, insert the key and hold it in the ON position to depress the plunger. Line up the locking set screw groove and push the cylinder in place. Turn the key to the OFF position and push the cylinder in until the plunger snaps into the detent.
11. Insert the side locking screw. Turn the key to the ON position to ensure the cylinder functions properly in both the ON and OFF positions.

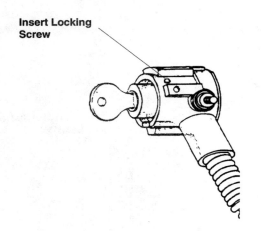

Insert Locking Screw

12. Test the switch and cable with the testing procedure on page 1-203.

Replacing Armored Cable Ignition Wire (1928 to Mid-1930)

This cable has the distributor connector on one end and brass plunger on the other end.

1. Place the <u>switch end</u> (plunger) of the cable in a vise. With a vise grip pliers, twist the end housing off the cable and pull it out far enough to cut the wire.
2. Tap the plunger and insulator out through the front of the housing.
3. Cut the wire off flush at the crimped end and drill a hole 3/8" deep into the crimped plunger end. Clean the hole and solder a new 30" wire in it (use # 14 gauge automotive fine strand heat resistance wire).
4. Place the distributor end of the armor cable in a vise and twist the distributor end housing off the cable. Pull the old wire out of the armor cable and cut it off about 2" from the end of the housing (distributor end housing).
5. Feed the free end of the wire from the plunger end through the armor cable. Twist the plunger end housing onto the armor cable.
6. Pull the wire snug at the distributor end and splice the end of the wire with the distributor end cut wire. Insulate the splice with heat-shrink. Twist the armor cable into the distributor end housing.
7. Continuity test the cable. The cable should show continuity from one tip to the opposite end tip. Test either tip to the armor cable for short circuit to the armor. The center cable should not test shorted to the outside armor cable. The plunger end of the cable can now be twisted into the ignition switch housing. The plunger end must seat all the way into the switch.
8. Test the switch and cable with the testing procedure on page 1-203.

Replacing Armored Cable Ignition Wire (Mid 1930 Through 1931)

1. Remove the cable from the switch end as described in the "Disassembly and Repair " procedure.
2. Place the distributor end of the armor cable in a vise and twist the distributor end housing off the cable. Pull the old wire out of the armor cable and cut it off about 2" from the end of the housing (distributor end housing).
3. Feed a new 30" long wire through the armor cable.
4. At the distributor end, splice the end of the wire with the distributor wire. Insulate the splice with heat-shrink. Twist the armor cable into the distributor end housing.

IGNITION SWITCH (POP-OUT)

5. Continuity test the cable. The cable should show continuity from one tip to the opposite end tip. Test either tip to the armor cable for short circuit to the armor. The center cable should not test shorted to the outside armor cable. The switch end of the cable can now be twisted into the ignition switch housing. See "Disassembly and Repair".

Installing Ignition Cable and Switch

1. Route the distributor end of the armor cable through the gas tank trough from the instrument panel side.
2. Place the ignition switch into the rear of the instrument panel and attach with three screws (6-32 X 1/4).
3. Attach the red harness wire to the switch screw terminal.
4. Attach the instrument panel to the dash with four (4) screws (10-32 X 1/2 oval head).

6. Screw the distributor onto the armor cable.

NOTE
If the ignition cable is screwed in too far, the cable housing will sometimes short out against the bottom bracket on the lower plate. Screw in the ignition cable only far enough to allow the spring loaded end to make good contact with the lower plate bracket.

7. Place the distributor with shaft into the cylinder head, carefully aligning the shaft slot with the tab on the distributor drive gear. When correctly positioned, the small pin on the bottom of the distributor housing must fully seat into the pin hole in the top of the cylinder head. The bottom of the distributor body must rest down fully on the cylinder head.

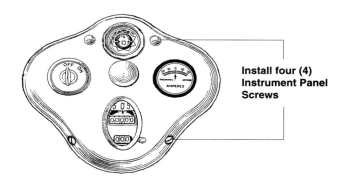

Install four (4) Instrument Panel Screws

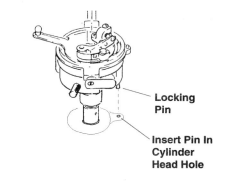

Locking Pin

Insert Pin In Cylinder Head Hole

5. Check the rubber grommet on the armor cable to make sure it is correctly positioned in the terminal box. This prevents the armor cable from shorting against the terminal box posts.

NOTE
The terminal box posts are always hot (6 volt potential).

IGNITION SWITCH (POP-OUT)

8. Install the distributor locking screw and jam nut into the side of the head. Screw in the locking screw only far enough to lock the distributor in place with no movement. Adjusting the lock screw too tight can cause binding on the distributor shaft, damaging the shaft and bushing. Lock the screw in place with the jam nut.

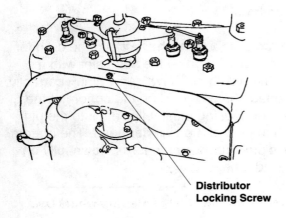

Distributor Locking Screw

9. Attach the ignition cable clamp to the center head stud and torque the stud nut to 55 ft.lbs.

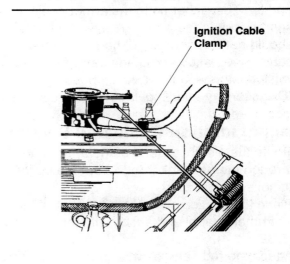

Ignition Cable Clamp

Service and Repair

KING PINS

Worn king pins and bushings can cause front end shimmy and hard steering. Many times only the bushings and thrust bearings will need to be replaced. Loose (worn) king pins can be checked by raising the front wheels off the ground, and grabbing the wheel at the top and bottom. Try rocking the wheel back and forth, top to bottom. If movement is detected, the bushings and possibly the king pins should be replaced. Before testing for loose king pins, make sure the front wheel bearings are not loose.

Replacing the king pin bushings and king pins requires removing the front wheels, brakes, backing plates, and spindles. Parts involved include spindle bolt (king pin), bushings, shims, thrust bearings, and felt washer and cup. A special king pin bushing reamer will be needed to ream the bushings after they have been installed. The two bushings on each spindle must be reamed in-line with each other. The parts that will need to be replaced can only be determined after removal of the spindles and inspection of each part.

Replacing the front king pins and bushings can be a fairly simple task. To familiarize yourself with the task, read through the following procedure in its entirety before starting.

Front Spindle Removal

1. Jack up the front end and place jack stands under the front axle near the spring perches. Remove the front wheels.

2. On the left front side of the car remove the drag link from the spindle arm ball by removing the cotter pin and unscrewing the drag link end plug.

3. Remove the clevis pin attaching the front brake rod to the actuating arm.

4. Remove the front wheel axle nut, wheel bearings, and drum.

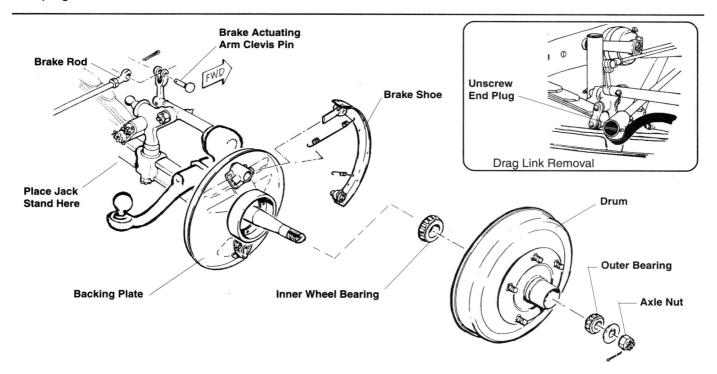

Removing Drum and Brake Shoes

KING PINS

Front Spindle Removal (con't)

5. Remove the three (3) brake shoe springs (1 long and 2 short) and remove the two brake shoes.

   NOTE
   The brake shoes can be easily removed by pulling down on the bottom of the shoe, releasing it from the operating wedge. The springs can then be removed by hand and the shoes removed from the backing plate.

Removing Backing Plate

1. Remove the operating wedge stud nut [5/8 socket], located on the back side of the backing plate. The operating wedge stud and operating wedge can now be removed. The operating pin will then drop out of the king pin.

   NOTE
   Be sure to retain any operating pin shims (pill) that may be in the operating wedge dimple, and the operating pin felt washer.

2. Remove the four (4) backing plate bolts (inside grease baffle) and castle nuts [9/16 socket]. The grease baffle and backing plate can now be removed from the spindle.

3. The tie-rod end can now be removed from the spindle arm. Remove the cotter pin from the end of the tie-rod and screw out the end plug. The tie-rod can then be lifted off the spindle arm ball. Remove the rubber grease seal and metal cap from the spindle arm.

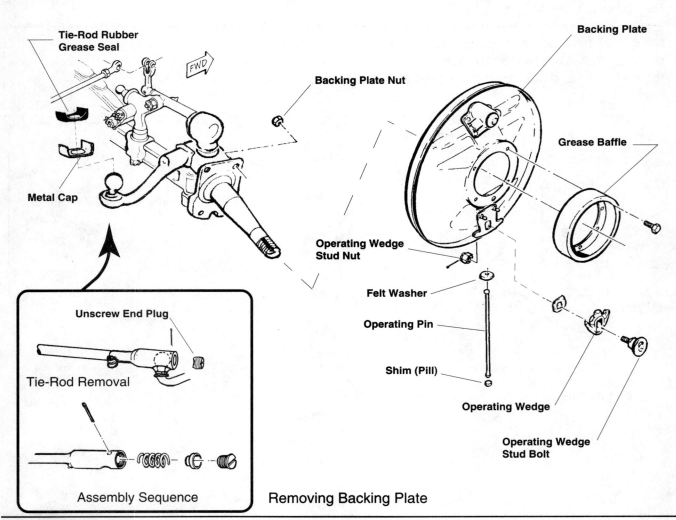

Removing Backing Plate

Service and Repair

KING PINS

Removing Spindle

1. Remove the spindle locking pin nut [9/16 socket] and lock washer. Reinsert the locking pin nut, screwing in only 1/2 the thread length. The nut is used to knock out the grooved locking pin. With a small hammer, hit the end of the nut to drive out the pin. A drift punch may be needed to completely drive out the locking pin.

2. Remove the actuating arm nut [9/16 socket] and lock washer from the back side of the spring perch. With large pliers or pipe wrench rotate the king pin cup (top portion of king pin) outward (toward front) a few degrees to release the actuating arm. Remove the actuating arm from the spring perch and king pin cup.

CAUTION

The king pin must be rotated slightly outward to allow the actuating arm bolt to release from the spring perch without damaging the threads on the actuating arm bolt.

3. Pull the king pin straight up and remove the spindle from the axle. Retain the thrust bearing, shims, and felt cup washer.

4. Inspect the ball studs on the spindle arms. If they are worn out of round, it is best to replace the ball studs. Out of round ball studs will cause hard steering and ineffective alignment of the front end. Out of round ball studs must be replaced to achieve proper steering. The old ball studs can be cut off, the spindle arm drilled, and new ball studs welded in.

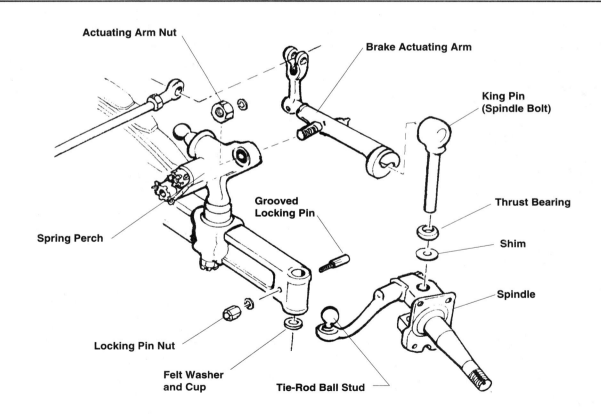

Removing Spindle

Service and Repair

KING PINS

Installing New Bushings

1. Thoroughly clean all dirt and grease from the spindle. Drive out both bushings in the spindle with a drift punch or press.

2. Press in the two (2) king pin bushings.

   CAUTION

   Each bushing must be pressed in. Using a hammer to insert bushings will damage the bushing. If a press is not available, a work bench vise can be used to easily press in the bushings. The hole in the bushing must line up with the grease fitting hole as the bushing is pressed in.

3. After the bushings have been pressed in, clamp the spindle in a vise so the bushings can be reamed to size. The two bushings must be reamed in-line. Ream the bushings using a .812 in-line bushing reamer. The bottom end of the reamer is smaller (.798) and serves as a pilot shaft into the bottom bushing as the top bushing is reamed. Continue to clean the shavings as the bushings are being reamed to prevent scoring the bushing walls.

4. After the bushings have been reamed, thoroughly clean the spindle of all shavings. Insert grease through the grease fitting to clean all shavings from the bushing grease hole.

5. Plug both bushings with paper towels and paint the spindle body. Clean any paint residue from inside the bushings before assembly.

6. Attach spindle arms to the spindle if they were removed for ball stud replacement.

Installing Spindles and King Pins

1. If the old king pin shows signs of excessive wear, it should be replaced (.810 min.). Before installing the spindle on the axle, slip the king pin through the new bushings on the spindle to check the fit in the bushing. Slip the thrust bearing on the king pin when checking for bushing fit. This will match the correct part of the king pin shaft to the bushing. No movement (side play) should be detected. Replace the king pin if any play is detected. If new king pins are installed, it may be necessary to lap the new king pins into the bushings with valve grinding compound. Thoroughly clean all components after lap fitting.

2. Apply a coat of grease to the king pin shaft, thrust bearing, and inside the bushings.

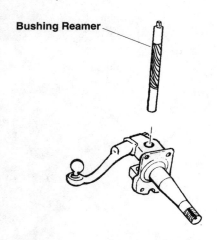

Reaming Bushings

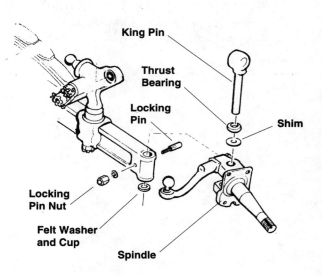

Installing Spindle and King Pins

KING PINS

3. Place the spindle on the axle. Insert the king pin, new thrust bearing (open side facing down), and shim through the spindle and axle, through the felt washer cup, and into the lower bushing. Always replace the thrust bearing with a Timken T-83 bearing. The replacement foreign made bearings should not be used.

NOTE

The new thrust bearings are thinner than the original bearings. One or two shims will be needed to take up the difference. This will allow the thrust bearings to support the total weight of the car, producing easy and smooth steering. The grooved locking pin securely fastens the king pin to the axle. The weight of the car then creates a downward force on the king pin, placing the car's weight on the thrust bearing, between the king pin upper cup and the top of the spindle. If the thrust bearing is too thin, the weight of the car will be transferred to the bottom of the axle, at the felt washer and cup. This is not a bearing surface and will cause stiff and hard steering. The front end weight of the car should be totally supported on the thrust bearing. Adding a shim or two under the thrust bearing will shift the weight to the bearing.

4. Insert the end of the brake actuating arm into the king pin cup and then rotate the actuating arm bolt into the spring perch. Allow the king pin to rotate to prevent damaging the actuating arm bolt threads when inserting into the spring perch. Apply nut and lock washer to the actuating arm bolt. Securely tighten.

5. Rotate the king pin to align the king pin locking pin groove with the hole in the axle.

6. Insert the grooved locking pin through the front of the axle to lock the king pin in place. Hammer the locking pin all the way in before applying the lock washer and nut. (This will prevent applying excessive force on the bolt threads.)

7. Apply the locking pin lock washer and nut. Securely tighten. Check thrust bearing operation as follows before continuing assembly:
   a.) Place a floor jack under the spindle and raise just enough to support the total weight of the car on the jack.
   b.) Try to move (rotate) the thrust bearing on top of the axle and the felt washer cup under the axle. The felt washer cup should rotate freely and the thrust bearing, supporting the car's weight, should not rotate. If the thrust bearing can be moved, add a shim under the thrust bearing.
   c.) Lower the front end back onto the jack stands. Grabbing the spindle axle, rotate the spindle back and forth to ensure free movement.

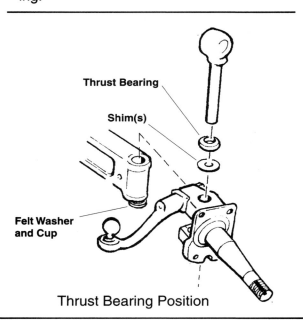

Thrust Bearing Position

KING PINS

8. Place a metal cap and rubber grease seal over the spindle arm ball stud. (The rubber grease seal usually needs replacing.)

9. Place the end of the tie-rod over the spindle arm ball stud and screw in the end plug. After the end plug contacts the ball, screw in the end plug an additional 1 to 1-1/2 turns. Align the end plug slot with the cotter pin holes in the tie-rod. Insert the cotter pin and secure it in place.

NOTE
The tie-rod ball spring should be compressed 25% for correct tension. Steering is affected if this adjustment is too loose or too tight.

10. Place the backing plate and grease baffle on the spindle and attach with four (4) bolts (3/8-24 X 7/8) and nuts [9/16 socket]. Securely tighten all nuts and insert cotter pins.

11. Push the operating pin up into the center of the king pin. Insert a felt washer over the operating pin, and into the backing plate access hole.

12. Hold the operating pin up while attaching the operating wedge with wedge stud, stud washer (spacer), and castle nut [5/8 socket]. Securely tighten the stud nut and insert a cotter pin. Check for free movement (up and down) of the operating wedge.

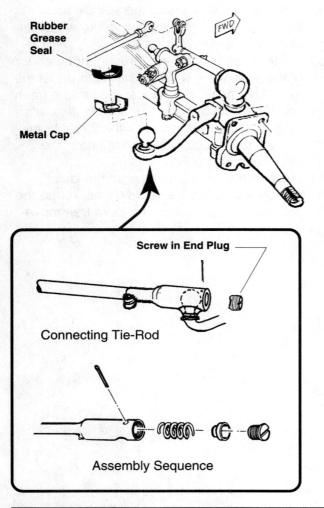

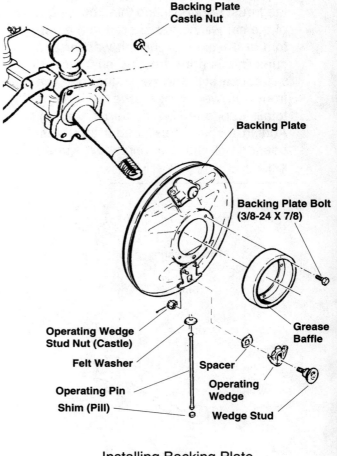

Installing Backing Plate

Service and Repair

Installing Brake Shoes

1. Clean all components on the brake shoes before installing on backing plates.

2. Place each brake shoe adjusting shaft into the top adjuster housing on the backing plate.

3. Pull the two shoes together to allow the top (long) spring to be easily attached between the shoes.

4. Pull the bottom of the shoe in and attach the short spring from the shoe to the spring stud. The bottom of the shoe can then be pushed outward and slipped onto the roller track, with the rollers contacting the operating wedge. This can all be done without tools.

5. Pack all wheel bearings with grease. Install the inner wheel bearing, hub, outer wheel bearing, key washer, and axle nut. Tighten the axle nut until a heavy drag is felt on the wheel. Then back off the axle nut one castle position from the cotter pin hole. Install the cotter pin.

6. Install the drag link on the left spindle. Screw in the drag link end plug and tighten sufficiently to compress the internal spring 25% (usually 1 to 1-1/2 turns past contact with the ball stud). Install the cotter pin.

7. Attach both brake rods to brake actuating arms with clevis pin and cotter pin.

8. Install both front wheels.

9. Adjust the brakes in accordance with the "Brake Adjusting Procedure" (See Section II).

10. After king pins and bushings have been installed, readjust the front toe-in. See Section II.

11. Remove the jack stands and test drive.

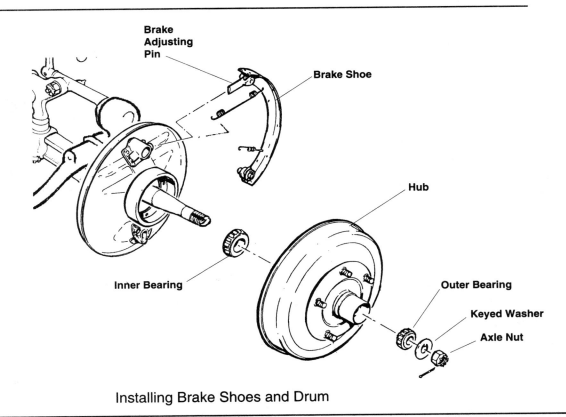

Installing Brake Shoes and Drum

HEADLIGHTS

The headlight used in 1928/1929 differs from the 1930/1931 headlight. The 1928/1929 headlights are parabolic-shaped plated steel, while the 1930/1931 headlights are made of stainless steel with a hemisphere shape. The flexible conduit from the head light shell to the radiator shell was 7/16" diameter in 1928, then changed to 1/2" diameter in 1929 through 1931. The headlights are held in place on the light bar by a nut and lock washer (1/2-20)[3/4 wrench]. The same nut holds the horn in place on the driver's side of the light bar. Repairs to the headlights include removal and replacement of light bulbs, polishing or replacing the light reflectors, removing and replacing the headlight lens, replacing the light bulb socket and harness connector socket, and improving grounding connections.

Changing Headlight Bulbs

1. To access the headlight bulb, extend the spring catch at the bottom of the rim and slip it off the slotted seat. Pull up on the bottom of the rim to remove the rim from the top lens retainer clip.

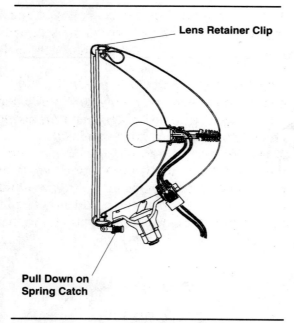

Lens Retainer Clip

Pull Down on Spring Catch

2. Removing the rim will expose the bulb and reflector. Push the bulb in and twist it to the left to remove it.

3. All 1928 and early 1929 headlights have a single-bulb socket which uses a two-filament bulb, while 1929 through 1931 headlights have two-bulb sockets. The center bulb is the high/low beam and the upper socket is the parking light. It is recommended that a 32-50 candle power bulb be used for normal beam.

4. If using a #1188 bulb (32-50 candle power), the longer filament goes on top when the bulb is correctly mounted.

Removing Lens

1. Inside the rim there are three (3) wire spring retainers that hold the glass lens in place. (The retainer springs are different sizes for 1928/1929 light rims and 1930/1931 light rims). These can be removed by extending one leg of the spring with needle nosed pliers and removing the spring clip. Remove the glass lens. The 1928 lens is fluted while the 1929 through 1931 lens is a prism type.

HEADLIGHTS

Removing Reflector

1. The reflector is removed by first removing the center headlight bulb and then slightly prying the sides of the reflector out of the pressed clips on each side of the light shell. The reflector will pull off the bulb spring socket.
2. Only silver plating is recommended for reflectors. If the reflector is dirty and needs cleaning, wash it gently with soap and water. Rub only using up and down motions. Never clean in a circular motion. Use silver polish if the reflectors are tarnished, again using only up and down motion.

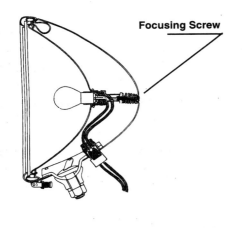

3. Removing the focusing screw at the rear of the shell will release the spring and light bulb socket.

Removing Connector Socket

1. The connector socket can be cleaned by wrapping a piece of fine emery paper around a 1/2" dowel to clean the inside of the socket. This can improve the connection.

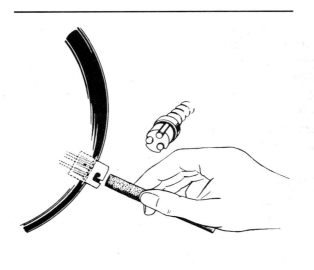

2. The connector socket can be removed and replaced if necessary. Depress the tongues on side of the socket located at the bottom of the socket (from inside the shell).
3. Inspect the spring contacts inside the light socket. Make sure they have good resilience and are not broken. Replace with new spring and contacts if not in good condition.
4. Check the conduit socket plug. Be sure the measurement from the back of the plug to the tip of the wire contact is 11/16". Some reproduction sockets are too long and will cause the socket spring to bow, shorting out the wiring.

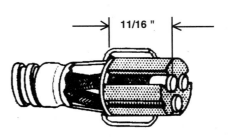

Service and Repair

HEADLIGHTS

Headlight Grounding

It's important to determine how well the light tube socket fits into the reflector, and how well the connector tube fits into the shell. These connections must be tight to properly ground the head lamps. If these sockets and connectors do not fit tightly, a grounding wire to the mounting bracket should be installed. A good ground connection should also be made at the headlight bar. The ground path must be positive and continuous from the lamp shell all the way to the frame. To add a grounding wire requires removing the headlight from the light bar as follows.

1. Remove the battery <u>ground cable</u> from the (+) battery post.

2. Remove the headlight conduit connectors (push and twist counterclockwise to release).

NOTE

Some headlight wiring may have been modified by eliminating the connector plug from inside the conduit socket. The wires would then be routed directly from the conduit into the headlight bucket and attached to the bulb sockets with wire nuts. The wires would have to be disconnected from behind the headlight reflector. To access the headlight bucket, release the front lens clip, pull the clip down (spring loaded latch) and lift up on lens rim to remove. Remove the center bulb and lift the reflector out of the headlight bucket.

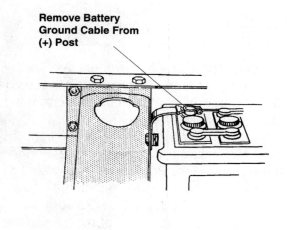

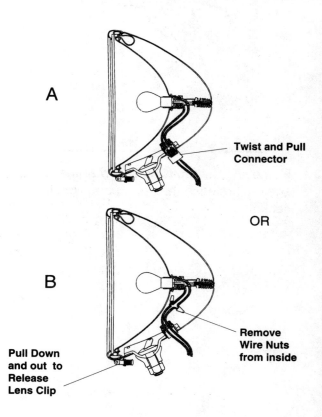

HEADLIGHTS

3. Remove the 1/2-20 nut and lock washer attaching the headlight to the light bar (3/4 wrench).
4. Remove the headlight rim, bulb, and reflector.
5. Remove the rear focusing screw at the rear of the shell to allow removal of the spring and bulb socket.
6. The connector socket can be removed by depressing the tongues on the side of the socket located at the bottom of the socket (from inside the shell).

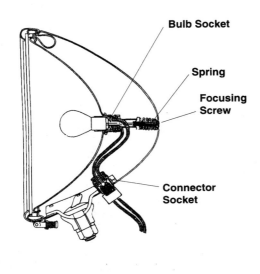

7. Drill out one of the rear 3/16 rivets attaching the swivel bolt to the inside spring bracket.
8. With a small file, square the holes in the shell and swivel bolt plate to accept the squared portion of a 3/16 carriage bolt.
9. Insert a 3/16 X 1 inch stainless steel carriage bolt. Lock the carriage bolt in with a 10-24 hex nut and lock washer.
10. Solder a short length of wire to the main head lamp socket and one to the parking light socket. Ground these two wires to the installed carriage bolt with a nut and lock washer.
11. Push the connector socket back into the shell (insert from the outside) until the side tongues snap inside, locking the connector in place.
12. Attach the bulb socket and spring with focusing screw (10-32).
13. Install the reflector, bulb, and rim. Replace the cork lens gasket on the reflector channel before installing the rim.

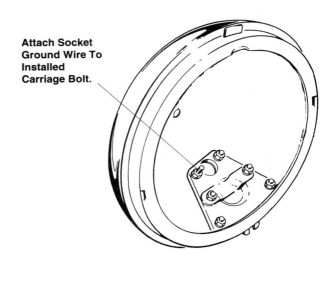

14. Position the headlight on the light bar and attach with nut and lock washer (1/2-20)[3/4 wrench].
15. Install the headlight conduit connectors (push and twist clockwise to lock).
16. Connect the battery ground strap.
17. Readjust headlight alignment (See "SERVICE ADJUSTMENTS.")

MOTOR MOUNTS

The Model A used a three point suspension for the engine. Correct installation of the motor mounts is important to maintaining correct alignment of the entire driveline. Any stress on the driveline caused by misalignment will create vibration. The rear motor mounts should provide a fairly rigid and stable support to the frame, while the front motor mount should allow the front of the engine to float. Replacing the motor mounts will not necessarily correct excessive engine vibration. Engine vibration is caused by an engine out of balance, misaligned driveline, warped flywheel housing, unbalanced flywheel and pressure plate, and even incorrect valve timing.

Both the front and rear motor mounts can be removed and/or replaced without removing the engine.

Removing Front Motor Mount

1. Place a floor jack under the oil pan for engine support while removing the front motor mount. Raise the front of the engine slightly.
2. Removing the fan belt will provide more room and access to the front motor mount. Loosen the generator mounting bolt and nut [3/4 socket].
3. If a generator holding bracket is installed, loosen the holding bracket bolt [9/16 socket] on the timing gear cover and swing the bracket away from the generator. Push the generator toward the engine to release belt tension.
4. Slip the belt off the generator pulley and then off the crank pulley. The belt can now be removed from the fan pulley.
5. Remove the two (2) front motor mount bolts [3/4 socket].
6. Remove the cotter pin and nut on the bottom of the front motor mount assembly. Remove the bottom spring and brass washer and pull the yoke out of the cross member. Check the bottom spring plate and the two (2) side suspension springs for cracks or brakes. Replace if weak or damaged.
7. Look for excessive wear around the lower stud where it goes through the frame cross member. Repair or replace if needed. Clean and inspect all parts and reassemble in accordance with the figure below.

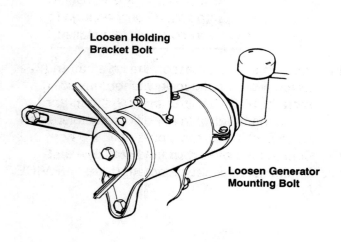

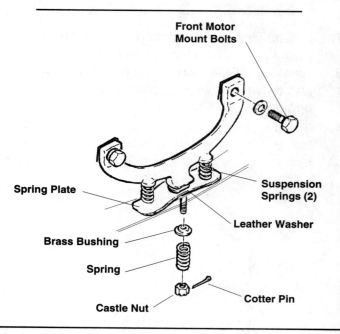

MOTOR MOUNTS

Removing Rear Motor Mounts

The rear motor mounts can be removed and replaced without removing the engine from the car.

1. Remove the safety wire from the four (4) rear engine mounting bolts and remove the bolts [3/4 inch short thin-wall socket] inside rear engine mounts, two (2) on each side of the flywheel housing.
2. Place a floor jack under the flywheel housing and raise it enough to release the weight of the engine from the motor mounts.

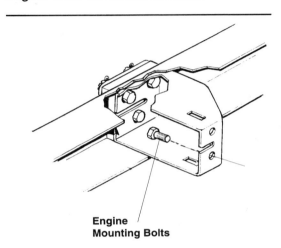

Engine Mounting Bolts

3. Remove the three (3) castle nuts and bolts [1/2" wrench] through the frame and remove the outer steel plate and rubber pad. Drive the bolts and steel sleeves out of the frame and motor mounts.
4. Lift the flywheel housing (with the floor jack) enough to lift the side arms off the motor mount.
5. Spray WD40 or other lubrication on the inside of the frame to allow the motor mount to slide forward. Drive the motor mount toward the front of the car to remove it.

Rear Motor Mount Installation

Properly functioning rear motor mounts will help reduce engine vibration. If the rubber pads on the rear motor mounts (between bracket and frame) are hard and cracked, they should be replaced. Replace both rubber pads and the mounting bolt sleeves.

The new rubber pads do not line up with the frame holes properly. The hole extrusions should be cut off flush with the pad and the bottom right angle of the pad removed. Be sure to insert the metal sleeves for the bolts. This will keep the motor mounts and bolts centered on the frame and provide a certain amount of floating action so the rubber pads can absorb the engine vibration.

1. Inspect each motor mount for cracks. Weld all breaks and cracks as needed.
2. Replace all rubber pads and bolt sleeves.
3. Trim the inside rubber pad as described above and check the fit and hole alignment.
4. Lightly lubricate the rubber pad with soap. Position the rubber pad on the frame and drive the motor mount into place from the front side.

NOTE

The frame may need spreading to allow installation of the motor mount with new rubber pads. Block one side of the engine with a 2X4 and use a bottle jack on the working side. Place the bottle jack between the frame and the transmission. Spread the frame only enough to allow the motor mount to be installed.

5. Insert the steel sleeves through all three (3) frame holes and place the three mounting bolts (5/16-24 X 1-3/8) through the motor mount and frame. Install the outside rubber pad, steel plate, and castle nuts. Do not tighten the castle nuts until both flywheel mounting bolts have been installed.

MOTOR MOUNTS

6. From under the car, insert the two rear motor mount bolts (1/2-13 X 1-3/8" drilled) on each side of the flywheel housing [3/4 socket]. Tighten firmly and safety wire.

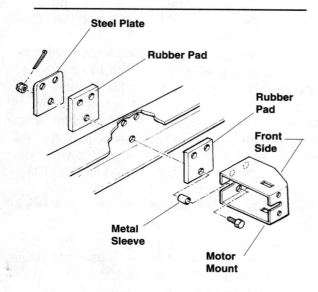

Original Motor Mount Installation
(Left Side Viewed From Rear)

7. Tighten all three (3) frame bolts [1/2" socket] and insert cotter pins.
8. Lower and remove the floor jack from under flywheel housing.

Float-A-Motor Installation

1. If the rear engine motor mount brackets are being replaced with Float-A-Motor brackets, attach the flywheel housing bracket to the flywheel with two bolts (1/2-13 X 1-3/8" drilled) on each side of the flywheel housing [3/4 socket]. Tighten firmly and safety wire.
2. Install the Float-A-Motor frame bracket, using the same rubber pads, sleeves, bolts, and outer steel plate as used for the original motor mount. Mount the frame bracket so the bevel edge faces the front of the car.
3. Place a rubber bushing and bushing cap on each side of the flywheel bracket and lower the engine onto the motor mount.

4. Place a single bolt through the bushing caps, rubber bushings, and motor mount brackets. Tighten the center bolt nut on both motor mounts.
5. After installing the motor mounts, check clearance between the firewall and the right end of the accelerator bracket (1/8 to 1/4" clearance). If the accelerator bracket contacts the firewall, readjust (lower) the front motor mount by tightening the center motor mount nut on the bottom of the assembly.

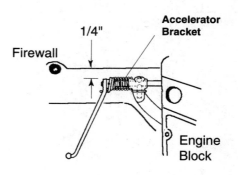

6. Check clearance between the brake cross shaft and the bottom of the transmission. The brake cross shaft should move freely with no interference (contact) from the bottom of the transmission. Adjust the Float-A Motor center mounting bolt to obtain proper clearance above the brake cross shaft.

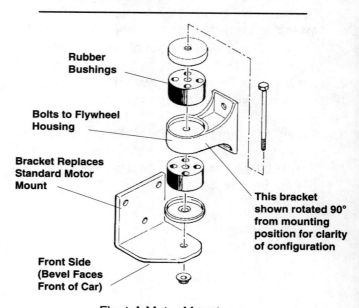

Float-A Motor Mounts
(Right Side Viewed From Front)

Service and Repair   1-222

MUFFLER

The Model A muffler and tail pipe is a one-piece welded construction. It is important that the muffler be correctly clamped to the manifold to prevent exhaust leaks. An after market copper/asbestos gasket should be used between the manifold and the muffler pipe connection. Most manifolds are warped (dropped) down at the rear exhaust flange. This can make it difficult to make a good connection to the manifold and keep the muffler and tail pipe parallel to the frame. Hold the flange of the new muffler against the manifold flange to check the angle of the muffler and pipe, with the muffler flange square against the manifold flange. With the tail pipe hump touching the frame (holding bracket location), the muffler flange should squarely fit the manifold flange. If the angle of the flange causes a gap at the manifold connection, the muffler and manifold cannot be clamped together tightly enough to prevent a manifold leak. This problem is nearly always caused by a drooping manifold. With the proper fixture (muffler shop), the neck of the muffler can be re-bent to fit the angle of the manifold.

Muffler Removal and Installation

1. From under the car loosen the bolt and nut on the muffler frame clamp [9/16 wrench].
2. Remove the two (2) bolts on the muffler clamp (9/16 wrench) and remove both halves of the clamp.

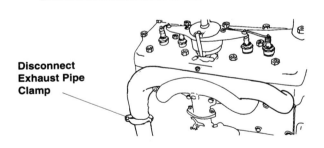

Disconnect Exhaust Pipe Clamp

3. Remove the rear tail pipe bracket bolt and nut. Slide the bracket off the tail pipe.

4. Slide the tail pipe bracket over the new tail pipe as shown. Both ends of the clamp sit on top of the lower frame rail.

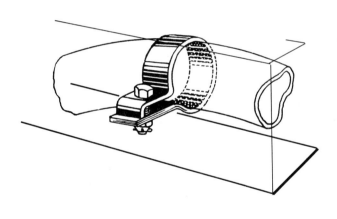

5. Bolt the bracket loosely to the frame. Do not tighten at this time.

MUFFLER

6. Place a copper/asbestos gasket over the front muffler inlet pipe flange. Position the gasket so the raised center portion faces down into the muffler pipe.
7. Raise the inlet pipe to the manifold flange and apply the two halves of the manifold clamp. The larger flange on the clamp is placed around the muffler flange and the smaller clamp flange is placed around the manifold flange.

8. Install the muffler clamp using two (2) bolts (3/8-16 X 1-7/8") and nuts [9/16 socket]. The clamp must grip the full circle of the muffler flange. The clamp provides a tight fit for the exhaust seal and also must support the weight of the muffler as a holding clamp. Therefore, it is important for the clamp to grip the entire flange on the muffler. If there is a mismatch between the muffler flange and exhaust manifold, release the tail pipe bracket and re-clamp the manifold bracket.
9. Securely tighten the manifold clamp bolts evenly on both sides.
10. Lift the rear tail pipe into position to allow the tail pipe bracket to be reinstalled. Tighten the bracket bolt (3/8-24 X 1-1/4")[9/16 socket] and nut and insert cotter pin.

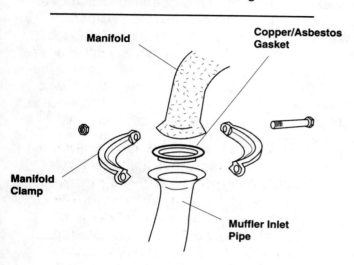

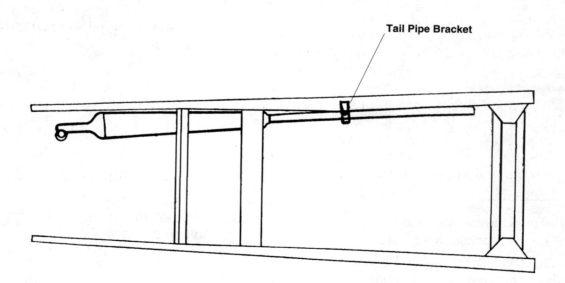

Service and Repair

OIL PAN GASKET

Removing Oil PAN

1. Drain the oil pan by removing the bottom drain plug. After draining, install the drain plug and tighten it.
2. Remove the engine side pans. The engine pans are attached to the frame on each side with three (3) 1/4-28 X 1/2" hex head bolts [7/16 wrench], lock washers and nuts, and two attaching ears under two oil pan bolts [1/2" socket].
3. From under the car, remove all twenty (20) oil pan bolts [1/2 socket] and lock washers. Remove the oil pan and oil pump. The pan can be lowered down at the rear and moved away from the tie-rod. (About one quart of oil remains in the oil pan baffle. Keep upright.) The oil pump will drop out of the block and remain in the oil pan.
4. Scrape all old gasket material off the top edge of the oil pan. Pry the baffle tray out of the pan so all sludge can be cleaned out of the bottom of the pan. Flush the pan with solvent.
5. Clean and inspect the oil pump before reinstalling (See "Oil Pump" section).

Replacing Oil Pan and Gasket

1. Place the pump shaft into the block in alignment with the locating pin. The pump can be held in position using a small jack placed between the frame and the block with a 1/4 inch rod inserted in the side plug hole and pressing against the pump housing.

NOTE

The plug located in the engine block near the oil pump has a dry seal fine taper pipe thread (3/8-27F-PTF). Do not insert a set screw in this location. The pump was not designed to have a set screw hold it rigid. The spring located on the bottom of the pump holds the pump in position flexibly. If a set screw is used, the pump end plate and gears will wear prematurely. If a bolt of the wrong thread size is inserted into the plug hole, the threads will be damaged, resulting in oil leakage.

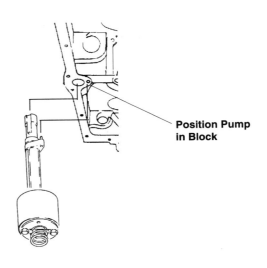

Position Pump in Block

OIL PAN GASKET

2. Take extreme care when installing the pan gaskets. Correct installation of the pan gaskets is essential to prevent oil pan leaks. Check the mating flange of the oil pan to make sure it is not bent, and that the entire flange surface is clean and flat.
3. Thoroughly clean all old gasket material from the pan and the bottom the engine block.
4. Insert the half round asbestos gasket from the gasket set (oil soaked) in the front recess of the oil pan. (New neoprene seal may be available.)

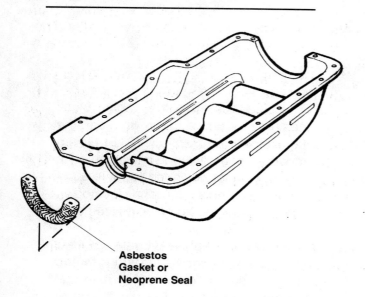

Asbestos Gasket or Neoprene Seal

5. Put a thin coat of Permatex gasket sealer on both sides of the two pan gaskets and set the two gaskets in place <u>on the block surface</u>. Make sure the end tabs on each gasket half fit all the way into the rear main bearing gasket groove.

6. Place the soaked rear main cork gasket around the rear main bearing cap. Make sure that both ends of the cork sit **on top** of the pan gasket tabs. Place a little gasket sealer in the area where the rear main cork gasket meets the pan gasket.
7. Carefully lift the pan into place on the gaskets, placing one pan bolt and lock washer on each side of the pan and finger tighten. Now install the remaining 5/16-18 X 3/4 hex head bolts [1/2" socket] and 5/16 lock washers. Tighten all bolts evenly. Torque to 20 ft. lbs.
8. Install both engine dust pans from under the car. Attach the two dust pan tabs under two of the oil pan bolts, and attach the other side to the frame with three 1/4-28 X 1/2' Hex Hd bolts, lock washers and square nuts. Make sure the engine pan bolts have been securely tightened after inserting the dust pan tabs.
9. Add four (4) quarts of oil through the oil filler tube. Check the oil dip stick. Add only enough oil to bring the oil level up to the "F" on the dip stick. DO NOT OVER FILL.

OIL PUMP

The key to the lubrication system is the flow of oil from the bottom of the oil pan to the valve chamber. The valve chamber supplies the oil to all main bearings, the timing gears, and the valve guides. The oil pump delivers a measured amount of oil from the oil pan to the valve chamber. The oil pump is driven by the distributor drive gear located in the valve chamber.

Two changes were made to the oil pump during production. In April 1928 the diameter of the shaft hole in the pump body was increased from 9/16" to 5/8" and the relief removed from the pump shaft. The clearance between the shaft and body forms the passage through which the pump delivers oil to the valve chamber. Formally the clearance was obtained by relieving the shaft. The clearance in the later pump is obtained by a larger shaft bore in the oil pump body, and a straight shaft (no relief). When replacing a shaft in a pump body equipped with a relieved shaft, be sure to replace it with the same type of shaft. The later straight shaft would not allow sufficient area for oil flow. The second change took place in November 1929. The pump shank was reinforced by adding four ribs up the shank. In this configuration, the size of the two shaft bushings were changed. The bushings in the earlier pumps were 21/32" diameter. The bushings in the ribbed shaft are 5/8" diameter.

There is very little that goes wrong with the oil pump. When the engine gets overhauled, the pump should be disassembled for thorough cleaning and the two shaft bushings replaced.

Removing Oil Pump

1. Drain the oil pan by removing the bottom drain plug. After draining, install drain plug.
2. Remove the engine side pans. The engine pans are attached to the frame on each side with three (3) 1/4-28 X 1/2" Hex Hd bolts [7/16 wrench], lock washers and nuts, and two attaching ears under two oil pan bolts [1/2" socket].
3. From under the car, remove all twenty (20) oil pan bolts [1/2 socket] and lock washers. Remove oil pan and oil pump. The pan can be lowered down at the rear and moved away from the tie-rod. (About one quart of oil remains in the oil pan baffle. Keep upright.) The oil pump will drop out of the block and remain in the oil pan.

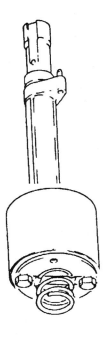

Service and Repair

OIL PUMP

Pump Design Changes

In April 1928 the diameter of the shaft hole in the pump body was increased from 9/16" to 5/8" and the relief (A) removed from the pump shaft. After April 1928 the shaft is a straight 1/2" shaft (B).

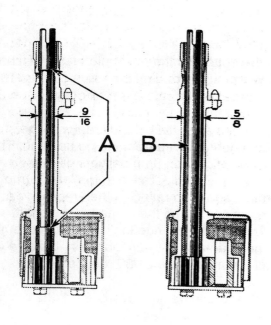

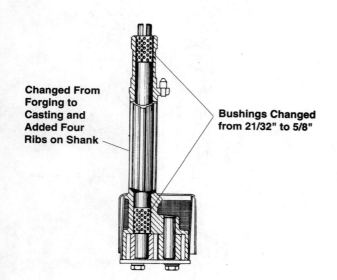

November 1929 Bushing Change

Oil Pump Disassembly and Overhaul

1. Remove the two (2) screws (1/4-28 X 7/16 fillister head) and lock washers from the top of the filter screen cover.
2. Lift the cover and gasket over the top of the shaft. Remove The filter screen.
3. Remove the four screws (1/4-28 X 1/2)[7/16 wrench] and lock washers from the bottom of the pump. The spring, cover plate, gasket, gear, and gear shaft can now be removed from the pump case.
4. Clean all parts with solvent.
5. The two shaft bushings can be removed from the case using a 5/8 diameter flat washer. Grind two sides off the washer for 7/16" wide at the flat sides.

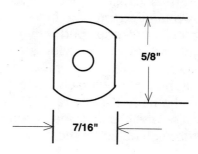

6. Drop the washer into the shaft hole, slipping the washer past the bushing at the flat sides. With the washer sitting on top of the bushing, a 1/2" rod can be inserted down the shaft hole and placed on top of the washer to drive out the bushing. Do the same to remove the bushing from the other end.
7. Press in new bushings. The earlier pumps used .656 O.D bushing. After Nov. 1929 the bushing was changed to .625 O.D., .500 I.D., one (1) inch long.

Service and Repair

OIL PUMP

8. Reassemble the pump in accordance with the illustration below. If the bottom cover plate shows wear, turn the plate over to install. Use new gaskets for assembly.

9. Place the pump shaft into the block in alignment with the locating pin. The pump can be held in position using a small jack placed between the frame and the block, with a 1/4 inch rod inserted in the side plug hole and pressing against the pump housing.

NOTE

The plug located in the engine block near the oil pump has a dry seal fine taper pipe thread (3/8-27F-PTF). Do not insert a set screw in this location. The pump was not designed to have a set screw hold it rigid. The spring located on the bottom of the pump holds the pump in position flexibly. If a set screw is used, the pump end plate and gears will wear prematurely. If a bolt of the wrong thread size is inserted into the plug hole, the threads will be damaged, resulting in oil leakage.

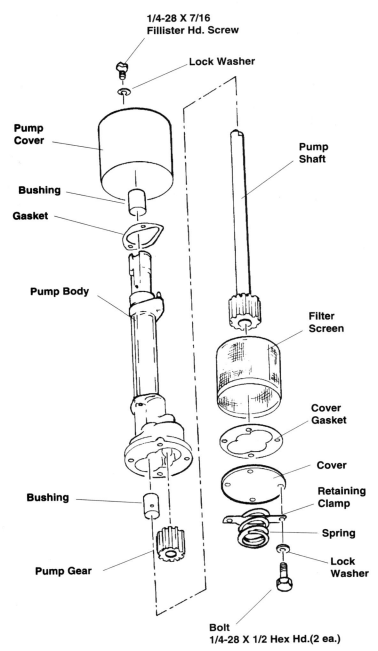

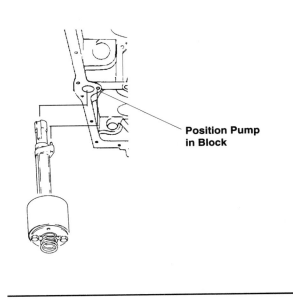

Position Pump in Block

Service and Repair

OIL PUMP

10. Take extreme care when installing the following pan gaskets. Correct installation of the pan gaskets is essential to prevent oil pan leaks. Check the mating flange of the oil pan to make sure it is not bent, and that the entire flange surface is clean and flat.
11. Insert the half round asbestos gasket from the gasket set (oil soaked) into the front recess of the oil pan. (New neoprene seal may be available.)

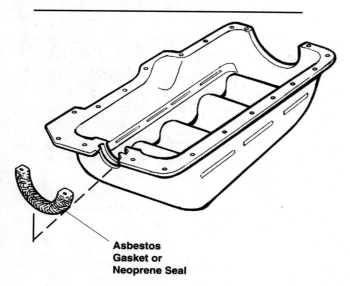

Asbestos Gasket or Neoprene Seal

12. Put a thin coat of Permatex gasket sealer on both sides of the two pan gaskets and set the two gaskets in place <u>on the block surface</u>. Make sure the end tabs on each gasket half fit all the way into the rear main bearing gasket groove.
13. Place the soaked rear main cork gasket around the rear main bearing cap. Make sure that both ends of the cork sit **on top** of the pan gasket tabs. Place a little gasket sealer in the area where the rear main cork gasket meets the pan gasket.
14. Carefully lift the pan into place on the gaskets, placing one pan bolt and lock washer on each side of the pan and finger tighten. Now install the remaining 5/16-18 X 3/4 hex head bolts [1/2" socket] and 5/16 lock washers. Tighten all bolts evenly. Torque to 20 ft. lbs.
15. Install both engine dust pans from under the car. Attach the two dust pan tabs under two of the oil pan bolts, and attach the other side to the frame with three 1/4-28 X 1/2' Hex Hd bolts, lock washers and square nuts. Make sure the engine pan bolts have been securely tightened after inserting the dust pan tabs.
16. Add four (4) quarts of oil through the oil filler tube. Check the oil dip stick. Add only enough oil to bring the oil level up to the "F" on the dip stick. DO NOT OVER FILL. Nearly five (5) quarts will be needed if the oil pan baffles were emptied before the oil pan was installed.

PEDALS - BRAKE/CLUTCH

Two different size pedal shafts were used during the model A production. A 3/4" shaft was used from beginning of production until November 1928. December 1928 through the end of production used a 7/8" pedal shaft. The brake and clutch should have no lateral movement. Install new bushings if lateral movement exists. Bronze bearing bushings with dimples to hold grease should be used.

Removing Brake and Clutch Pedals

1. Remove the front floor mat (or carpet) and shifting tower cover plate, attached to the floor boards with three (3) clips. Remove both sections of the front floor boards (12 flathead screws).
2. Remove both battery cables (ground first) and battery hold-down bracket from the battery and remove the battery. (Always remove the ground strap before removing battery cable.)
3. Remove the stop light linkage and brake rod from the brake pedal arm.

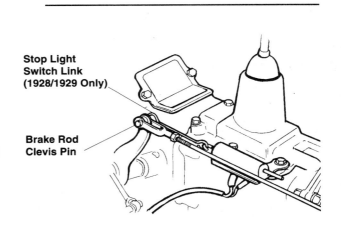

Battery Hold-Down Bracket

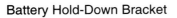

Ground Strap To (+) Post

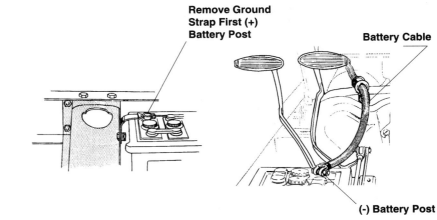

Battery Cable To (-) Post

PEDALS-BRAKE / CLUTCH

4. From under the car, remove the clutch arm clevis pin and release the clutch arm.

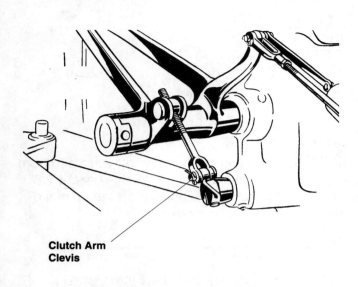

Clutch Arm Clevis

5. Remove the brake and clutch pedals by removing the cotter pin and shaft pin on the end of the pedal shaft. Remove the end cap and slide the two pedals and spring washer (after May 29) off the pedal shaft.

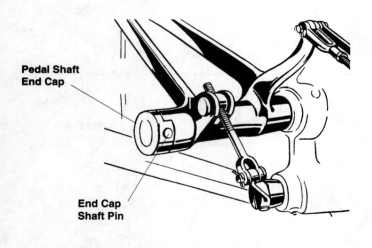

Pedal Shaft End Cap

End Cap Shaft Pin

6. Drive the bushings out of both pedal shafts. Press in new bushings (for either 3/4" or 7/8" shaft) on each pedal. Bearing bronze bushings with dimples to hold grease should be used. Ream the bushing for 3/4" shaft to .749, and for 7/8" shaft ream to .874. This will allow for shaft wear.

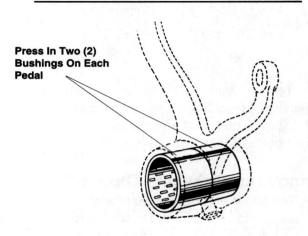

Press In Two (2) Bushings On Each Pedal

7. Lubrication fittings were installed on the brake and clutch pedals after May 1930. After installing bushings, remove the grease fittings and drill a 19/64" hole through the bushing. Reinstall the grease fittings.

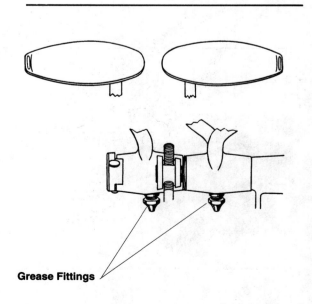

Grease Fittings

PEDALS-BRAKE / CLUTCH

8. Apply grease to the shaft and inside each pedal bushing. Slide the brake pedal on the shaft, followed by a spring washer (after May 1929) and the clutch pedal.

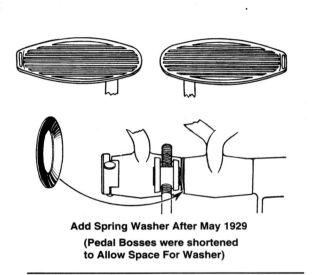

Add Spring Washer After May 1929
(Pedal Bosses were shortened to Allow Space For Washer)

9. Attach the pedal shaft end cap and shaft pin (1/4 X 1-9/16" for 7/8 shaft). Install cotter pin in shaft pin.
10. From under the car attach the clutch arm clevis pin and cotter pin.

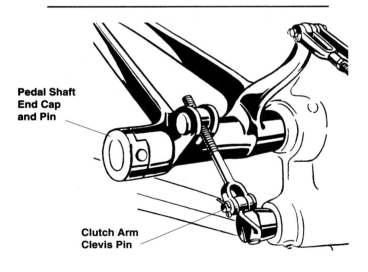

Pedal Shaft End Cap and Pin

Clutch Arm Clevis Pin

11. Install the brake rod and clevis pin on the brake pedal arm. Attach stoplight linkage.

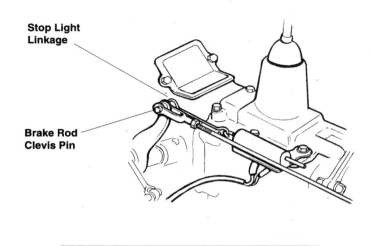

Stop Light Linkage

Brake Rod Clevis Pin

12. Install the battery and attach both battery cables. Secure the battery with the hold down brackets.
13. Install both floor board sections with twelve (12) flat head screws (12-24 X 1-1/8").
14. Place the shifting tower metal plate over the shifter and attach to the floor boards with the three floor board clips.
15. Install floor mats and screw on the accelerator pedal.

RADIUS BALL CAP ASSEMBLY

The radius ball cap assembly must be correctly positioned and properly installed to provide the correct caster alignment at the front axle (5 degrees). If the radius ball is worn or loose in the ball cup, the front end caster cannot be maintained. Likewise, if the ball is held rigid in the ball cup, due to incorrect installation, the radius rods will bend or twist when driving on rough roads or hitting a pot hole in the road. The radius ball must fit snugly to the ball cap but must be allowed to flex on the mounting bolt springs. The after-market rubber ball modification for the radius ball is not advisable. In most cases the front caster will be lost with the mod kit. Ford's original idea still works best.

1. Remove the two (2) cotter pins and nuts [3/4 socket] from the bottom of the radius rod ball socket. Remove the two springs, spacers, and caps. Support the radius rod ball end on a 2 X 4 wood block to temporarily hold it in place.

2. If the radius ball is loose in the ball cup, a shim can be made from a fender washer by using a ballpeen hammer to shape the washer to fit the bottom curvature of the ball.

3. Reassemble the radius ball in the cap assembly as shown, placing the cap with the hole on top (allows oil to seep into the ball cup) in the flywheel housing cavity, the radius ball then placed in the cap, the spacers placed over the studs and the lower cap placed under the radius ball, sliding over the spacers. The springs are placed over the spacers, against the lower cap. Screw the nut down until it just contacts the spacer and insert the cotter pin. This will allow spring movement of the lower cap, allowing it to move up and down the spacer when driving on rough roads.

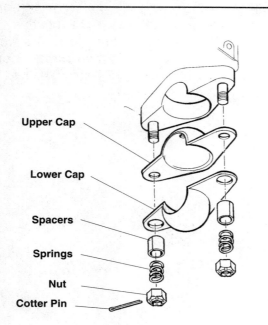

RADIATOR

The radiator is usually the main cause for overheating, although other conditions can cause overheating (See "Troubleshooting" section.) The more obvious causes of radiator problems are a clogged radiator, loose fins on the radiator tubes which prevent efficient transmission of heat from the tubes to the fins and hence to the air, and leaks in the radiator. The lack of a baffle plate or incorrectly installed baffle in the top of the radiator below the filler neck can cause water to be pumped out the overflow tube, constantly reducing the volume of water. Check the radiator fins and straighten any bent ones. This can be done with duckbill pliers. Many times the radiator can be satisfactorily repaired by boiling it out and rodding the tubes. This involves removing the tanks and should be done by a qualified radiator shop. The radiator can also be re-cored, using your original top and bottom tanks and straps. When the radiator is re-cored, be certain to use a 3-row core. The 2-row cores do not provide satisfactory cooling. Also be certain that the re-cored radiator is not changed in height. This will affect the fit and alignment of the hood. The 1928/1929 radiator core measures 19-3/4" between the upper and lower tanks. The 1930/1931 radiator core measures 22-1/4" between the tanks. Never use an ordinary enamel to paint the radiator. This will restrict the efficient radiation of heat. Use a tar base paint, sparingly applied. A good radiator should flow test at 36 to 38 gallons per minute.

Radiator Flow Test (in Car)

1. Drain the radiator water. The drain petcock is located on the bottom of the water return pipe.

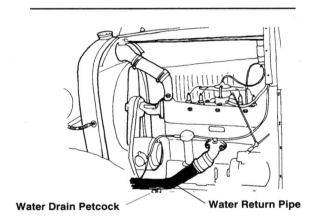

Water Drain Petcock   Water Return Pipe

2. Loosen the hose clamps on the water return pipe and remove the pipe. Do not remove the short hose attached to the lower radiator pipe. Remove the upper radiator hose and plug the top radiator neck.
3. Plug the lower radiator hose with a rubber ball.
4. Fill the radiator with water (about 1-1/2 gallons). If it takes much less than 1-1/2 gallons, the radiator has insufficient capacity.
5. Remove the ball and the water should empty in 4 seconds or less. If it takes longer, the radiator is partially clogged and should be removed for cleaning and possible repairs.

Overflow Tube and Baffle

A missing radiator baffle and incorrectly placed overflow tube will cause loss of water from the overflow tube. Location of the overflow tube and the baffle is important in retaining water level. The baffle blocks the water pressure flow to the overflow tube, caused by water pump pressure. Replacing the baffle should be done as shown.

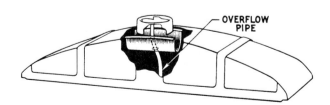

RADIATOR

Removing Radiator

1. Drain the radiator and remove the upper and lower radiator hoses.
2. Remove the bottom section of the front floor board (6 flathead screws) for access to the battery terminals.
3. Remove the battery ground strap from the (+) battery post.

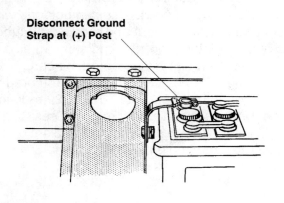

Disconnect Ground Strap at (+) Post

4. Move to the front of the car and remove the four screws holding the front splash apron and remove the front apron. This will allow easier access to the radiator mounting bolts later.

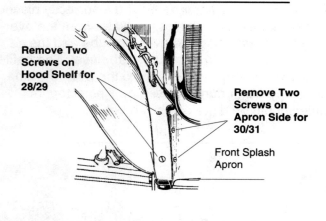

Remove Two Screws on Hood Shelf for 28/29

Remove Two Screws on Apron Side for 30/31

Front Splash Apron

5. Remove the horn cover by removing the single round head screw on the back cover (10-32 x 3/4 screw). Remove the two horn wires from the terminal under the horn motor (pull out type).
6. Remove the headlight conduit connectors (push and twist counterclockwise to release).

NOTE

Some headlight wiring may have been modified by eliminating the connector plug from inside the conduit socket. The wires would then be routed directly from the conduit into the headlight bucket and attached to the bulb sockets with wire nuts. The wires would have to be disconnected from behind the headlight reflector. To access the headlight bucket, release the front lens clip, pull the clip down (spring loaded latch) and lift up on the lens rim to remove it. Remove the center bulb and lift the reflector out of the headlight bucket.

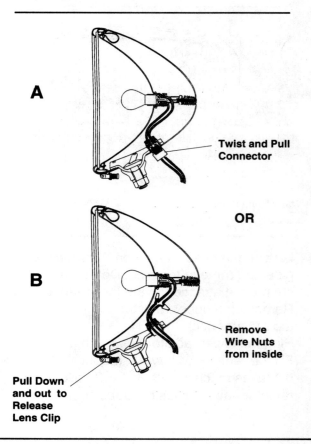

A — Twist and Pull Connector

OR

B — Remove Wire Nuts from inside

Pull Down and out to Release Lens Clip

Service and Repair 1-236

RADIATOR

7. Pull the headlight wires back through the conduit to the inside of the radiator shell, leaving the metal conduit and grommets attached to the radiator shell. Do the same for both headlight harness wires and the horn harness wires.
8. Remove the radiator cap.
9. Under the hood, remove the two screws and nuts from the hood rear hold down bracket.

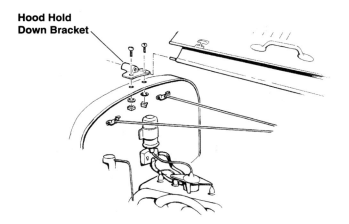

Hood Hold Down Bracket

10. Remove the hood and place it in a safe location on cardboard or carpet to prevent chipping the paint. Do not lay the hood down on the side louver panels. It's best to stand the hood up on the back edge to prevent warping or creasing the top panels.

11. Remove the radiator shell by removing the two (2) screws and nuts on each side of the radiator, attaching the shell to the radiator brackets. Slide the radiator shell straight up and off the radiator.
12. Remove the cotter pin from the two radiator mounting bolts. Using a 3/8 ratchet drive with a 6-inch extension and 9/16 inch deep socket, reach under the front cross member and place the 9/16 inch socket on the head of the radiator mounting bolt. Hold the nut on top with a 9/16 inch box wrench and ratchet the bolt from the bottom. Remove the bolt, spring, and nut from each side of the radiator.

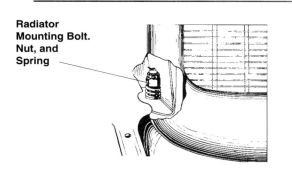

Radiator Mounting Bolt, Nut, and Spring

13. Remove and retain the rubber pads under the radiator mounting brackets (both sides). Move the radiator to one side to clear the fender and lift the radiator and shell off the frame. On the 28 models, a fan shroud may be attached to the radiator. This can be removed after the radiator has been removed from the car.

Service and Repair

RADIATOR

Installing Radiator

1. Set the radiator on the front cross member. Place a rubber pad under both radiator mounting brackets. The front frame cross member is different on 1928/1929 than on 1930/1931. The 1928/1929 cross member has a raised pad for the radiator mounting brackets. The 1930/1931 cross member pad is recessed. Use a 1/8" pad for a 1928/1929 radiator/frame, and a 1/16" pad for a 30/31 radiator/frame. A piece of old inner tube works fine.

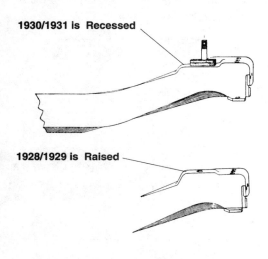

2. Install the radiator mounting bolts, nuts and spring assembly as shown below. Tighten the bolts only enough to install cotter pins in the mounting bolts.

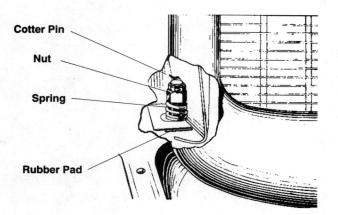

3. Secure the water return pipe hoses to the radiator lower pipe and the water inlet neck on the engine block. Securely tighten all four hose clamps.
4. Slip the top radiator neck into the top hose and install the hose clamps. Do not tighten these hose clamps until the radiator support rods have been installed and the hood installed and adjusted.
5. Attach the ends of the support rods into the radiator bracket with a nut and lock washer on each side of the bracket [1/2" wrench].

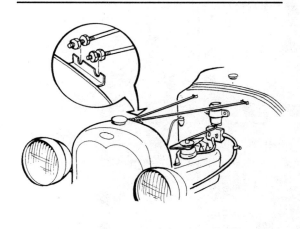

6. The radiator shell and fan shroud may not have been removed from the radiator during disassembly. If the shell was removed from the radiator, reinstall it at this time, attaching with four (4) pan head screws (12-24 X 19/32") and square nuts.

RADIATOR

7. Set the hood in place and attach with two (2) screws, lock washers, and nuts (12-24 X 5/8" Round Head) on the rear hold down bracket.

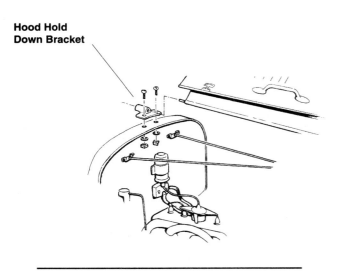

8. After the hood has been installed and properly aligned, securely tighten both front radiator support rod nuts. Securely tighten the two radiator hose clamps on the upper radiator hose (radiator to goose neck). Check all four (4) hose clamps on the water return pipe hoses. Ensure all hose clamps are tight.
9. Route the wiring harness through the radiator shell to the headlights and horn. Connect the horn wires.
10. Connect the headlight conduit connectors (push and twist clockwise to connect).

NOTE
Some headlight wiring may have been modified by eliminating the connector plug from inside the conduit socket. The wires would then be routed directly from the conduit into the headlight bucket and attached to the bulb sockets with wire nuts. The wires would have to be connected from behind the headlight reflector. To access the headlight bucket, release the front lens clip (spring loaded latch) and lift up on the lens rim to remove it. Remove the center bulb and lift the reflector out of the headlight bucket.

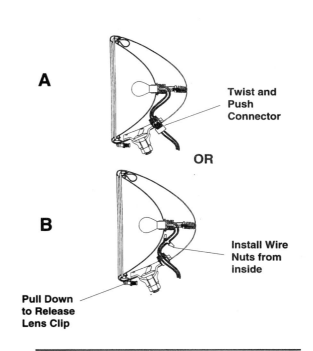

11. Attach three harness wires to the generator cutout terminals (terminal box wire, horn and headlight harness wire).

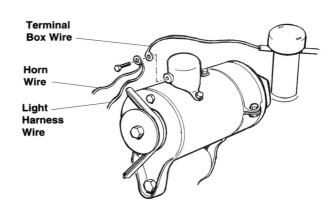

12. Reconnect the battery ground strap and pour three (3) gallons of water in the radiator. Start the engine and let run for approximately 15 minutes or until operating temperature is reached. Check all water connections for leaks (hose connections). Tighten connections as needed.

Service and Repair

RADIATOR SHELL

RADIATOR SHELL

The Model A used three different radiator shells during production of the passenger car. (Trucks used a different radiator shell.) The 1928 and 1929 radiator shells were the same except for minor changes in the crank hole opening, and a change in the size of the headlight and horn wire conduit holes. The 1928/1929 radiator shells were originally nickel plated, although, many have been changed to chrome plating for durability. The 1930 and 1931 radiator shells were made of polished stainless steel. The 1930 shell had a fairly flat front surface with no inserts. The 1931 shell had a painted recessed insert in both the upper and lower face of the shell. These inserts were usually painted body color. The 1930/1931 radiator shells were 2" taller than the 1928/1929 shells to accommodate the taller 1930/1931 radiators. To remove the radiator shell requires removing the hood, radiator cap, and the horn and headlight wiring harness and conduit from the shell. The radiator shell must be removed from the radiator for replacement of the Ford medallion on the front of the shell.

Removing Radiator Shell

1. Remove the front floor mat (or carpet) and shift lever plate.
2. Remove the bottom section of the front floor board (6 flathead screws) for access to the battery terminals.
3. Remove the battery ground cable from the (+) battery post.

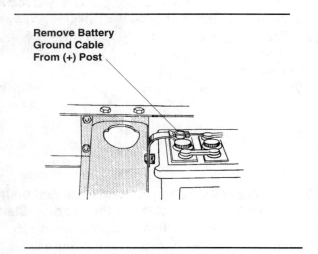

4. Remove the horn cover by removing the single round head screw on the back cover (10-32 x 3/4 screw). Remove the two (2) horn wires from the terminal under the horn motor (pull out type).
5. Remove the headlight conduit connectors (push and twist counterclockwise to release).

NOTE

Some headlight wiring may have been modified by eliminating the connector plug from inside the conduit socket. The wires would then be routed directly from the conduit into the headlight bucket and attached to the bulb sockets with wire nuts. The wires would have to be disconnected from behind the headlight reflector. To access the headlight bucket, release the front lens clip, pull the clip down (spring loaded latch) and lift up on the lens rim to remove it. Remove the center bulb and lift the reflector out of the headlight bucket.

RADIATOR SHELL

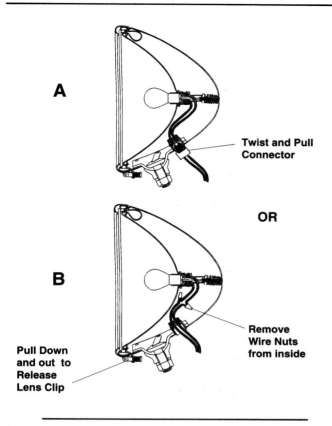

6. Pull the headlight wires back through the conduit to the inside of the radiator shell, leaving the metal conduit and grommets attached to the radiator shell. Do the same for both headlight harness wires and the horn harness wires.

7. Remove the radiator cap.
8. Under the hood, remove the two (2) screws and nuts from the hood rear hold down bracket.

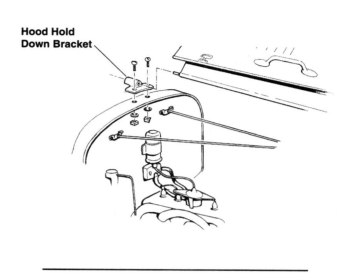

9. Remove the hood and place it in a safe location on cardboard or carpet to prevent chipping the paint. Do not lay hood down on the side louver panels. It's best to stand the hood up on the back edge to prevent warping or creasing the top panels.

10. Remove the radiator shell by removing the two (2) screws and nuts on each side of the radiator, attaching the shell to the radiator brackets. Slide the radiator shell straight up and off the radiator.

RADIATOR SHELL

Installing Radiator Shell

1. Slide the shell down over the radiator, attaching with four (4) pan head screws (12-24 X 19/32") and square nuts.
2. Set the hood in place and attach with two (2) screws, lock washers, and nuts (12-24 X 5/8" round head) on the rear hold down bracket.

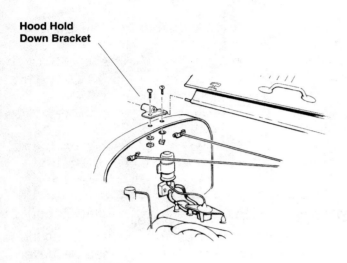

Hood Hold Down Bracket

3. Route the wiring harness through the radiator shell to the headlights and horn. Connect the horn wires.
4. Connect the headlight conduit connectors (push and twist clockwise to connect).

NOTE

Some headlight wiring may have been modified by eliminating the connector plug from inside the conduit socket. The wires would then be routed directly from the conduit into the headlight bucket and attached to the bulb sockets with wire nuts. The wires would have to be connected from behind the headlight reflector. To access the headlight bucket, release the front lens clip (spring loaded latch) and lift up on the lens rim to remove it. Remove the center bulb and lift the reflector out of the headlight bucket.

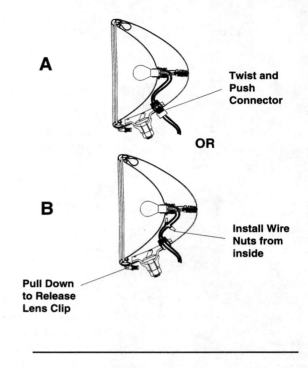

A — Twist and Push Connector

OR

B — Install Wire Nuts from inside / Pull Down to Release Lens Clip

5. Install the radiator cap.
6. Connect the battery ground cable to the (+) battery post.

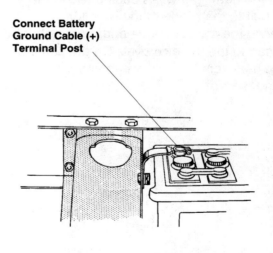

Connect Battery Ground Cable (+) Terminal Post

7. Install the front floor board and floor mat. Secure the floor board with six (6) flat head screws (12-24 X 1-1/8") and cup washers.

Service and Repair 1-242

RADIUS RODS

The front radius rod (wishbone) provides stability to the front axle and maintains a true alignment of the front axle perpendicular to the driveline. If the front radius rod becomes bent, the perpendicular alignment is lost, which can cause excessive tire wear, hard steering, and/or wandering. The front radius rod also establishes the caster alignment on the front axle. A bent radius rod or worn and incorrect assembly of the radius ball cap assembly will greatly affect the front caster setting. A bent radius rod should always be replaced and not straightened. The radius rods are hollow and will nearly always lengthen when straightened. Removing the front radius rod (wishbone) requires removing the front axle.

The rear radius rods maintain a true perpendicular alignment of the torque tube (driveline) with the rear axle. The rear radius rods are made LEFT and RIGHT side. Should one of the rear radius rods get bent, do not attempt to straighten it. Replace it with a straight radius rod. The rear radius rods can be removed without removing the rear end assembly. When the bolt hole in the front of the radius rod will not align with the bolt hole at the front end of the torque tube, preventing the bolt from being inserted, it is an indication that one or both radius rods are or have been bent. The only cure is to replace the radius rod.

Removing Front Radius Rod

1. Remove the four (4) screws holding the front splash apron and remove the front apron.

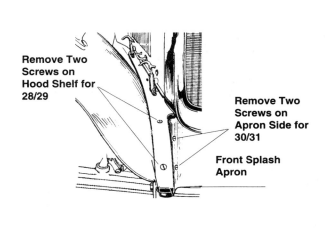

2. Jack up the front end and place jack stands on each side under the frame, just to the outside of the front radius rod.

3. Place a floor jack under the front axle and raise it enough to allow removal of both front wheels.
4. On the left front side of the car remove the drag link from the spindle arm ball by removing the cotter pin and unscrewing the drag link end plug.
5. Remove the cotter pin and screw out the top plug in both shock links. Remove both shock links from the spring perches.

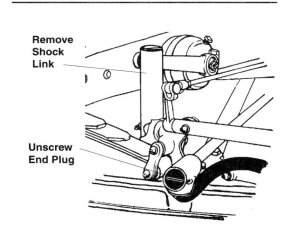

RADIUS RODS

6. Remove the clevis pins attaching the front brake rods to the actuating arms.
7. Remove the front wheel axle nuts, wheel bearings, and drums.
8. Remove the three (3) brake shoe springs (1 long and 2 short) and remove the two brake shoes.

NOTE

The brake shoes can be easily removed by pulling down on the bottom of the shoe, releasing them from the operating wedge. The springs can then be removed by hand and the shoes removed from the backing plate.

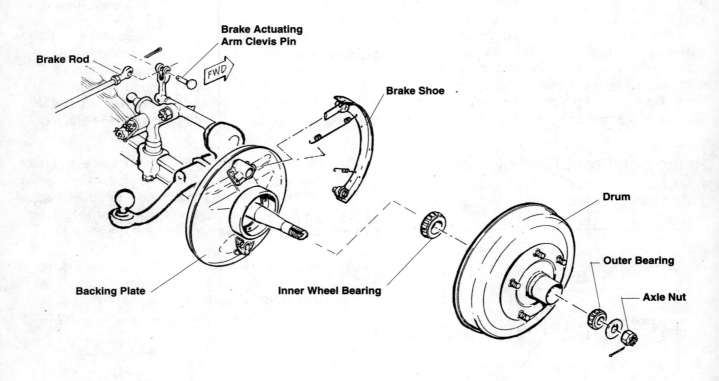

Removing Drum and Brake Shoes

Service and Repair

RADIUS RODS

9. Remove the operating wedge stud nut [5/8 socket], located on the back side of the backing plate. The operating wedge stud and operating wedge can now be removed. The operating pin will then drop down out of the king pin.

NOTE
Be sure to retain any operating pin shims (pill) that may be in the operating wedge dimple, and the operating pin felt washer.

10. Remove the four (4) backing plate bolts (inside grease baffle) and castle nuts [9/16 socket]. The grease baffle and backing plate can now be removed from the spindle.

11. The tie-rod end can now be removed from the spindle arm. Remove the cotter pin from the end of the tie-rod and screw out the end plug. The tie-rod can then be lifted off the spindle arm ball.

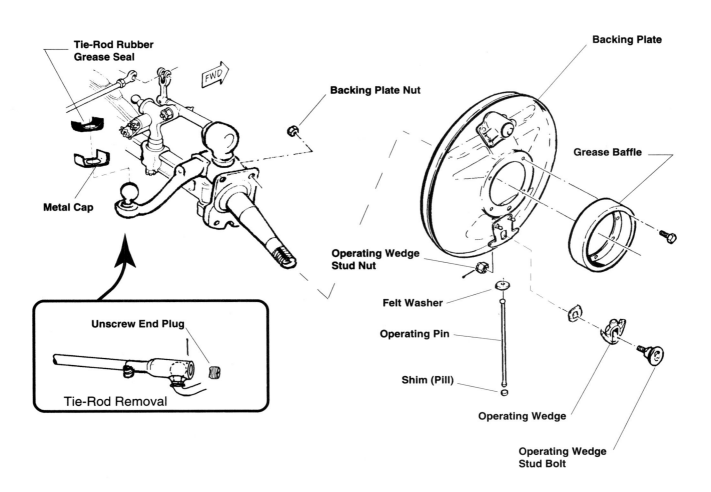

Removing Backing Plate

RADIUS RODS

12. Remove the spindle locking pin nut (9/16 socket) and lock washer. Reinsert the locking pin nut, screwing in only 1/2 the thread length. The nut is used to knock out the grooved locking pin. With a small hammer, hit the end of the nut to drive out the pin. A drift punch may be needed to completely drive out the locking pin.

13. Remove the actuating arm nut (9/16 socket) and lock washer from the back side of the spring perch. With large pliers or pipe wrench rotate the king pin cup (top portion of king pin) outward (toward front) a few degrees to release the actuating arm. Remove the actuating arm from the spring perch and king pin cup.

CAUTION

The king pin must be slightly rotated outward to allow the actuating arm bolt to release from the spring perch without damaging the threads on the actuating arm bolt.

14. Pull the king pin straight up and remove the spindle from the axle. Retain the thrust bearing, shims, and felt cup washer.

15. Repeat steps 8 through 14 to remove the opposite wheel and spindle assembly.

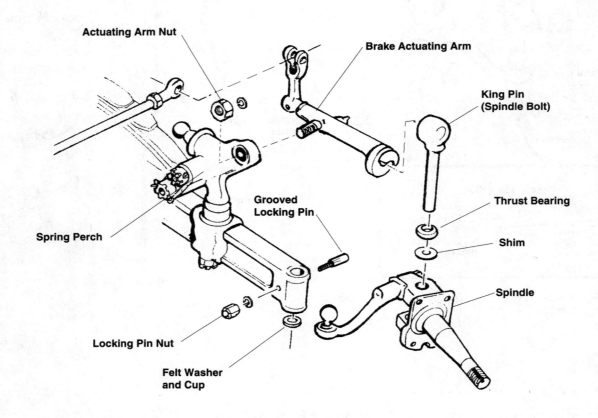

Removing Spindle

Service and Repair

RADIUS RODS

16. Remove the two (2) cotter pins and nuts [3/4 socket] from the bottom of the radius rod ball socket. Remove the two springs, spacers, and caps. Support the radius rod ball end on a 2 X 4 wood block to temporarily hold it in place.

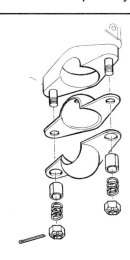

17. Lower the floor jack under the front axle to allow the ends of the leaf spring to rise above the axle. Place a small block of wood under both spring eyes (between the axle and spring eye).
18. Slowly raise the floor jack under the axle, spreading the spring ends on the wood blocks.

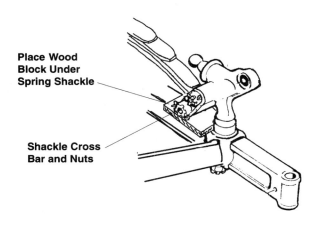

Place Wood Block Under Spring Shackle

Shackle Cross Bar and Nuts

19. Remove the cotter pins and nuts [5/8 socket] from the back side of the spring shackles. Remove the shackle cross bar.

20. Continue raising the axle to spread the spring until most tension is released from the spring shackles. Drive the spring shackles out through the front of the spring eyes and spring perch.
21. Lower the floor jack and remove the axle and radius rod (wishbone).
22. Remove the cotter pin and nut [15/16 socket] on the bottom of each spring perch and drive the spring perch out of the axle and radius rod.

NOTE
Lots of heat and WD-40 may be needed to remove the spring perches from the axle. It's best to have a machine shop press them out.

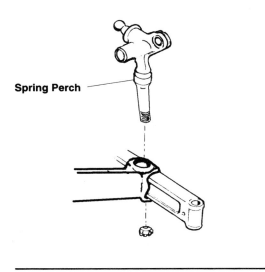

Spring Perch

23. Separate the radius rod (wishbone) from the axle. The axle and radius rod must be checked and absolutely straight before reassembling.

RADIUS RODS

Installing Front Radius Rod

1. Attach the radius rod to the axle with the spring perch bolts. Attach nuts (special convex shape) to spring perch bolts. The two spring perches must be very closely aligned or the spring shackles will not line up with the spring eyes when attaching the front leaf spring. To obtain alignment between the two spring perches, clamp a straight edge (angle iron) against the shackle bushing hole on both perches. Then torque the two perch nuts to 100 ft. lbs.

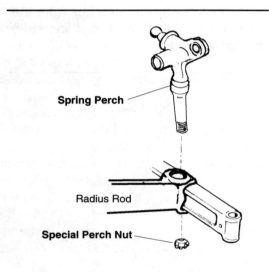

2. Before attaching the axle to the leaf spring, insert the spring shackle (new or used) through the spring eye bushing and spring perch bushing to ensure correct fit. The fit should be an easy slip through. If the shackle is a tight fit in the bushing, the bushing will need to be reamed. A slightly loose fit is okay.
3. Place the axle on the floor jack and raise it far enough to allow a spring shackle to be inserted in one end of the spring and spring perch. Apply the shackle bar and nuts on the back side of the shackle. Do not tighten the nuts at this time.
4. Place wood blocks under each end of the spring (spring eyes) and raise the axle until the other spring shackle can be easily inserted through the spring eye and spring perch. Apply the shackle cross bar and nuts [5/8 socket].
5. Tighten the nuts on both shackles just enough to allow the cotter pins to be inserted.

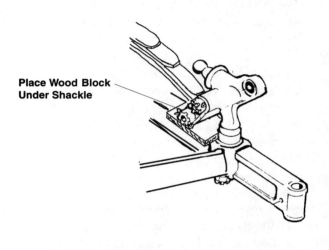

6. Install the radius rod ball on the bottom of the flywheel housing. Place the ball cup with the hole on the top side of the radius ball. Insert the two spacers, springs, and nuts [3/4 wrench] as shown below. Tighten the two (2) castle nuts until they touch the spacers, then insert cotter pins.

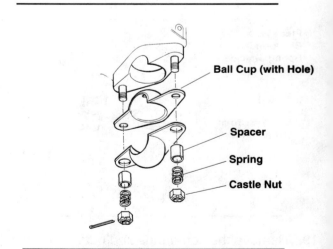

RADIUS RODS

7. Place the spindle on the axle. Apply a coat of grease to the king pin shaft and insert the king pin, new thrust bearing (open side facing down), and shim through the spindle and axle, through the felt washer cup, and into the lower bushing.

NOTE

The new thrust bearings are thinner than the original bearings. One or two shims will be needed to take up the difference. This will allow the thrust bearings to support the total weight of the car, producing easy and smooth steering. The grooved locking pin securely fastens the king pin to the axle. The weight of the car then creates a downward force on the king pin, placing the car's weight on the thrust bearing, between the king pin upper cup and the top of the spindle. If the thrust bearing is too thin, the weight of the car will be transferred to the bottom of the axle, at the felt washer and cup. This is not a bearing surface and will cause stiff and hard steering. The front end weight of the car should be totally supported on the thrust bearing. Adding a shim or two under the thrust bearing will shift the weight to the bearing.

8. Insert the end of the brake actuating arm into the king pin cup and then rotate the actuating arm bolt into the spring perch. Allow the king pin to rotate to prevent damaging the actuating arm bolt threads when inserting into the spring perch. Apply nut and lock washer to the actuating arm bolt. Securely tighten.
9. Rotate the king pin to align the king pin locking pin groove with the hole in the axle.
10. Insert the grooved locking pin through the front of the axle to lock the king pin in place. Hammer the locking pin all the way in before applying the lock washer and nut. (This will prevent applying excessive force on the bolt threads.)
11. Apply the locking pin lock washer and nut. Securely tighten. Check the thrust bearing operation as follows before continuing assembly:
   a.) Place a floor jack under the spindle and raise it just enough to support the total weight of the car on the jack.
   b.) Try to move (rotate) the thrust bearing on top of the axle and the felt washer cup under the axle. The felt washer cup should rotate freely and the thrust bearing, supporting the car's weight, should not rotate. If the thrust bearing can be moved, add a shim under the thrust bearing.
   c.) Lower the front end back onto the jack stands. Grabbing the spindle axle, rotate the spindle back and forth to ensure free movement.

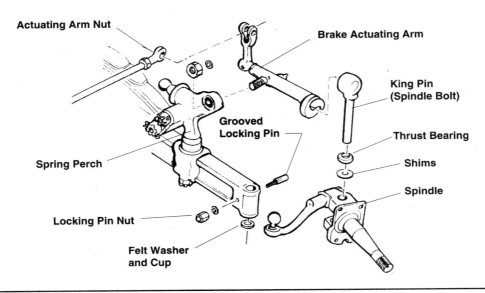

RADIUS RODS

12. Place a metal cap and rubber grease seal over the spindle arm ball stud. (The rubber grease seal usually needs replacing.)

13. Place the end of the tie-rod over the spindle arm ball stud and screw in the end plug. After the end plug contacts the ball, screw in the end plug an additional 1 to 1-1/2 turns. Align the end plug slot with the cotter pin holes in the tie-rod. Insert a cotter pin.

NOTE
The tie-rod ball spring should be compressed 25% for correct tension. Steering is affected if this adjustment is too loose or too tight.

14. Place the backing plate and grease baffle on the spindle and attach with four (4) bolts (3/8-24 X 7/8) and nuts [9/16 socket]. Securely tighten all nuts and insert cotter pins.

15. Push the operating pin up into the center of the king pin. Insert a felt washer over the operating pin and into the backing plate access hole.

16. Hold the operating pin up while attaching the operating wedge with a wedge stud, stud washer (spacer), and castle nut [5/8 socket]. Securely tighten the stud nut and insert cotter pin. Check for free movement (up and down) of the operating wedge.

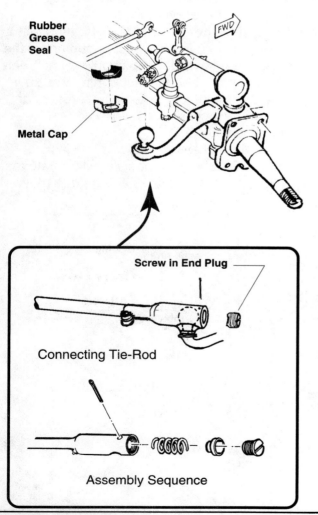

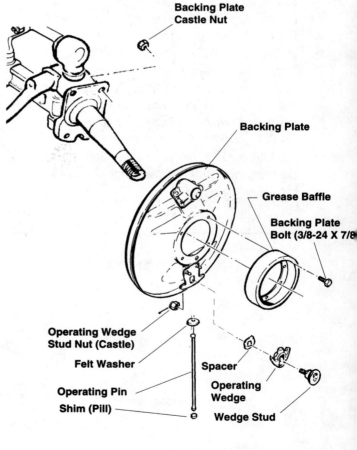

Installing Backing Plate

Service and Repair

RADIUS RODS

17. Clean all components on the brake shoes before installing them on the backing plates.

18. Place each brake shoe adjusting shaft into the top adjuster housing on the backing plate.

19. Pull the two shoes together to allow the top (long) spring to be easily attached between the shoes.

20. Pull the bottom of the shoe in and attach the short spring from the shoe to the spring stud. The bottom of the shoe can then be pushed outward and slipped onto the roller track, with the rollers contacting the operating wedge. This can all be done without tools.

21. Pack all wheel bearings with grease. Install the inner wheel bearing, hub, outer wheel bearing, key washer, and axle nut. Tighten the axle nut until a heavy drag is felt on the wheel. Then back off the axle nut one castle position from the cotter pin hole. Install a cotter pin.

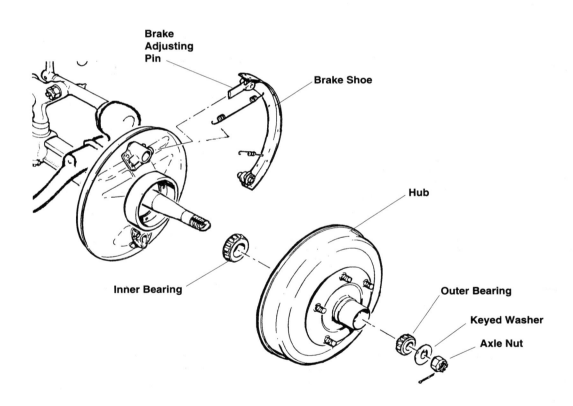

Installing Brake Shoes and Drum

Service and Repair

RADIUS RODS

22. Assemble and install both front shock links as shown below. Screw in the end plug and insert a cotter pin.

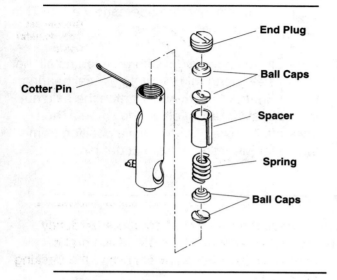

23. Install the drag link on the left spindle. Screw in the drag link end plug and tighten it sufficiently to compress the internal spring 25%. (Usually 1 to 1-1/2 turns past contact with the ball stud.) Install a cotter pin.

24. Attach both brake rods to the brake actuating arms with clevis pin and cotter pin.

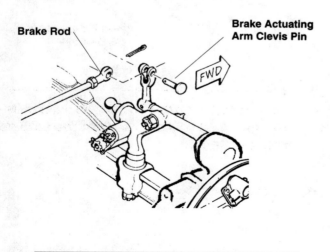

25. Adjust brakes in accordance with the "Brake Adjusting Procedure". (See Section II.)

26. After completion of front end assembly, readjust front toe-in. See Section II, Service Adjustments.

27. Attach the front splash apron with four screws (**28/29 Model** use 1/4-20 X 1-1/4" oval head) (**30/31 Model** use 1/4-20 X 1/2" round head).

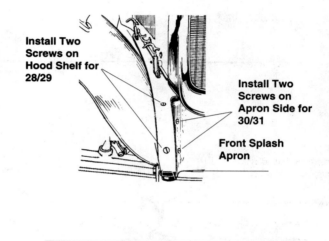

28. Remove jack stands and test drive.

RADIUS RODS

Removing Rear Radius Rods

1. Block the front wheels and release the emergency brake.
2. Jack up the rear end of the car and place jack stands under the frame, just behind the running board brackets. Remove both rear wheels.
3. Disconnect the brake rod anti-rattlers from the radius rods (bolt and lock washer, 9/16 socket).

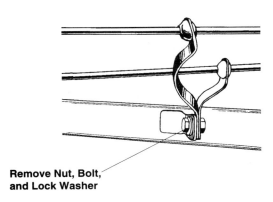

Remove Nut, Bolt, and Lock Washer

4. Remove both rear axle nuts [15/16 wrench] and remove both rear wheel drums.

NOTE
A rear wheel hub puller may be needed to remove the drums from the axle.

Remove Drum

5. Disconnect the speedometer cable (screw out the cap) from under the torque tube.

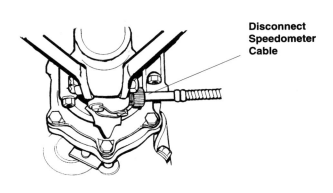

Disconnect Speedometer Cable

6. Remove the clevis pin from the emergency brake connecting link on the wheel brake assembly. This will allow access to the backing plate nuts.

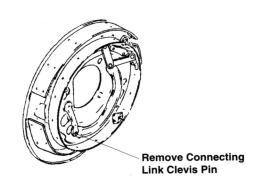

Remove Connecting Link Clevis Pin

7. Remove the two (2) front backing plate bolts and nuts [9/16 socket]. The front two bolts hold the radius rod.

Service and Repair

RADIUS RODS

8. Remove the radius rod bolt and nut (7/8 wrench) at the front of the torque tube. Set both radius rods aside.

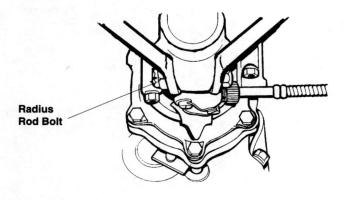

Radius Rod Bolt

Installing Rear Radius Rod

1. Place both radius rods on the end of the axle housings and attach them with two (2) long-shouldered backing plate bolts.
2. Install the front radius rod bolt through the radius rods and torque tube (9/16-18 X 3-1/8") [7/8 wrench]. Tighten castle nut and insert a cotter pin.
3. Connect the speedometer cable to the speedometer gear cap.

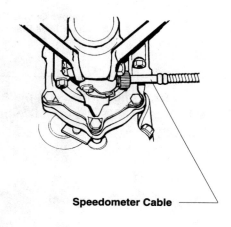

Speedometer Cable

4. Ensure that all four (4) backing plate nuts are tight.
5. Connect the emergency brake connecting link with a clevis pin.

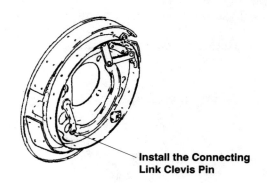

Install the Connecting Link Clevis Pin

6. Attach the brake rod anti-rattler springs to the rear radius rods (5/16-24 X 11/16")[1/2 wrench].

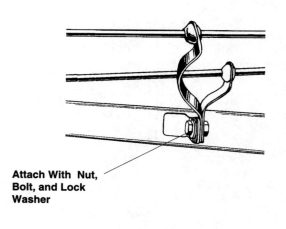

Attach With Nut, Bolt, and Lock Washer

RADIUS RODS

7. Inspect the axle key for wear. The axle key should be replaced if it does not fit tight in the axle groove. Install the axle key with the beveled end toward the inside of the axle.
8. Install the rear drum with fiber axle seal, flat washer, and castle nut (5/8-18)[15/16 wrench]. Torque the axle nut to 125ft/lbs. and install a cotter pin.
9. Install both rear wheels and torque the lug nuts to 64 ft. lbs.
10. Check the rear brake adjustment (See "Section II, Service Adjustments").
11. Remove all jacks and blocks from under the car. Apply grease to all rear grease fittings.

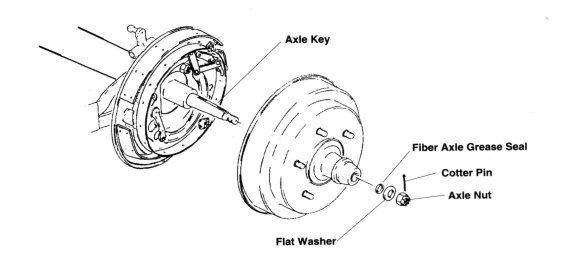

Service and Repair

SHOCKS

The only purpose of the shock absorber is to retard the movement of the spring. They reduce the compression of the spring caused by a bump in the road, and to a greater extent, reduce the amount of spring rebound. It is the spring rebound that throws the car and occupants skyward when you hit a bump in the road. In order for the shocks to operate fully, it is important that the spring shackles be free moving and the bushings kept well greased.

The Model A double acting shock absorbers operate entirely on the principle of hydraulic resistance. Hydraulic fluid is forced from one chamber to another by the movement of the shock arm. The working chamber is automatically kept full by the fluid in the reservoir. The working chamber provides the shock absorbing action, consisting of a forged steel chamber divided into two equal sections by a stationary shaft. A rotating wing shaft operates integrally with the shock absorber arm and is rotated by movement of the arm. The rotation of the shaft forces the fluid from one compartment to the other. The rate of flow is controlled by the size of the opening between the compartments. This opening is enlarged or restricted by adjustment of the needle valve. This is why correct needle valve adjustment is so important.

The shocks can almost always be rebuilt if they still have fluid in them. If they are dry and wobbly, they are probably too rusted and worn to repair. Rebuilding consists of disassembling for thorough cleaning and replacing seals and packing. Most shocks that have to be heated to remove the cover are either too rusty to thoroughly clean or are worn beyond repair. A special spanner wrench can be made to remove the cover.

The markings "C.W." (clockwise) and "A.C." (anti-clockwise) are stamped on the side of the reservoir of each shock. When installing, be sure the shocks marked "C.W." are installed at the right front and left rear of the frame. Shocks marked "A.C." are installed at left front and right rear.

Removing Shocks

The wheel should be removed for easy access to the shock and link. The shock should first be tested on the car to determine condition of the shock. If it is determined that the shock needs repairing, the shock should be removed, repaired, and reinstalled before going to the next shock. This will prevent mixing of components between clockwise shocks and anti-clockwise shocks.

1. Remove the wheel lug nuts to remove the wheel.
2. Remove the shock link by removing the cotter pin in the top and screwing out the top plug. This will loosen the spring tension and allow the link to be removed from the shock arm ball and the perch ball.

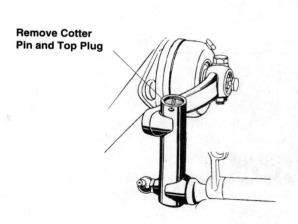

Remove Cotter Pin and Top Plug

SHOCKS

3. Make sure the shock arm is tight on the shaft. Test the shock to determine its condition before removing it from the car.
4. To test the shock first pull the arm all the way down, then push the arm up quickly, repeating the operation three or four times. If little or no resistance is encountered on the down stroke, screw the needle valve all the way in and again check the resistance. The resistance on the up stroke should be considerably less than the resistance on the down stroke. Check that the fluid level is to the bottom of the fill hole. If needed, fill and retest.
5. If very little resistance is encountered, the shock should be removed for repairs.
6. Remove the two castle nuts and cotter pins from the back side of the frame for the shock mounting bolts (5/8 socket). Move the shock to the work bench for further disassembly.

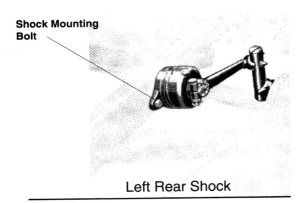

Left Rear Shock

7. Remove the shock arm castle nut and bolt (3/8-24 X 1-7/8)[9/16 wrench] to allow removal of the arm. The shock arm cannot be removed without complete removal of the bolt.

Disassembling Shock
1. Remove the filler plug and drain all fluid.
2. Use a power wire brush to clean all paint and rust from the threads around the outside of the reservoir.
3. Use a punch and make an identifying mark on the flat part of the shaft, and another punch mark (in line) on the cover apron and on the cast body in line with the cover marking. These identifying or reference marks will be used during reassembly for correct alignment of the parts.
4. Clamp the shock in a large bench vise. The ring just above the exposed threads is a lock ring for the reservoir cover. Use a special spanner or lock ring wrench to loosen the lock ring. Turn the lock ring 1/4 turn clockwise to screw it away from the cover. This may require lots of force.
5. After loosening the lock ring, remove the cover. This will require the use of a special cover wrench and lots of force to remove.
6. Remove the wing shaft gasket (seal) and the O-ring from around the reservoir (above the lock ring).
7. The mounting ears for the shock are closest to the top. Note that the two air vents on the flange cover are at the top of the shock when the flange cover is fully seated in the reservoir body. This is reference for reassembly. Also note the position of the dimple in the shaft (for shock arm bolt) relative to the top of the shock. This will show orientation of the wing shaft during reassembly. As a guide when reassembling, locate the position of the flange cover in relation to the reservoir base with a punch or small chisel mark on the reservoir body and the flange cover.
8. Check the air vents and replenishing valve in the flange cover. This can be done by screwing down the needle (adjusting) valve until it seats and placing a wrench on the wing shaft and pumping it back and fourth several times. If it is working properly, the fluid will be forced out of the air vents, and the replenishing valve will draw in air. This operation will also help clean out the vents.

SHOCKS

9. Unscrew the needle valve packing nut and then screw out the needle valve.
10. Unscrew the flange cover using a 1-9/16 socket with 3/4 drive. It may take lots of force to remove the flange cover.
11. In removing the rotating wing shaft, note the position of the bolt notch in the wing shaft in relation to the stationary wing in the reservoir body. In reassembly, replace the wing shaft in the same position.
12. Drain the remainder of fluid from the reservoir body.
13. Rinse all parts in carburetor cleaner.
14. Check to see that the air vents and replenishing valve in the flange cover are clear. The air vent plugs can be removed for cleaning if necessary.

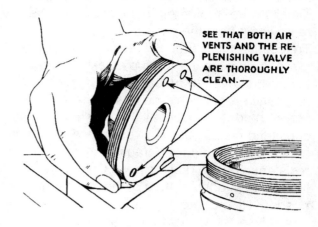

SEE THAT BOTH AIR VENTS AND THE REPLENISHING VALVE ARE THOROUGHLY CLEAN.

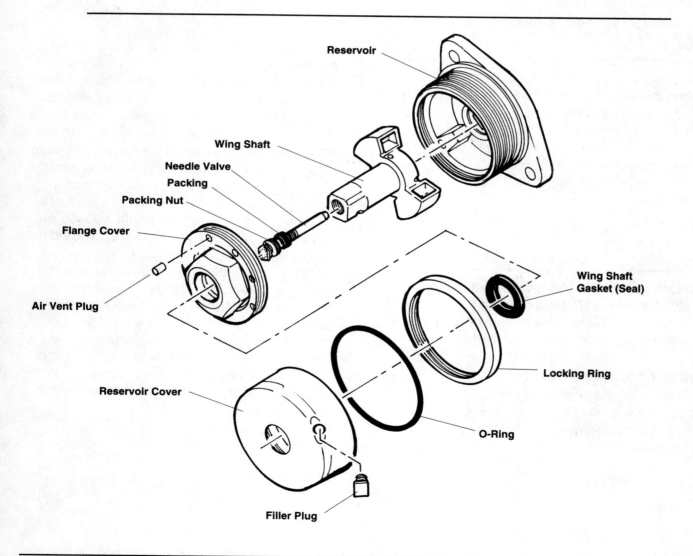

Service and Repair 1-258

SHOCKS

15. The air vent plugs can be easily removed from the flange cover with a drift punch as shown.

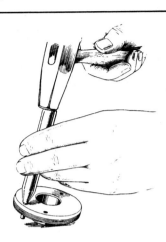

Removing Vent Plugs

16. Clean up the plugs and run a small three-corner file down the groove in the plug to clear the air vent.
17. The plugs must be installed with the grooved side facing out. Drive the plugs in until the top is flush with the cover. The inner end of the plug is then staked to securely hold it in place. The staking operation should be crosswise to the groove to avoid any possibility of closing the groove.

Installing Vent Plugs

18. Clean the replenishing ball check valve in the flange cover. A dental pick can be used to clean and clear the ball check valve.
19. Clean the ball check valves in both stationary wings inside the reservoir base. These can be checked for operation by squirting (aerosol can) carburetor cleaner through the check valve. They should be clear in one direction only.

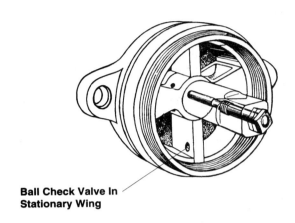

Ball Check Valve In Stationary Wing

20. Chase the packing nut threads in the top of the wing shaft with a 1/2-20 NF tap. Do not run the tap too deep or you will damage the needle valve threads.
21. Make final check of the wing shaft to make sure all passages have been cleared. Blow compressed air through all passages to clear.
22. Thoroughly clean all parts with denatured alcohol and blow dry with air.

SHOCKS

Assembling Shock

1. Place the wingshaft in its original position. (Wing shafts were fitted by selective fit and are not interchangeable.)
2. Center the wing shaft in the center of its rotation. The bolt notch on the shaft should be at 9 o'clock for C.W. shocks and at 3 o'clock position for A.C. shocks. Fill all the compartments with fluid to the top of the wing shaft.
3. Screw on the flange cover. Screw it down tight (it should bottom out) and then line up the previously punched reference marks. The marks should be very close at this point. The two air bleed valve holes should be at the top.
4. Place the wing shaft seal over the shaft.
5. Place new packing around the needle valve and insert the valve into the top of the wing shaft. Screw the packing nut down tight. Run the needle valve adjusting nut down to the bottom seat and back off 1/4 turn.
5. Lightly lubricate the outside threads of the reservoir body and screw on the lock ring, beveled side up. Screw down to near the bottom of the threads on the reservoir body.
6. Screw on the reservoir cover until it contacts the wing shaft seal.
7. Slide the O-ring over the cover and into the recess between the cover and lock ring. Tighten the cover enough to line up the previous made reference mark on the cover, with the mark on the body. The fill plug must be in the top quadrant of the body and lined up about 20° off vertical on the side of the wing shaft bolt notch.
8. Bring the lock ring up in contact with the O-ring seal and snug up with a spanner wrench. When tightening, be sure the O-ring does not slip out of the groove.
9. Clean all oil and residue off the outside body and spray paint black. The shock is now ready for installation.

Installing Shock

1. Mount the shock to the frame with two (2) bolts, castle nuts, and cotter pin (7/16-20 X 1-1/8", elongate head with one side trimmed to fit body curvature)[5/8 socket]. When installing, be sure the shocks marked "C.W." are installed at the right front and left rear of the frame. Shocks marked "A.C." are installed at left front and right rear.

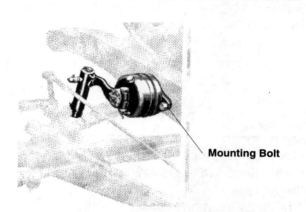

A.C. Installed at Left Front

2. Install shock arm with bolt and castle nut (3/8-24 X 1-7/8)[9/16 wrench]. This connection must be very tight on the shock shaft. There must be no movement between the shock arm and the shaft.
3. Remove the filler plug and fill with shock fluid to the bottom of the filler hole. Replace the filler plug.
4. Test the operation of the shock. Close the needle valve on its seat and move the shock arm up and down several times to bleed air out of the chambers. Open the fill plug to check level. Fill to the bottom of the fill hole and install the fill plug. Open the needle valve 1/4 turn and check operation of the shock. The action should be stiffer on the down stroke. If the internal check valves are working properly, you will have a 60/40 operating shock.

SHOCKS

5. Install the shock link with the end plug on the top. Install new rubber grease seals on the shock arm ball and perch ball. Install and assemble the shock link as shown. Pack the shock link with grease before installing. The rear shock links will tilt about 15° back from vertical when installed with correct frame and body load. If the rear shock link is vertical, the rear spring is either overloaded or is weak and sagging.
6. Install the wheel and lug nuts. Torque the lug nuts to 64 lbs.

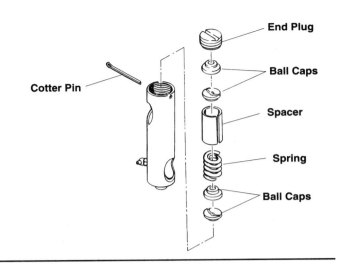

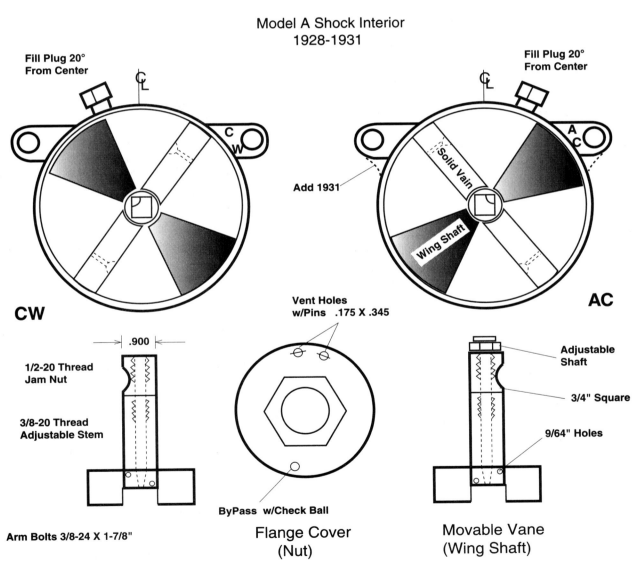

Illustration provided by Richard Bleak, Auburn Calif.

Service and Repair

SPARE TIRE CARRIERS

Eighteen (18) different rear spare tire carriers were used during production of the Model A. All A1379 carriers are interchangeable with all 1928 and 1929 year coupes and roadsters. All A1379-B carriers are interchangeable with all 1930 and 1931 year coupes and roadsters. All A1380 and A1380-B carriers are interchangeable with all sedans except Briggs body sedans. Most changes made to the carrier were made to add strength to the carrier.

The front fender wheel carrier can be installed on the left or the right side. Factory installed carriers were riveted to the frame. The front wheel carriers can be mounted to the frame with 5/16 bolts and castle nuts and cotter pin. The carrier rod for 1928/1929 is mounted vertically through the top of the splash apron into the frame mounted bracket. The carrier rod for 1930/1931 is mounted horizontally through the side of the splash apron into the frame mounted bracket.

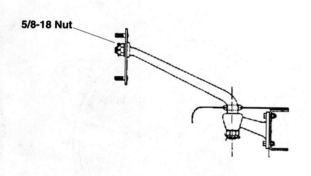

1928/1929 Carrier Mounting

1928/1929 Right Side Carrier

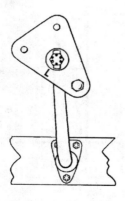

1930/1931 Carrier Mounting
Side View

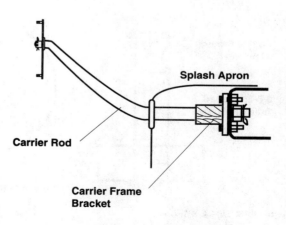

1930/1931 Carrier Mounting
Front View

SPARE TIRE CARRIERS

Rear Wheel Carriers

ALL SEDANS and PHAETONS
(except Briggs Fordor 60-A, B, C and 160-A, B, C

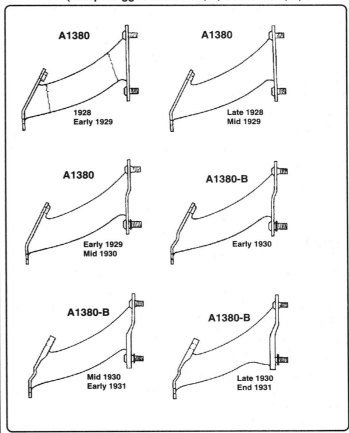

COUPE, ROADSTER, CABRIOLET

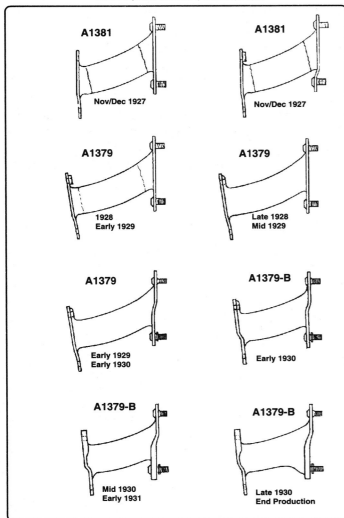

Briggs FORDOR 60-A, B, C

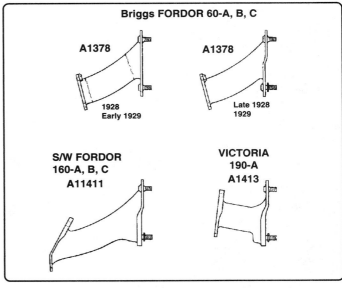

Lower Carrier -To-Body Bolt - 3/8-24 X 1"
Upper Carrier -To-Body Bolt - 7/16-20 X 2-1/4

SPEEDOMETER DRIVE GEARS

Two gears are used to drive the Model A speedometer; a drive gear on the drive shaft, and a reduction ratio gear at the torque tube. The drive gear is a splined fit on the front end of the drive shaft, just behind the transmission. The drive shaft drive gear is the same for all model years. The reduction ratio gear is located in a casing that bolts to the torque tube beneath the drive gear. There are four (4) different reduction ratio gears to correspond to the four different rear end ratios. The reduction ratio gear can be changed within the gear casing as described on the next page. The following figure defines the different speedometer reduction ratio gear assembly's and corresponding rear end ratios. The speedometer cable end that screws into the reduction ratio gear assembly is different for 1928/1929 and 1930/1931. The 1928/1929 speedometer cables have a round keyed end that fits into the casing shaft. The 1930/1931 speedometer cables have a square cable end that fits into the casing shaft. A worn reduction ratio gear can be removed from the casing and replaced, or if the differential ratio is changed, the reduction ratio gear in the speedometer drive assembly casing must also be changed to give an accurate reading at the speedometer. To replace the speedometer drive gear on the drive shaft requires removing the differential/rear end assembly.

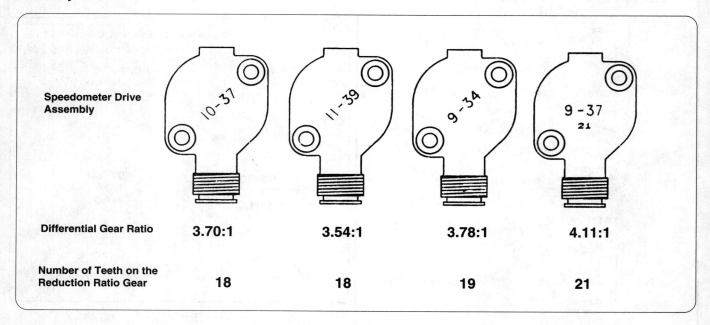

Speedometer Drive Assembly	10-37	11-39	9-34	9-37
Differential Gear Ratio	3.70:1	3.54:1	3.78:1	4.11:1
Number of Teeth on the Reduction Ratio Gear	18	18	19	21

SPEEDOMETER DRIVE GEAR

Removing and Replacing Reduction Ratio Case Assembly and Gear

1. Uncrew the speedometer cable from the gear cap assembly. Remove the two (2) bolts and lock washers (1/2" socket) from the speedometer gear cap. Remove the ratio gear case assembly and set it aside.

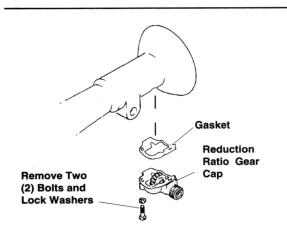

2. To remove the gear from the case, use a thin knife or very thin screwdriver blade to carefully pry the end cap off the case. With the end cap removed, the gear shaft will slide out the front and the gear can be lifted out.

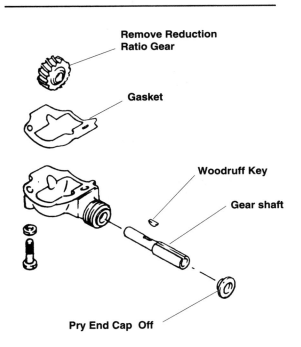

3. When installing a new ratio reduction gear on the shaft, ensure the woodruff key is in place on the shaft to lock the gear to the shaft.
4. With the gear and shaft placed in the casing, tap the end cap back into the casing.
5. Install the speedometer gear cap and gasket with two bolts and lock washers [1/4-28 X 1", 7/16 wrench]. Safety wire the two bolt heads.
6. Connect the speedometer cable to the speedometer gear cap assembly.

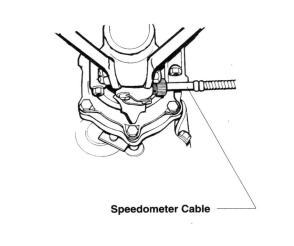

Speedometer Cable

Removing Speedometer Drive Shaft Gear

Removing the speedometer drive shaft gear requires removing the differential/rear end assembly for access to the drive gear located in the end of the torque tube. The following procedure describes removing the differential/rear end assembly for access to the drive shaft gear.

SPEEDOMETER DRIVE GEAR

1. Block the front wheels and release the emergency brake.
2. Jack up the rear end of the car and place jack stands under the frame, just behind the running board brackets. Remove both rear wheels.
3. Disconnect the service brake rod and emergency brake rod (remove clevis pins) at both rear wheels.

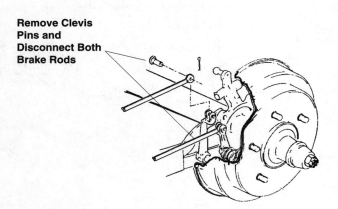

Remove Clevis Pins and Disconnect Both Brake Rods

Remove Brake Rods

4. Disconnect the brake rod anti-rattlers from the radius rods (bolt and lock washer), [1/2 socket].

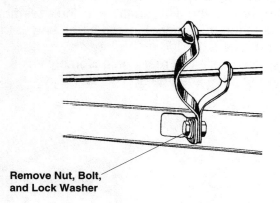

Remove Nut, Bolt, and Lock Washer

5. Remove the cotter pin from the top of the shock link and screw out the end plug for removal of the shock link from the shock arm and the axle housing.

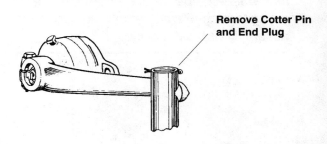

Remove Cotter Pin and End Plug

Remove Shock Arm

6. Uncrew the speedometer cable from the gear cap assembly. Remove the two (2) bolts and lock washers [1/2 socket] from the speedometer gear cap. Remove the ratio gear case assembly and set aside.

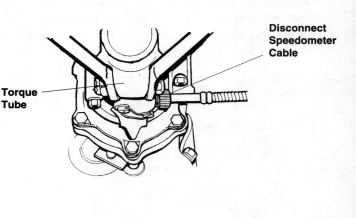

Disconnect Speedometer Cable

Torque Tube

Service and Repair

SPEEDOMETER DRIVE GEAR

7. Remove the two (2) bolts [9/16 socket] and nuts on each side of the U-joint outer cover.
8. Remove the six (6) bolts and nuts [9/16 socket] from around the U-joint outer cover. Remove both halves of the outer cover.

Removing and Replacing Speedometer Drive Gear

1. Remove the retaining clip ring from the front of the drive shaft, just in back of the spline. Slide the speedometer drive gear, thrust washer, and roller bearing off the end of the drive shaft.
2. Replace any defective components and reassemble as shown.

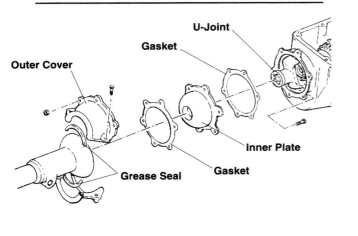

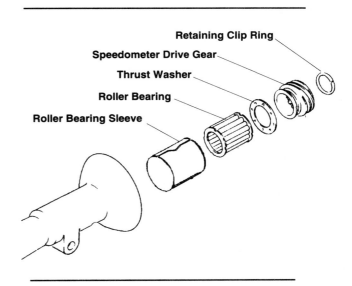

9. Place a floor jack under the differential housing.
10. Remove the four hanger nuts (7/8 wrench) to allow removal of the spring from the cross member.

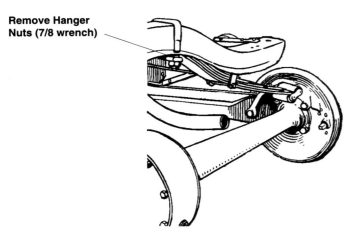

Service and Repair

SPEEDOMETER DRIVE GEAR

Installing Rear End Assembly

1. Check the U-joint at this time for excessive end and side play. The U-joint should be replaced if the joints are loose, showing signs of wear. (Refer to "U-joint Replacement")
2. Pack a liberal amount of grease around the U-joint.
3. Place gaskets and inner cover over the U-joint on the back side of the transmission as shown below.

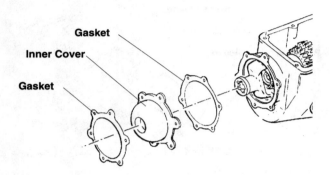

4. Place the differential housing on a floor jack and raise the assembly until the end of the drive shaft can be inserted into the U-joint. The drive shaft is a splined fit into the U-joint. Rotating the rear axles will cause the drive shaft to turn, allowing the drive shaft spline to align with the U-joint.

5. After the drive shaft and U-joint have been mated, raise the differential to position the spring in the rear cross member. Position the two U-bolt brackets on the U-bolt hangers. Attach with four (4) castle nuts (9/16-18)[7/8 wrench]. Install cotter pins.

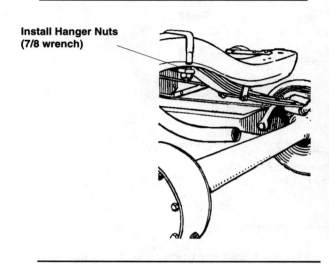

6. Place new grease seals (felt or cork) in the U-joint outer cover. Clamp the two halves around the torque tube and install the two side bolts, lock washers, and nuts (3/8-24 X 1"), [9/16 socket]. Do not tighten at this time.

SPEEDOMETER DRIVE GEAR

7. Install the six (6) bolts, nuts, and lock washers around the U-joint cover (3/8-24 X 1-1/4"), [9/16 socket]. Now firmly tighten all eight (8) bolts and nuts. Pump a liberal amount of grease into the bottom grease fitting for the U-joint until it comes out where the speedometer gear cap mounts.

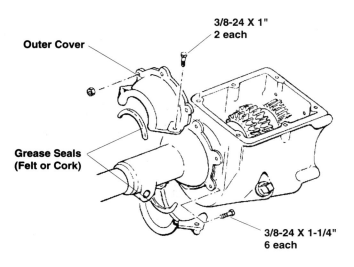

8. Install the speedometer gear cap and gasket with two (2) bolts and lock washers (1/4-28 X 1"), [7/16 wrench]. Safety wire the two bolt heads.
9. Connect the speedometer cable to the speedometer gear cap.

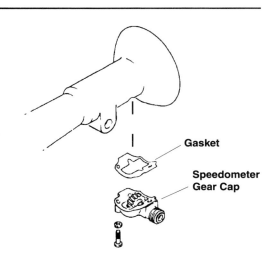

10. Attach the brake rod anti-rattler springs to the rear radius rods (5/16-24 X 11/16")[1/2 wrench].

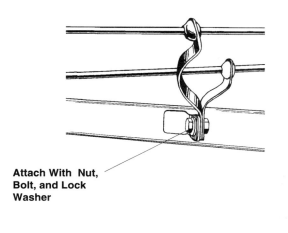

11. Attach all four (4) rear brake rods with clevis pins and cotter pins.

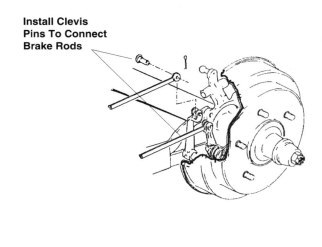

SPEEDOMETER DRIVE GEAR

12. Assemble and install both rear shock links as shown below. Screw in end plug and insert cotter pin.

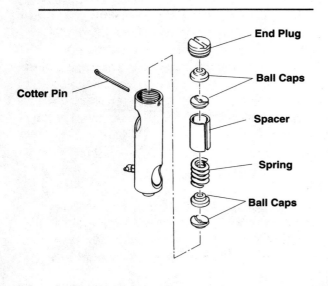

13. Install both rear wheels and torque lug nuts to 64 ft. lbs.
14. Check rear brake adjustment (See "Section II, Service Adjustments").
15. Remove all jacks and blocks from under the car. Apply grease to all rear grease fittings.
16. Check tire pressure and test drive.

SPEEDOMETER

Two different style speedometers were used during Model A production. An oval shaped speedometer made by Stewart Warner (Model 600) and by Waltham Mfg. was used in the smooth instrument panel from 1928 until June 1930. The round speedometer face was made by Stewart Warner, Waltham Mfg., and NorthEast, and was used in the ribbed instrument panel from mid 1930 to the end of production.

The speedometer is a delicate watch-like instrument that requires special tools for disassembly and repair. Most failures in the speedometer are due to dried up lubrication and worn gears. Special tools are needed to disassemble the inner workings for gear removal and lubrication. Purchasing a replaceable (rebuilt) unit is the most practical solution to a faulty speedometer. This section describes removal of the speedometer from the car and disassembly to allow the speedometer and odometer numbers (decals) to be replaced. Even at this level, extreme care must be taken so as not to damage the speedometer hairspring and pivot shaft.

OPERATIONAL NOTE

The oval speedometer contains a trip indicator. To reset the trip indicator, pull the reset rod out (located in lower right corner) to engage the trip indicator wheel gear. Turn clockwise to reset the indicator wheels to "000". Push the rod back in to disengage. **CAUTION:** *Never engage the reset rod (pull out) while the car is in motion. This will strip the reset gear. Reset the trip indicator only when stopped.*

Speedometer Removal and Disassembly

1. Remove the battery ground cable from the (+) battery terminal.

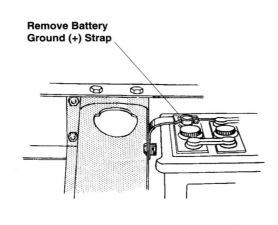

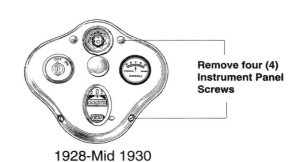

1928-Mid 1930

Mid 1930 -1931

2. Remove the speedometer cable hold-down clip, located on the firewall next to the choke rod. This will allow the speedometer cable to be pulled up when instrument panel is released.

3. Remove the four (4) 10-32 X 1/2 oval head screws from the instrument panel. Carefully pull the instrument panel away from the dash (gas tank) and unscrew the speedometer cable connector from behind the speedometer.

4. Pull the Instrument Panel out far enough for access to the ammeter terminals on the back side of the panel. Remove the two 8/32 nuts from the ammeter terminals and remove the yellow, yellow/black, and instrument light wires from the ammeter terminals.

SPEEDOMETER

5. Remove three (3) screws from around the original pop-out ignition switch to release the entire switch from the instrument panel.

   NOTE

   If a replacement type ignition switch has been installed, only the two wires (red and black) need to be removed from the switch, leaving the switch attached to the panel.

6. Move the instrument panel to the work bench for removal of the speedometer.
7. On the back side of the instrument panel, remove the two (2) speedometer retaining screws (1/4-20 X 1/2" round head screws, lock washers, and square nuts). Lift the speedometer from the instrument panel.

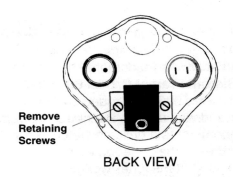

8. Cut the wire and remove the lead seal from the post on the back cover.
9. The front plated cover is a tight press-on fit over the front edge of the rear cover. Turn the speedometer upside down, and use a metal bar to tap around the outer edges to push the cover off. With the front cover off, the face plate can be lifted off the instrument.

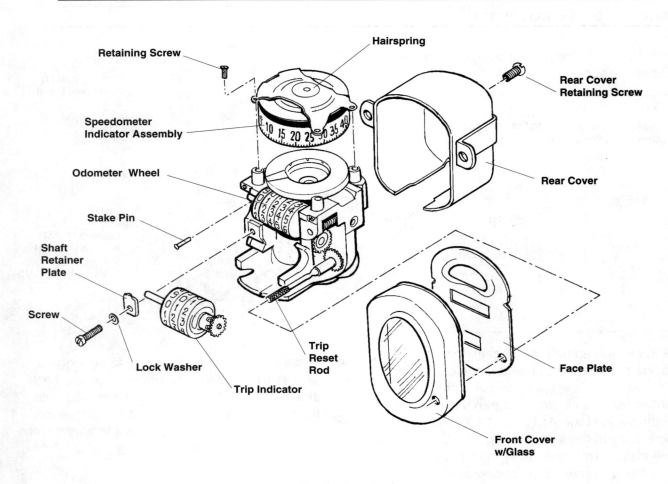

Oval Speedometer

Service and Repair

SPEEDOMETER

10. Remove the rear cover retaining screw located in the center of the rear cover. Very carefully slide the speedometer out of the rear cover. The most delicate part of the speedometer is the speedometer indicator assembly that contains the hairspring and jeweled pivot shaft. Handle with care.

Removing Oval Speedometer Indicator Wheels

1. Remove the four mounting screws for the speedometer indicator assembly. Carefully remove the old decals from the indicator wheel and replace with new number decals.
2. To remove the trip indicator wheels, remove the single screw, lock washer, and small retainer plate over the trip indicator shaft. The trip indicator wheel assembly can now be removed for number decal replacement.
3. The odometer is held in place with a small stake pin. Pry the pin out and remove the odometer wheel assembly for decal replacement.
4. Reassemble as shown in the illustration.

Removing Round Speedometer Indicator Wheels

1. Remove the two (2) mounting screws for the speedometer indicator assembly. Carefully remove the old decals from the indicator wheel and replace with new number decals.
2. To remove the odometer wheels, remove the single screw, lock washer, and small retainer plate over the odometer indicator shaft (bottom side). The odometer wheel assembly can now be removed for number decal replacement.
3. Reassemble as shown in the illustration.

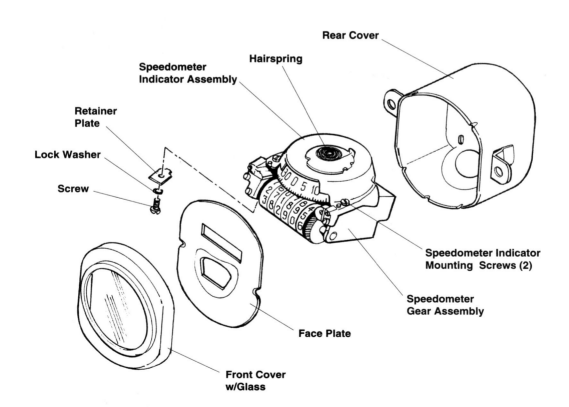

Round Speedometer

Service and Repair

SPEEDOMETER

Installing Speedometer

1. Place the speedometer on the back side of the instrument panel and attach with two (2) screws, lock washers, and square nuts (1/4-20 X 1/2").

> **CAUTION**
>
> Do not over tighten the mounting screws or use longer than 1/2" long screws. Longer screws will make indentations in the front of the instrument panel when screwed in too far.

2. Place the instrument panel at the dash and attach the pop-out ignition switch to the panel with three (3) screws (6-32 X 9/32") and lock washers.

> **NOTE**
>
> Attach the red and black wires to the switch terminals (either terminal) for a replacement type ignition switch.

3. Attach the yellow wire to the ammeter DISCHARGE (-) terminal post, and the yellow/black wire with instrument light wire attached to the (+) CHARGE terminal post on the ammeter.

4. Screw the speedometer cable into the backside of the speedometer.

5. Place the instrument panel against the dash and attach with four (4) 10-32 X 1/2" oval Hd screws.

6. Attach the speedometer cable hold-down clip to the firewall (12-24 X 1/2" round head screw and lock washer).

7. Reconnect the battery ground strap to the (+) terminal on the battery.

SPRING - FRONT

A well maintained front spring with correct arch will provide a smooth ride and aid in handling and front end steering. Spring condition can be checked in several ways. The ground clearance (height) of the car is one indication of spring condition. With the front tires fully inflated, measure the front end height from the center of the bumper to ground. 1928/1929 should be 18-11/16 ±1/2". 1930/1931 should be 18-1/2±1/2". (Tire manufacturer and size may vary these measurements) Check spring flexibility. The front shock arms must be disconnected to check flexibility. Press down on each bumper bracket to check flexibility. There should be about six (6) inches of up and down travel without excessive force. One of the best indications of a weak and sagging spring is to measure the clearance from the bottom of the spring eye to the top of the axle. There should be a minimum of 1/4" clearance. If the clearance is less than 1/4" or the spring eye is sitting on the axle, it is an indication that the spring has lost most of its arch and is sagging. A weak spring pushes out and down on the shackles, forcing the ends of the spring (spring eyes) to rest on the axle. If the tie-rod is rubbing against the drag link when the wheels are turned from side to side, it is an indication the spring is sagging or the shackle bushings are badly worn. This condition must be corrected to prevent the tie rod from wearing through from the two rods rubbing. If the above checks are not within limits, the spring should be removed for replacement or re-arching. The front spring can be easily removed without the use of a spring spreader.

Removing Front Spring

1. Remove four screws holding the front splash apron and remove the front apron.

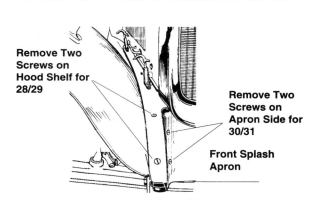

Remove Two Screws on Hood Shelf for 28/29

Remove Two Screws on Apron Side for 30/31

Front Splash Apron

2. Jack up the front end and place jack stands on each side under the frame, just to the outside of the front radius rod.
3. Place a floor jack under the front axle and raise it enough to allow removal of both front wheels.

4. Remove the cotter pin and screw out the top plug in both shock links. Remove both shock links from the spring perches.

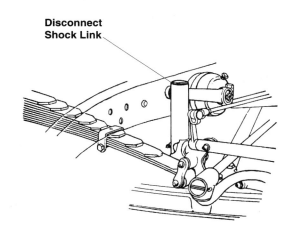

Disconnect Shock Link

Service and Repair

SPRING - FRONT

5. Lower the floor jack under the front axle to allow the ends of the leave spring to raise above the axle. Place a small block of wood under both spring eyes (between the axle and spring eye).

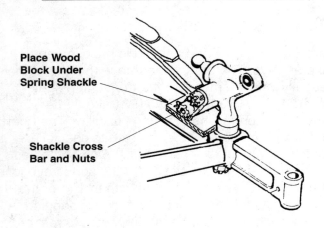

Place Wood Block Under Spring Shackle

Shackle Cross Bar and Nuts

6. Apply a little grease to the top of the wood blocks and slowly raise the floor jack under the axle, spreading the spring ends on the wood blocks.
7. Remove the cotter pins and nuts [5/8 socket] from the back side of the spring shackles. Remove the shackle cross bar.
8. Continue raising the axle to spread the spring until most tension is released from the spring shackles. Drive the spring shackles out through the front of the spring eyes and spring perch.

9. Lower the floor jack to separate the axle from the spring.
10. Remove the four (4) castle nuts under the spring hanger (3/4 wrench) U-bolts. Remove the spring from the front cross member.
11. Lay the spring on the shop floor and measure the free length height and width as shown below. Make note of these measurements for re-arching reference.

Disassembly and Arching

1. Place a 6" C-clamp on each side of the center bolt.
2. Remove the spring clips on each side of the spring.

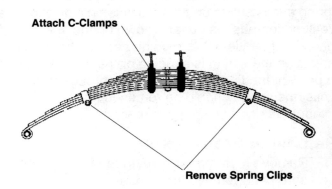

Attach C-Clamps

Remove Spring Clips

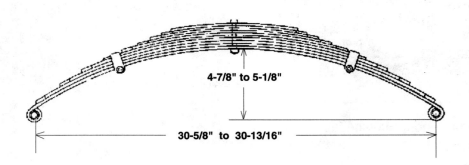

4-7/8" to 5-1/8"

30-5/8" to 30-13/16"

Free Length Measurements (10 Leaf Spring)

SPRING - FRONT

3. Slowly loosen the center bolt while alternately loosening the C-clamps. If large C-clamps are not available, place a single clamp on the spring to hold it tightly clamped together. Then remove the center bolt and replace it with a 12" length of 5/16 All-Thread rod, with nut and flat washer on each end. Remove the C-clamp and slowly release the All-Thread nut on one side to release spring tension and separate the leaves.
4. Clean all grease and dirt from each leave with a strong detergent or solvent. Wire brush all heavy rust from each leave.
5. Remove the shackle bushings from the spring eyes on the main leave. Press in new bushings.
6. Grind the underside edge of each leave to a smooth bevel. This will prevent the ends of the leave from digging into the leave below it.

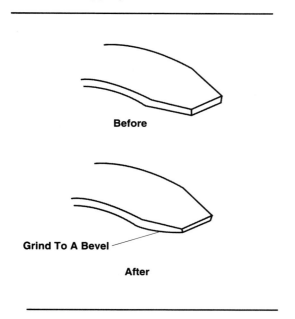

7. Grind the edge off the top of each leave where the leave above it may have dug in and left a ridge.
8. Place each leave on a large piece of paper and draw an outline of the arch for reference.
9. Start with the Main (bottom) leave. Clamp it in a vise vertically, about 3" from the center hole. (Do not bend (arch) the leave any closer than 3" from each side of the center hole.)
10. Clamp a large crescent wrench to the top (end) of the leave and make a strong pull in the direction of arch. Repeat the bending process about every 1/2" to about eight (8) inches from the end. Turn the leave end-for-end and arch the other half.
11. Compare the arch to the paper pattern. Measure the arch height of the leave. It should have increased 1/4" to 3/8".
12. Repeat the arching process until the desired arch is achieved. Make several passes. Do not try to arch it all in one pass.
13. Proceed to the next spring leave and check it for fit by placing it on it's side next to the leave just finished. The gap in the center between the two leaves should be close to what was previously outlined. The spring leaves are made of different thickness to achieve the proper flexibility.
14. When all leaves have been subjected to the re-arching process, and they appear to nest uniformly when placed next to each other, they are ready for final treatment.
15. Paint each leave with a rust oxidizer (a good product for this is called EXTEND) to neutralize and seal the rust.
16. Paint the <u>bottom</u> of each leave (except bottom of main leave) with SLIP-PLATE (made by John Deere Mfg). SLIP-PLATE is a graphite paint lubricant that provides an excellent dry lubricant that will allow the spring to be painted later after assembly. After assembly the spring can be painted and sealed from rusting.

Service and Repair

SPRING - FRONT

Front Spring Assembly

1. Stack each leave in order and put the center bolt in place.

   NOTE

   Replace the center bolt if the old bolt is rusted. This must be a square head bolt to fit into the frame cross member correctly. A square hole is punched into the cross member to correctly center and hold the spring in the centered position. Use a 5/16-18 X 2-3/4" square head bolt for 10 leave spring. Some replacement springs have a round head bolt that will fit the cross member hole.

2. Place a large C-clamp near the center bolt to draw the spring tight. Insert the center bolt, nut and lock washer (5/16-18).
3. Attach the spring clips on each end of the spring, with the clip dimple placed over the spring end with a hole in it.
   (clip bolt - 1/4-20 X 2-3/8")
4. Paint the entire spring with black RUSTOLEUM.

Installing Front Spring

1. Before installing the front spring, replace the shackle bushings in the axle spring perches.
2. Place the spring shackle in each spring perch and spring eye bushing to ensure correct fit. The fit should be an easy slip through. A tight fit will create difficulty when hanging the spring and inserting the shackles.
3. Cut an 8" strip of body welt to be placed between the spring and front cross member. Cut a hole in the center to clear the center bolt head. Glue the welt to the top leave. Coat the top of the welt with grease.
4. Position the spring in the front cross member. Place the crank bearing on top of the cross member, insert the front spring U-bolts, and lower plate under the spring. Attach with four (4) castle nuts (1/2-20 castle nut)[3/4 wrench]. Install cotter pins.

   NOTE

   It is very important that the spring bolt head be fully positioned in the hole in the cross member.

NOTE

Crank bearing plate and U-bolts: Square until Feb 1930; round after 1930 to end of production.

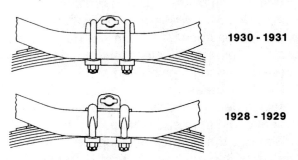

1930 - 1931

1928 - 1929

5. Place the axle on the floor jack and raise far enough to allow a spring shackle to be inserted in one end of the spring and spring perch. Apply shackle bar and nuts on the back side of the shackle. Do not tighten nuts at this time.
6. Place wood blocks under each end of the spring (spring eyes) and raise the axle until the other spring shackle can be easily inserted through the spring eye and spring perch. Apply shackle cross bar and nuts [5/8 socket].

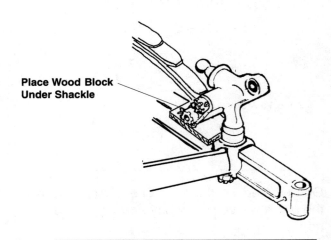

Place Wood Block Under Shackle

7. Tighten the nuts on both shackles just enough to allow the cotter pins to be inserted.
8. Install both front wheels. Torque lug nuts to 64 lbs.
9. Remove the jack stands and floor jack.
10. Push down on each bumper bracket to test flexibility of the spring. There should be about 6" of up and down travel.

SPRING - FRONT

11. Assemble and install both front shock links as shown below. Screw in the end plug and insert a cotter pin.

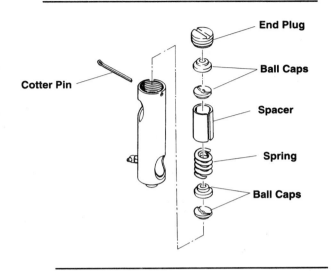

12. Attach the front splash apron with four screws (**28/29 Model** use 1/4-20 X 1-1/4" Oval Head) (**30/31 Model** use 1/4-20 X 1/2" Round Head).

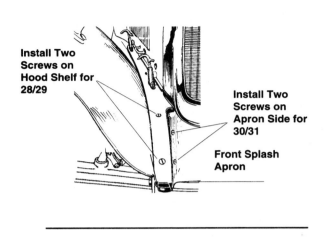

13. The splash apron should now be above the axle, plenty of clearance between the tie rod and drag link, and the measurement from center of bumper to ground should be:

   1928/1929 - 18-1/2 ±1/2"
   1930/1931 - 18-11/16 ±1/2"

SPRING - REAR

The rear spring used a different leave count for the different body styles.
- All Sedans (Tudor and Fordor), Delivery - 10 Leaves
- Coupes, Phaetons, Cabriolets, Victoria - 8 Leaves
- Roadsters - 7 Leaves

Removal of the rear spring requires the use of a special spring spreader.

Rear Spring Removal

1. Block the front wheels and release the emergency brake.
2. Jack up the rear end of the car and place jack stands under the frame, just behind the running board brackets. Remove both rear wheels.
3. Disconnect the service brake rod and emergency brake rod (remove clevis pins).

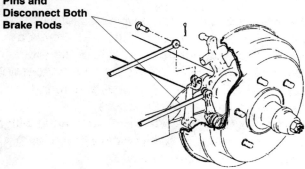

Remove Clevis Pins and Disconnect Both Brake Rods

4. Remove the rear shock arms from the shock (Remove shock arm bolt [9/16 socket] and pull the arm off the shock shaft.)

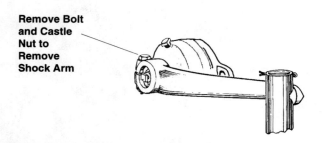

Remove Bolt and Castle Nut to Remove Shock Arm

5. Disconnect the brake rod anti-rattlers from the radius rods (bolt and lock washer), [9/16 socket].

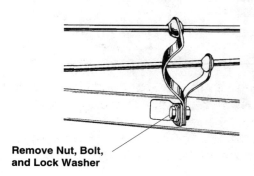

Remove Nut, Bolt, and Lock Washer

6. Place a floor jack under the differential housing (banjo) for support while removing the spring shackles.
7. Place a full length Model A spring spreader on the rear spring and adjust it sufficiently to allow the spring shackles to be removed.

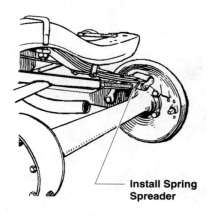

Install Spring Spreader

SPRING - REAR

8. To remove the spring shackle, remove the two rear shackle nuts [11/16 socket] and remove the shackle cross bar. With spring tension removed by the spring spreader, the shackle can be driven out of the spring perch and spring eye.

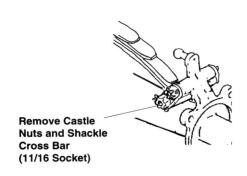

Remove Castle Nuts and Shackle Cross Bar (11/16 Socket)

9. Remove the spring spreader and lower the floor jack under the differential to allow removal of the spring.
10. Remove the four hanger nuts (7/8 wrench) to allow removal of the spring from the cross member.

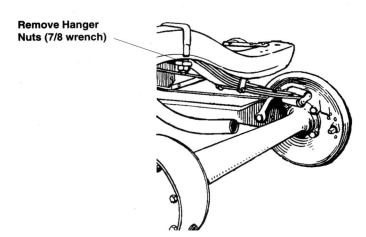

Remove Hanger Nuts (7/8 wrench)

NOTE
A pry bar may be needed to pry the spring out of the cross member.

Rear Spring Disassembly and Repair

1. Wrap a chain around the spring as a safety precaution before removing the center bolt. Place an 8" C-clamp on each side of the center bolt.
2. Place another C-clamp just above each spring clip. Remove both spring clips.

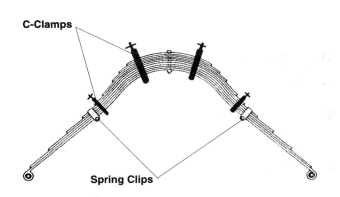

C-Clamps

Spring Clips

3. Remove the center bolt and replace it with a 24" length of 3/8 ALL-THREAD rod. Screw a flat washer and nut on each side of the rod.
4. Slowly loosen the C-clamps and the bottom nut on the ALL-THREAD rod to release spring tension and separate the leaves
5. Clean all grease and dirt from each leave with a strong detergent or solvent. Wire brush all heavy rust from each leave.
6. Remove the shackle bushings from the spring eyes on the main leave. Press in new bushings.

SPRING - REAR

7. Grind the underside edge of each leave to a smooth bevel. This will prevent the ends of the leave from digging into the leave below it.

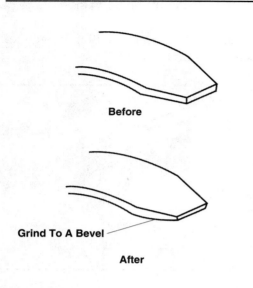

Before

Grind To A Bevel

After

8. Grind the edge off the top of each leave where the leave above it may have dug in and left a ridge.
9. Paint each leave with a rust oxidizer (a good product for this is called EXTEND) to neutralize and seal the rust.
10. Paint the bottom of each leave (except bottom of main leave) with SLIP-PLATE (made by John Deere Mfg). SLIP-Plate is a graphite paint lubricant that provides an excellent dry lubricant that will allow the spring to be painted later after assembly. After assembly the spring can be painted and sealed from rusting.
11. Stack each leave in order and place the 3/8 ALL-THREAD rod through the center hole of the spring leaves.
12. Tighten the center rod nuts until the C-clamps can be attached just above the spring clips.
13. Wrap a chain around the spring as a safety precaution. Alternately tighten the center nut and C-clamps to compress the spring.
14. After the spring has been drawn up tight, install both spring clips (use clip bolts 1/4-20 X 2-7/8") and then reposition the two center C-clamps about 3" on either side of the center bolt. Adjust all slack out of the chain wrap and lock it in place with a bolt and nut.
15. Remove the center rod and insert a new spring bolt (3/8-16 X 2-7/8" w/lock washer). Firmly tighten the nut and lock washer. Remove C-clamps and chain.
16. Paint the entire spring with gloss black RUSTOLEUM paint.

Installing Rear Spring

1. Check the shackle bushings on the rear axle spring perches. Replace bushings if needed.
2. Place the spring shackle in each spring perch and spring eye bushing to ensure correct fit. The fit should be an easy slip through. A tight fit will create difficulty when hanging the spring and inserting the shackles.
3. Cut a 6" strip of body welt to be placed between the spring and cross member. Cut a hole in the center to clear the center bolt head. Glue the welt to the top leave. Coat the top of the welt with grease.
4. Position the spring in the rear cross member. Position the two U-bolt brackets on the U-bolt hangers. Attach with four (4) castle nuts (9/16-18)[7/8 wrench]. Install cotter pins.
5. Install the spring spreader on the rear spring between the two spring eyes.

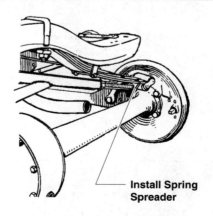

Install Spring Spreader

Service and Repair

SPRING - REAR

6. Raise the differential on the floor jack to allow the spring shackles to be installed. Attach the right spring shackle first. (Shackle grease fittings face the outside, rear of the car.) Apply the cross bar and two (2) castle nuts (7/16-20) [11/16 wrench] but do not tighten the nuts at this time.

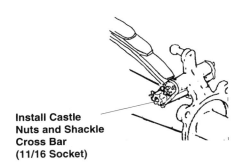

Install Castle Nuts and Shackle Cross Bar (11/16 Socket)

7. Adjust the spring spreader to allow installation of the left spring shackle. Apply the cross bar and castle nuts. Tighten all four (4) castle nuts only enough to allow cotter pins to be inserted. The shackles will not flex if the shackle bolts are too tight. Remove the spring spreader. Grease all four grease fittings on the shackles.

8. Attach the brake rod anti-rattler springs to the rear radius rods (5/16-24 X11/16")[1/2 wrench].

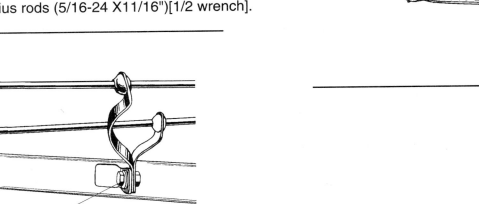

Attach With Nut, Bolt, and Lock Washer

9. Attach all four (4) rear brake rods with clevis pins and cotter pins.

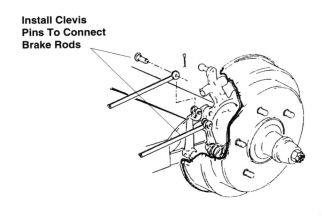

Install Clevis Pins To Connect Brake Rods

10. Install the rear shock arms on the shocks [9/16 socket].

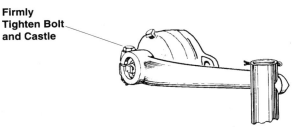

Firmly Tighten Bolt and Castle

SPRING - REAR

11. Assemble both rear shock links as shown below. Connect the links to the shock arm and spring perch ball. Screw in the end plug and insert a cotter pin.

12. Install both rear wheels and torque the lug nuts to 64 ft. lbs.

13. Remove all jacks and blocks from under the car. Apply grease to all rear grease fittings.

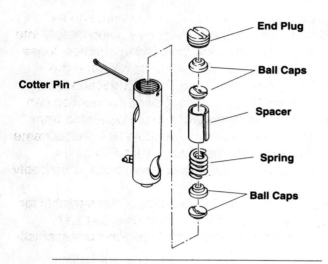

STARTER

STARTER MOTOR

Symptoms of starter motor defects are slow cranking speed, failure to crank, and unusual noise during cranking. All of these symptoms can also be caused by defects elsewhere. Before going deeply into the starter, check the other possibilities. These include discharged battery, defective battery cables, loose or corroded cable connections, and jammed or broken starter bendix drive. Often on the Model A the ground connection between the engine and frame develops excessive resistance. The connection is designed to be mainly through the engine mounts and engine splash aprons. The ground connection can be improved with the addition of a heavy ground cable (use a #2 or larger battery cable) connected from the frame to the bell housing. This can be easily connected from the battery ground cable bolt on the frame cross member to one of the bell housing to flywheel housing bolts directly behind the starter. If all the above has been checked and made OK, and you still have poor starter action, the starter motor is probably the problem.

The following procedures describe removing the starter from the car, bench testing, disassembly for cleaning, and brush replacement. If it is determined that the starter requires more than cleaning and brushes replaced, the starter should be taken to a qualified starter/generator repair shop for more sophisticated analysis and repairs.

Removing Starter Motor

1. Remove the front floor mat (or carpet) and shift lever plate, attached to the floor board with three clips.
2. Remove the bottom section of the front floor board [6 flathead screws] for access to the battery terminals.
3. Remove the battery <u>ground cable</u> from the (+) battery post first, then remove the cable from the (-) terminal post.
4. Unscrew the starter push rod from the starter switch and push it all the way up.
5. Remove the oil dip stick.
6. Remove the battery cable and harness wire from the starter switch [5/8 box wrench].
7. Remove the starter motor bolts [three bolts, 9/16 socket]. Remove the top bolt last. It will support the weight of the starter motor while the other two are being removed. (Starter Motor weighs 21 lbs.) Lift the starter up and pull the motor and bendix drive assembly out of the flywheel housing.

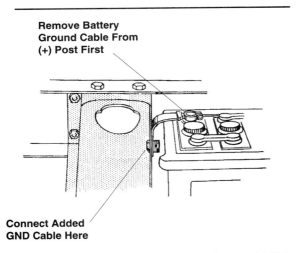

Remove Battery Ground Cable From (+) Post First

Connect Added GND Cable Here

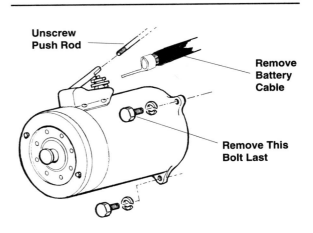

Unscrew Push Rod

Remove Battery Cable

Remove This Bolt Last

Service and Repair

STARTER

8. The starter bendix drive must be removed for starter motor bench testing. Bend down the locking ear on the special lock washer that locks the hex head bolt to the motor shaft at the front of the bendix drive. Remove the front bolt, bendix drive and woodruff key from the shaft.
9. Remove the starter switch (four 10-32 X 5/16 screws).

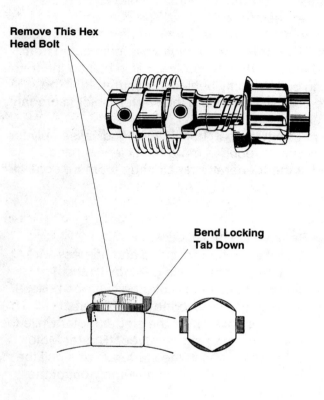

Remove This Hex Head Bolt

Bend Locking Tab Down

Bench Testing

1. The first bench test is a simple hand spin of the starter shaft. There should be no gritty or scraping feeling as the shaft is turned. The shaft should turn easily with two fingers. If not, the shaft bushings may need replacing. A dragging or rubbing may mean a bent shaft or loose field pole shoes. These defects need to be corrected before going to the electrical bench tests.

2. **No-Load Current Draw Test** - For this test you will need a fully charged 6 volt battery, heavy duty jumper cables, and an inductive ammeter reading up to 100 Amps.

CAUTION

During this test there will be sparks generated. Keep the battery and starter motor as far apart as possible. Make and break the connection at the starter, not the battery to prevent a possible explosion from battery gases.

3. Connect the battery cables to the two battery terminal posts.
4. Clamp the (+) battery cable to the starter motor case. Attach the inductive ammeter to this cable.
5. Hold the starter firmly with one hand and touch the (-) cable to the copper starter terminal. Allow the starter motor 5 or 6 seconds to stabilize its speed, then read the ammeter. The ammeter should read 50 amps. Up to 60 amps is acceptable. More than 60 amps indicates a problem. Additional repairs should be made by a qualified repair shop.

6. **No-Load RPM Test** - Hold the starter firmly with one hand and touch the (-) cable to the copper starter terminal.
7. Allow the starter motor about 10 seconds to stabilize its speed, then listen. The shaft should be turning at 4000 RPM. When at stabilized speed, the starter should give off a fast smooth whirring sound. Almost a whine, with no squeals or chirps, and only modest vibration. You should be able to comfortably hold the motor on the bench with one hand.
8. A bent shaft will look blurred and fuzzy. If instead of a smooth whirr, you get slow, rough running, screeches, groans, or grinding noises, a complete rebuild is needed.

STARTER

Replacing Brushes
1. Loosen the screw on the side of the cover band and slide it back to remove it.
2. The brushes are held in place with spring clips. Visually inspect each brush in the holder. If the brush is 1/4 inch or longer below the holder, the brushes do not need replacing.
3. To replace a brush, use a wire hook to lift the spring up off the brush and then lift the brush out of the holder. Insert the new brush into the holder and release the spring.

Disassembly, Inspection and Cleaning
1. The brushes should be removed as described above.
2. Remove the two long bolts from the rear plate (1/4-20 X 6-3/4 long).
3. Slide the brush holder end plate off the armature shaft. Set aside.
4. Slide the front end plate off the armature shaft and gently lift the armature out of the case.
5. Use a soft brush and compressed air to clean the armature, end plates and bushings. A solvent can be used on all components except the armature windings. Some insulating coatings may break down with solvent.
6. Clean and smooth the copper commutator with 300 grit sandpaper (Do not use emery cloth). Blow or brush away all sanding residue.
7. Inspect the insulation on the field brush leads. Repair breaks or thin spots in the insulation by wrapping with cotton string and then coating with a glue that is resistant to both oil and temperatures up to 400 ° F. Do not use electricians tape. The high temperatures and oily atmosphere will loosen the tape adhesive, causing the tape to separate and end up under a brush.
8. Test the brush springs for a 2 lb. pull. An easy way to check is to hang the end plate (which weighs almost exactly 2 pounds) by each brush spring with a wire S-hook. The spring should just barely lift off the holder, or not at all. If it lifts more than 1/8", the spring is too weak and should be replaced.
9. Check the bushings in each end plate. Replace bushings if their is more than .002 inches clearance between the shaft and bushing. The end plate bushing for end that bolts to flywheel housing were two sizes: (1) 1928 and early 1929 starters used I.D. .627, O.D. .688, 1.155 inches long. (2) 1929 through 1931 starters used I.D. .627, O.D. .753, 1.155 inches long. Brush end plate bushing is I.D. .640, O.D. .753, .592 inches long.

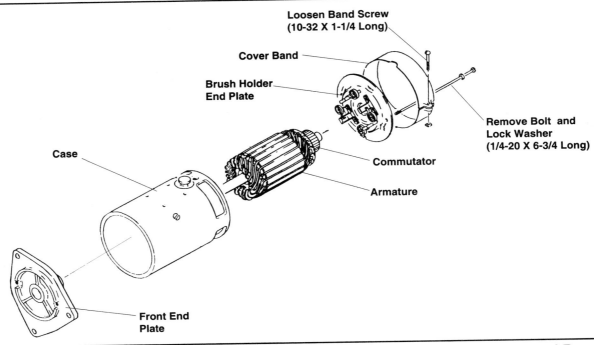

Service and Repair

STARTER

Reassembly

1. Carefully lift the armature into the case. Make sure the 5/8 fiber washer is installed on the shaft next to the commutator.
2. Slide the front end plate onto the shaft and up against the case.
3. Place the brush holder end plate on the rear commutator shaft and push the plate against the case.
4. Align both end plate tabs with the slots in the case and insert the two long bolts through the rear end plate (1/4-20 X 6-3/4). Tighten both bolts (with lock washer under bolt head).
5. Lift each spring clip and insert the brushes into the holder. Take care to center the springs on the back of the brushes. Off-center springs can cause brushes to hang up in the holders.
6. With a light and a mechanics mirror, make sure the brush leads are positioned so as not to rub on the spinning armature.
7. Spin the armature shaft by hand. It should turn smoothly with no rubbing or gritty feeling.
8. Slip the band cover over the case open slots and tighten the side screw (10-32 X 1-1/4 round head)
9. Run the No-Load bench test for rpm and current draw.
10. Slip the bendix drive onto the shaft (with #6 woodruff key) and bolt it to the shaft with special bolt and tabbed lock washer.
11. Place a new tabbed lock washer on the front spring bolt. The tab on the lock washer should be bent to lock the bolt in place. The tab on the washer must be bent upward until it presses tightly against a flat side of the bolt head.

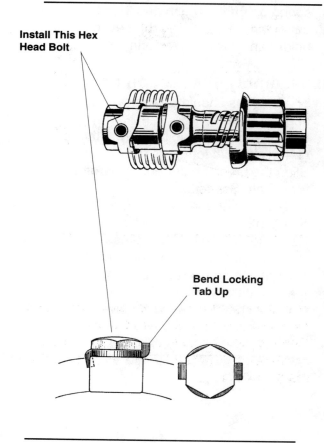

Install This Hex Head Bolt

Bend Locking Tab Up

Service and Repair

STARTER

Installing Starter Motor

1. Install the starter motor with three (3) bolts and lock washers (3/8-16 X 1") [9/16 socket]. Install the top-outside bolt first. This will hold the starter motor in place while the other two bolts and lock washers are being installed.

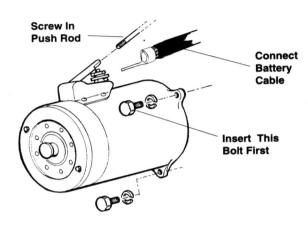

2. Mount the starter switch to the motor with four (4) 10-32 X 5/16 round head screws.
3. Connect battery cable and harness wire to the starter switch. Screw the starter push rod to the starter switch.

4. Connect the battery cable (from the starter switch) to the (-) battery post.

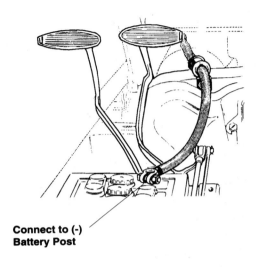

5. Connect the battery ground strap to the (+) battery post.

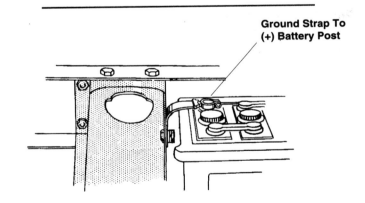

6. Install the front floor board and floor mat. Secure the floor board with six (6) flat head screws [12-24 X 1-1/8"] and cup washers.
7. Slip on the shifting tower boot and emergency handle boot. Screw the knob on top of the shifting tower and screw on the accelerator pedal (top cap).

Service and Repair

STEERING ASSEMBLY

The Model A steering gear box affects only about 70% of the car's ability to steer and handle correctly. The following items also affect the steering and should be checked when making repairs to the steering system: sector housing-to-frame mounting bolts (loose); pitman arm bolt (loose); pitman arm and spindle arm ball studs worn (out of round); incorrect tension on drag link and tie-rod end plugs; worn king pin bushings; spindle thrust bearings incorrectly set; incorrect toe-in adjustment; and incorrect caster.

Two different steering gear columns were made for the Model A, a 7-tooth sector and worm gear and a 2-tooth sector and worm gear. The 7-tooth sector and worm gear was used primarily in 1928/1929 year models. The 2-tooth sector and worm gear were used primarily in 1930/1931 year models. A few 2-tooth sector types made by GEMMER Mfg. were installed in Model A's for a couple of months in early 1929.

The 7-tooth sector type can be identified by the one-piece (all welded) steering column and gear box, including the sector shaft housing.

The 2-tooth sector type is made in three pieces, the steering column housing, the gear box, and the sector housing. The column attaches to the gear box with a clamp. The sector housing attaches to the gear box with four attaching studs and nuts.

The components are not interchangeable between the two types of steering assemblies. The 2-tooth sector steering column is one inch longer than the 7-tooth sector column. The 7-tooth sector steering column has a splined shaft steering wheel. The 2-tooth steering column has a keyed shaft (woodruff key) steering wheel. Only minor adjustments can be properly made to both types of steering assemblies while mounted in the car. Refer to Section II for (in car) steering adjustments. The complete steering assembly must be removed from the car for overhaul and complete adjustment.

Both types of steering column assemblies can be removed from the car by using the same step-by-step procedures that follow. Both steering assemblies can be removed from the car using either of two procedures. One procedure requires removing the horn rod and steering wheel so the column can be guided down between the clutch and brake pedals and out through the engine compartment. The second procedure allows you to leave the horn rod and steering wheel in place, while removing the clutch and brake pedals to allow the gear box and column to be pulled into the drivers compartment and out through the driver's door.

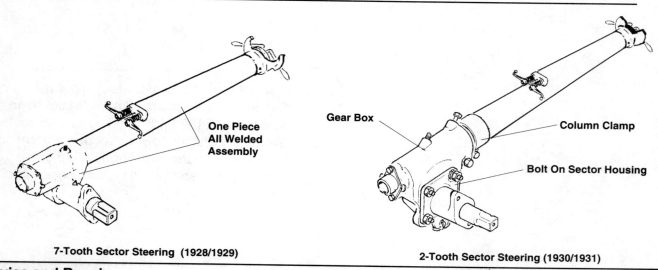

7-Tooth Sector Steering (1928/1929)   2-Tooth Sector Steering (1930/1931)

STEERING

Removing Steering Assembly
(Through Engine Compartment)

This method of removing the steering column assembly from the car requires removing the horn rod and steering wheel, allowing the column to be pulled out through the engine compartment.

1. Remove (unscrew) the gear shift knob to allow removal of the shifter column boot. Slip off the shifter column boot and the emergency handle boot.
2. Remove (unscrew) the accelerator pedal (top cap).
3. Remove the front floor mat (or carpet) and shifting tower cover plate, attached to the floor boards with three (3) clips. Remove both sections of the front floor boards (12 flathead screws).
4. Remove both battery cables from the battery and remove the battery.

NOTE
Removing the battery is not absolutely necessary, but is a safety precaution and will allow more room when maneuvering the column past the pedals.

5. From under the car, disconnect the drag link at the pitman arm by removing the end cotter pin and unscrewing the drag link end plug. Slightly turn the steering wheel to the left to allow removal of the drag link from the pitman arm ball.

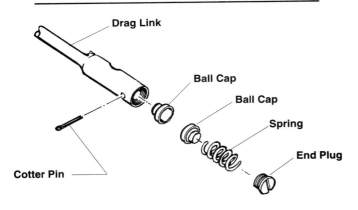

6. Turn the steering wheel left, far enough to allow access to the pitman arm castle nut. Remove the cotter pin and castle nut [5/8 socket]. Turn the steering wheel back to center position to allow removal of the pitman arm bolt. The bolt must be fully removed before the pitman arm can be removed from the sector shaft.

NOTE
It may be necessary to slightly spread the split housing on the pitman arm to allow removal from the sector shaft.

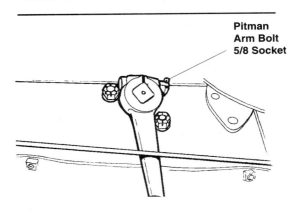

7. From under the hood on the left side remove the short throttle linkage and longer spark control linkage from the steering column arms.

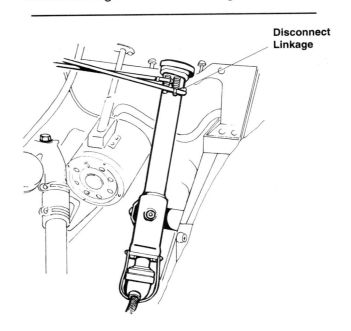

Service and Repair

STEERING

8. Release the bail wire from the light switch (push bail wire down) at the end of the steering column. Pull the light switch bulb from the end of the steering column.
9. Push up slightly on the switch spider to remove the retaining clip, spider, and spring from the end of the horn rod.

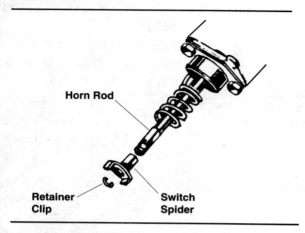

10. Pull the horn rod from the center of the steering wheel.

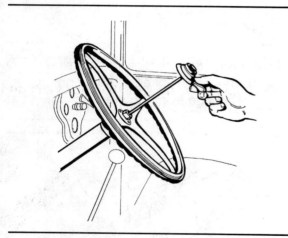

NOTE
When the horn rod is removed, oil may run out the horn rod hole at the end of the column. Allow the oil to drain before continuing.

NOTE
The head room in the coupe or pickup may not be sufficient to allow removal of the horn rod and steering wheel until further disassembly is completed.

11. Remove the steering wheel nut [15/16 socket] and remove the steering wheel.

NOTE
1928 and 1929 steering wheels were splined to the shaft. 1930 and 1931 steering wheels were keyed to the shaft. A steering wheel puller and Liquid Wrench may be necessary to pop the steering wheel loose from the shaft.

12. From under the hood remove the oil filler tube and oil dip stick to provide room for the steering column to pass through. The oil filler tube is a press fit. It may be necessary to use a rubber mallet to knock the filler tube out. Cover the oil filler tube hole with duct tape.
13. Unscrew the starter push rod from the starter switch.

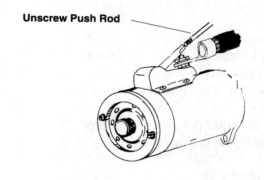

14. Remove the battery cable and harness wire from the starter switch [5/8 box wrench].
15. Remove the starter motor [three bolts, 9/16 socket].

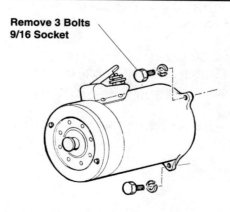

STEERING

16. From under the fender, remove the two sector housing-to-frame castle nuts and bolts [9/16 socket].

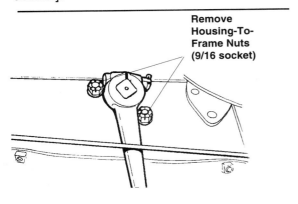

Remove Housing-To-Frame Nuts (9/16 socket)

17. From inside the car remove the two (2) screws at the steering column bracket.
18. *[Coupes and Pickups Only]* Pull the sector shaft from the frame and then carefully pull the column toward the front of the car, allowing enough room to remove the horn rod and steering wheel, if not already done.
19. After removing the sector housing away from the frame, the steering column and gear box can be removed through the engine compartment by lifting the gear box up and pulling it toward the generator, while maneuvering the upper column and control rods past the brake and clutch pedals.

Removing Steering Assembly
(Through Driver's Side Front Door)

This method of removing the steering column assembly from the car requires removing the brake and clutch pedals, allowing you to leave the horn rod and steering wheel attached until after the column has been removed from the car.

1. Remove (unscrew) the gear shift knob to allow removal of the shifter column boot. Slip off the shifter column boot and the emergency handle boot.
2. Remove (unscrew) the accelerator pedal (top cap).

3. Remove the front floor mat (or carpet) and shifting tower cover plate, attached to the floor boards with three (3) clips. Remove both sections of the front floor boards [12 flathead screws].
4. Remove both battery cables from the battery and remove the battery.
5. Remove the stop light linkage and brake rod from the brake pedal arm.

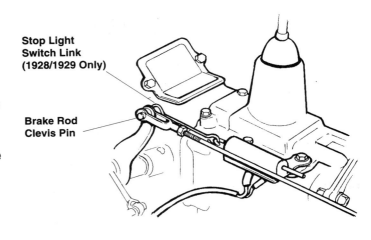

Stop Light Switch Link (1928/1929 Only)

Brake Rod Clevis Pin

6. From under the car, remove the clutch arm clevis pin and release the clutch arm.

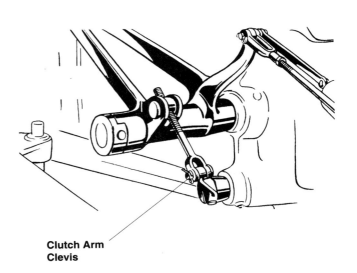

Clutch Arm Clevis

STEERING

7. Remove the brake and clutch pedals by removing the cotter pin and shaft pin on the end of the pedal shaft. Remove the end cap and slide the two pedals and spring washer off the pedal shaft.

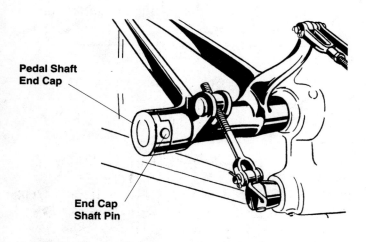

8. From under the car, disconnect the drag link at the pitman arm by removing the end cotter pin and unscrewing the drag link end plug. Slightly turn the steering wheel to the left to allow removal of the drag link from the pitman arm ball.

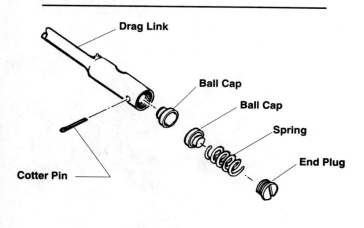

9. Turn the steering wheel left, far enough to allow access to the pitman arm castle nut. Remove the cotter pin and castle nut [5/8 socket]. Turn the steering wheel back to center position to allow removal of the pitman arm bolt. The bolt must be fully removed before the pitman arm can be removed from the sector shaft.

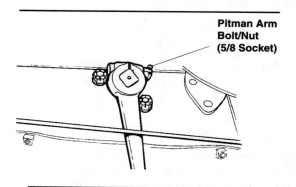

NOTE
It may be necessary to slightly spread the split housing on the pitman arm to allow removal from the sector shaft.

10. From under the hood on the left side remove the short throttle linkage and longer spark control linkage from the steering column arms.

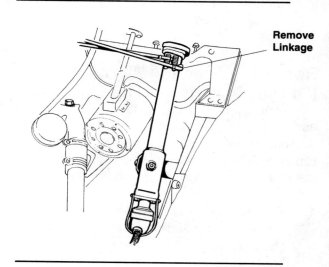

11. Release the bail wire from the light switch (push bail wire down) at the end of the steering column. Pull the light switch bulb from the end of the steering column.

Service and Repair

STEERING

12. Unscrew the starter push rod from the starter switch.

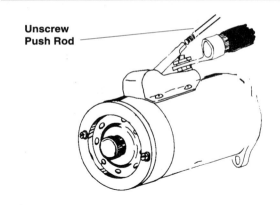

13. Remove the battery cable and harness wire from the starter switch [5/8 box wrench].
14. Remove the three (3) starter motor mounting bolts to remove the starter motor (9/16 socket).

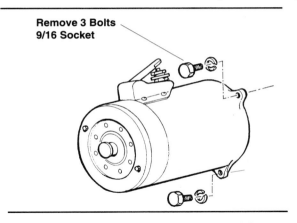

15. From inside the car remove the two (2) screws holding the steering column bracket. Remove the bracket and rubber bushing.

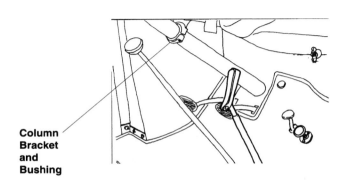

16. From under the left front fender, remove the two sector housing-to-frame castle nuts and bolts [9/16 socket].

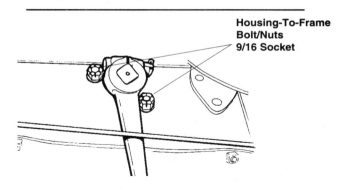

17. Pull the steering sector shaft out of the frame and then maneuver the gear box under the firewall and into the driver's compartment. Keep the steering wheel end of the column in a low position and towards the driver-side door. The assembly can be pulled out through the driver's door (left side), steering wheel first.

2-Tooth Sector Steering Assembly Overhaul

1. If not already completed, remove the horn rod by pressing up on the spring loaded spider to remove the retaining clip at the end of the column.

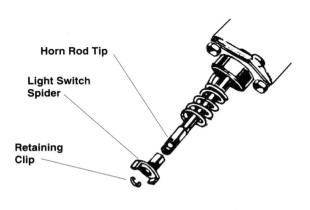

Service and Repair

STEERING

2. Pull the horn rod out of the column.
3. Remove the steering wheel nut [15/16 socket] to remove the steering wheel.

NOTE

The steering wheel is on a tapered shaft, held in place with a woodruff key. A steering wheel puller may be needed to release the steering wheel.

4. Remove the column clamp bolt and nut [1/2 socket]. Ensure the clamp is loose on the column housing.
5. Slide the column off the steering shaft.

NOTE

The upper column bushing (woven webbing) may be tight on the shaft. If necessary, screw the steering wheel nut back on the shaft, just far enough to cover the threads. With a brass mallet, knock the shaft through the upper column bushing. Take extreme care not to damage or distort the upper shaft threads or the hole in the center of the shaft.

6. Remove the two bolts and lock washers from the light switch bracket on the bottom end of the gear box [7/16 socket]. Remove the bracket, end plate, and gaskets.

NOTE

Any oil in the gear box will drain out when the end plate is removed.

7. On the back side of the gear box, remove the sector end play adjusting screw, jam nut [3/4 wrench], and lock washer.
8. Remove the four (4) sector housing nuts and washers [5/8 wrench]. Remove the adjusting cone from the upper right hand mounting stud.

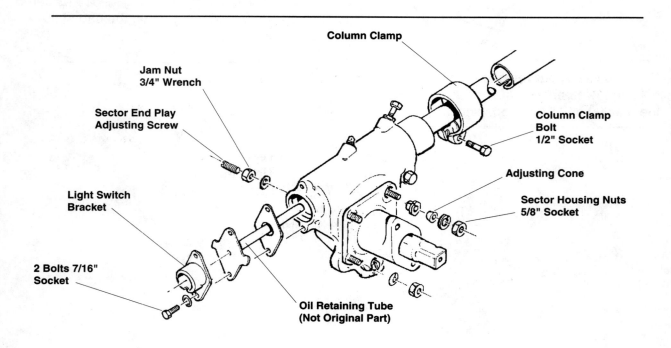

Service and Repair

STEERING

9. Lift the sector housing off the studs and sector shaft. To remove the housing, push the sector shaft through the housing. After the housing has been removed, the sector shaft, brass thrust washer, and cork gasket can be removed.
10. Remove the upper race locking bolt, nut and lock washer [9/16 socket]. Pull the upper race from the housing.

NOTE

The upper race may be wedged tightly into the upper housing. The housing is split where the upper race locking bolt goes through. Using a large chisel or wedge, spread the housing at the split. Hammer the chisel in parallel with the race, being careful not to damage the race. The housing will spread apart sufficiently to allow the upper race to be removed.

11. The steering shaft with worm gear, upper race, and two tapered bearings can then be removed from the housing. Thoroughly clean all parts with cleaning solvent.

NOTE

The early 2-tooth sector steering assemblies used a cylindrical 9-roller bearing in place of the later style tapered 13-roller bearing. The angle of the bearing and race on the 9-roller bearing (25°) is different than the 13-roller tapered bearing (15°). Steering assemblies found with 9 roller bearings must have all internal components replaced, which include worm gear, upper and lower race, and the two tapered bearings. The early style races and bearings are no longer made. The early worm gear can also be identified by the presences of a shoulder on the end of the worm bearing race. The bearing race on the later worm gear is smooth to the end.

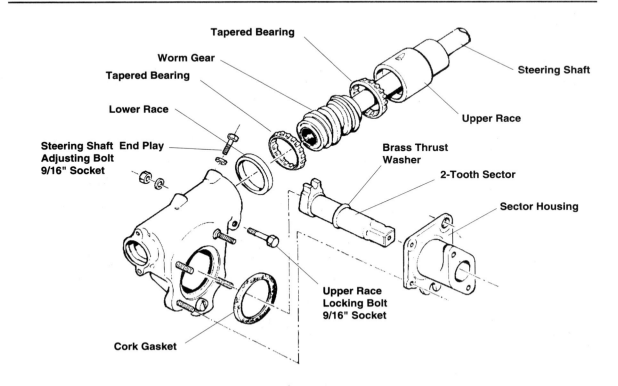

Service and Repair

STEERING

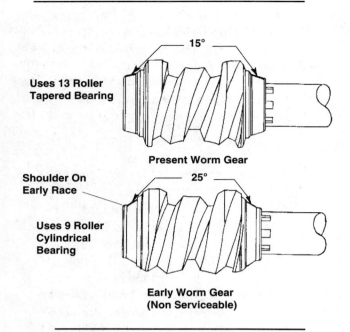

Uses 13 Roller Tapered Bearing
Present Worm Gear
Shoulder On Early Race
Uses 9 Roller Cylindrical Bearing
Early Worm Gear (Non Serviceable)

12. Inspect the lower race (inside the housing) for pitting. The lower race will have to be removed and replaced if the surface is not smooth, or if pitting is observed.
13. The lower race can be removed from the housing with a 1/8" drift punch through the end plate bolt holes. Punch the race out evenly using both bolt holes.

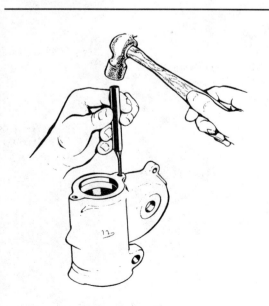

Removing Lower Race

14. Insert the new race through the top of the housing. Tap the race down (squarely) using a 1-3/8" 1/2 drive socket (1-7/8" O.D.). Install the socket up side-down on an extension shaft, using the bottom, flat side of the socket to drive down the race. The race must be set completely and squarely with the bottom machined surface of the housing.
15. Inspect the worm gear upper and lower race surfaces. Replace the worm gear if the bearing surfaces are worn or pitted. The worm gear must be pressed off and a new one pressed on the shaft. When pressing the worm gear off and on the shaft, extreme care must be taken not to bend the shaft. The shaft and worm must remain straight wit hin .002".
16. Inspect the upper race for pits and non conforming surface. Many upper races will crack at the race surface, near the end play adjusting bolt pad. The race must be replaced if any cracks are detected.
17. Inspect both tapered bearings. Replace if worn or pitted.
18. Inspect the sector shaft. Some wear on the outer edges of the two teeth is acceptable. The shaft bearing surface should be smooth with minimal wear. The sector shaft should be replaced if the bearing surface is pitted, rough, or shows signs of excessive wear. The standard shaft measures 1.125" diameter. Replace if less than 1.123" diameter.
19. If the sector housing has pressed-in brass bushings, it is advisable to replace the housing with one that has inserted needle bearings and outer oil seal. The needle bearings are made for a 1.125" diameter shaft. Replace the shaft if it is less than 1.123" diameter. This will provide easier steering, less wear, and an excellent oil seal for the shaft. The brass bushings should always be replaced if the needle bearing is not being used. Press in the modern type outer oil seal. This is the only way to prevent oil from seeping out from around the sector shaft.
20. Thoroughly clean and paint the gear box housing and sector shaft housing.

STEERING

Assembling 2-Tooth Gear Box

1. Check that the screwdriver slotted centralization rivet can be moved to the right and left of center. The screwdriver slot in the rivet usually remains in the straight vertical position. Readjustment is usually not necessary unless the worm gear or sector shaft has been replaced. Place the slot in the straight vertical position to begin assembly. Check that the upper race will slip easily into the upper part of the housing. If necessary, open the housing slit (with wedge or chisel) enough to allow the race to slide into the housing without difficulty.
2. Apply a small amount of Lubriplate on a tapered bearing and drop it into place on the lower bearing race.

NOTE
Do not use any lithium grease in the steering assembly. The gear box will be filled with 600W oil after assembly and installation in the car.

3. Slip a tapered bearing and the upper race over the top of the steering shaft and down onto the worm gear. Place the worm gear and shaft into the housing, seating the worm gear on the lower bearing, and the upper race pushed into the housing, seated against the upper bearing. Be sure to line up the adjusting pad on the race with the adjusting bolt hole in the top of the housing.
4. On top of the housing, screw in the steering shaft end play adjusting bolt (7/16-20 X 1-7/16") and jam nut. Screw in the adjusting bolt [9/16 socket] while checking end play of the steering shaft, then back off 1/8 turn.

CAUTION
Adjusting this bolt too tight after end play has been removed can cause the upper race to crack. This adjustment can only be correctly made with the column housing removed from the steering shaft.

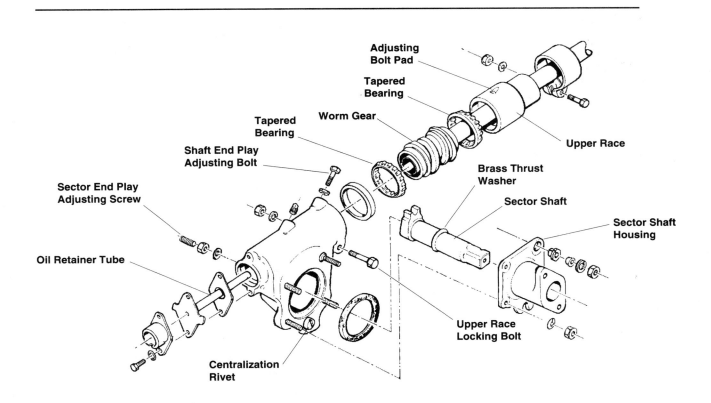

STEERING

5. Tighten the jam nut [5/8 wrench] against the housing. Recheck for end play. Check for free rotation (no binding) of the steering shaft. Repeat steps 4 and 5 if necessary.
6. Insert and tighten the upper race locking bolt, lock washer, and nut (3/8-24 X 1-15/16")[9/16 socket].

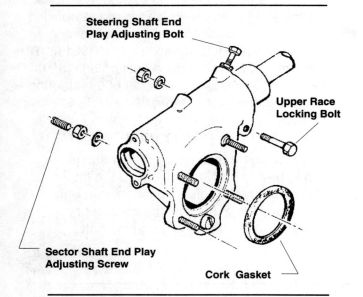

7. Apply a light coat of lubrication on the top surface of the sector housing cork gasket. Place the gasket in the round recess in the steering gear housing. The lubrication on the cork gasket will allow the sector housing to rotate on the gasket during the following adjustments.

8. Slip the brass thrust washer over the sector shaft, pushing it up against the 2-tooth casting. Apply a light coat of Lubriplate on the sector shaft and set the shaft into the gear housing.
9. Place the sector shaft housing over the sector shaft and housing studs. Insert the sector adjusting sleeve and cone over the upper right housing stud. Position the slit in the adjusting sleeve so that it faces the adjusting bolt on top of the housing.

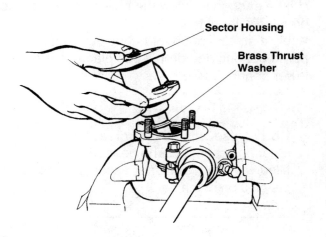

10. Apply lock washers and nuts (3/8-24) on each of the four studs. Before tightening the four (4) nuts, make sure the sector end play adjusting screw (on back side of housing) has not been installed. Securely tighten all four mounting nuts [9/16 wrench].
11. Grind off any projections from the end of the sector shaft end play adjusting screw. Screw in the sector shaft end play adjusting screw (9/16-18 X 15/16"), jam nut [3/4 wrench], and locking washer. Grab the end of the sector shaft and move it in and out while making the adjustment. Screw the end play adjusting screw in until the sector shaft end play is removed. Hold the screw in place while tightening down the jam nut [3/4 wrench].
12. After adjustment, rotate the steering shaft from stop-to-stop to ensure free travel with no binding. Repeat steps 11 and 12 above if necessary.

STEERING

Sector Worm Mesh Adjustment

The following adjustment is made to align and properly mesh the sector teeth with the worm gear. To correctly detect lateral play while making this adjustment, the pitman arm must be securely attached to the sector shaft.

1. Install the pitman arm on the end of the sector shaft. Install the special bolt (7/16-20 X 1-15/16) and nut [5/8 wrench]. Securely tighten to remove all movement between the sector shaft and the pitman arm.
2. Rotate the steering shaft from the left stop to the right stop, while counting the number of turns on the shaft (approximately 3 full turns). Rotate the shaft counter clockwise 1-1/2 turns (to center of rotation). Line up the keyway, next to the threaded end of the shaft, with the end play adjusting bolt on top of the gear box housing. This will be referred to as center position.
3. With the steering shaft at center position, rotate the pitman arm back and forth to check for play in the sector to worm mesh. This adjustment is made with the adjusting sleeve nut, located on the upper-right sector housing stud. This is an eccentric sleeve that moves the position of the sector housing, thereby changing the position of the sector teeth to the worm gear. This adjustment is made to remove all lateral play in the sector shaft when positioned at center travel.

   a. Loosen the three (3) housing cover nuts 1/4 turn [5/8 wrench].
   b. Loosen the housing cover adjusting nut 1/4 turn [5/8 wrench].
   c. Turn the eccentric adjusting sleeve nut [7/8 wrench] clockwise very gradually while rotating the pitman arm back and forth to detect sector play. Stop adjustment when all play in the sector shaft is eliminated. Do not adjust beyond zero movement point. It may be necessary to back off the adjustment and re-approach the adjustment again. Always approach and finish the adjustment in a clockwise direction.
   d. After adjustment, tighten the housing cover adjusting nut first, then tighten the other three housing nuts.
   e. Rotate the steering shaft from stop-to-stop to ensure free travel with no binding. If binding is felt at any point, repeat steps a through d until correct adjustment is made. The following sector tooth centralization adjustment may be necessary to obtain correct sector worm adjustment.

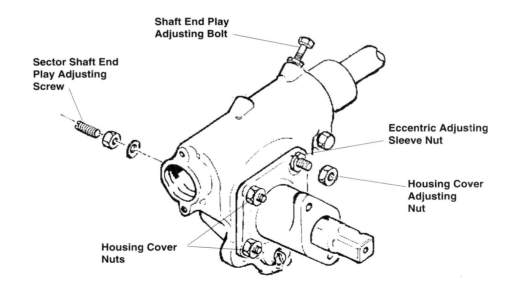

STEERING

Centralization of Sector to Worm

This adjustment centers the sector teeth to the worm. The sector teeth must be centered on the worm for correct sector worm mesh adjustment.

1. Rotate the steering shaft clockwise to the stop position, then back 1-1/2 turns. Line up the shaft keyway with the end play adjusting bolt on top of the gear box housing (center position).
2. Rotate the steering shaft 1/2 turn clockwise from center. Shake the pitman arm to check the amount of play. Rotate the steering shaft back to center position and then counter clockwise 1/2 turn from center. Shake the pitman arm to check the amount of play.
   The following adjustment is made to equalize the amount of play on both sides of center.
   a. Return the steering shaft back to center. Loosen the four (4) housing nuts 1/4 turn.
   b. Turn the centering adjusting rivet to the right (clockwise) 1/8 turn if more play was detected to the right of center. Turn the adjusting rivet to the left (counter clockwise) 1/8 turn if more play was detected to the left of center. Retighten all four housing nuts after adjustment.
   c. Repeat steps 1 and 2 above to check centering.
3. The sector worm mesh adjustment must be repeated after this adjustment.

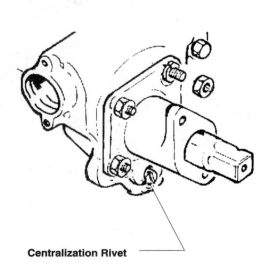

Centralization Rivet

Steering Column Housing Repairs

Steering column parts include the column housing, control rod quadrant, upper bushing, control rods (spark and gas), and the control rod springs and arms. The steering column parts can only be repaired or replaced with the column housing removed from the steering shaft.

Removing Control Rods and Upper Bushing

1. The control rods are held in by the spring loaded control rod arms. Soft pins attach the arms to the control rod. DO NOT ATTEMPT TO DRILL OUT THE PINS. The pins can be easily sheared. Attach a 3/16 socket [1/4" drive] to a 6-inch extension. Place the socket against the end of the control rod and knock the control rod through the control arm, shearing off the pin. Once started, it may be necessary to use a drift punch to fully drive the control rod through the control arm. The arm and spring can then be removed from the rod. A punch can be used to remove the remaining pieces of pin from the arm.

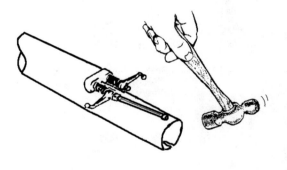

STEERING

2. Pull the control rods out of the upper bushing.
3. The upper bushing may be held in place with a screw on each side of the control rod quadrant. The screws must be removed before driving out the upper bushing. If no screws are present, the upper bushing is a press fit.
   Using a 1/2" X 48" steel rod, drive out the upper bushing from the bottom end of the column housing. The upper bushing is made of pot metal and may break during removal.
4. Inspect the column housing for cracks. Cracks will normally appear where the control rods protrude from the housing. Weld all cracks. Clean and repaint the housing.

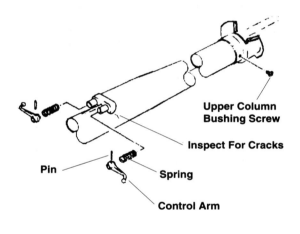

Installing Control Rods and Upper Bushing

1. Slip both control rods into the upper bushing before installing the bushing into the column. Then slip a rubber sleeve (3/8" I.D. X 1/2" long) on each control rod, approximately 14 inches down from the top. The rubber sleeves will prevent the control rods from rattling against the steering shaft. DO NOT LEAVE THEM OFF.
2. Insert the control rods through the upper end of the column. Before the upper bushing is placed into the column, the control rods can be sighted and guided into the tubes in the column.
3. After the control rods have been inserted into the tubes, push the upper bushing into the column housing. Some bushings are held in with a screw on each side of the column. Others are made to be driven in (tight fit), requiring no screws. When driving in the upper bushing, align the two control rod holes so they are at the top front side of the column.

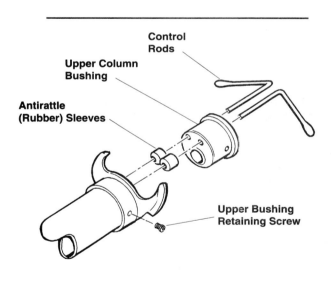

Service and Repair

STEERING

4. Slip the control arms on the control rod (with no spring) to check alignment of the control arm pin hole and pin fit to the control rod.
5. File or grind a bevel on one end of the pin. Slip the pin through both control arm and rod to ensure everything fits without a struggle.
6. Remove the pin and control arm from the end of the rod. Now place the spring and control arm over the rod and use a 7/16" nut driver to push the control arm up to the pin hole. Drop in the pin.

NOTE

The control arm ball on the spark control rod faces down. The control arm ball for the accelerator control rod faces up.

The column is now ready to be slipped onto the steering shaft.

Installing Column on Steering Shaft
(Final Assembly)

1. Place the column clamp over the steering shaft and slide it down to the steering gear housing.
2. Slide the column down over the steering shaft, placing the top end of the shaft through the upper bushing. The bushing is lined with a cotton webbing material. Carefully guide the end of the steering shaft through the bushing. The lower column will slip over the upper race shaft. The column clamp fits over the column, with the bolt hole on the bottom of the column. Insert the clamp bolt (5/16-24 X 1-7/8") lock washer, and nut [1/2" socket]. Tighten the clamp bolt, securing the column housing to the gear box.
3. The end plate should be replaced with the new end plate with oil retainer tube. This will prevent oil from leaking into the wiring harness. Smear a little Permatex gasket sealer on the end plate gasket and place the end plate and gasket in the end of the steering assembly.

7/16 Nut Driver

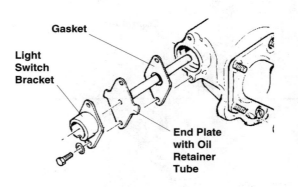

STEERING

4. Place the light switch bracket on the end plate and attach both end plate and light switch bracket with two (2) bolts (1/4-20 X 5/8") and lock washers [7/16 socket].

NOTE

The steering wheel and horn rod can be installed on the steering column now or after the assembly has been installed back in the car.

5. Place a 3/16 X 3/4" woodruff key in the key way groove and insert the steering wheel.
6. Screw on the special thin 5/8-18 nut to hold the steering wheel to the shaft. This only needs to be a snug fit. Do not overtighten. Due to the thin wall at the end of the shaft, the threads could be damaged if overtightened. (It's possible to twist the threaded end off the shaft.) Use "Loctite" rather than over-torquing.
7. Insert the horn rod through the center of the shaft. Check that horn rod rotates freely in steering shaft. On the end of the horn rod, insert the spring, light switch spider, and retainer clip.

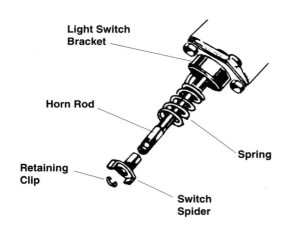

7-Tooth Sector Steering Assembly Overhaul

1. If not already completed, remove the horn rod by pressing up on the spring loaded spider to remove the retaining clip at the end of the column.
2. Pull the horn rod out of the column.
3. Remove the steering wheel nut [3/4 socket] and remove the steering wheel.

NOTE

The steering wheel is on a splined shaft. A steering wheel puller may be needed to release the steering wheel.

4. On the back side of the gear box, remove the three (3) housing cover bolts [7/16 socket] and lift off the housing cover.

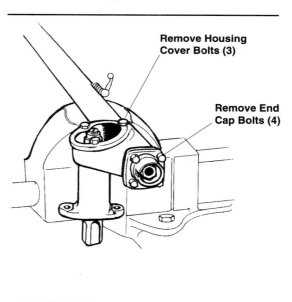

Service and Repair

STEERING

5. Drain the oil from the housing and lift out the 7-tooth sector and thrust washer. Do not misplace the thrust washer. New thrust washers are not available.

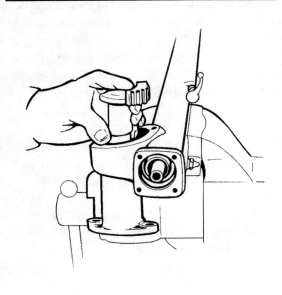

6. Remove the four (4) bolts at the end of the column [7/16 socket], and pull out the lower bearing assembly. Retain the brass shims that come off when the bearing assembly is removed. Remove the oil seal retainer nut (5/8 socket) from the center of the bearing assembly. Remove and discard the oil seal.

7. Remove the steering shaft and two (2) thrust bearings from the bottom end of the column.

NOTE

The upper column bushing (woven webbing) may be tight on the shaft. If necessary, screw the steering wheel nut back on the shaft, just far enough to cover the threads. With a brass mallet, knock the shaft through the upper column bushing. Take extreme care not to damage or distort the upper shaft threads or the hole in the center of the shaft.

8. The control rods are held in by the spring-loaded control rod arms. Soft pins attach the arms to the control rod. DO NOT ATTEMPT TO DRILL OUT THE PINS. The pins are soft and will easily shear off by hitting the end of the rod with a hammer. The arm and spring can then be removed from the rod. A punch can be used to remove the remaining pieces of pin from the arm.

9. Pull the control rods out of the upper column bushing.

10. The upper column bushing is held in place with a screw on each side of the control rod quadrant. The screws must be removed before driving out the upper bushing. Using a 1/2" X 48" steel rod, drive out the upper column bushing from the bottom end of the column housing. The upper column bushing is made of pot metal and may break during removal.

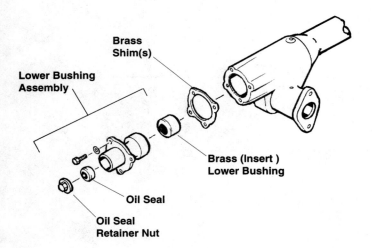

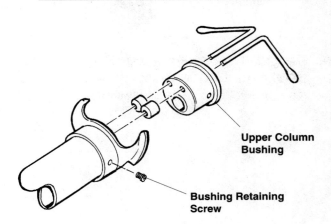

STEERING

11. After the upper column bushing has been removed, the upper shaft bushing can be removed. Insert a 1/2" X 48" steel rod through the top end of the column and drive out the brass upper shaft bushing.

   NOTE

   Removal and replacement of the brass upper shaft bushing may not be necessary. Replace this bushing only if extremely worn. Installation of the upper shaft bushing can be difficult. Accurate alignment between the upper and lower shaft bushings is critical. Misalignment can cause binding of the steering shaft.

   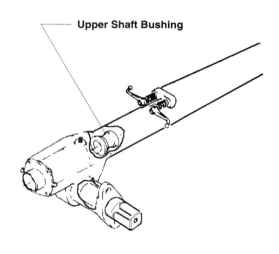

12. Clean and repaint the housing. If needed, replate or replace the two control rods. Inspect the upper bushing. Replace if necessary.

Assembling 7-Tooth Steering Gear

1. Inspect the end of the steering shaft below the worm gear. The end of the shaft rides in the lower shaft bushing and must be smooth. If grooves are worn into the shaft, this end of the shaft must be turned down on a lathe and a new bushing reamed to fit (lower bushing assembly). The shaft can be turned down to 5/8" O.D. minimum.

   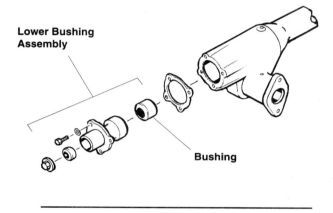

2. Remove the two bushings in the sector shaft housing and replace with new bushings.

   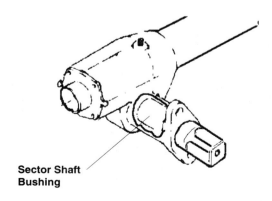

Service and Repair

STEERING

3. Inspect the 7-tooth sector shaft. If the shaft is pitted or worn, the sector must be replaced.
4. If the upper shaft bushing is to be replaced, insert the bushing from the lower end of the column and drive it in until it seats.

NOTE

Check the fit of the upper shaft bushing on the steering shaft before installing in the column.

5. To reassemble the steering assembly, slip a new thrust bearing over the end of the steering shaft and slide it down against the worm gear.
6. Insert the steering shaft with thrust bearing through the bottom end of the column and through the shaft upper bushing. Push the shaft up into the column until the thrust bearing rest against the upper shaft bushing.
7. Install a new bushing in the lower bushing assembly. Ream the bushing to fit the lower end of the steering shaft.
8. Insert a thrust bearing against the bottom end of the worm gear. Insert the lower bushing assembly with three (3) brass shim washers under the lower bushing assembly. Attach lower bearing assembly with four (4) bolts (1/4-28 X 21/32") and lock washers [7/16 socket].

NOTE

When installing the lower bushing assembly, make certain that the oil hole that is drilled into it at an angle has its open end toward the top of the steering gear housing.

9. Steering shaft end play must be checked at this point of assembly. With the lower shaft bushing assembly bolted in place, grab the top end of the steering shaft and try moving it up and down in the column. Add or delete brass shims from under the lower shaft bushing assembly to adjust out steering shaft end play. With correct adjustment, the steering shaft should rotate freely, with no binding and no end play.

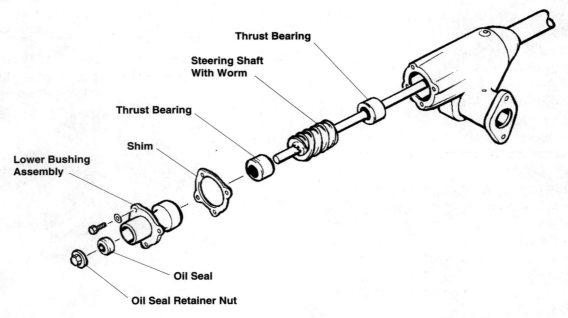

Steering Shaft Assembly

Service and Repair

STEERING

10. Slip both control rods into the upper bushing before installing the bushing into the column. Slip a rubber sleeve (3/8" I.D. X 1/2"long) on each control rod, approximately 14 inches down from the top. The rubber sleeves will prevent the control rods from rattling against the steering shaft. DO NOT LEAVE THEM OFF.

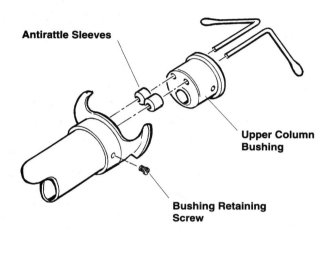

11. Insert the control rods through the upper end of the column. Before the upper bushing is placed into the column, the control rods can be sighted and guided into the tubes in the column.
12. After the control rods have been inserted into the tubes, push the upper bushing into the column housing. The bushing is held in with a screw on each side of the column. When driving in the upper bushing, align the two control rod holes so they are at the top front side of the column. Insert the two (2) side retaining screws.
13. Before installing the springs and control arms on the ends of the control rods, check the fit of the new control arm pins. Slide the control arm on the end of the spark and throttle control rod and insert the pin, making sure the pin alignment is correct on both the arm and the rod. After the pin fit check, remove the control arm from the rod ends.

14. Insert the springs over the end of the rods. Use a 7/16" nut driver (this really makes it easy) to push the control arms up to the pin hole.

NOTE
The control arm ball on the spark control rod faces down. The control arm ball for the accelerator control rod faces up.

15. Line up the control arm and rod pin holes and drop in the pin.

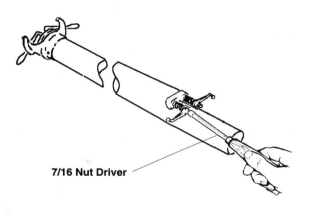

16. Place the steering wheel and steering wheel nut on the upper splined shaft. Tighten the nut just enough to hold the steering wheel tight on the splined shaft. Do not overtighten. The threaded end can be twisted off.

Service and Repair

STEERING

17. Slip the sector thrust washer over the sector shaft, with the grooves in the washer towards the toothed end of the sector. Place the sector shaft into the housing and mesh the sector teeth with the worm gear.

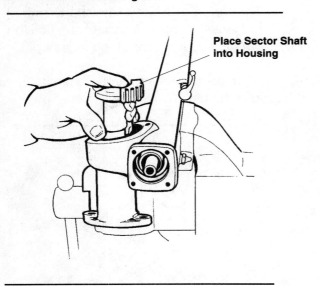

Place Sector Shaft into Housing

18. Loosen the sector thrust screw lock nut [3/4 wrench] and screw out all adjustment of the thrust screw.
19. Install the housing cover and gasket with three (3) bolts (1/4-28 X 21/32") and lock washers [7/16 socket].

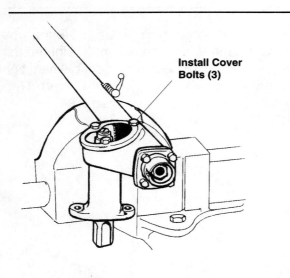

Install Cover Bolts (3)

20. Screw in the sector shaft end play adjusting screw. Grab the end of the sector shaft and move it in and out while making the adjustment. Screw the end play adjusting screw in until the sector shaft end play is removed. Hold the screw in place while tightening down the jam nut (1/2-20)[3/4 wrench].

NOTE
Steering shaft end play and sector shaft end play are the only two adjustments that can be made to the 7-tooth steering assembly.

21. Check sector/worm play. There is no adjustment for this, but now is the time to check it. If it is out of tolerance, the 7-tooth sector and worm gear will need to be replaced. The sector and worm gear should be replaced as a matched pair for best results.
    a. Sector/worm play is measured as backlash. The backlash is measured at the outer circumference of the steering wheel. Temporarily attach the pitman arm to the end of the sector shaft. Ensure there is no play in the sector shaft to pitman arm mating.
    b. Rotate the steering wheel to center travel (approximately 1-1/2 turns from either stop).
    c. Grab the end of the pitman arm and hold it firmly to prevent it from turning.
    d. Rotate the steering wheel in either direction and measure the free travel (before the pitman arm moves) on the outer circumference of the steering wheel. If free travel exceeds 1 to 1-1/2 inches, replace the sector shaft. Make sure both end play adjustments have been properly made before checking back lash.
    e. Remove the pitman arm from the end of the sector shaft.

STEERING

22. Insert the horn rod through the steering shaft. Check that horn rod rotates freely in steering shaft. At the lower end of the steering column, place a neoprene oil seal over the end of the horn rod. Insert the oil seal retainer nut and screw it into the lower bushing assembly.

NOTE
The oil seal provides a seal around the horn rod, preventing gear lube oil from leaking out around the horn rod. Tightening the retainer nut squeezes the neoprene seal tighter around the horn rod.

23. Over the end of the horn rod, insert the spring, switch spider, and retainer clip.

Replacing 7-Tooth Worm Gear

The lower end of the steering shaft is splined. The worm gear is press fit on the splined shaft.

1. Remove the worm gear retaining ring from the end of the shaft, at the lower end of the worm.
2. Press the worm gear off the shaft and insert a new worm gear (press fit).
3. Insert the gear retaining ring.

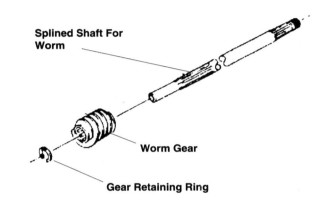

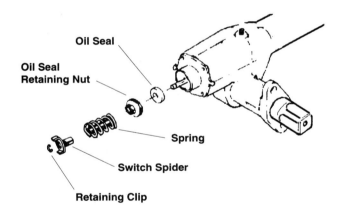

Service and Repair

STEERING

Installing Steering Assembly in Car

The 7-tooth steering assembly and 2-tooth steering assembly can both be installed in the car using the following step-by-step procedure. Installing the steering assembly with the steering wheel and horn rod installed requires removing the brake and clutch pedals from the pedal shaft.

1. Remove both battery cables from the battery and remove the battery.
2. Remove the stoplight linkage and brake rod from the brake pedal arm.

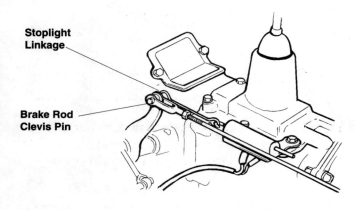

3. From under the car, remove the clutch arm clevis pin and release the clutch arm.

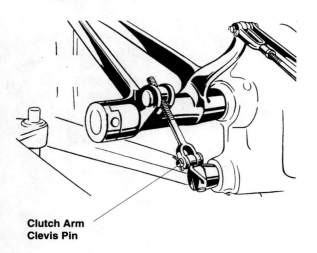

4. Remove the brake and clutch pedals by removing the cotter pin and shaft pin on the end of the pedal shaft. Remove the end cap and slide the two pedals and spring washer (after May 1929) off the pedal shaft.

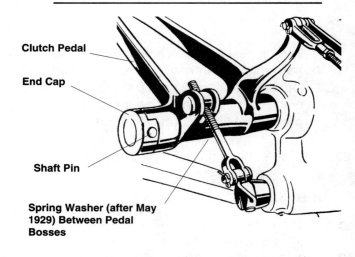

5. Place the steering assembly through the driver's side door and guide the lower end of the column under the firewall and into the engine compartment.
6. Place the sector housing against the frame and insert the two (2) frame bolts (3/8-24 X 1")[9/16 wrench] and castle nuts. Do not tighten the frame bolts until after the column bracket screws have been tightened.

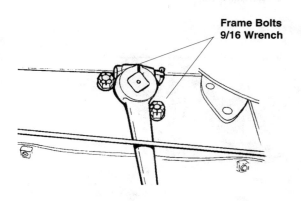

STEERING

7. Wrap the column bracket bushing around the column and attach the bracket with two (2) screws (5/16-24 X 1" Fillister head.)

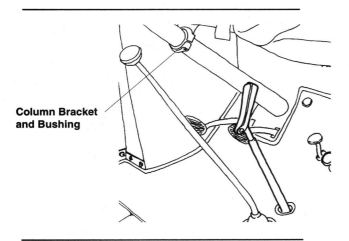

Column Bracket and Bushing

8. Tighten the two (2) frame-to-housing castle nuts and insert cotter pins [9/16 wrench].
9. Place the pitman arm on the end of the sector shaft (pitman arm ball toward inside). Insert the pitman arm bolt and castle nut (7/16-20 X 1-15/16)[5/8 socket]. Firmly tighten and insert cotter pin.

NOTE

The pitman arm <u>must</u> fit tight on the sector shaft. Tighten the pitman arm nut enough to eliminate <u>all</u> movement between the pitman arm and the sector shaft.

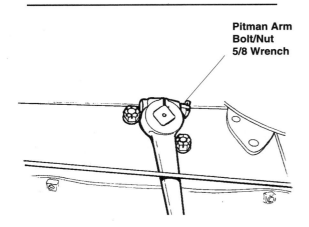

Pitman Arm Bolt/Nut 5/8 Wrench

10. Install the starter motor (3 bolts, 3/8-16 X 1") [9/16 socket].

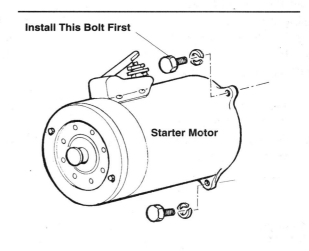

Install This Bolt First

Starter Motor

11. Attach the battery cable and harness wire to the starter switch stud [5/8 wrench].
12. Screw the starter push rod into the starter switch.

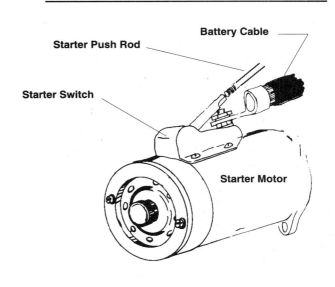

Starter Push Rod
Battery Cable
Starter Switch
Starter Motor

1-313   Service and Repair

STEERING

13. Place the light switch on the end of the steering column. Lock the switch in place with light switch bail wire.

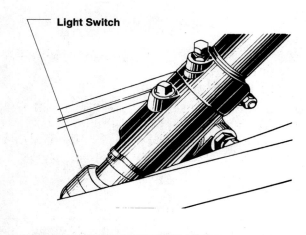

Light Switch

14. Attach the spark and throttle linkage rods to the control arms on the steering column.

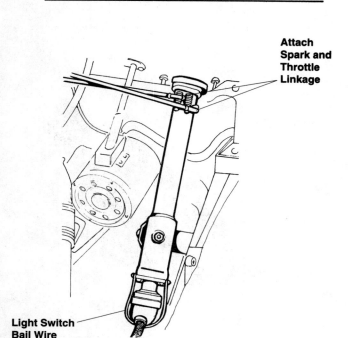

Attach Spark and Throttle Linkage

Light Switch Bail Wire

15. Install the oil filler tube and oil dip stick if previously removed.

16. Attach the drag link to the pitman arm ball (apply grease to the ball before attaching). Screw in the drag link end plug. Turn the steering wheel to the right until the pitman arm ball fully seats in the end of the drag link. Tighten the end plug until full contact is made with the internal spring, and the spring is pressing against the ball cap, then rotate the end plug one more full turn. Insert a cotter pin.

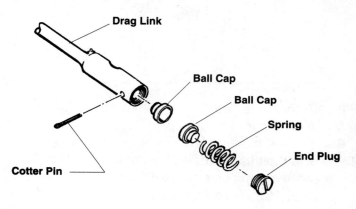

Drag Link, **Ball Cap**, **Ball Cap**, **Spring**, **End Plug**, **Cotter Pin**

17. From inside the car, slide the brake pedal on the pedal shaft. Apply a spring washer and then slide the clutch pedal on the shaft.

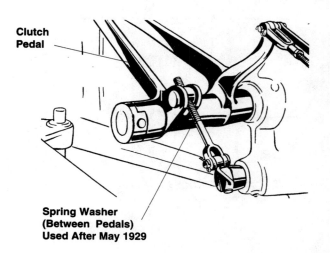

Clutch Pedal

Spring Washer (Between Pedals) Used After May 1929

Service and Repair   1-314

STEERING

18. Attach the pedal shaft end cap and shaft pin. Install a cotter pin in the shaft pin.
19. From under the car attach the clutch arm clevis pin and cotter pin.

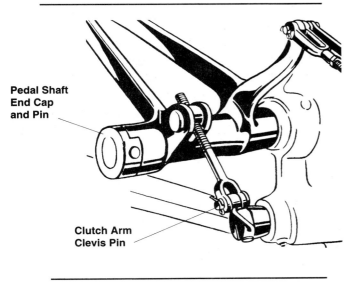

20. Install the brake rod and clevis pin on the brake pedal arm. Attach stop light linkage.

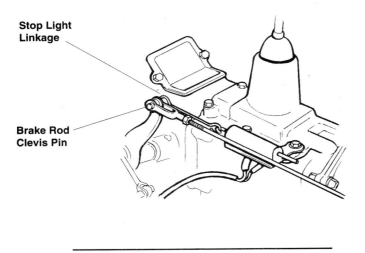

21. Install the battery and attach both battery cables. Install battery hold down brackets.
22. Install both floor board sections with 12 flat head screws (12-24 X 1-1/8").
23. Place the shifting tower metal plate over the shifter and attach it to the floor boards with the three floor board clips.
24. Install floor mats and screw on the accelerator pedal.
25. Slip on the shifting tower boot and emergency handle boot.
26. Screw on the shifter knob.
27. From under the hood, remove the oil filler plug on the steering gear box (1/4" pipe plug) and fill with 600W gear lube. DO NOT USE GREASE. The 7-tooth sector gear box takes 7-3/4 oz. The 2-tooth sector gear box takes 4-1/2 oz.

NOTE
When filling the gear box with gear lube, raise the front wheels off the ground and slowly rotate the steering wheel from stop to stop. This will allow the heavy oil to run through the gears easier.

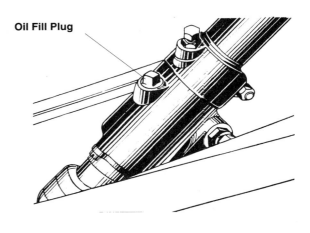

Service and Repair

STEERING WHEEL

Two different steering wheels were used during Model A production. The 1928/1929 steering wheel has a 17-1/2" diameter. The 1930/1931 steering wheel has a 17" diameter and the horn/light switch is recessed into the center of the steering wheel, unlike the 1928/1929 that is fully exposed. The 1928/1929 steering wheel is a splined fit to the steering shaft when used with the 7-tooth sector steering gear box. In Jan/Feb 1929 Ford test-installed a few 2-tooth sector gear boxes (made by GEMMER MFG), and then continued to use up the supply of 7-tooth sector gear boxes through 1929 to about Feb 1930. The 2-tooth gear boxes made by both Ford and GEMMER were used from Jan 1930 through the end of production. This information on steering gear boxes is relevant to the different steering wheels. The 7-tooth sector gear box always had a splined steering wheel, and the 2-tooth sector gear box always had a tapered/woodruff keyed steering wheel. So the early 1929 2-tooth (GEMMER) steering wheels were a tapered/woodruff key fit to the steering shaft. The 7-tooth sector steering gear boxes that were carried over into early 1930 used 1930 steering wheels that were splined fit to the steering shaft. All 2-tooth sector gear boxes used from 1930 through 1931 used the 1930 style steering wheel with the tapered /woodruff key fit to the steering shaft.

The tapered/woodruff keyed steering shaft used on all 2-tooth sector gear boxes is smaller in diameter than the steering shaft used on the 7-tooth gear boxes. Because of the smaller diameter shaft (thinner wall), the steering wheel nut threads on the shaft can be easily twisted off. Use caution when applying the steering wheel nut on the tapered /keyed shaft. Do not overtighten. Use LOCTITE and only snug down on the nut.

The horn rod must be removed for access to the steering wheel nut. A steering wheel puller is usually needed to remove the steering wheel from the shaft.

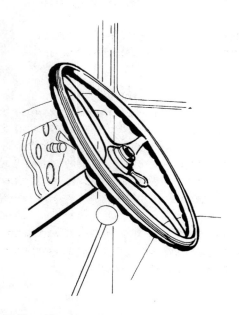

1928/1929 Steering Wheel

1930/1931 Steering Wheel

STEERING WHEEL

Removing Steering Wheel

To remove the horn rod and steering wheel from a closed car (coupe, sedan or pickup) requires removing the entire steering column from the car. There is not sufficient room to pull the horn rod from the steering column. See "Steering" section for removal of the steering column. The top can be lowered on "open" cars for removal of the horn rod.

1. Release the bail wire from the light switch (push bail wire down) at the end of the steering column. Pull the light switch bulb from the end of the steering column.
2. Push up slightly on the switch spider to remove the retaining clip, spider, and spring from the end of the horn rod.

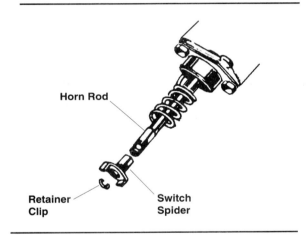

3. Pull the horn rod from the center of the steering wheel.

NOTE
When the horn rod is removed, oil may run out the horn rod hole at the end of the column. Allow the oil to drain before continuing.

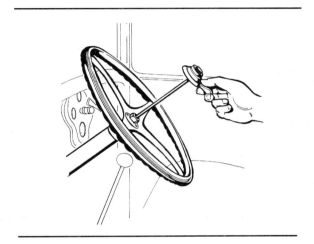

NOTE
The head room in coupes and pickups is not sufficient to allow removal of the horn rod and steering wheel. The steering column must be removed to remove the horn rod and/or steering wheel.

4. Remove the steering wheel nut [15/16 socket] and remove the steering wheel.

NOTE
In 1928 and 1929 steering wheels were splined to the shaft. In 1930 and 1931 steering wheels were keyed to the shaft. A steering wheel puller and Liquid Wrench may be necessary to pop the steering wheel loose from the shaft.

5. Some cracks in the steering wheel can be filled and repaired with body putty and then painted with a black enamel paint.

STOPLIGHT SWITCH

The stoplight switch on the 1928/1929 Model A is mounted on the side of the transmission shifting tower. A special clevis pin is used to attach the brake rod to the pedal. A hook on the stoplight switch pull rod clips over the head of the special clevis pin. When the brake pedal is depressed the short link from the pedal to the switch pulls the switch contacts closed. The mounting holes on the switch are elongated to allow some adjustment in the engagement of the stoplight switch. This switch is not intended as a repairable item, although, tabs on the back side of the cover can be bent up to allow removal of the cover and access to the switch contacts. The two green wires from the main wiring harness are attached to the two (2) screws on the bottom side of the switch.

The stoplight switch on the 1930/1931 Model A is mounted on the back side of the center cross member, just above the brake cross shaft. A special actuating rod from the brake pedal has an extension beyond the cross shaft attaching clevis that keeps the stoplight switch actuating rod pushed in. In this position the switch contacts are held open. Since the switch actuating rod is spring loaded, when the brake pedal is depressed, the brake rod pulls forward, allowing the switch rod to extend out, closing the switch contacts. There is no adjustment for this switch.

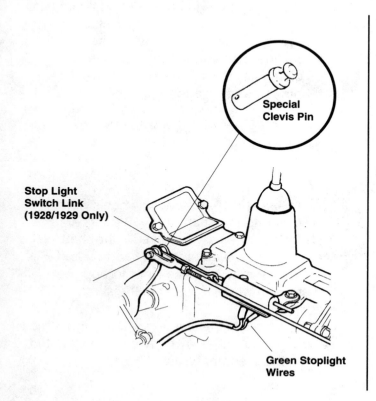

1928/1929 Stoplight Switch Mounting

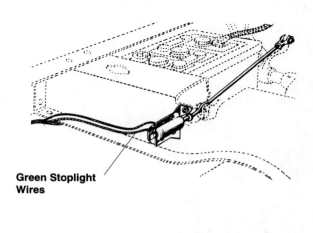

1930/1931 Stoplight Switch Mounting

TERMINAL BOX

The terminal box is the electrical junction between the instrument panel wiring harness and the engine compartment harness. The two brass wing nuts (10-32) that hold the cover on the box are screwed to the two terminal posts for wire connections. These two wing nuts are hot (6 volt potential) at all times. These two terminal posts are an extension of the ammeter. Electrically the ammeter is placed between these two terminal posts. It is essential that a rubber grommet be placed around the ignition cable to prevent the cable from shorting against either terminal post. The terminal box is mounted to the firewall with four (4) screws (10-32 X 3/8") from the back side of the firewall. See the "Wiring" section for wire connections inside the terminal box.

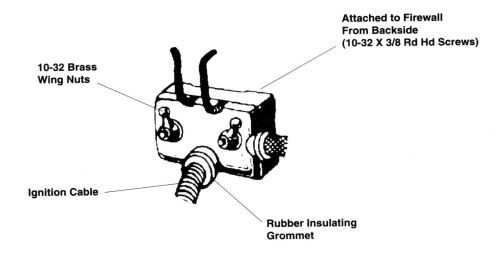

THROWOUT BEARING

The clutch throwout bearing is located inside the bell housing on the front end of the transmission. The bearing (Bower P/N 2065) is pressed on a slider housing that slides on the transmission front bearing retainer. When the clutch pedal is depressed, the throwout bearing is pressed against the pressure plate fingers, thereby disengaging the clutch plate. Since the pressure plate is bolted to and rotates with the flywheel, the throwout bearing provides a rotating bearing surface to press in on the rotating pressure plate fingers.

There is 1100 ft. lbs. of pressure is applied against the throwout bearing when it is engaged with the pressure plate. If a loud squeal is heard when the clutch is engaged, indicates that the throw out bearing is defective and should be replaced immediately. The throwout bearing is rotating at the same RPM as the engine when the clutch is engaged. A defective throwout bearing could possibly overheat, as it is rotating at 1200 to 2000 RPM with 1100 ft. lbs. of pressure applied. A defective throwout bearing could cause serious damage to the clutch assembly. The throwout bearing should be replaced any time the engine or transmission is removed for repairs.

The grease fitting on the throwout bearing collar housing (viewed through the inspection plate on top of the bell housing) <u>does not</u> lubricate the throwout bearing. This grease fitting lubricates the throwout bearing slider on the transmission front bearing retainer. To replace the throwout bearing requires removing the differential/rear end assembly and transmission, or removing the engine.

Removing Throwout Bearing-By *Removing Rear End Assembly*

1. Remove both sections of the front floor boards [12 flathead screws].
2. Remove the clevis pin attaching the rod at the bottom of the emergency brake handle.
3. Remove the six (6) bolts [1/2" socket] and lock washers on top of the shifting tower and lift the tower off the transmission housing.
4. Remove the brake pedal clevis pin, disconnecting the brake actuating rod and stoplight switch.
5. Remove the clutch pedal clevis pin, disconnecting the clutch arm.
6. Tap out the pedal shaft collar pin and remove the pedal shaft collar. Slide the clutch and brake pedals and spring washer off the shaft.

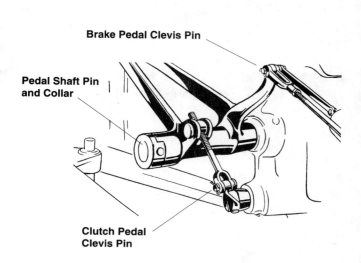

THROWOUT BEARING

7. Remove the transmission drain plug (bottom of transmission) and drain all oil. Replace the drain plug.
8. Place a floor jack under the transmission for support.
9. The transmission can be removed from the car by removing the differential with drive shaft (rear end assembly). To remove the rear end assembly follow the procedures for "Rear End Assembly Removal" steps 1 through 11A, page 1-88.
10. After removing the rear end assembly, disconnect the front radius ball under the bell housing.

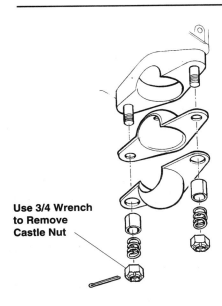

Use 3/4 Wrench to Remove Castle Nut

11. Remove the eleven (11) bell housing to flywheel housing bolts [9/16 socket] and separate the bell housing from the flywheel housing. The splined transmission drive shaft will separate from the clutch assembly. The complete transmission assembly with bell housing can be rolled out from under the car on a floor jack.

12. Release the throwout bearing spring and slide the throwout bearing hub assembly (with throwout bearing) off the bearing retainer sleeve.

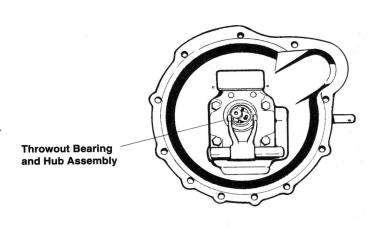

Throwout Bearing and Hub Assembly

13. Thoroughly clean the sliding shaft for the throwout bearing and the bearing housing assembly. Replace the throwout bearing (p/n Bower 2065). The bearing is a press fit on the hub.
14. Lightly grease the housing and reinsert the throwout bearing and slider assembly. Attach the retaining spring. Make sure the slider assembly slides smoothly on the shaft.

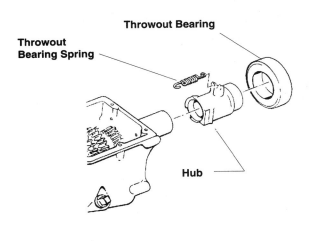

Throwout Bearing Spring, **Throwout Bearing**, **Hub**

Service and Repair

THROWOUT BEARING

Installing Transmission w/Throwout Bearing - *With Rear End Assembly Removed*

1. Place the two sliding gears in neutral position. Place the transmission and bell housing on a floor jack and slide it under the car.
2. Raise the transmission/bell housing level with the flywheel housing.
3. Remove the bell housing cover plate so the splined transmission drive shaft can be viewed.
4. Viewing through the bell housing top cover plate, align the transmission drive shaft spline with the clutch spline. Push the transmission drive shaft into the clutch spline.
5. Install the eleven (11) bell housing to flywheel bolts (3/8-16 X 1")[9/16 socket] and lock washers.
6. Attach the radius ball under the bell housing.

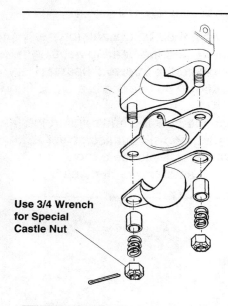

Use 3/4 Wrench for Special Castle Nut

7. Install the rear end assembly by following step-by-step instructions under "Installing Rear End Assembly" beginning on page 1-97, steps 1 through 5B.
8. Remove the temporary cardboard cover from the top of the transmission and pour in 1-1/2 pints of 600W gear oil. Do not fill above the oil fill hole.

9. Place a transmission cover gasket on top of the transmission. Install the shifting tower, using six (6) bolts and lock washers (4 each 5/16-18 X 3/4, 2 each 5/16-18 X 1-3/8")[1/2" socket]. Make sure the shifting forks seat correctly in the two sliding gear collars.

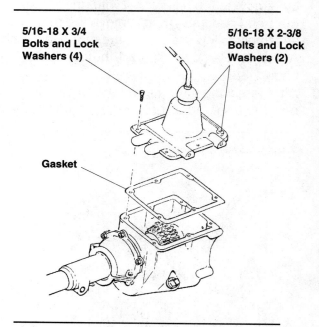

5/16-18 X 3/4 Bolts and Lock Washers (4)

5/16-18 X 2-3/8 Bolts and Lock Washers (2)

Gasket

10. Attach the emergency brake actuating rod to the emergency brake handle with a clevis pin. Lock with a cotter pin.
11. Slide the brake and clutch pedals on the pedal shaft, inserting a thin spring washer between the two pedals (after May 1929).
12. Install the pedal shaft collar on the end of the shaft and insert the collar pin. Insert a cotter pin through the end of the collar pin.

THROWOUT BEARING

13. Attach the clutch arm to the clutch pedal adjusting yoke with a clevis pin. Lock with a cotter pin.

NOTE

Adjust the clutch pedal with the pedal adjusting yoke for 1" free pedal travel before the clutch engages.

14. Attach the brake actuating rod and stoplight linkage to the brake pedal arm with a clevis pin. Lock with a cotter pin.

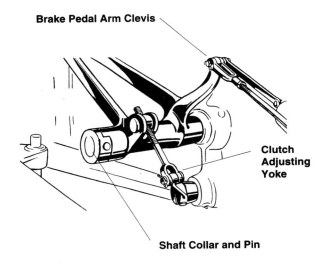

15. From inside the car apply a small amount of grease to the clutch throwout bearing. This grease fitting is accessible under the inspection plate located in front of the emergency brake handle (on top of the bell housing). Install the inspection plate (two screws, 5/16-18 X 3/8).

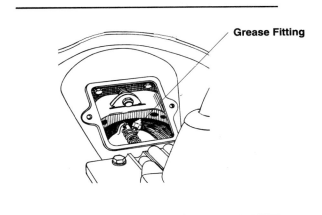

16. Install the front floor boards, shift lever plate, and floor mat. Secure the floor board with twelve (12) flat head screws (12-24 X 1-1/8") and cup washers.

17. Slip on the shifting tower boot and emergency handle boot. Screw the knob on top of the shifting tower.

Service and Repair

TIMING GEAR

The timing gear is made of fiber composition and mates with the steel crank gear. This provides a quiet gear mesh but creates wear of the fiber timing gear. The timing gear requires a .003" to .004" backlash clearance. A knocking sound similar to a rod knock can be an indication of a loose or worn timing gear (in excess of .010" backlash). The timing gear is located behind the timing gear cover at the front of the engine. A loose timing gear can be detected by removing the timing pin from the cover, reinserting the pin backwards into the pin hole, and pressing the pin hard against the timing gear (while the engine is running). If the gear is loose, the knocking sound will nearly stop when the timing pin is pressed against it.

The timing gear can be replaced without removing the engine or radiator. The gear can be accessed by removing the fan belt and timing gear cover. The timing gear nut is a standard right hand thread.

1. Remove the harness wires from the cutout. Tape the ends of the wires to prevent shorting.

2. Loosen the generator mounting bolt and nut [3/4 socket]. If a generator holding bracket is installed, loosen the holding bracket bolt [9/16 socket] on the timing gear cover and swing the bracket away from the generator. Push the generator toward the engine to release belt tension.

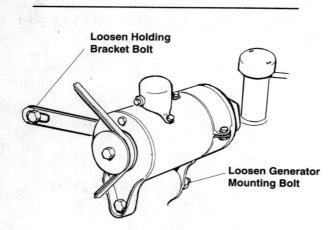

3. Slip the belt off the generator pulley and then off the crank pulley. The belt can now be removed from the fan pulley.

4. Place a floor jack under the engine pan for support. Remove the front two (2) motor mount bolts (3/4 wrench) and lock washers.

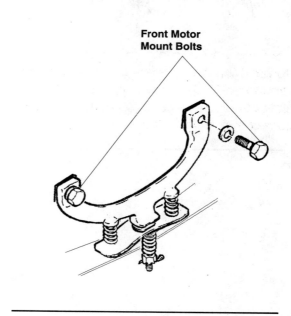

TIMING GEAR

5. Remove the front four (4) pan bolts and the seven (7) bolts [9/16 socket] and lock washers from the front timing gear cover and remove the cover. The front timing gear cover is under slight spring tension. After removing the cover, remove the spring plunger and spring recessed in the back side of the cover.

6. Remove the two (2) bolts [5/8 socket] and lock washers from the side timing gear cover and remove the side cover.

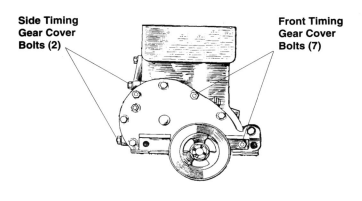

7. Remove the timing gear nut (standard right hand thread.) The timing gear is held onto the end of the cam shaft with two steel pins. The gear can be pulled off the pins.

8. Place a new timing gear on the end of the cam shaft and push the gear onto the two aligning pins.

CAUTION

The two timing gear aligning pins are slightly off center. The timing gear will only align with the two pins one way. If the gear does not align precisely with the pins, rotate the gear 180° and reinsert. Forcing could cause damage.

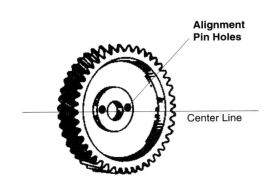

9. Carefully align the timing gear mark with the crank gear mark. Firmly tighten the timing gear nut.

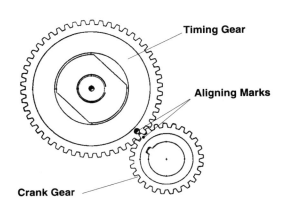

Service and Repair

TIMING GEAR

10. Insert the asbestos rope gasket into the bottom of the timing gear cover.

11. Insert the thrust spring into the camshaft thrust plunger and place it into the timing gear cover recess.

NOTE
Check the thrust spring for correct compression tension (35 - 38 lbs).

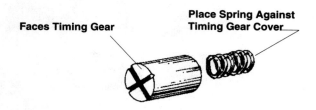

12. Apply a thin coat of Permatex gasket sealer to the timing gear cover gasket and apply to timing gear cover.

13. Bolt the front timing gear cover in place with seven (7) 3/8" dome head bolts [9/16 socket] and lock washers.

14. Install the side timing gear cover using two (2) 7/16 hex dome head bolts [5/8 socket]. The top bolt is 1-3/8" long and the bottom bolt is 2-1/8 " long.

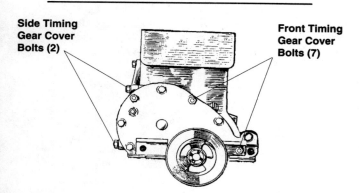

15. Install the front four (4) pan bolts (5/16-18 X 3/4 hex hd bolts)[1/2 socket].

16. Insert the front two (2) motor mount bolts (1/2-13 X 1 3/8") and lock washers [3/4 socket].

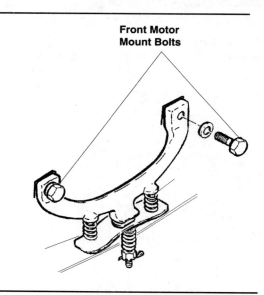

17. Remove the floor jack from under the engine pan.

18. Place a new belt over the fan pulley, and then under the crank pulley. With the generator pushed up against the engine block, slip the belt over the generator pulley.

19. Pull the generator away from the block to apply tension on the belt. Set the generator holding bracket against the generator and tighten the holding bracket bolt on the timing cover [9/16 socket].

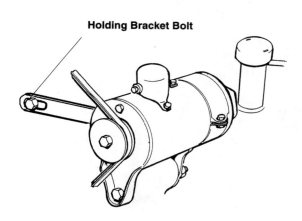

TIMING GEAR

20. Pull hard on the generator while tightening the generator mounting bolt [3/4 socket]. Push on the belt at a point half way between the fan pulley and the generator pulley. Correct tension would allow the belt to be pushed in 1/2".

21. After correct belt tension is set, push the generator holding bracket against the generator and tighten the bracket bolt on the timing gear cover. Retighten the generator mounting bolt.
22. Connect the harness wires to the cutout.
23. Set the distributor timing in accordance with the "Timing Procedure, Section II".

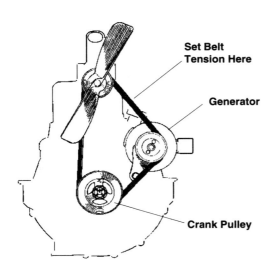

Belt Routing

Service and Repair

TRANSMISSION SHIFTING TOWER

Repairs that can be made to the shifting tower include the shifting forks, gear shift lever ball, gear shift lever spring, and the detent plunger and spring assembly. A worn or faulty shifting tower can be one of the causes of the transmission slipping out of gear. The ball on the end of the shifting lever should be a 1/2" <u>round</u> ball. When the ball becomes square due to wear, the shifting forks will not travel the full distance to fully engage the transmission gears. Likewise, if the detent plunger spring is weak or broken, the shifting fork shafts will not hold in the detents, allowing the transmission to jump out of gear. If the shifting forks are bent or badly worn the shifting fork shaft will not fully engage into the detents or allow full engagement of the gears, allowing the transmission to jump out of gear.

Shifting Tower Disassembly

1. Remove the detent plunger screw plug. (WD-40 and an impact screwdriver may be needed.)
2. Place a small drift punch into the center of the shifting fork tubular rivet and drive the rivet out the bottom of the shaft.
3. Place a screwdriver into the shifting fork shaft groove and drive the shaft out through the front of the housing. The second shaft should now slide out easily, with no pressure from the detent caps and spring assembly. The two (2) detent caps and spring can be removed from the side detent screw plug hole.
4. Using a shifting tower spring compressor, remove the shifting lever spring keeper and spring.
5. Weld up the shifting lever ball and file it to a 1/2" round ball.
6. Check that the 6" shift lever spring is not broken or compressed. It must have a minimum free length of 6".
7. Replace the detent caps if the ball tips are badly worn.
8. Replace the detent spring.

Shifting Tower Assembly

1. Insert the shifting lever through the top of the housing, making sure the shift lever pin fully seats in the slot in the top of the housing.
2. Place the 6" shifting lever spring over the lever end ball and mount the special shifting tower spring compressor to the housing. Compress the spring, insert the spring keeper, and remove the spring compressor.
3. Insert the wide spaced detent shifting fork shaft into the left side of the housing (viewed from the bottom side, the opposite side from the detent screw plug hole).
4. Slide the shifting fork on to the shaft and push the shaft into the back of the housing, flush with the front end of the housing.

NOTE

The forks are identical and slide onto the shafts in opposite directions. The tubular rivet pin hole will only line up correctly in one direction. The front fork has the pin hole to the rear and the rear fork has the pin hole toward the front.

5. Before inserting the narrow spaced detent shaft, insert the detent plunger assembly through the side hole (two detent caps and spring).
6. Compress the plunger assembly while inserting the narrow spaced detent shaft. Slide the shifting fork on the shaft and push the shaft in until it is flush with the front side of the housing. Make sure the detents on both shafts face each other, toward the middle of the housing.
7. Line up the shifting forks with the rivet hole in the shaft and insert the tubular rivet from the bottom side of the shaft. Spread the hollow end of the rivet to lock it in place. Install the tubular rivet for the second shifting fork in the same manner.

TRANSMISSION

8. Pour 1-1/2 pints of 600W gear oil into the transmission. Do not fill above the oil fill hole.
9. Place a transmission cover gasket on top of the transmission. Install the shifting tower, using six (6) bolts and lock washers (4 each 5/16-18 X 3/4, 2 each 5/16-18 X 1-3/8")[1/2" socket]. Make sure the shifting forks seat correctly in the two sliding gear collars.
10. Engage the clutch and shift through the three forward gears and reverse gear to check that all gears engage properly.
11. Bolt the emergency brake handle to the side of the shifting tower using two (2) bolts and lock washers (3/8-16 X 13/16")[9/16 socket].

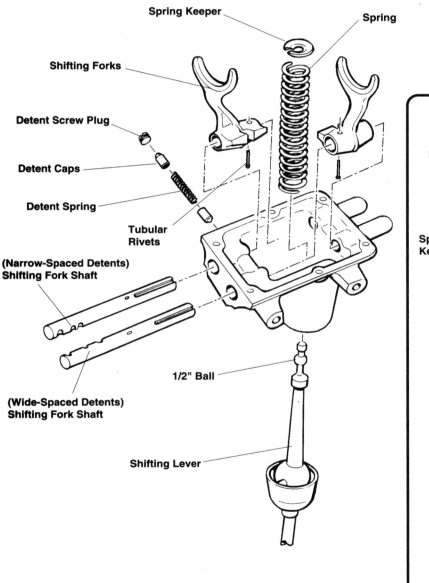

Transmission Shifting Tower

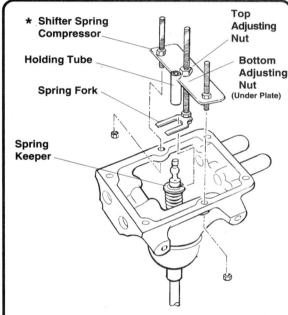

1. Slide the spring fork under the spring keeper, on top of the top spring coil.
2. Position the holding tube over the shifting lever ball and bolt the spring compressor assembly to the housing with the two outside rods and nuts as shown.
3. Raise the top adjusting nut up about 1 inch and turn the bottom adjusting nut clockwise to lower the center rod and fork, thereby pushing the spring down. The spring keeper can be safely removed with the spring held captive. Adjusting the top rod nuts allows safe removal of the tool.

Spring Compressor Tool

★ Made by Auto Care & Restoration
3824 Alma Ave., Redding, Ca. 96002
(1-800-452-1027)

Service and Repair

TRANSMISSION

Repairs to the transmission must be made with the transmission removed from the car. The Model A transmission is a simple design, and removing it from the car is actually more work than taking it apart.

The transmission can be removed from the car in either of two ways: removing the engine, or removing the differential and driveline. If the engine has been removed for repairs, it is easy to disconnect the transmission from the driveline and extract the transmission from under the car. If the engine is in the car and does not require removal for repairs, it is probably more convenient to remove the rear end assembly (differential and driveline) to enable removal of the transmission. Both procedures are explained below.

Production Design Changes

Several design changes were made to the transmission during production. Review the following design changes for compatibility before replacing components for repair.

Transmission Case — JAN 1929 Added bosses on both ends of the case for the cluster gear and eliminated the brass thrust washers at each end. (*Ford Service Bulletin -Jan 1929, pg. 311*)

Reverse Idler Gear/Shaft — JAN 1929 New reverse idler gear and shaft for better oiling. When old shaft needs replacing, idler gear must be replaced. New idler gear can be used with old style shaft. (*Ford Service Bulletin-Jan 1929, pg. 312*)

Transmission Case — SEPT 1929 Eliminated shoulder for main shaft bearings stop at each end of case. Added groove for snap rings (bearing stop) to replace machined shoulder. (*Ford Service Bulletin - Sept 1929, pg. 379*)

Bearing Oil Baffle — SEPT 1929 Larger oil baffles added to front and rear main shaft bearings to help prevent oil leaking past main shaft bearings. (*Ford Service Bulletin - Sept 1929, pg. 379*)
(**Note:** *When replacing main shaft ball bearings, replace with "one side sealed" type to prevent oil leaking from transmission.*)

Cluster Gear Shaft Spacer — OCT 1929 Eliminated two collar spacers that were pressed into cluster gear shaft hole. Replaced with single cylindrical loose fit spacer. (*Ford Service Bulletin - Oct. 1929, pg. 387*)

Shaft Retainer — NOV 1929 Cluster gear shaft and reverse idler shaft retainer bar made thinner. Cluster gear shaft and idler gear shaft also changed to accommodate thinner retainer. (*Ford Service Bulletin - Nov. 1929, pg. 391*)

Rear Bearing Retainer — JUNE 1929 Changed bolt hole pattern for rear bearing retainer, U-joint cover, and outer cover top half. (*Ford Service Bulletin - June 1929, pg. 350*)

TRANSMISSION

Transmission Removal-*By Removing Engine*

1. The transmission can be removed by removing the engine. To remove the engine, follow the procedure given for "Engine Removal".
2. After the engine has been removed, remove the clevis pin attaching the rod at the bottom of the emergency brake handle.

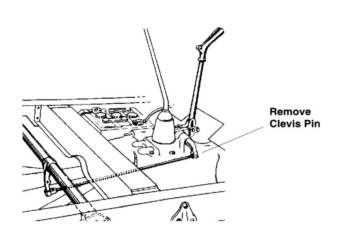
Remove Clevis Pin

3. Remove the six (6) bolts [1/2" socket] and lock washers on top of the shifting tower and lift the tower off the transmission housing.

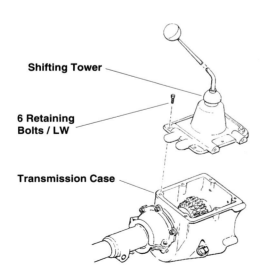
Shifting Tower
6 Retaining Bolts / LW
Transmission Case

4. Remove the brake pedal clevis pin, disconnecting the brake actuating rod and stoplight switch.
5. Remove the clutch pedal clevis pin, disconnecting the clutch arm.
6. Tap out the pedal shaft collar pin and remove the pedal shaft collar. Slide the clutch and brake pedals and spring washer (after May 1929) off the shaft.

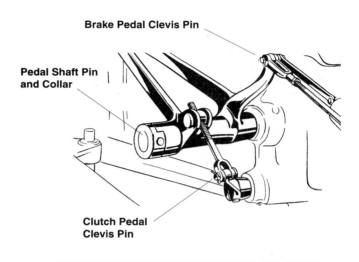
Brake Pedal Clevis Pin
Pedal Shaft Pin and Collar
Clutch Pedal Clevis Pin

7. Remove the transmission drain plug (bottom of transmission) and drain all oil. Replace the drain plug.
8. Place a floor jack under the transmission for support.
9. Remove the two (2) nuts [3/4 socket], springs, and spacers from the radius ball cap located under the bell housing. Separate the radius ball from the bell housing.

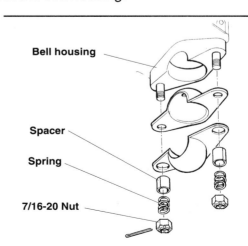
Bell housing
Spacer
Spring
7/16-20 Nut

Service and Repair

TRANSMISSION

10. Remove the two (2) bolts [9/16 socket] and nuts on each side of the U-joint outer cover.
11. Remove the six (6) bolts and nuts [9/16 socket] from around the U-joint cover.
12. Pull the bell housing, transmission, and U-joint assembly forward, pulling the splined U-joint off the drive shaft. The complete transmission assembly can be rolled out from under the car on a floor jack.

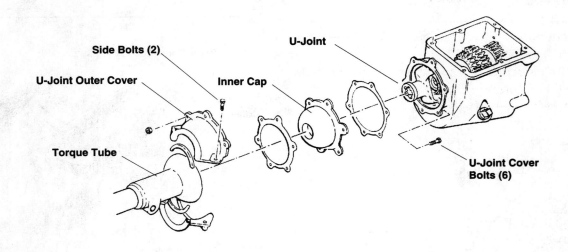

Separating Transmission from Driveline

Transmission Removal-*By Removing Rear End Assembly*

1. Remove (unscrew) the gear shift knob. Slip off the emergency brake handle boot and shifter boot. Remove (unscrew) the accelerator pedal (top cap).
2. Remove the front floor mat (or carpet) and shift lever plate, attached to the floor board with three (3) clips.
3. Remove both sections of the front floor boards [12 flathead screws].
4. Remove the clevis pin attaching the rod at the bottom of the emergency brake handle.

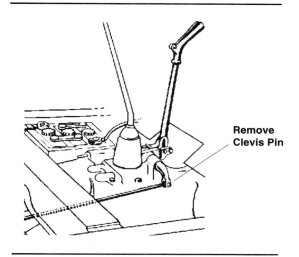

5. Remove the six (6) bolts [1/2" socket] and lock washers on top of the shifting tower and lift the tower off the transmission housing.

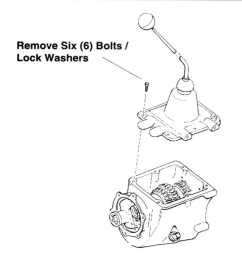

6. Remove the brake pedal clevis pin, disconnecting the brake actuating rod and stoplight switch.
7. Remove the clutch pedal clevis pin, disconnecting the clutch arm.
8. Tap out the pedal shaft collar pin and remove the pedal shaft collar. Slide the clutch and brake pedals and spring washer off the shaft.

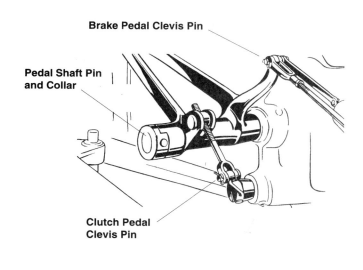

9. Remove the transmission drain plug (bottom of transmission) and drain all oil. Replace the drain plug.

TRANSMISSION

10. Place a floor jack under the transmission for support.
11. The transmission can be removed from the car by removing the differential with drive shaft (rear end assembly). To remove the rear end assembly follow the procedures for "Rear end Assembly Removal" on page 1-88.
12. After removing the rear end assembly, disconnect the front radius ball under the bell housing.

Transmission Disassembly

1. Release the throwout bearing spring and slide the throwout bearing hub assembly (with throwout bearing) off the bearing retainer sleeve.
2. Remove the bell housing from the transmission case by removing the four (4) bell housing to transmission case bolts [5/8 socket] and lock washers. Lift the bell housing off the transmission.

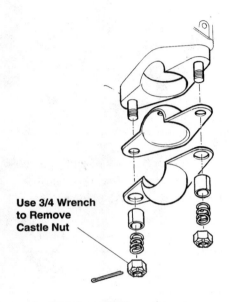

13. Remove the eleven (11) bell housing to flywheel housing bolts [9/16 socket] and separate the bell housing from the flywheel housing. The splined transmission drive shaft will separate from the clutch assembly. The complete transmission assembly with bell housing can be rolled out from under the car on a floor jack.

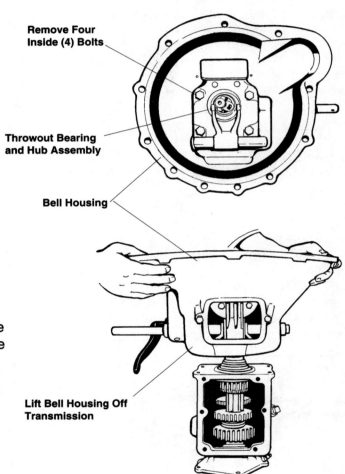

Removing Bell Housing

Service and Repair   1-334

TRANSMISSION

3. Remove the four (4) bolts [1/2" socket] and lock washers attaching the front bearing retainer. Remove the bearing retainer and gasket.

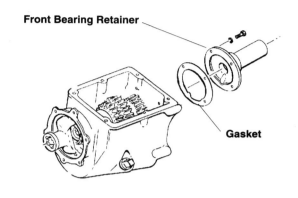

4. Lift out the main drive gear (with attached bearing) and pilot bearing from transmission.

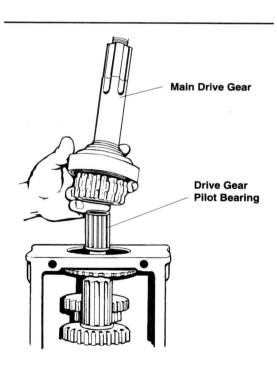

5. Remove the bolt [9/16 socket], lock washer and large washer attaching the U-joint to the rear of the main shaft. Remove the U-joint.

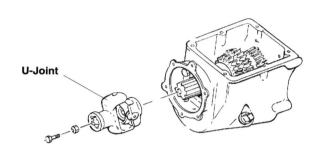

6. Cut and remove the safety wire on the four (4) rear bearing retainer bolts, and remove the bolts [5/8 socket] and bearing retainer.

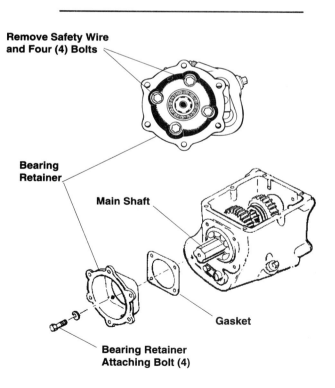

Service and Repair

TRANSMISSION

7. Withdraw the main shaft with main shaft bearing attached. The reverse/low and 2nd/high gears will slide off the main shaft and can be removed from the case.

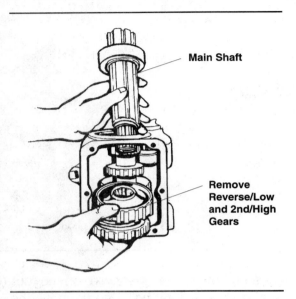

8. Remove the cluster gear (counter gear) and idler gear shaft retainer bolt and slide off the retainer [9/16 socket].

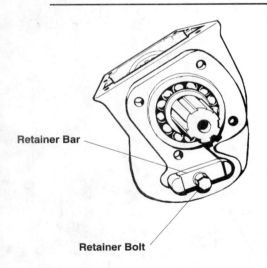

9. Remove the cluster gear shaft by tapping it out through the front of the transmission.

CAUTION
The cluster gear shaft is slightly larger diameter (.001") at the front end and should only be removed through the front of the transmission case. Forcing the shaft out the rear may crack the case.

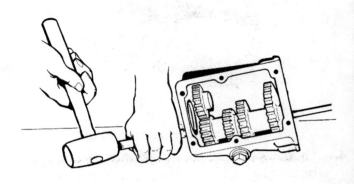

10. The cluster gear can now be lifted out of the case and the two needle bearings and spacer withdrawn from the ends of the gear.
    Prior to Jan 1929 Remove the two brass thrust washers at each end of the cluster gear.

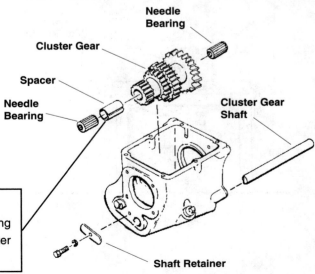

NOTE
Prior to Oct 1929 the needle bearing spacer was pressed into the cluster gear shaft hole.

Service and Repair   1-336

TRANSMISSION

11. Withdraw the reverse idler gear shaft from the transmission case and lift out the reverse idler gear.

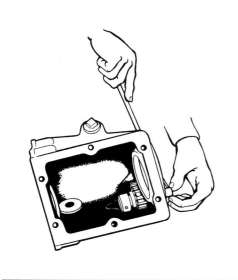

12. *Sept 1929 Through Production* Remove the snap rings from the main bearing hole at both ends of the transmission case.
13. Thoroughly clean all parts for inspection.

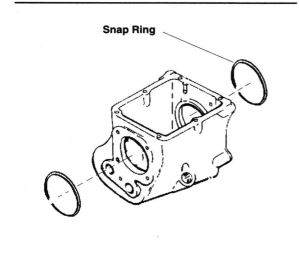

Assembling Transmission

Several design changes in parts took place during production of the Model A transmission. Before starting assembly, refer to page 1-330, "Production Design Changes" to determine the correct parts needed for the transmission in repair.

A full inspection should be made of all parts to determine usability and replacement needs.

Inspection

1. Inspect the two main shaft ball bearings. If they are pitted, galled or discolored, replace them. If they look okay, apply a light oil and turn each bearing slowly. If you feel a catch, or the bearings are not silky smooth, or they are loose in their cage, replace them. When replacing either the main shaft or main drive gear ball bearings, use the new type that are sealed on one side to prevent oil leaks from the transmission around the shaft. The two ball bearings must be pressed on or off. Always place the sealed side towards the outside of the case.

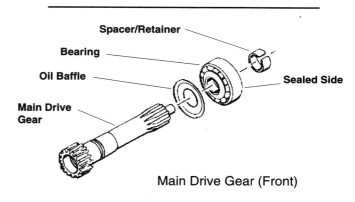

Main Drive Gear (Front)

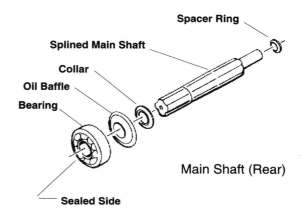

Main Shaft (Rear)

Service and Repair

TRANSMISSION

2. Check the fit of the two gears (low/reverse gear and 2nd/high gear) on the splined main shaft. The clearance between gear and shaft must be no more than .002" for proper operation. Check this tolerance by lubricating the gears and shaft, then holding the shaft upright and sliding the gears onto it. They should just slide of their own weight, or require a little help. If they slip down instantly, they're too loose. The gears and main shaft should be replaced as a matched set.
3. Check the teeth on all the gears for pitting, grooves, missing or chipped teeth, or severely rounded edges. Severely rounded edges can cause the transmission to slip out of gear under load. The gears are to be replaced if severely worn, or if there are chipped and missing teeth.
4. Check the shifting forks on the shifting tower to make sure they are not bent or badly worn. Check the detent assembly to make sure it is functioning properly and smoothly. Replace the detent springs if necessary.
5. Check the fit of the reverse idler gear to shaft. If the fit is loose, replace the idler gear bushing.
6. Check the end of the main drive gear (flywheel pilot bearing end) for excessive wear, pitting or ridges. Slide a new flywheel pilot bearing on the shaft end to check fit. *This is one of the most overlooked areas on the transmission and vital to correct operation.* Pilot bearing to shaft fit must be no more than .002". Excessive wear on the shaft causes transmission growl, misalignment of gear teeth, and slipping out of gear. The main drive gear should be replaced if pilot bearing fit is out of tolerance.

Check For Flywheel Pilot Bearing Fit

Main Drive Shaft

Assemblie

Before starting assemblie, ensure all transmission parts and work area are clean. One small filing or speck of grit can ruin a bearing or pit a gear, so make sure your work area, transmission case, and all parts are surgically clean before assemblie.

1. Paint the transmission case, bell housing, rear bearing retainer, and shifting tower housing, Ford engine green.
2. Place the reverse idler gear in the transmission case with the flush side of the gear facing the rear of the transmission.
3. Insert the reverse idler shaft through the case and gear, turning it so that the flat side of the shaft faces the cluster gear shaft hole.

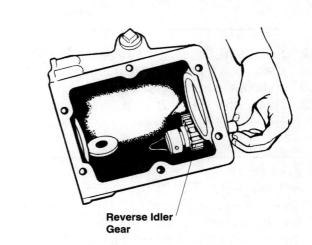

Reverse Idler Gear

Service and Repair

TRANSMISSION

4. Place the cluster gear needle bearings and spacer into each end of the cluster gear assembly (<u>always</u> replace needle bearings with new). The longer bearing (1-11/16" long) goes into the end with the small gear. The shorter bearing (1-7/16" long) goes into the larger gear end.

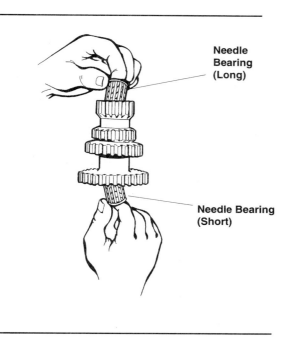

5. Place the cluster gear into the transmission case so the small gear is at the rear, meshed with the reverse idler gear.
6. Slide the cluster gear shaft (notched end first) through the front of the transmission case, through the roller (needle) bearings and spacer, into the hole in the back of the case. Make sure the notched flat area on the end of the shaft is facing the reverse idler shaft, then tap the shaft into the rear hole in the transmission.

NOTE

Early transmissions (prior to Jan 29) used brass thrust washers at each end of the cluster gear. Install the thrust washers if required, prior to installing the cluster gear shaft.

7. Position the flat retainer for the cluster gear shaft and idler gear shaft between the flat sides of the shaft and securely tighten the attaching bolt and lock washer (3/8-16 X 13/16) [9/16 socket].

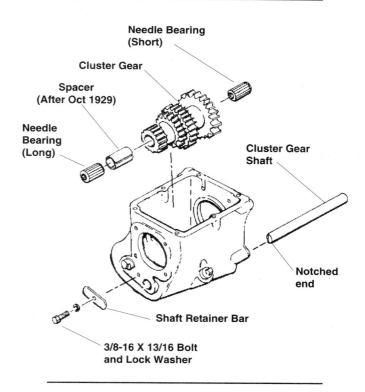

8. <u>After Sept 1929</u> Insert a main bearing snap ring in the groove at both ends of the case in the main shaft bearing holes. Replace new if worn thin.

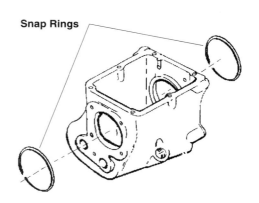

1-339 Service and Repair

Transmission

9. Stand the transmission case on the front face. Place the 2nd/high gear (smaller gear) in the case with the shifting collar up. Put the reverse/low gear (larger gear) on top of the smaller gear with its shifting collar down (shifting collars facing each other). Make sure the splines on both gears are aligned.

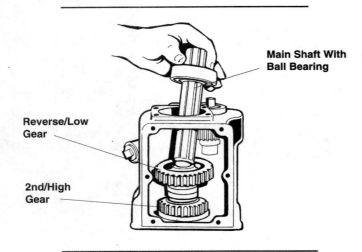

10. Slide a spacer ring on the end of the main shaft.

CAUTION
If this ring is left out, the needle pilot bearing in the main drive gear will be destroyed. Replace with new ring if there are signs of wear.

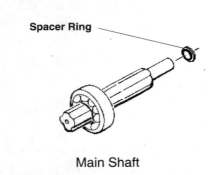

11. Place the main shaft through the top of the case (rear) until the main roller bearing seats in the case against the snap ring. Make sure the shafts spline align with the gears below (see top figure).

12. Place a bearing retainer gasket on the rear of the transmission case and install the bearing retainer (lubricating fitting on bottom) with four (4) bolts (7/16-20 X 1")[5/8" socket]. Securely tighten and safety wire the four bolt heads.

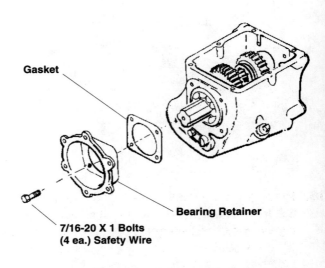

13. Place a pilot needle bearing over the end of the main shaft just installed (always install a new pilot needle bearing. This bearing gets the most abuse when other areas are worn).

14. Place the main drive gear through the front of the case and over the pilot bearing on the main shaft.

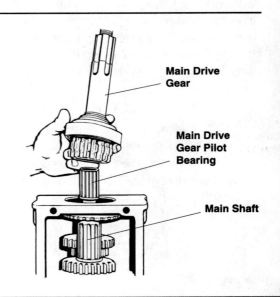

TRANSMISSION

15. Place a gasket and the main drive shaft bearing retainer on the front of the transmission case and install four (4) bolts and lock washers (5/16-18 X 3/4")[1/2"socket].

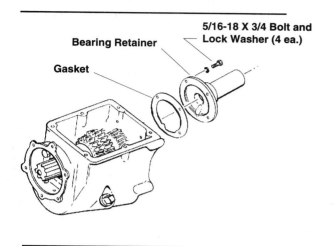

16. Place the transmission/bell housing gasket on the front of the transmission and set the bell housing on the transmission case. Install four (4) bolts and lock washers and securely tighten (7/16-14 X 1-1/14")[5/8 socket].

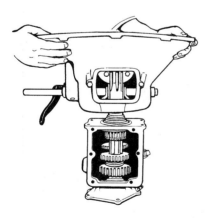

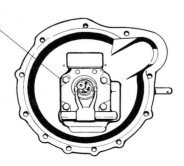

17. Apply a light film of grease over the front bearing retainer sleeve and slide it on the throwout bearing hub assembly. Ensure the hub assembly slides freely on the sleeve. Attach the hub with the throwout bearing spring. Install a new throwout bearing (Bower 2065).

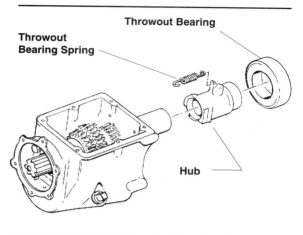

18. Slip the U-joint on the end of the rear shaft. Attach with bolt and lock washer (3/8-24 X 1")[9/16" socket] and knuckle retainer. Securely tighten.

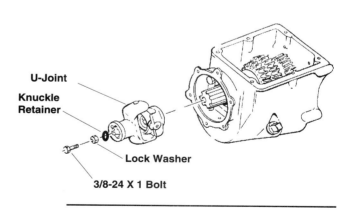

19. Insert the oil drain plug in the bottom of the transmission (3/4 X 5/16" square pipe plug). Tape a cardboard cover over the top of the transmission to prevent foreign material (bolts, dirt, grit etc.) from falling into the transmission. The transmission is ready to be installed.

Service and Repair

TRANSMISSION

Installing Transmission-*With Engine Removed*

1. Place the two (2) sliding gears in neutral position. Place the transmission with bell housing on a floor jack and slide it under the car.
2. Place a gasket on each side of the U-joint inner cap. Place the U-joint inner cap with gaskets over the U-joint on the rear of the transmission.
3. Line up the spline of the U-joint with the drive shaft spline and push the U-joint onto the drive shaft.
4. Install new cork gaskets in the two halves of the U-joint outer cover. Place the two outer cover halves over the torque tube flange and bolt together with two (2) bolts, lock washers and nuts (3/8-24 X 1")[9/16" socket]. Bolt the transmission and driveline together with six (6) bolts and castle nuts (3/8-24 X 1-7/32). Insert cotter pins.
5. Apply six to eight pumps of grease through the grease fitting on the bottom of the rear bearing retainer cap.
6. Remove the temporary cover from the top of the transmission and pour in 1-1/2 pints of 600W gear oil. Do not fill above the oil fill hole.
7. Place a transmission cover gasket on top of the transmission. Install the shifting tower using six (6) bolts and lock washers (4 each 5/16-18 X 3/ 2 each 5/16-18 X 1-3/8")[1/2" socket]. Make sure the shifting forks seat correctly in both sliding gear collars.

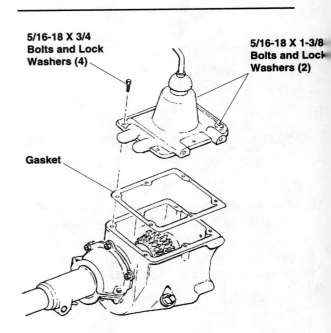

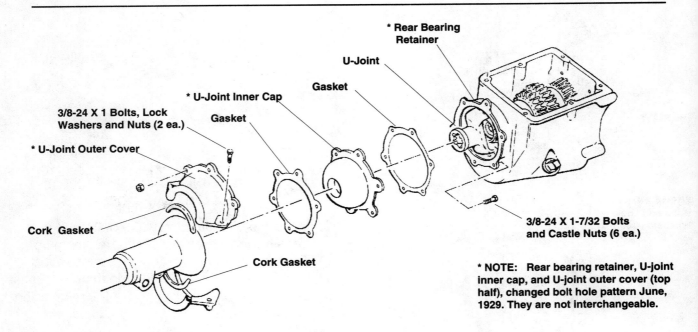

Transmission To Driveline Connection

* NOTE: Rear bearing retainer, U-joint inner cap, and U-joint outer cover (top half), changed bolt hole pattern June, 1929. They are not interchangeable.

TRANSMISSION

8. Install the engine by following the steps under "Engine Installation".
9. Reattach the radius ball under the bell housing.

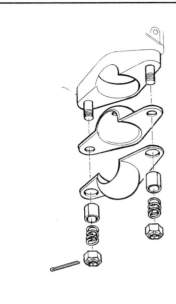

10. Attach the emergency brake actuating rod to the emergency brake handle with a clevis pin. Lock with a cotter pin.

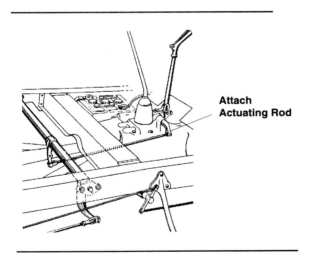

Attach Actuating Rod

11. Slide the brake and clutch pedals on the pedal shaft, inserting a thin spring washer between the two pedals (after May 1929).
12. Install the pedal shaft collar on the end of the shaft and insert the collar pin. Insert a cotter pin through the end of the collar pin.

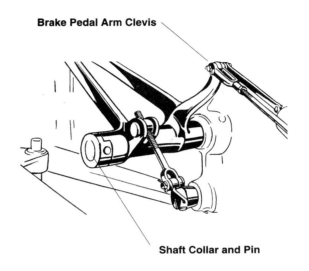

Brake Pedal Arm Clevis

Shaft Collar and Pin

13. Attach the clutch arm to the clutch pedal adjusting yoke with the clevis pin. Lock with a cotter pin.

NOTE
Adjust the clutch pedal with the pedal adjusting yoke for 1" free pedal travel before the clutch engages.

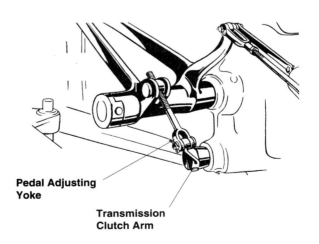

Pedal Adjusting Yoke
Transmission Clutch Arm

Service and Repair

TRANSMISSION

14. Attach the brake actuating rod and stoplight linkage to the brake pedal arm with a clevis pin. Lock with a cotter pin.
15. From inside the car apply a small amount of grease to the clutch throwout bearing slider shaft. This grease fitting is accessible under the inspection plate located in front of the emergency brake handle (on top of the bell housing). Install the inspection plate (two (2) screws, 5/16-18 X 3/8).

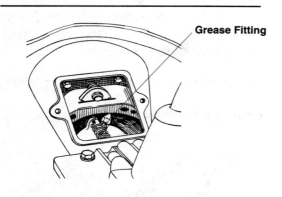

Grease Fitting

16. Install the front floor boards, shift lever plate, and floor mat. Secure the floor board with twelve (12) flat head screws (12-24 X 1-1/8") and cup washers.

17. Slip on the shifting tower boot and emergency handle boot. Screw the knob on top of the shifting tower.

18. From under the hood, set the distributor timing in accordance with the "Timing Procedure, Section II."

19. Pour three (3) gallons of water into the radiator and two (2) quarts of oil through the oil filler tube. Check the oil dip stick. Add only enough oil to bring the oil level up to the "F" on the dip stick. DO NOT OVER FILL.

Installing Transmission-*With Rear End Assembly Removed*

1. Place the two (2) sliding gears in neutral position. Place the transmission and bell housing on a floor jack and slide it under the car.
2. Raise the transmission/bell housing level with the flywheel housing.
3. Remove the bell housing cover plate so the splined transmission drive shaft can be viewed.
4. Viewing through the bell housing top cover plate, align the transmission drive shaft spline with the clutch spline. Push the transmission drive shaft into the clutch spline.
5. Install the eleven (11) bell housing to flywheel bolts (3/8-16 X 1")[9/16 socket] and lock washers.
6. Attach the radius ball under the bell housing.

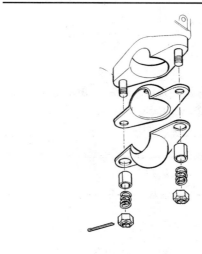

7. Install the rear end assembly by following the step-by-step instructions under "Installing Rear End Assembly".
8. Remove the temporary cardboard cover from the top of the transmission and pour in 1-1/2 pints of 600W gear oil. Do not fill above the oil fill hole.

TRANSMISSION

9. Place a transmission cover gasket on top of the transmission. Install the shifting tower, using six (6) bolts and lock washers (4 each 5/16-18 X 3/4, 2 each 5/16-18 X 1-3/8")[1/2" socket]. Make sure the shifting forks seat correctly in both sliding gear collars.

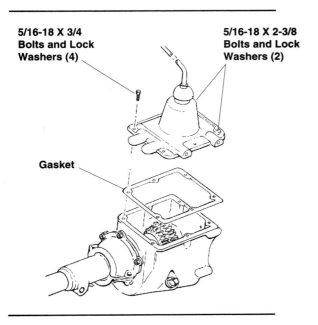

10. Attach the emergency brake actuating rod to the emergency brake handle with a clevis pin. Lock with a cotter pin.

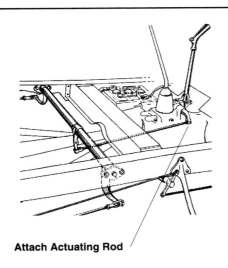

11. Slide the brake and clutch pedals on the pedal shaft, inserting a thin spring washer between the two pedals (after May 1929).
12. Install the pedal shaft collar on the end of the shaft and insert the collar pin. Insert a cotter pin through the end of the collar pin.
13. Attach the clutch arm to the clutch pedal adjusting yoke with a clevis pin. Lock with a cotter pin.

NOTE
Adjust the clutch pedal with the pedal adjusting yoke for 1" free pedal travel before the clutch engages.

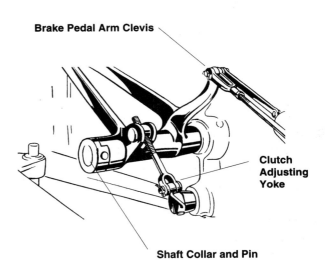

Service and Repair

TRANSMISSION

14. Attach the brake actuating rod and stop light linkage to the brake pedal arm with a clevis pin. Lock with a cotter pin.
15. From inside the car apply a small amount of grease to the clutch throwout bearing slider shaft. This grease fitting is accessible under the inspection plate located in front of the emergency brake handle (on top of the bell housing). Install the inspection plate (two (2)screws, 5/16-18 X 3/8).
16. Install the front floor boards, shift lever plate, and floor mat. Secure the floor board with twelve (12) flat head screws (12-24 X 1-1/8") and cup washers.
17. Slip on the shifting tower boot and emergency handle boot. Screw the knob on top of the shifting tower.

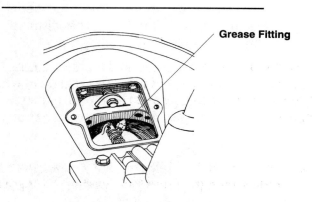

Grease Fitting

Table 1-5. Transmission Assembly Hardware

Hardware (Bolts, Washers, Nuts, Studs)	Qty	Size (Wrench)
Shifting Tower To Transmission Case	4	5/16-18 X 3/4 (1/2)
Shifting Tower To Transmission Case	2	5/16-18 X 1-3/8 (1/2)
Lock Washer	6	5/16
Oil Drain Plug	1	3/4 X 5/16 Sq Pipe Plug
Oil Fill Plug	1	3/4 X 5/16 Sq Pipe Plug
U-Joint Outer Cover Halves	2	3/8-24 X 1 (9/16)
Lock Washer	2	3/8
Nut	2	3/8-24
U-Joint Outer Cover To Transmission	6	3/8-24 X 1-7/32 (9/16)
Nut	6	3/8-24, Castle (9/16)
U-Joint To Main Shaft (Rear)	1	3/8-24 X 1 (9/16)
Lock Washer	1	3/8
Bell Housing To Transmission	4	7/16-14 X 1-1/4 (5/8)
Lock Washer	4	7/16
Main Shaft Bearing Retainer (Rear)	4	7/16-20 X 1 Drilled (5/8)
Main Drive Shaft Bearing Retainer (Front)	4	5/16-18 X 3/4 (5/8)
Lock Washer	4	5/16
Shaft Retainer Bar	1	3/8-16 X 13/16 (9/16)
Lock Washer	1	3/8

Service and Repair

UNIVERSAL JOINT (U-JOINT)

The universal joint (U-joint) is a double-jointed knuckle that transmits torque at different angles between the transmission and drive shaft. The U-joint is located directly behind the transmission and rotates with the drive shaft in a grease filled housing. A loose, worn and defective U-joint will cause a clunking noise when the drive shaft is turning, or sometimes a whining noise. The differential/rear end assembly must be removed for access to the U-joint.

Removing U-Joint

1. Block the front wheels and release the emergency brake.
2. Jack up the rear end of the car and place jack stands under the frame, just behind the running board brackets. Remove both rear wheels.
3. Disconnect the service brake rod and emergency brake rod (remove clevis pins) at both rear wheels.
4. Disconnect the brake rod anti-rattlers from the radius rods (bolt and lock washer), [1/2 socket].

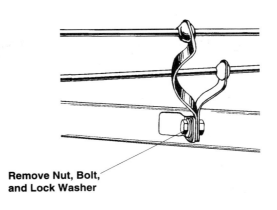

Remove Nut, Bolt, and Lock Washer

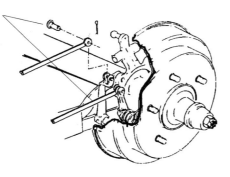

Remove Clevis Pins and Disconnect Both Brake Rods

Remove Brake Rods

Service and Repair

U-JOINT

5. Remove the cotter pin from the top of the shock link and screw out the end plug for removal of the shock link from the shock arm and the axle housing.

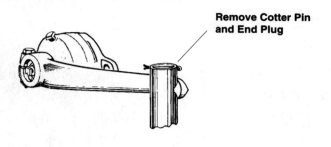

Remove Shock Arm

6. Uncrew the speedometer cable from the gear cap assembly.

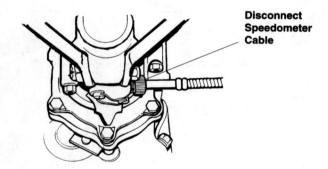

7. Remove the two (2) bolts [9/16 socket] and nuts on each side of the U-joint outer cover.
8. Remove the six (6) bolts and nuts [9/16 socket] from around the U-joint outer cover. Remove both halves of the outer cover.

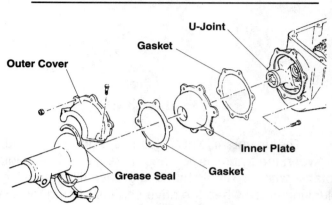

9. Place a floor jack under the differential housing.
10. Remove the four hanger nuts (7/8 wrench) to allow removal of the spring from the cross member.
11. Slide the rear end assembly out from under the car.

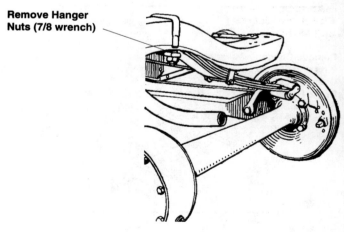

Service and Repair   1-348

U-JOINT

12. Remove the bolt [9/16 socket], lock washer and large washer attaching the U-joint to the rear of the transmission. Remove the U-joint.

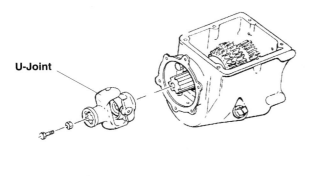

13. When the inside ring and bushing assembly becomes worn and loose, the U-joint should be replaced. A noisy U-joint can be caused by the lug or tongue on the front knuckle retainer riding on top of the splines of the U-joint instead of seating down in between the splines as shown below.

14. Slip a new U-joint on the end of the rear shaft. Attach with a bolt and lock washer (3/8-24 X 1") [9/16" socket] and knuckle retainer. Securely tighten.

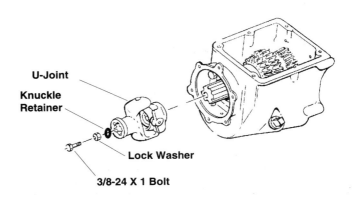

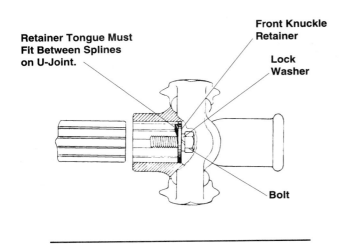

Service and Repair

U-JOINT

Installing Rear End Assembly

1. Pack a liberal amount of grease around the U-joint.
2. Place gaskets and inner cover over the U-joint on the back side of the transmission as shown below.

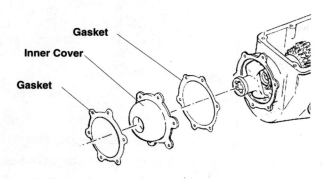

3. Place the differential housing on a floor jack and raise the assembly until the end of the drive shaft can be inserted into the U-joint. The drive shaft is a splined fit into the U-joint. Rotating the rear axles will cause the drive shaft to turn, allowing the drive shaft spline to align with the U-joint.

4. After the drive shaft and U-joint have been mated, raise the differential to position the spring in the rear cross member. Position the two U-bolt brackets on the U-bolt hangers. Attach with four (4) castle nuts (9/16-18)[7/8 wrench]. Install cotter pins.

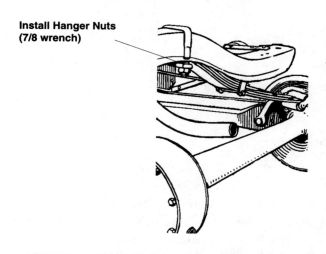

5. Place new grease seals (felt or cork) in the U-joint outer cover. Clamp the two halves around the torque tube and install the two side bolts, lock washers, and nuts (3/8-24 X 1"), [9/16 socket]. Do not tighten at this time.

Service and Repair

U-JOINT

6. Install the six (6) bolts, nuts, and lock washers around the U-joint cover (3/8-24 X 1-1/4"), [9/16 socket]. Now firmly tighten all eight (8) bolts and nuts. Pump a liberal amount of grease into the bottom grease fitting for the U-joint.

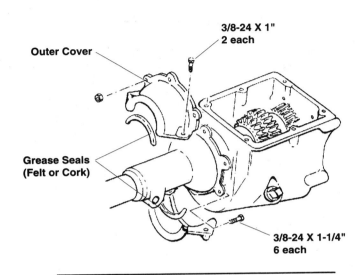

7. Connect the speedometer cable to the speedometer gear cap.
8. Attach the brake rod anti-rattler springs to the rear radius rods (5/16-24 X 11/16")[1/2 wrench].

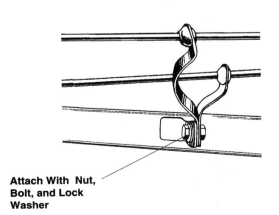

9. Attach all four (4) rear brake rods with clevis pins and cotter pins.

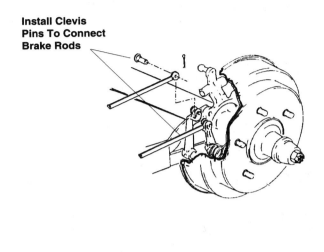

10. Assemble and install both rear shock links as shown below. Screw in the end plug and insert cotter pin.

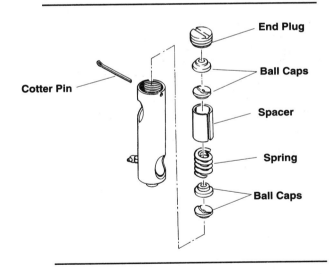

11. Install both rear wheels and torque the lug nuts to 64 ft. lbs.
12. Check the rear brake adjustment (See "Section II, Service Adjustments").
13. Remove all jacks and blocks from under the car. Apply grease to all rear grease fittings.
14. Check tire pressure and test drive.

Service and Repair

WATER PUMP

The Model A uses a thermo-siphon cooling system. This means that the coolant is not only pumped through the system but also circulates by the hot water from the block forcing the cooler water down the radiator and into the water jackets in the block. Without the proper pumping action of the impeller in the water pump, efficient cooling will not take place. A shaft with excessive end play can permit the impeller to contact the inside of the head and grind out the tolerance between the impeller blades and the head, to the point where pumping action is reduced. The allowable amount of end play in the pump shaft is from .006 to .010 inches. Excessive end play is caused by wear on the end of the shaft, and on the pad on the inside of the head where the shaft contacts and rotates against the pad. The pump shaft can be built up to compensate for wear on the head pad. Build up the shaft end with braze rather than hard surfacing. Hard surfacing will cause more wear on the head pad. If the shaft end is built up with brass, it will wear before the cast iron material in the head.

Another method of eliminating end play is to press a race sleeve on the pump shaft for the front Torrington needle bearing, thereby providing a collar to lock the shaft in a fixed position. These procedures are described below.

Removing Water Pump (with 2-Blade Fan installed)

The water pump, with a two blade fan installed, can be removed by disconnecting the two front radiator support rods and pulling the radiator forward enough to remove the water pump. If a four blade fan is installed, the radiator will have to be removed to remove the water pump.

1. Drain the radiator water. The drain petcock is located on the bottom of the water return pipe, under the generator.

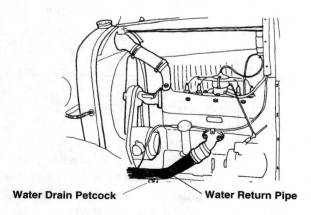

Water Drain Petcock   Water Return Pipe

2. Under the hood, remove the two screws and nuts from the hood rear hold down bracket.

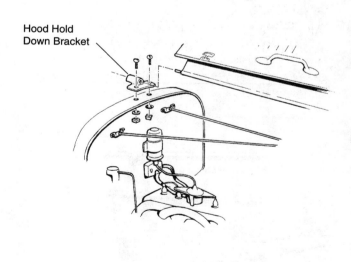

Hood Hold Down Bracket

3. Remove the hood and place it in a safe location on cardboard or carpet to prevent chipping the paint. Do not lay the hood down on the side louver panels. It's best to stand the hood up on the back edge to prevent warping or creasing the top panels.

Service and Repair

WATER PUMP

4. Loosen the two (2) nuts [1/2 inch wrench] on the front end of the two radiator support rods. Pull the two rods up out of the radiator bracket.

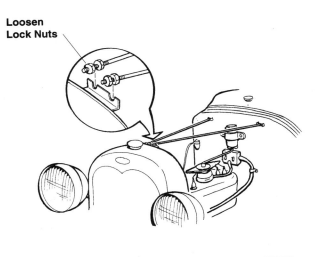

Loosen Lock Nuts

5. Loosen the hose clamp on the top radiator hose. Pull the radiator forward enough to pull the radiator neck out of the hose.
6. Loosen the generator mounting bolt and nut [3/4 socket].
7. If a generator holding bracket is installed, loosen the holding bracket bolt [9/16 socket] on the timing gear cover and swing the bracket away from the generator. Push the generator toward the engine to release belt tension.

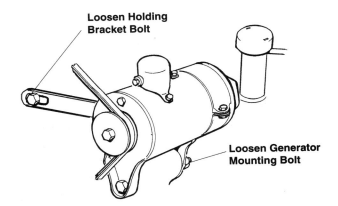

Loosen Holding Bracket Bolt

Loosen Generator Mounting Bolt

8. Slip the belt off the generator pulley and then off the crank pulley. The belt can now be removed from the fan pulley.

9. Remove the four (4) nuts [9/16 wrench] and lock washers that attach the water pump to the front of the cylinder head. Remove the water pump.

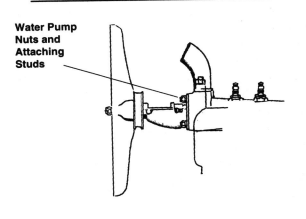

Water Pump Nuts and Attaching Studs

WATER PUMP

Removing Water Pump (with 4-Blade Fan installed)

If a four blade fan is installed, the radiator will have to be removed to remove the water pump.

1. Complete steps 1 through 8 of the previous procedure (Removing Water Pump w/2-Blade Fan).
2. Disconnect the ground cable from the battery (+) terminal post. (For safety when disconnecting the wiring harness.)

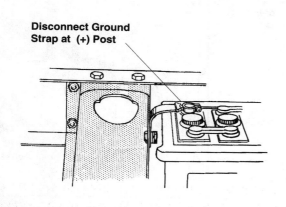

Disconnect Ground Strap at (+) Post

3. Move to the front of the car and remove the horn cover by removing the single round head screw on the back cover (10-32 x 3/4 screw). Remove the two horn wires from the terminal under the horn motor (pull out type).
4. Remove the Headlight conduit connectors (push and twist counterclockwise to release).

NOTE

Some headlight wiring may have been modified by eliminating the connector plug from inside the conduit socket. The wires would then be routed directly from the conduit into the headlight bucket and attached to the bulb sockets with wire nuts. The wires would have to be disconnected from behind the headlight reflector. To access the headlight bucket, release the front lens clip, pull the clip down (spring loaded latch) and lift up on the lens rim to remove it. Remove the center bulb and lift the reflector out of the headlight bucket.

5. Pull the headlight wires back through the conduit to the inside of the radiator shell, leaving the metal conduit and grommets attached to the radiator shell. Do the same for both headlight harness wires and the horn harness wires.

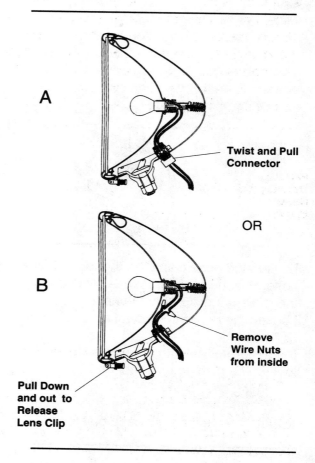

A — **Twist and Pull Connector**

OR

B — **Remove Wire Nuts from inside**, **Pull Down and out to Release Lens Clip**

Service and Repair   1-354

WATER PUMP

6. To remove the radiator, first remove the radiator shell by removing the two (2) screws and nuts on each side of the radiator, attaching the shell to the radiator brackets. Then remove the cotter pin from the two radiator mounting bolts. Using a 3/8 inch ratchet drive with a 6-inch extension and 9/16-inch deep socket, reach under the front cross member and place the 9/16-inch socket on the head of the radiator mounting bolt. Hold the nut on top with a 9/16 inch box wrench and ratchet the bolt from the bottom. Remove the bolt, spring, and nut from each side of the radiator.

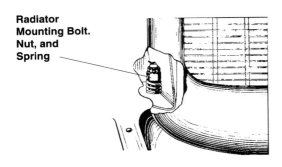

Radiator Mounting Bolt, Nut, and Spring

7. Remove and retain the rubber pads under the radiator mounting brackets (both sides). Move the radiator to one side to clear the fender and lift the radiator and shell off the frame. On the 28 models, a fan shroud may be attached to the radiator. This can be left in place when removing the radiator.
8. Remove the four (4) nuts [9/16 wrench] and lock washers that attach the water pump to the front of the cylinder head. Remove the water pump.

Water Pump Disassembly

1. Remove the cotter pin and nut on the front of the water pump shaft (5/8 wrench). Remove the fan blade from the water pump tapered and keyed shaft. Retain the woodruff key in the end of the shaft.

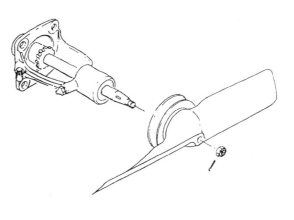

2. Unscrew the packing nut and pull the pump shaft and impeller out the rear of the housing, while removing the packing nut. Retain the impeller washer.
3. Punch the front felt retainer cup out the front with a punch from the rear shaft hole.
4. Remove both felt retainer cups, felt washers, felt retainer flat washers, needle bearing and bearing sleeve from the front of the housing.
5. Drive the rear bushing out the rear of the housing.
6. Rinse the housing in solvent and clean all grease from inside the housing. Pump a little grease through both grease fittings to make sure they are clear. Paint the housing engine green. The housing is ready for reassembly.
7. Inspect the impeller fins to make sure they are not broken or ground down. If the shaft is worn more than .005 inches where the needle bearing and rear bushing ride, the shaft should be replaced. If the pad inside the cylinder head is worn, the end of the shaft will have to be brazed to take up the clearance. This will be adjusted during assembly.

Service and Repair

WATER PUMP

Water Pump Assembly

1. Press the rear bushing into the housing, making sure the grease hole in the bushing aligns with the housing grease hole.
2. Check the impeller to shaft fit. The impeller is pined to the shaft and should be a tight fit.
3. Put the impeller washer on the shaft, up against the impeller and locked in the V-groove. Insert the shaft through the rear bushing to the front. The end play of the shaft to the cylinder head pad should be checked at this time.
4. Place the pump housing, with shaft and impeller installed, on the cylinder head with a water pump gasket. Push the shaft in and out to check end play clearance between the cylinder head pad and the end of the shaft.
5. The end play should be .006 to .010 inches. Braze the end of the shaft and grind smooth. Repeat the process until the specified clearance is obtained.
6. Pull the shaft out far enough to insert the packing and packing nut.
7. From the front, install a felt retainer cup, felt washer, flat retainer washer, bearing sleeve (align with grease fitting hole), needle bearing (well greased), flat retaining washer, felt washer, and felt retainer cup (which is the front cap).
8. Insert a woodruff key and the fan blade onto the shaft. Install castle nut and a cotter pin.

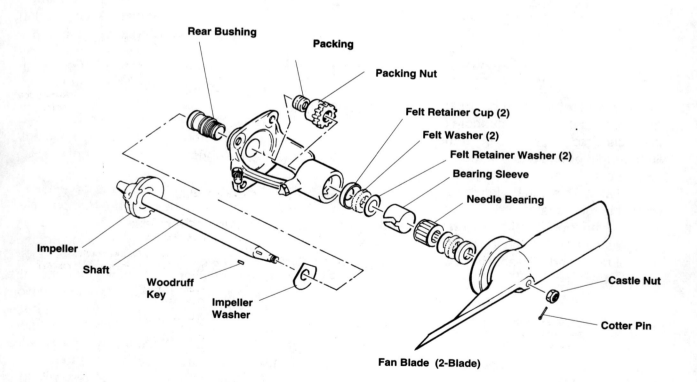

WATER PUMP

Modified Pump Shaft

This modification locks the pump shaft in the front needle bearing housing, thereby eliminating increased shaft end play brought about by wear on the end of the shaft or at the cylinder head pad. This modification requires special tooling equipment to knurl the shaft. The additional parts needed are:

- New Stainless Steel Shaft (.6250 Dia.)
- Torrington Needle Bearing #B-1412
- Bearing Race # IR-1016
- Brass Thrust Washers, 2 ea. .620 I.D.

1. After the housing has been readied for assembly, the bearing race (IR1016) must be pressed onto the shaft. (The impeller is pinned to the shaft last.) The shaft should be knurled for a tight fit and the race pressed onto the shaft 1-3/4" from the front reference point. See diagram.

2. Press the rear bushing into the housing, making sure the grease hole in the bushing aligns with the housing grease hole.
3. The modified shaft is installed through the front of the housing. First place a felt cup, felt washer, and brass thrust washer (replaces flat steel retainer washer), into the front housing.
4. Insert the Torrington needle bearing #B-1412 (well greased).
5. Now insert the modified shaft through the front needle bearing, and insert the packing and packing nut before the shaft is inserted through the rear bearing. The race on the front of the shaft should bottom against the brass thrust washer just installed.
6. Now install the second brass thrust washer, felt washer, and felt retainer cup (which is the front cap).

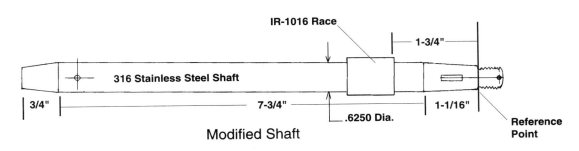

Modified Shaft

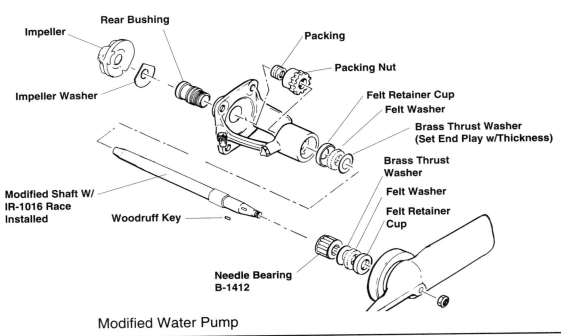

Modified Water Pump

Service and Repair

WATER PUMP

7. Install the impeller washer and impeller on the back of the shaft. DO NOT DRIVE THE PIN ALL THE WAY THROUGH. Tap the impeller pin in just far enough to hold the impeller in place. Now check the end play of the shaft. The end play is adjusted with the thickness of the brass thrust washers on the back side of the needle bearing race. The impeller stops the shaft in the forward motion. The brass thrust washer against the pressed on front bearing race stops the shaft in the back motion.

NOTE
The end play can also be set by changing the assembly sequence and pressing the race on the shaft after the impeller and shaft have been installed from the rear.

Installing Water Pump w/2-Blade Fan

1. Apply the water pump gasket to the cylinder head with a small amount of Permatex gasket sealer on both sides. Mount the water pump with four (4) nuts (3/8-24) and lock washers [9/16 socket].
2. Pull the radiator back in place and install the top radiator hose. (Do not tighten the top hose clamps at this time.) Tighten the two (2) hose clamps on the bottom radiator hose.
3. Attach the two (2) radiator support rods. Tighten the two front nuts only enough to hold the two rods in place.

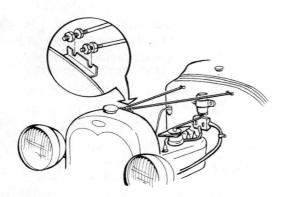

4. Set the hood in place and attach with two (2) screws, lock washers, and nuts (12-24 X 5/8" Round Head) on the rear hold down bracket.
5. After the hood has been installed and properly aligned, securely tighten both front radiator support rod nuts. Securely tighten the two radiator hose clamps on the upper radiator hose (radiator to goose neck).
6. Place the fan belt over the fan pulley, and then under the crank pulley. With the generator pushed up against the engine block, slip the belt over the generator pulley.
7. Pull the generator away from the block to apply tension on the belt. Set the generator holding bracket against the generator and tighten the holding bracket bolt on the timing cover [9/16 socket].
8. Pull hard on the generator while tightening the generator mounting bolt [3/4 socket]. Push on the belt at a point half way between the fan pulley and the generator pulley. Correct tension would allow the belt to be pushed in 1/2".
9. After correct belt tension is set, push the generator holding bracket tight against the generator and tighten the bracket bolt on the timing gear cover. Retighten the generator mounting bolt.

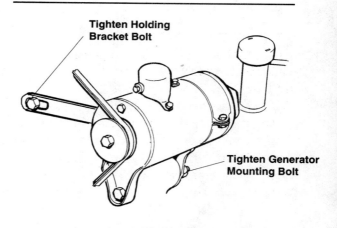

10. Pour three (3) gallons of water into the radiator. Start the engine, and let it run for approximately 15 minutes or until operating temperature is reached. Check all water connections for leaks (hose connections). Tighten connections as needed.

WATER PUMP

Installing Water Pump w/4-Blade Fan

1. Apply the water pump gasket to the cylinder head with a small amount of Permatex gasket sealer on both sides. Mount the water pump with four (4) nuts (3/8-24) and lock washers [9/16 socket].
2. Set the radiator on the front cross member. Place a rubber pad under both radiator mounting brackets (28/29 use 1/8" pad, 30/31 use 1/16" pad). A piece of old inner tube works fine. Install the radiator mounting bolts, nuts and spring assembly as shown below. Tighten the bolts only enough to install cotter pins in the mounting bolts.

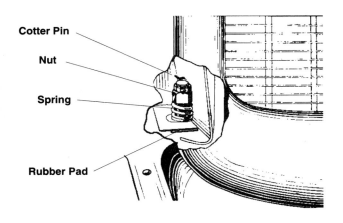

3. Place a short radiator hose over the end of the water return pipe and lower radiator hose pipe and attach with two (2) hose clamps.
4. Slip two (2) hose clamps over the long radiator hose and install the hose from the top radiator neck to the goose neck. Do not tighten these hose clamps until the radiator support rods have been installed and the hood installed and adjusted.

5. Attach the two (2) radiator support rods. Tighten the two front nuts only enough to hold the two rods in place [1/2" wrench].

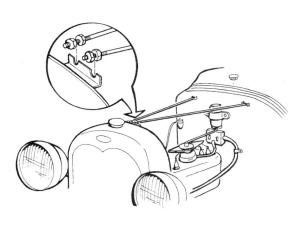

6. The radiator shell and fan shroud may not have been removed from the radiator during disassembly. If the shell was removed from the radiator, reinstall at this time, attaching with four (4) pan head screws (12-24 X 19/32") and square nuts.
7. Route the wiring harness through the radiator shell to the headlights and horn. Connect the horn wires.
8. Connect the headlight conduit connectors (push and twist clockwise to connect).

NOTE

Some headlight wiring may have been modified by eliminating the connector plug from inside the conduit socket. The wires would then be routed directly from the conduit into the headlight bucket and attached to the bulb sockets with wire nuts. The wires would have to be disconnected from behind the headlight reflector. To access the headlight bucket, release the front lens clip (spring loaded latch) and lift up on the lens rim to remove it. Remove the center bulb and lift the reflector out of the headlight bucket.

WATER PUMP

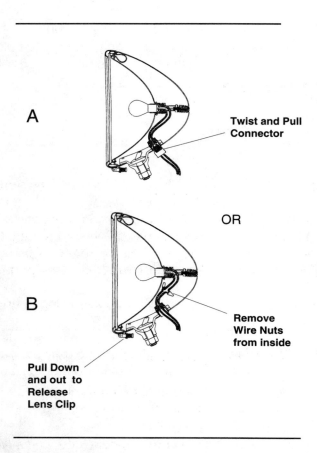

A — Twist and Pull Connector

OR

B — Remove Wire Nuts from inside
Pull Down and out to Release Lens Clip

9. Set the hood in place and attach it with two (2) screws, lock washers, and nuts [12-24 X 5/8" Round Head] on the rear hold down bracket.

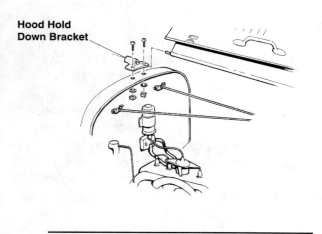

Hood Hold Down Bracket

10. After the hood has been installed and properly aligned, securely tighten both front radiator support rod nuts. Securely tighten the two radiator hose clamps on the upper radiator hose (radiator to goose neck).

11. Place the fan belt over the fan pulley, and then under the crank pulley. With the generator pushed up against the engine block, slip the belt over the generator pulley.

12. Pull the generator away from the block to apply tension on the belt. Set the generator holding bracket against the generator and tighten the holding bracket bolt on the timing cover [9/16 socket].

13. Pull hard on the generator while tightening the generator mounting bolt [3/4 socket]. Push on the belt at a point half way between the fan pulley and the generator pulley. Correct tension would allow the belt to be pushed in 1/2".

14. After correct belt tension is set, push the generator holding bracket tight against the generator and tighten the bracket bolt on the timing gear cover. Retighten the generator mounting bolt.

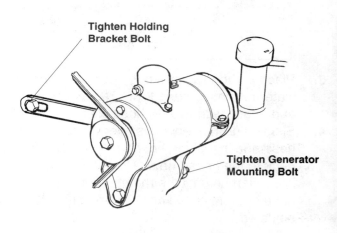

Tighten Holding Bracket Bolt

Tighten Generator Mounting Bolt

15. Reconnect the battery cable and then pour three (3) gallons of water into the radiator. Start the engine and let it run for approximately 15 minutes or until operating temperature is reached. Check all water connections for leaks (hose connections). Tighten connections as needed.

Service and Repair

WHEEL BEARINGS

The front wheel bearings should be removed and repacked with grease every 5,000 miles. The front wheel bearings are tapered (inner and outer) and are not greased through grease fittings. The front outer wheel bearing is the most susceptible to becoming dry and failing. When a front wheel bearing becomes dry and overheats, it usually results in the bearing welding it'self to the spindle, causing severe damage to the spindle and bearing races. By the time the warning noise is heard, it's too late. This can be avoided by packing the front bearings every 5,000 miles. Proper adjustment of the front wheel bearing nut is important to the life of the bearing and the retention of grease.

The rear wheel bearing is a roller bearing and is conveniently greased through a grease fitting during maintenance intervals.

Front Wheel Bearing

1. Remove the front wheel lug nuts and remove both front wheels.
2. Remove the axle cotter pin, axle nut (7/8-14 castle)[1-1/4" wrench] and washer. Remove the outer bearing, drum, and inner bearing.
3. Pack the inner and outer bearings with a high grade bearing grease.
4. Slip the inner bearing onto the front spindle, making sure it seats completely against the spindle backing.
5. Place the drum over the spindle axle, and insert the outer bearing, keyed axle washer, and castle nut.
6. Tighten the axle nut until a heavy drag on the drum is felt. Then back off on the castle nut until a very light drag is felt. Insert the cotter pin. The drum should spin free with no detectable side play.

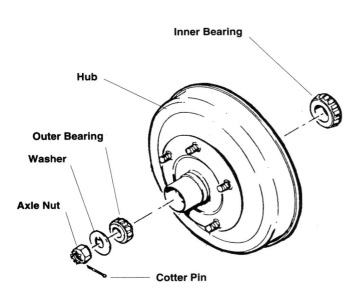

WHEEL BEARINGS

Rear Wheel Bearing

1. Release the emergency brake. Remove the cotter pin, washer, and grease seal (fiber washer) from the end of the axle.
2. Use a hub puller to remove the rear drum.
3. Grease is applied to the rear axle bearing through a grease fitting. If the grease seal or the bearing is badly worn or damaged, the bearing can be removed from the drum and replaced.
4. Remove the grease seal and bearing retainer ring. The roller bearing will lift out of the drum.
5. Insert a new roller bearing (with grease) into the hub.
6. Insert the grease seal so the inner lip on the seal faces the inside (toward bearing). Insert the steel retainer ring.
7. Insert an axle key (beveled edge toward inside, key must be tight fit in axle groove) and the drum.
8. Insert the fiber grease seal washer in the end of the drum (must seat into the drum, flush with the outer edge). Insert the steel washer and axle nut (5/8-18)[15/16 wrench]. Torque the rear axle nut to 125 ft/lbs. Insert cotter pin.

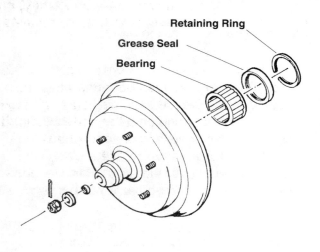

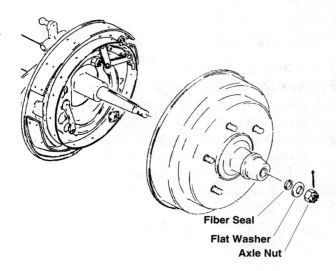

WINDOW GLASS AND REGULATOR

Hard to crank and sticking door window glass is usually caused by a worn and dry, or gummed up window regulator, or a door glass that does not fit the window channel correctly. The window crank handle operates a set of gears to raise and lower the regulator arm attached to a steel channel holding the glass. The lifting action at the bottom of the glass is always beyond center. It is farthest from center when the arm is parallel with the steel channel below the glass, and therefore exerts a side pressure when in motion up or down. As the glass is being raised, the top corner of the glass is being crowded hard against the felt glass channel. If the glass is not wide enough for proper fit between the felt channels, the glass is thrown out of alignment and will bind and eventually tear the felt channel. The glass should fit snugly between the channels, allowing only a small amount of clearance. A narrow glass giving trouble by binding can be corrected by removing the glass moldings and door panel and narrowing the glass opening with cardboard shims inserted between the felt channel and the door post. The door panel (cardboard covered w/upholstery) and window glass must be removed to successfully fix the problem. A worn and gummed up window regulator should be removed for cleaning and/or replacement to ease window cranking.

Removing Regulator

1. Remove the inside door handle and window crank. Most inside door handles are held in place with a single screw in the center of the shaft. To remove the window crank, push in the escutcheon and remove the pin that holds the crank to the regulator shaft.
2. Remove the inside door window sill (4 screws).
3. Remove the door cardboard panel by inserting a screwdriver blade between the door frame and the cardboard panel next to each spring clip and popping the spring clip out of the door frame hole. Use some patience here. Remember that the door panel is cardboard and will tear if you are not careful. The panel retaining clips are formed spring clips. The clips will pop out of the holes in the door fairly easy by placing the blade of a screwdriver against the shank (under the head of the clip) and then carefully prying out with the screw driver.
4. After all clips have been released and the door panel removed, roll the window half way up (or half way down) and check for side movement of the glass. Take hold of the glass at the top edge and move it from side to side in the channels. The glass should fit in the side channels with 1/16 " or less side play.
5. If the window glass is too loose in the channels it will allow the glass to cock forward as the window is rolled up and bind at the front edge of the channel. This can be corrected by replacing the two side window channels and/or shimming the channels to fit the glass. To either replace the channels or shim the channels requires removing the window glass from the door.

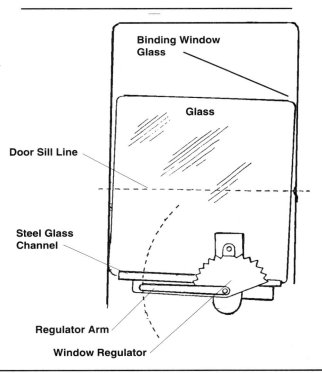

WINDOW GLASS/REGULATOR

6. To remove the window glass, remove the top door sill (3 screws).
7. To remove the regulator, roll the window all the way up.
8. Remove the three (or four) screws that hold the regulator in place. Before removing the last attaching screw, reach up behind the door frame and hold onto the glass channel and regulator. The glass channel must remain above the regulator to allow removal of the regulator.
9. After all screws have been removed, pull the regulator into the door (under the glass channel). The regulator can then be lowered to the bottom of the door and removed through the opening in the door frame. The regulator arm wheel will slide out of the window U-channel through a cutaway in the bottom of the channel. The window glass can be pushed all the way up and removed through the top of the door.
10. Thoroughly soak and clean the regulator in solvent. If the gear teeth are excessively worn, new regulators are available. Don't be too quick to buy a new regulator. The original regulator will usually fit and perform better if not excessively worn. Most of the time the original regulator will work fine after a thorough cleaning and lubrication.
11. After a thorough cleaning, spray the spring and inside mechanism liberally with WD-40. Put a light coat of grease on the regulator teeth.
12. Insert the crank handle and crank the regulator to both stops. It should crank smooth and easy from stop to stop.
13. Install new window channels in the door if needed. Insert the window glass through the top of the door and check for correct fit (1/16" side play or less with window half down). If needed, the side channels can be shimmed to fit the glass.
14. Remove the glass and one side channel.
15. Cut a strip of cardboard 1/2" wide X 16" long and glue to the back side of the channel or inside the door frame.
16. Reinstall the channel in the door frame and install the glass. Check clearance at the top, center, and bottom position of the glass. Shim the opposite channel if necessary. Usually shimming one side will fix the problem.

NOTE
Cardboard shim thickness is dependent on the amount of window side play.

Installing Window Regulator

1. Apply a small amount of grease along the inside of the U-channel at the bottom of the glass (where the regulator arm wheel rides).
2. Insert the window glass in the window channel and then lower the glass to the bottom of the door.
3. Raise the window above the bottom about 4" and place the regulator behind the door frame (below the glass channel), and insert the regulator arm wheel in the window bottom U-channel. There is a cutaway in the channel to allow access of the regulator arm wheel.
4. Push the window glass to the top position, insert the regulator crank shaft through the hole in the door panel and install the regulator screws and star washers.
5. Install the door top sill (3 screws).
6. Place the large retention spring over the regulator shaft, the small end against the door and the large end facing out.
7. Place the cardboard door panel over the regulator shaft and inside door handle rod. Press in each attaching spring clip around the door panel.
8. Install the bottom sill plate along the top edge of the door panel (4 screws).
9. Install the door handle and window crank. The window crank should turn effortlessly, raising the window to the top position with very little resistance and no binding.

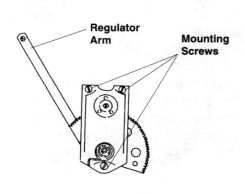

Regulator

Service and Repair

WIRING

The Model A uses a simple electrical system consisting of three (3) harnesses: a main wiring harness, an instrument panel harness, and a terminal box-to-generator harness. There are no wires returning current to the battery positive post. The metal body and frame carry the return current to the battery. A few short lengths of wire are used in some circuits, such as the pigtail wire used in the distributor, a wire for the instrument panel light, and a short wire from the coil to the terminal box. Each wire end has a connector that is fastened with a lock washer and nut to insure they remain tightly fastened. Electrically, the two terminal box posts are equal to the ammeter terminals. The yellow wire is always the battery circuit. The following procedures describe the routing and hookup of each harness and its purpose. Disconnect the battery before disconnecting or connecting harness wires.

Terminal Box-To-Generator Harness

This harness connects the battery voltage to the terminal box and terminal box to the generator. Before February 1930, this harness is in a metal conduit that runs from the junction box to the generator. After February 1930 the harness is in a black lacquered loom.

1. Connect the yellow wire spade terminal to the passenger side terminal box post.
2. Connect the yellow /black wire spade terminal to the driver side terminal box post.
3. Connect the yellow wire from the middle of the harness to the starter switch terminal.
4. Connect the yellow/black wire round connector to the cutout terminal on the generator.

Instrument Panel Harness

This harness connects the ammeter to the terminal box and the ignition switch to the coil.

1. Connect the yellow wire spade terminal to the passenger side terminal box post.
2. Connect the yellow /black wire spade terminal to the driver side terminal box post.
3. Connect the red wire spade terminal to the coil (+) post.
4. Connect the yellow/black wire round connector to the ammeter discharge post.
5. Connect the yellow wire round connector to the ammeter charge post.
6. Connect the red wire round connector to the ignition switch.

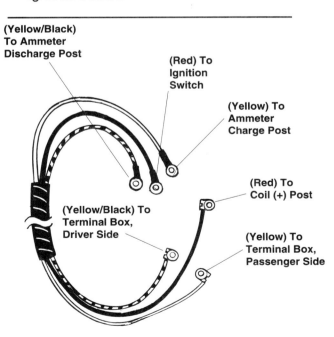

Terminal Box-To-Generator Harness

Instrument Panel Harness

WIRING

Main Harness

This harness connects power through the light switch base to the headlights, tail lights, stoplights, cowl lights, and the horn. This harness picks up battery voltage from the generator cutout connection for distribution through the light switch connector.

1. Install the main harness connector block in the light switch metal housing.
2. Lay the harness along the frame toward the radiator. Forward of the light switch, the harness runs under the lower portion of the frame and is clipped under the hood latch.
3. Connect the spade connector (yellow wire) to the cutout terminal.

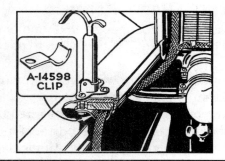

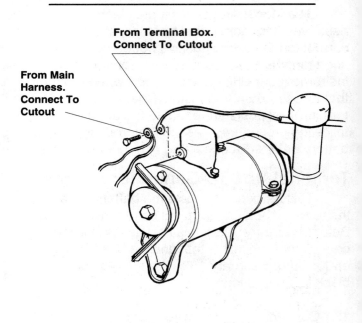

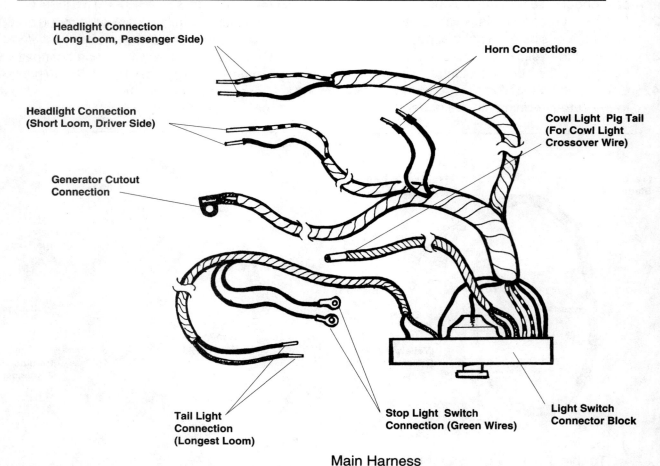

Main Harness

Service and Repair   1-366

WIRING

4. Route the two horn wires (blue/yellow and a yellow) under the lower radiator shell bracket and up the inside of the radiator shell to the lower conduit hole in the shell. Push the two wires through the conduit to the horn.
5. Route the shorter headlight harness wires (black/red and black/green) alongside the horn harness inside the radiator shell to the upper conduit hole in the shell. Push the wires through the conduit. When the wires come out of the conduit, separate them into the light plug. This will align the wires with the socket in the headlight.
6. Route the longer headlight harness wires along the bottom of the radiator to the passenger side of the car. Attach the harness to the bottom side of the radiator with three (3) wire clips attached to the radiator. Then route the wires up along the inside of the radiator shell to the conduit hole. Push the wires through the conduit to the right headlight. When the wires come out of the conduit, separate them into the light plug.
7. Route the longest loom under the car next to the frame to the tail light (left side).
   Note: A crossover wire will need to be added if there is a right side tail light. The black wire connects to the tail light and the green wire connects to the stoplight. The two green wires coming out of the middle of this loom connect to the two screw terminals on the bottom of the stoplight switch.

Coil (Black) Wire
1. Connect the spade connector terminal to the driver side terminal box post. Route the wire out the top of the terminal box to the (-) post on the ignition coil on the firewall.

Cowl Light Crossover
1. If the car is equipped with cowl lights, the main harness will have a short black wire with female sleeve extending from the harness near the light switch housing. The cowl light crossover wire will plug into the black wire sleeve.
2. Route the wires to each side of the car along the back side of the firewall to the cardboard cowl panels (inside cowl panels). Remove the cowl panels for connection to the cowl lights.

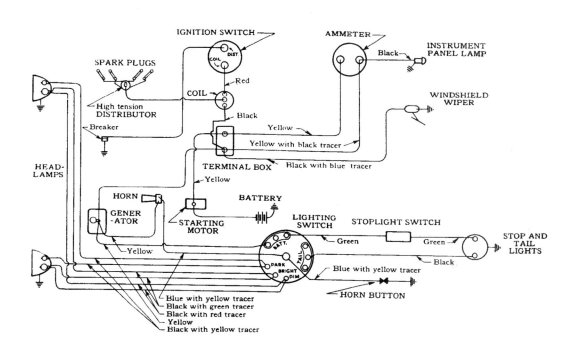

SECTION II
SERVICE ADJUSTMENTS

INTRODUCTION

This sections includes all adjustment and alignment procedures needed for servicing the Model A. Every adjustment is based on the original Ford specifications. Although, some procedures have been changed for the convenience of the home shop Model A owner. Full adjustment should be made on each component after it has been serviced or repaired. Some adjustments should be made on a regularly scheduled basis, as identified in the procedure.

SERVICE BRAKE ADJUSTMENT

Adjustment of the Model A brakes is only effective if the entire brake system is within tolerance and in specified operating condition. Before any adjustments are made to the brakes, the entire mechanical system should be inspected and corrected if necessary. If adjusting the brakes does not provide satisfactory braking, see "Section I, SERVICE and REPAIR, BRAKES" (page1-33) for a complete description on servicing the brake system. Service brake adjustment should be checked every 5,000 miles.

The following items will affect brake adjustment:
- Incorrect brake rod length
- Brake shoe wear
- Drums worn too thin
- Worn actuating lever bushings
- Worn clevis eyes and pins
- Worn cross shaft bushings
- Unequal brake adjusting shaft length
- Worn operating pin
- Worn roller track on backing plate
- Out of round drums
- Insufficient forward tilt on front actuating arm
- Worn brake pedal bushings and shaft
- Bent brake rods

A brake pedal adjusting board[1] is needed to make an effective and accurate adjustment.

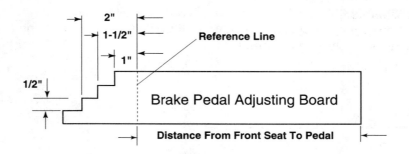

Brake Adjustment

NOTE

Always make adjustments with the brakes cold.

1. Place a jack under all four wheels (under the axles, not the frame).
2. Place the gear shift lever in neutral and release the hand brake.
3. Turn the adjusting wedge clockwise on the back of the backing plate until the brakes start to drag, then back the adjusting wedge out 2 or 3 notches, or enough to allow the wheels to rotate without drag. Always spin the wheel in the forward direction when testing for drag.

NOTE

A slight drag in one or two spots at 1/4 or 1/2 revolution will do no harm. Use judgement in determining a free spinning wheel.

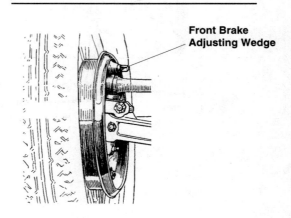

---

1. Brake Pedal Adjusting Board was the idea of Peter Crosby, Huntington, Vermont

SERVICE BRAKE ADJUSTMENT

4. Make certain the brake cross shaft is in a vertical position and is in the center of its travel.

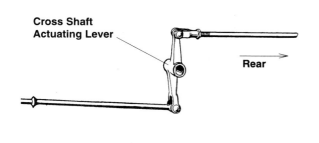

5. Remove the rear brake rod clevis pin at the cross shaft actuating lever.
6. Unlock the clevis jam nut on the brake rod so the clevis can be adjusted. Pull the rear brake rod forward enough to take up all free travel (without actuating the brakes).
7. Adjust the clevis on the brake rod until the hole in the clevis lines up with the hole in the cross shaft lever arm pin hole, allowing the clevis pin to be inserted. Tighten the jam nut against the clevis.

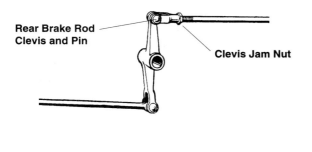

8. Repeat steps 5, 6, and 7 to remove free travel from the other rear brake rod.
9. Remove the front brake rod clevis pin at the front brake rod actuating arm.
10. Pull the front brake actuating arm back to take up free travel. With no free travel, the actuating arm should be positioned 15 degrees <u>forward</u> of perpendicular.

NOTE

Correct adjustment of the front brake cannot be made until the front brake actuating arm is 15 degrees forward with no free play. This can be corrected by replacing a worn brake operating pin (See "Section I, Service and Repair, Brakes" (page 1-33).

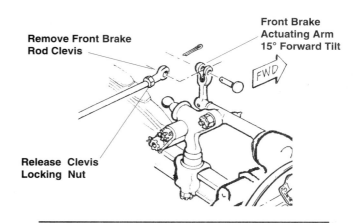

11. Release the front brake rod clevis locking nut. Pull the brake rod forward and adjust the clevis to line up with the front actuating arm pin hole and reinsert the clevis pin. Tighten the jam nut against the clevis.
12. Repeat steps 9, 10, and 11 to remove free travel from the other front brake rod.

SERVICE BRAKE ADJUSTMENT

13. Make sure new cotter pins have been installed in all four clevis pins that were removed.

NOTE
The brake pedal adjusting board should be used for the following adjustments.

14. Insert the brake pedal adjusting board and check that the fully extended brake pedal is at the reference line, then set the pedal in position ① (pedal depressed 1").

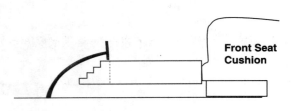

Pedal Board at Reference Mark

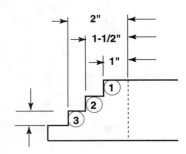

Pedal Board Notch Positions

15. Turn the adjusting wedge on the rear wheels until the rear brakes just begin to hold. Adjust both rear wheels accordingly.

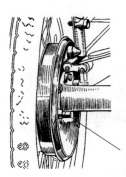

Rear Brake Adjusting Wedge (Turn Clockwise To Tighten)

16. Move the pedal adjusting board to position ② (pedal depressed 1-1/2"). The two rear brakes should be <u>very</u> tight, but not locked.

17. Adjust the front brake adjusting wedge until the front brakes just begin to hold.

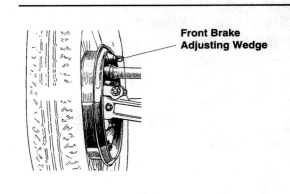

Front Brake Adjusting Wedge

Service Adjustments

SERVICE BRAKE ADJUSTMENT

18. Move the pedal adjusting board to position ③ (pedal depressed 2").

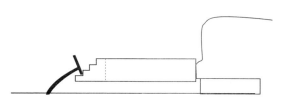

Pedal Depressed 2"

19. Rear brakes should be locked solid. Front brakes should have very heavy drag (not locked).
20. Check all four tires for correct tire pressure (34 lbs). Make sure all cotter pins have been installed.
21. Lower the car off the jack stands and test drive. At 20-25 MPH apply full brake pressure. The rear wheels should skid evenly, without pulling to either side. The front wheels should leave little or no skid marks. (A light skid mark on the front brakes will give better stopping.)
22. If the car pulls to one side during the stop test, turn the adjusting wedge in one click (clockwise) on the opposite side of the pull and retest.
23. After the braking test, return to the shop and jack up each wheel. Spin each wheel to see that it is not binding.

No amount of adjustment will provide good stopping with a worn out brake system. If the above adjustments can not be satisfactorily made, see "Section I, Service and Repair, Brakes" (page 1-33).

Pedal Adjusting Board Results

① Rear Brake Just Starts To Hold

② Rear Brakes Very Tight (Not Locked)
   Front Brakes Just Start To Hold

③ Rear Brakes Locked
   Front Brakes Very Tight (Not Locked)

CASTER ADJUSTMENT

CASTER ADJUSTMENT

Since steering is the hardest part of driving, anything that can be done to reduce the effort adds greatly to the comfort of driving. To give ease and certainty of steering, the Model A front axle is given a slant (caster) of 5 degrees. The purpose of the caster is to give the front wheels a tendency to maintain the straight ahead position on a level road. <u>The caster is maintained by the front radius rod,</u> mounted to hold the front axle at the proper angle. Therefore, if the radius rod position is changed, the caster is changed. Too much caster makes a car steer hard and is conducive to shimmy. Not enough caster (or reverse caster) causes the front wheels to wander and dive (like a car that is driven backwards) and the car must be steered continually. Caster can be easily measured to determine if it is within specification. If the caster measures more than ± 1° of 5 degrees, the fault is either at the radius ball or a bent radius rod. Check to see that the radius ball is correctly installed (see "Section 1, Service and Repair, Radius Ball Cap", (page 1-234). The after market (rubber ball) radius ball kit will usually adversely affect the front caster. Always install the original design radius ball cap components.

Measuring Caster

1. Place the car on a level driveway. Make a reference chalk mark on the front axle 5" to the inside of the spring perch bolt.

2. Measure and record the distance from the reference mark to the driveway. It should be between 11" to 12", depending on wheel size and variation of tire manufacturer size.

3. Use a string and plumb bob to locate a point directly below the axle reference point. Make a mark on the driveway and call it point A.

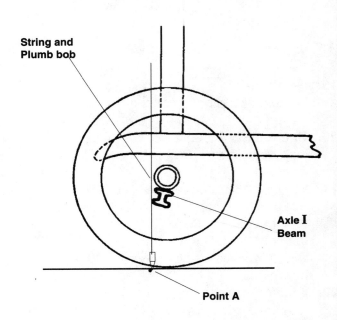

4. Lay a straight edge along the axle I beam, extended to the ground. Make a mark at ground point. Mark this point B.

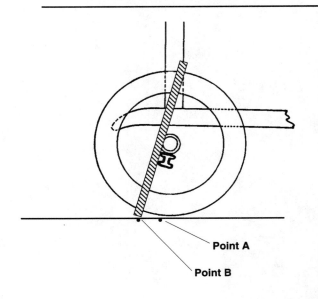

Measure the distance between point A and point B. The distance should be about 1 inch, depending on the height from the axle reference point to ground.

At a reference height of eleven (11) inches from the bottom ridge on the axle to ground, and a 1 inch spread between points A and B, is equivalent to 5° caster.

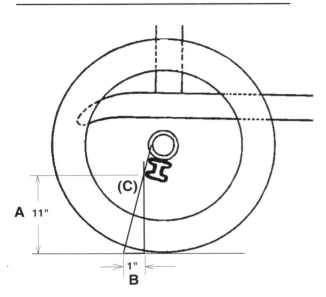

6. Caster is calculated as: $\frac{B}{A} = <(C)$

   TANGENT of $<(C)$ = Angle of Caster

   $\frac{1}{11} = .09$

   TANGENT OF .09 = 5.1 degrees Caster

CARBURETOR ADJUSTMENT

There are only two (2) in-service adjustments for the Zenith carburetor: (1) idle speed adjust, and (2) idle air mixture adjust. As indicated by their names, these adjustments affect only the idle circuit and have no effect on other functions of the carburetor. If the following adjustments cannot be satisfactorily made, see "Section I, Service and Repair, CARBURETOR", (page 1-57).

1. Start the engine and let it run at a fast idle until normal operating temperature is reached.
2. Fully retard the spark advance control rod on the left side of the steering column. (push all the way to the top most position.)
3. Turn the fuel mixture control (passenger side under gas tank) full clockwise to its seat position. Then back the mixture control out 1/4 turn or less.
   CAUTION: Never turn the fuel mixture control tight against the seat. The needle valve will be damaged.
4. Set the carburetor idle speed adjust screw for a slow idle in the full retard position.

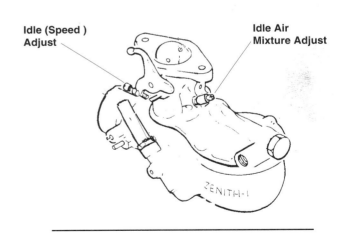

5. Slowly turn the idle air mixture screw in (CW) until the engine begins to stall. Note the position of the adjusting screw.

CLUTCH PEDAL ADJUSTMENT

6. Slowly turn the idle air mixture screw out (CCW) until the engine begins to stall. Note position of adjusting screw. Turn the screw half way between the two settings. Normal setting of the idle air mixture screw should be 1-1/2 turns from full clockwise position.

NOTE

If adjustment of the idle air mixture screw does not cause the engine to stall at some point in the adjustment, it is an indication that there is an air leak in the intake system. Look for air leaks around the throttle shaft (worn shaft), manifold to carburetor gasket, manifold to block gasket, and vacuum line leaks (to wiper motor).

7. Advance the spark control rod on the steering column to normal operating position (about 3/4 of the way down).
8. Adjust the idle adjust screw on the carburetor for the desired idle speed.

CLUTCH PEDAL ADJUSTMENT

When the clutch pedal is depressed, there must be 1" movement of the pedal before it starts to disengage the clutch. As the clutch facings wear, this clearance or play gradually becomes less. Consequently it should occasionally be checked.

1. Check pedal free play to determine how much adjustment is required.
2. Place a small hydraulic jack under the clutch actuating arm. Raise the arm enough to relieve tension on the pedal clevis rod. Remove the clevis pin from the pedal clevis rod.
3. Rotate the clevis rod in the trunnion nut to adjust pedal clearance. Turn the clevis rod in (clockwise) to increase pedal clearance. Turn the clevis rod out (counter clockwise) to decrease pedal clearance.
4. If the trunnion nut is badly worn, remove the clevis rod from the trunnion nut, turn the nut over and reinstall the trunnion and clevis rod.

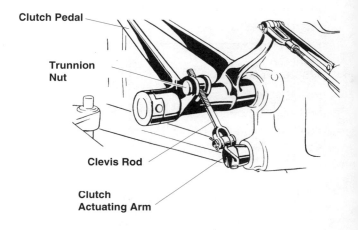

5. Reconnect clevis rod to clutch actuating arm. Check for 1" pedal clearance before it starts to disengage the clutch.

Service Adjustments

FAN BELT ADJUSTMENT

1. Loosen the generator mounting bolt and nut [3/4 socket].

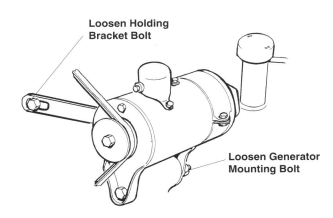

2. If a generator holding bracket is installed, loosen the holding bracket bolt [9/16 socket] on the timing gear cover.
3. Pull the generator away from the block to apply tension on the belt. Set the generator holding bracket against the generator and tighten the holding bracket bolt on the timing cover [9/16 socket].
4. Pull hard on the generator while tightening the generator mounting bolt [3/4 socket]. Push on the belt at a point half way between the fan pulley and the generator pulley. Correct tension would allow the belt to be pushed in 1/2" to 1".

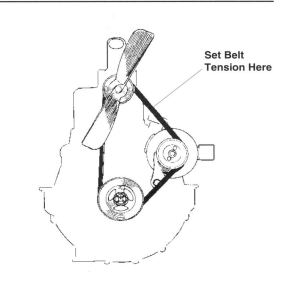

Belt Routing

5. After correct belt tension is set, push the generator holding bracket tight against the generator and tighten the bracket bolt on the timing gear cover. Retighten the generator mounting bolt.

FRONT WHEEL BEARING ADJUST

Front wheel bearings should be checked every 5,000 miles for grease and adjustment. Always repack bearings with grease when servicing for adjustment. A front wheel bearing adjusted too tight can cause premature failure.

1. Remove the front wheel lug nuts and remove both front wheels.
2. Remove the axle cotter pin, axle nut (7/8-14 castle)[1-1/4" wrench] and washer. Remove outer bearing, drum, and inner bearing.
3. Pack the inner and outer bearings with a high grade bearing grease.
4. Slip the inner bearing on the front spindle, making sure it seats completely against the spindle backing.
5. Place the drum over the spindle axle, and insert the outer bearing, keyed axle washer, and castle nut.
6. Tighten the axle nut until the inner and outer bearings are snug in their cones (8 to 10 ft.lbs torque on the axle nut).
7. Grasp the drum at top and bottom, apply side strain, and see that bearings are tight in the hub with no side play. A heavy drag will be noticeable when the drum is turned.
8. Turn the axle nut back one or two castle slots, insert a cotter pin, and try spinning the wheel. The wheel should spin freely.

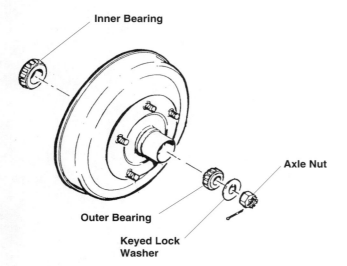

GENERATOR CHARGING RATE

Charging rate of the generator is set by moving an adjustable brush. Move the brush a small amount in the direction needed. Observe the charging rate as indicated on the ammeter. Charging rate for normal driving should be set at 10 Amps. For long trips set the charging rate to 8 Amps.

CAUTION
Never use a metal or sharp object to adjust the charging brush. Use a wood or non metallic stick to move the brush.

Power House Generator

1. Remove the rear cover. Lift the ends of the cover retaining wire out of the retaining holes at each end.. Lift the cover off the generator.
2. Loosen the field brush-holder lock screw (**A**) on the bottom brush. This is the only brush provided with a locking screw. All others are riveted.

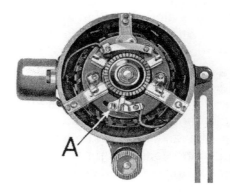

3. To increase the charging rate move the brush toward the engine (direction of rotation). To decrease the charging rate move the charging brush away from the engine.
4. After adjusting the charging rate, be sure to tighten the locking screw. Replace rear cover.

Service Adjustments

GENERATOR CHARGING RATE

Cylinder Style Generator

1. Loosen the screw on the rear cover band. Slide the cover off the back of the generator.

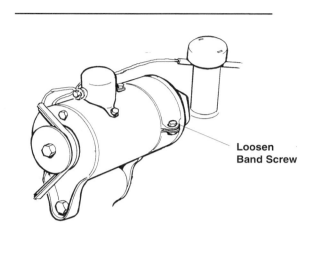
Loosen Band Screw

2. The charging brush is spring loaded. There is no locking screw for the movable brush. Move the brush up to decrease charging rate. Move the brush down to increase the charging rate.

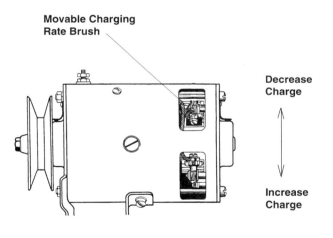
Movable Charging Rate Brush
Decrease Charge
Increase Charge

3. Replace the cover band and tighten the band screw.

HEADLAMP FOCUSING AND ALIGNMENT

A test bay must be available and can be set up in a garage as shown in the illustration below. A black line painted on the floor indicates the left tire position. Mark a center line 28" from the tire track. The face of the headlamp to the focusing wall must be 25 feet. On the focus wall, mark a line indicating the center line of the car. Mark a line 15" to each side of the center line. Each headlight will be centered on this line, setting them 30" apart. Mark a horizontal line across the top of the alignment lines, 37" above the floor line. (Early 1928 single filament headlamps with fluted lens were adjusted at 33" above the floor line.)

The headlamps are adjusted with the high beam (bright) only. The low beam will be correct with the high beam correctly adjusted.

1. Position the car with the left tire on the painted line, and the car positioned perpendicular to the focusing wall. All occupants must be out of the car for headlight alignment.
2. Park the car so the face of the headlamp is 25 feet from the focusing wall.

NOTE
The headlamp lens must be installed properly with the word "TOP" at the top of the of the headlight rim, and all lettering level and reading from the front of the car.

3. **Focus Adjustment** - Turn the headlights ON to bright position. Cover the right headlamp to allow focusing of the left headlamp.

Service Adjustments

HEADLAMP FOCUSING AND ALIGNMENT

4. Turn the focusing screw on the back of the headlamp to obtain an elongated elliptical spot of light on the focus wall, with its long axis horizontal. Adjust for a well defined cutoff across the top of the spot of the light as possible.

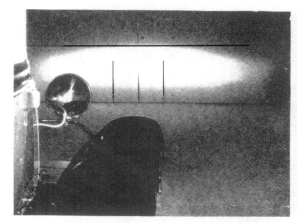

Focus and Alignment Position

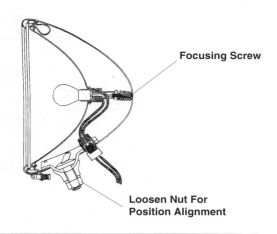

5. Cover the left headlamp and adjust the focus of the right headlamp as described in step 4.

6. **Alignment** - Loosen the nut at the bottom of the headlight bracket to allow the headlamp to be positioned.

7. Cover the right headlamp to adjust the left headlamp. Move the headlamp so the top of the elliptical spot touches the bottom of the horizontal adjustment line (37" above the floor).

8. Center the spot on the left vertical line, 15" to the left of the center line. Tighten the headlamp mounting nut.

9. Cover the left headlight. Adjust the right headlight, repeating steps 7 and 8.

10. Remove the cover from both headlamps. The beams should be on the same line, with the top of the beam 37 inches above the floor and the center of each spot 30 inches apart.

11. Turn the headlight switch to low beam position. The headlight beam should remain focused and aligned at a lower position.

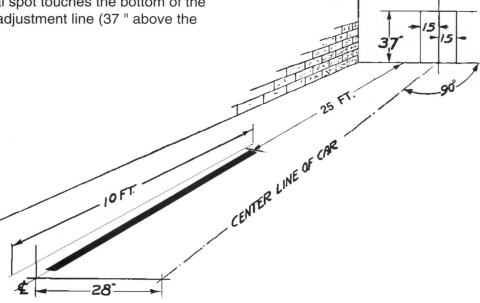

Service Adjustments

HORN ADJUST/SHOCK ADJUST

HORN ADJUST

To produce the most effective tone, it is necessary that the armature revolve at a high rate of speed. This speed is possible only when the horn is properly oiled, and the communicator and brushes are kept clean. For proper cleaning see Section I, Service and Repair, HORN, page 1-194.

1. Remove the rear cover screw to remove the rear cover.
2. Place a drop of light oil on the armature shaft felt oil pads (**B**).
3. Lightly spray the armature with tuner cleaner, and while placing the motor in motion by pressing the horn button, clean the commutator with a cloth.
4. With the motor in motion, turn the adjusting screw (**A**) to regulate the desired tone.
5. Replace the rear cover and screw. Do not excessively tighten the cover screw. It can adversely affect the tone adjustment.
6. After installing the rear cover, press the horn button to test the tone. Readjust the horn adjusting screw one notch at a time until desired tone is obtained.

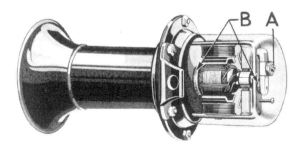

SHOCK ABSORBER ADJUSTMENT

The pointer on the shock absorbers appeared on shocks from the beginning of production to September 1928. After September 1928, the pointer and numbers were removed because of interference with the brake rod. The end of the needle valve was changed to a slotted end so it could be easily turned with a screwdriver (**A**).

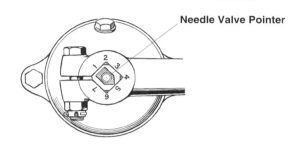

Beginning Production to Sept. 1928

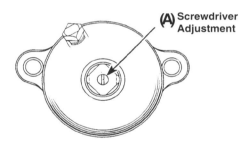

September 1928 to End of Production

1. Screw the needle in (clockwise) to increase resistance. Screw the needle out (counterclockwise) to decrease resistance.
2. **Warm Climate** - **(Front)** Screw the needle valve in until it seats, then back it out 5/8 to 3/4 turn. (Needle valve with pointer and numbers set at 2 to 3.
3. **(Rear)** Screw the needle valve in until it seats, then back it out 1/4 turn. (Needle valve with pointer set at 3 or 4.)
4. **Cold Climate** - **(Front)** Screw the needle valve in until it seats, then back it out 3/8 turn. (set to 5 with pointer).
5. **(Rear)** Screw the needle valve in until it seats, then back it out 1/2 to 5/8 turn. (set to 4 with pointer).

STEERING ADJUST

STEERING ADJUST

Two different steering gear columns were made for the Model A, a 7-tooth sector and worm gear and a 2-tooth sector and worm gear. The 7-tooth sector and worm gear was used primarily in 1928/1929 year models. The 2-tooth sector and worm gear were used primarily in 1930/1931 year models. Steering shaft end play and sector shaft end play are the only two adjustments that can be made to the 7-tooth steering assembly. Three adjustments can be made to the 2-tooth sector steering, Sector Shaft End Play, Steering Shaft End Play, and Sector Worm Mesh Adjustment. When making adjustments, the front wheels of the car should be jacked up and the drag link disconnected from the steering arm (pitman arm) in order to effect a satisfactory adjustment.

7-Tooth Steering Shaft End Play Adjust

1. Grab the steering wheel and try moving it up and down in the column. If it moves, add or delete brass shims from under the lower shaft bushing assembly to adjust out steering shaft end play.
2. To remove lower shaft bushing shims, first release the bail wire from the light switch (push bail wire down) at the end of the steering column. Pull the light switch bulb from the end of the steering column.

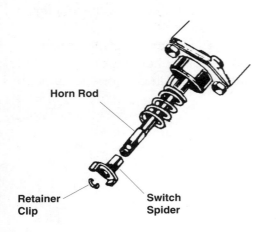

3. Push up slightly on the switch spider to remove the retaining clip, spider, and spring from the end of the horn rod.
4. Remove the four (4) bolts at the end of the column [7/16 socket], and pull out the lower bearing assembly. Retain the brass shims that come off when the bearing assembly is removed.
5. Remove the oil seal retainer nut (5/8 socket) from the center of the bearing assembly. Remove and replace the oil seal.

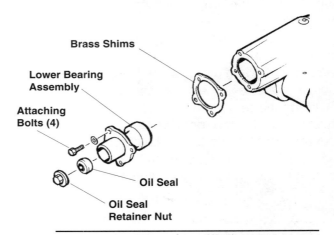

6. Remove one or two brass shims and reassemble the lower bushing assembly.
7. After reassembly, check steering shaft end play by repeating step 1. Steering shaft end play should not exceed .003". If it does or it feels rough, the steering worm thrust bearings may need replacing. See "Section I, Service and Repair, Steering".
8. Install the horn rod, spring, and switch spider. Install light the switch with bail wire.

STEERING ADJUST

7-Tooth Sector Shaft End Play Adjust

1. Disconnect the drag link at the pitman arm by removing the end cotter pin and unscrewing the drag link end plug. Slightly turn the steering wheel to the left to allow removal of the drag link from the pitman arm ball.

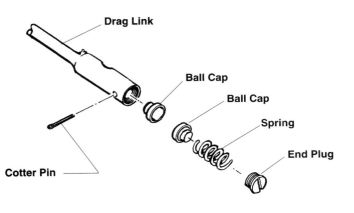

NOTE
The pitman arm must fit tight on the sector shaft. Tighten the pitman arm nut enough to eliminate all movement between the pitman arm and the sector shaft.

2. Grab the end of the sector shaft and move it in and out while making the adjustment. Loosen the lock nut and screw the end play adjusting screw in until the sector shaft end play is removed. Hold the screw in place while tightening down the jam nut [3/4 wrench].

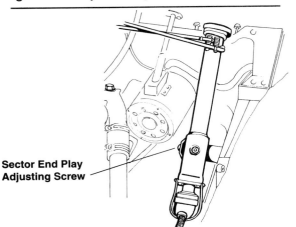

3. After adjustment, rotate the steering shaft from stop-to-stop to ensure free travel with no binding.
4. Reconnect the drag link to the pitman arm.

2-Tooth Sector Shaft End Play Adjust

When it is necessary to make any one of the three adjustments on the 2-tooth sector steering, the other two adjustments should also be checked. Adjustments should always be checked in the following order: Sector Shaft End Play, Steering Shaft End Play, and Sector Worm Mesh adjustment.

1. Disconnect the drag link at the pitman arm by removing the end cotter pin and unscrewing the drag link end plug. Slightly turn the steering wheel to the left to allow removal of the drag link from the pitman arm ball.

NOTE
The pitman arm must fit tight on the sector shaft. Tighten the pitman arm nut enough to eliminate all movement between the pitman arm and the sector shaft.

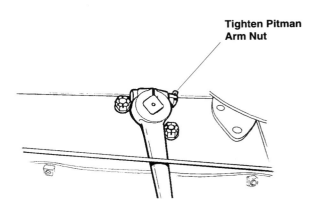

STEERING ADJUST

2. Check that the sector housing nuts are all tight. Turn the steering to either end stop and then back 1/8 turn.
3. Grab the end of the sector shaft and move it in and out while making the adjustment. Loosen the lock nut and screw the end play adjusting screw in until sector shaft end play is removed. Hold the screw in place while tightening down the jam nut [3/4 wrench].

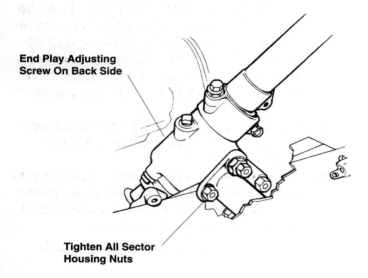

End Play Adjusting Screw On Back Side

Tighten All Sector Housing Nuts

4. After adjustment, rotate the steering shaft from stop-to-stop to ensure free travel with no binding.

2-Tooth Sector Steering Shaft End Play Adjust

When it is necessary to make any one of the three adjustments on the 2-tooth sector steering, the other two adjustments should also be checked. Adjustments should always be checked in the following order: Sector Shaft End Play, Steering Shaft End Play, and Sector Worm Mesh adjustment.
1. Turn the steering to either end stop and then back 1/8 turn.
2. Grab the steering wheel and try moving it up and down in the column. If it moves, the steering shaft end play needs adjusting.

3. Loosen the housing clamp bolt, column clamp bolt, and the adjusting bolt jam nut.
4. Turn down the adjusting bolt just enough to eliminate shaft end play, then back off 1/6 of a turn.

CAUTION
Adjusting this bolt too tight after end play has been removed can cause the upper race to crack.

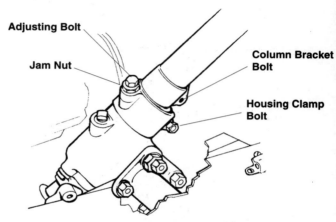

Adjusting Bolt

Jam Nut

Column Bracket Bolt

Housing Clamp Bolt

5. Hold the adjusting bolt with a wrench while tightening the jam nut. Securely tighten the housing clamp bolt and column bracket bolt.
6. Turn the steering wheel from extreme to extreme position and test for binding. Readjust if binding occurs.

2-Tooth Sector Worm Mesh Adjust

When it is necessary to make any one of the three adjustments on the 2-tooth sector steering, the other two adjustments should also be checked. Adjustments should always be checked in the following order: Sector Shaft End Play, Steering Shaft End Play, and Sector Worm Mesh adjustment.
1. Turn the steering wheel to the mid position of its turning limits.

STEERING ADJUST

NOTE

The pitman arm <u>must</u> fit tight on the sector shaft. Tighten the pitman arm nut enough to eliminate <u>all</u> movement between the pitman arm and the sector shaft.

2. With the steering shaft at center position, rotate the pitman arm back and forth to check for play in the sector to worm mesh.

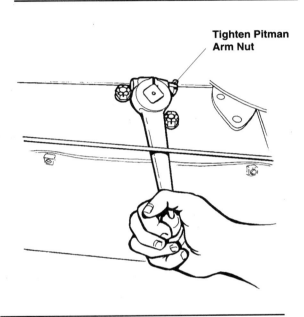

Tighten Pitman Arm Nut

3. This adjustment is made with the adjusting sleeve nut, located on the upper-right sector housing stud. This is an eccentric sleeve that moves the position of the sector housing, thereby changing the position of the sector teeth to the worm gear. This adjustment is made to remove all lateral play in the sector shaft when positioned at the center of travel.

4. To adjust sector mesh:
   a. Loosen the three housing cover nuts 1/4 turn [5/8 wrench].
   b. Loosen the housing cover adjusting nut 1/4 turn [5/8 wrench].
   c. Turn the eccentric adjusting sleeve nut [7/8 wrench] clockwise very gradually while rotating the pitman arm back and forth to detect sector play. Stop adjustment when all play in the sector shaft is eliminated. Do not adjust beyond the zero movement point. It may be necessary to back off the adjustment and re-approach the adjustment again. Always approach and finish the adjustment in a clockwise direction. The split in the eccentric adjusting nut should finish at about 2 o'clock position.
   d. After adjustment, tighten the housing cover adjusting nut first, then tighten the other three housing nuts.
   e. Rotate the steering shaft from stop-to-stop to ensure free travel with no binding. If binding is felt at any point, repeat steps a through d. until correct adjustment is made.

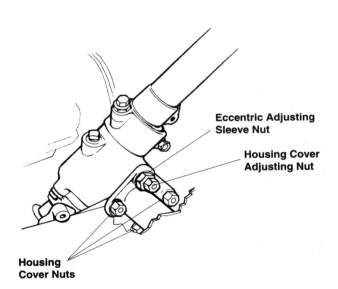

Eccentric Adjusting Sleeve Nut

Housing Cover Adjusting Nut

Housing Cover Nuts

Service Adjustments

IGNITION TIMING

IGNITION TIMING

1. Set the breaker point gap at .020 inches.
2. Check the rotor gap to distributor body contact points. Adjust at .025 inches

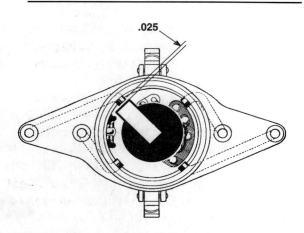

3. Turn ignition key OFF.
4. Place the gear shift lever in the neutral position.
5. Fully retard the spark lever on the steering column.
6. Screw out the timing pin located in the timing gear cover. Insert the opposite end of the pin (pointed end) into the timing pin hole.
7. With the starting crank, turn the engine over slowly while at the same time pressing in firmly on the timing pin. When the #1 piston reaches the top of the stroke (T.D.C.), the timing pin will drop into a small recess in the cam gear.

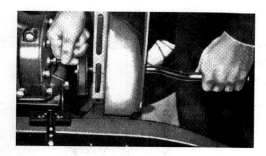

8. With the timing pin in place, remove the distributor cap, distributor body, and rotor.

9. Loosen the cam locking screw until the cam can be turned.

10. Replace the rotor on the cam and turn it until the rotor arm is opposite No. 1 contact point in the distributor body. (This identifies the correct cam lobe for timing.)

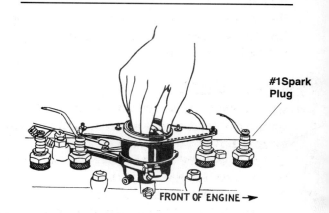

Service Adjustments

TOW-IN ADJUST

11. Remove the rotor and distributor body.
12. Connect a test light between the breaker point arm and a ground point.

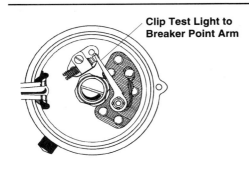

13. Turn the ignition key ON. Turn the distributor cam CCW until the points open (test lamp LIGHTS, and breaker point arm rubbing block is sitting on the cam high lobe).
14. Turn the cam CW until the points close. (Test lamp OFF). Lock the cam screw down and turn the cam CCW just enough to remove all backlash. The points should be in the "just closed" position. Repeat this step if necessary.
15. Slowly pull down on the spark advance rod until the points open, while counting each notch it passes. The test lamp should LIGHT (points open) at the 2nd quadrant notch. Repeat steps 13, 14, and 15 until the cam is correctly set. Replace the rotor and cap.

NOTE
This correctly sets the timing for the spark advance control rod at 3/4 down position on the column quadrant (normal driving position).

16. Remove the timing pin from the front timing gear cover, turn it around and screw it tight into the timing gear cover.

TOE-IN ADJUST
The front wheels should have a toe-in of 1/16"±1/32.

1. Jack the front end of the car up just enough to raise the front wheels off the ground.
2. Check both front wheels to make sure the front wheel bearings are not loose.
3. Place a piece of chalk against the tire thread and spin the tire to make an even line around the tire. Do the same for both front tires (exact location of the line is not important). Spin the tire and make a thin line in the center of the chalk mark with a nail.
4. At some point on the line, place a mark across the line on each tire, indicating a reference point.
5. Bring both reference points to the front, in horizontal line with the hub cap. Measure the distance between the reference marks on both wheels (**B**).
6. Move to the back side of the tire to a point directly behind the hubcap. Measure the distance between the lines on each tire (**A**). The difference between the front (B) and rear (A) measurement should be 1/16" ±1/32, with the front measurement (B) being the shortest.
7. If adjustment is required, remove the cotter pins and loosen the two tie-rod end clamp bolt nuts; then turn the tie-rod in or out until correct adjustment is obtained. The tie-rod has right-hand thread on one end and left-hand thread on the other end which simplifies the adjustment.

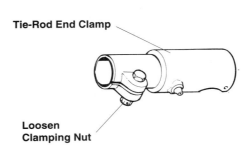

8. When correct toe-in is obtained, tighten the two tie-rod clamping bolt nuts and replace cotter pins.

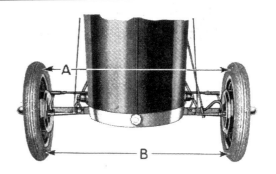

VALVE GRINDING AND ADJUSTMENT

VALVE GRINDING AND ADJUSTMENT

This subject is in two parts. The first topic describes grinding and seating the valves, and the second topic describes how to set valve clearance.

Grinding and Seating Valves

Grinding and seating the valves in the Model A requires removing the cylinder head.

1. To remove the cylinder head, refer to Section I, Service and Repair, Cylinder Head (page 1-80, step 1 through 22).
2. Shut off the gas valve.
3. Disconnect carburetor gasoline at the carburetor (9/16 wrench).
4. Remove the carburetor from the intake manifold (two (2) bolts), [1/2 inch wrench].
5. Remove the two bolts [1/2 socket] and brass washers attaching the oil return pipe.
6. Remove the ten (10) bolts [1/2 inch socket] and lock washers from around the valve cover and remove the cover plate. When removing the valve cover, there may be a small amount of oil left in the valve chamber. A shop towel may be needed for clean up when removing the cover.

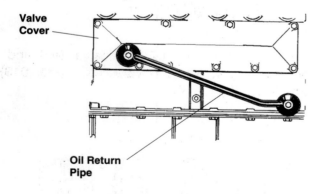

7. Remove all eight (8) valve spring keepers using a valve spring compressor to enable removal of the keepers from around the bottom mushroom of the valve.

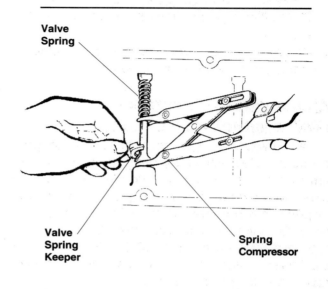

8. Lift each valve and inspect the valve seat in the block and the face of each valve. The valve will have to be removed if face grinding is needed on the valve or if the seat in the block needs to be reground. Remove the valve spring and valve guide (with valve guide remover) from the valve chamber. The valve can then be lifted straight up out of the block.
9. If the valves and seats do not require regrinding, the valves can be ground in (lapped) without removing the valve. This is easily done with a vacuum cup type valve grinder.

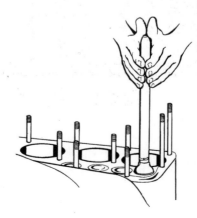

Service Adjustments

VALVE GRINDING AND ADJUSTMENT

10. Use a small amount of grinding compound to lap the valve seats. When a dull finish is seen on 2/3 of the valve face and the seat, the valve is properly lapped in. Prevent any grinding compound from getting into the valve guide.
11. Clean all compound from the valve face and seat.
12. Replace all valve springs and keepers. Check and adjust clearance on all valves.

Adjusting Valve Clearance (w/Adjustable Valve Lifters)

All valves, valve guides, springs, and keepers must be installed before adjusting valve clearance. All measurements are made with the lifter resting on the heel of the cam lobe (lowest point on the cam). This position is obtained when all four pistons are even in the cylinders, half way down the cylinder. At this point all four cylinders are 2-3/8" from the top of the cylinder. Check and record all valve clearances before making any adjustments.

Exhaust Valves : No's 1, 4, 5, 8 - set at .015"
Intake Valves   : No's 2, 3, 6, 7 - set at .013"

1. Place the gearshift lever in the neutral position.
2. Using the hand crank, turn the engine over until valve No. 8 and No. 3 are open, and pistons even, half way down the cylinder.
3. Measure valves No. 1 (Exh. .015") and No. 6 (Intk. .013).

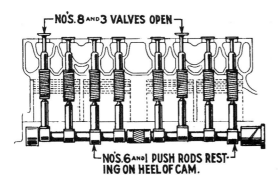

4. Turn the engine over 1/2 turn. Valve No. 7 and No. 5 are open. Measure valve No. 2 (Intk .013) and No. 4 (Exh. .015).

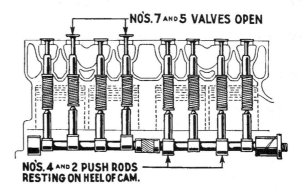

5. Turn the engine over 1/2 turn. Valve No. 1 and No. 6 are open. Measure valve No. 3 (Intk .013) and No. 8 (Exh. .015).

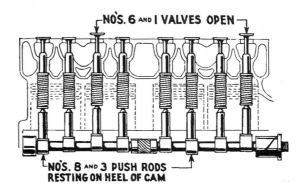

6. Turn the engine over 1/2 turn. Valve No. 2 and No. 4 are open. Measure valve No. 7 (Intk .013) and No. 5 (Exh. .015).

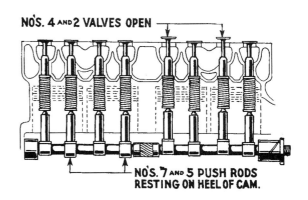

Service Adjustments

FLYWHEEL HOUSING VARIATION

FLYWHEEL HOUSING VARIATION MEASUREMENT

This measurement checks the alignment of the crankshaft end flange and the flywheel with the rear face of the flywheel housing. Misalignment of the flywheel housing creates a misalignment of the clutch housing (bell housing), which in turn causes a misalignment of the transmission drive gear with respect to the flywheel, clutch plate, and clutch pressure plate. This measurement can be made with a dial gauge or a crankshaft-to-housing gauge and a flywheel-to-housing gauge. The crankshaft end flange must be square with the flywheel housing rear face to within .006" maximum variation.

1. Thoroughly clean the mating surfaces of the flywheel housing and block. Place a paper gasket between the flywheel housing and the block. Securely bolt the housing to the block with four (4) attaching bolts (7/16-14 X 1-1/16" drilled hex head). Torque the bolts to 55 ft.lbs. Do not safety wire at this time.
2. Bolt the crank-to-flywheel housing gauge to the crankshaft flange using two of the flywheel attaching bolts (7/16-20 X 13/16 drilled head). Add spacers if necessary to allow the gauge to be absolutely tight against the crankshaft flange.

CAUTION

Do not allow the attaching bolts to extend more than 1/16" beyond the front side of the flange, causing possible damage to the rear main oil slinger.

3. Attach the throttle control bracket to the top of the flywheel housing at the two ears (7/16-14 X 1-3/4" hex head bolts and lock washers). Before tightening the two bolts, insert a horseshoe shaped shim (about .010" thick) under each ear, over the bolt shaft, and then securely tighten.
4. Set the adjusting bolt head on the gauge for .030" clearance from the flywheel housing rear face.
5. At about every 30°, check the clearance between the gauge adjusting bolt and the housing rear face. A maximum variation of .006" is allowable. Excessive variation can usually be adjusted out by varying the thickness of the horseshoe shims under the two ears for the throttle bracket. The flywheel housing should be replaced if the variation is greater than .006" around the housing rear face, usually caused by a warped housing.

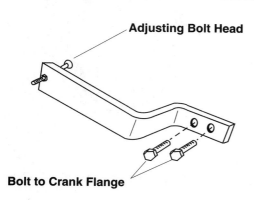

Crank-To-Flywheel Housing Gauge

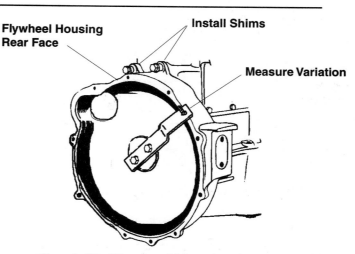

Crank-To-Flywheel Housing Variation Check

FLYWHEEL HOUSING VARIATION

6. After completing the crank-to-flywheel housing check, remove the gauge and safety wire the flywheel housing bolt heads.
7. Screw two short manifold studs into two adjacent holes in the crankshaft flange to use as guides when putting the flywheel in place on the crankshaft flange.

NOTE

The flywheel pilot bearing should be replaced before installing the flywheel (p/n GMN6203 DV).

8. Set the flywheel in place on the crankshaft flange. With the flywheel firmly seated over the dowels and against the crank flange, remove the two manifold studs and place the dowel retaining plate in the center of the flywheel. Insert the four (4) mounting bolts (7/16-20 X 13/16" with drilled hex head) and torque to 55 ft.lbs. Safety wire the bolt heads.

CAUTION

Do not allow the flywheel mounting bolts to extend more than 1/16" beyond the front side of the flange, causing possible damage to the rear main oil slinger.

9. Bolt the flywheel gauge across any two opposing holes in the flywheel annulus, and perform variation checks around the flywheel housing rear face, as done with the crankshaft-to-housing gauge.
10. The readings should be almost identical to those obtained from the crankshaft check. If the variation is more than .005", there will be too much wobble and the flywheel should be remachined or replaced.
11. After completing the flywheel variation check, remove the flywheel gauge and install the clutch and pressure plate, using twelve (12) bolts and lock washers (5/16-18 X 3/4" hex head). Torque to 20 ft.lbs.

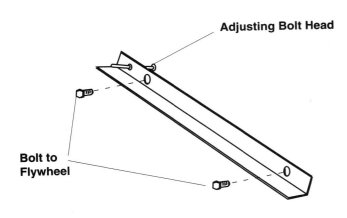

Flywheel-To-Housing Gauge

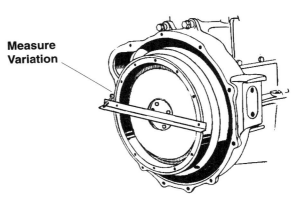

Flywheel-To-Housing Variation Check

Crank-To-Flywheel Housing and Flywheel-To-Housing Gauge Set Made by Auto Care & Restoration 3824 Alma Ave., Redding, Ca. 96002 (1-800-452-1027)

Service Adjustments

FLYWHEEL HOUSING VARIATION

SECITON III
LUBRICATION AND OIL

INTRODUCTION

The lubrication and oil system in the Model A requires constant attention as compared to modern cars of today. With no oil filtering for the crankcase or air filter for the carburetor, the engine oil must be changed frequently to reduce wear of engine components. The oil pump transfers oil from the oil pan to the valve chamber. Oil from the valve chamber drains to the crank bearings and back into the oil pan. The piston rods and cylinders receive oil by the splash method. With the many mechanical systems in the Model A, grease lubrication should be performed at every 500 miles. There are from 28 to 31 grease fittings on the model A, depending on the year of manufacture. Every point of lubrication is identified on the following pages.

LUBRICATION

EVERY 500 MILES

Location	Quantity	Grease Fitting	Location
Grease Gun			
1. Upper Spindle Arm (Left Side/Right Side)	2	4	A
2. Lower Spindle Arm (Left Side/Right Side)	2	5	A
3. Brake Actuator Arm (Front Axle - L/R Side)	2	5	B
4. Shock Link (Front /Rear - L/R)	4	2	B
5. Spring Shackle (Front - L/R)	2	5	B
6. Spring Shackle (Rear - L/R)	2	5	C
7. Tie-Rod Ends	2	3	D
8. Drag Link Ends	2	5	E
9. Rear Axle Bearing (Rear - L/R)	2	3	C
10. Rear Brake Actuator Arm (Rear - L/R, Behind Rear Radius Rod)	2	5	F
11. U-Joint (Under U-Joint Housing, Behind Trans)	1	3	G
12. Brake and Clutch Pedal Bushing	2	3	H
13. Emergency Brake Cross Shaft (Outside Frame - L/R)	2	4	J
14. Water Pump	2	3/1	K
Oil Can (squirt, SAE 30)			
15. Accelerator Control shaft	2		L
16. Distributor	1		M
17. Starter Crank Hole	1		N
Engine Oil (SAE 10W-30)			
18. Crankcase (Oil Pan, 4-1/2 Qts. at Oil Change)	5 Qts		O
3:1 Oil			
19. Horn (Oil Twice Yearly)	2		P

Grease Fittings

Five different types of lubricator fittings were used on the Model A cars. Two fittings are of the driver type which are pressed into a 5/16" diameter hole in the part. They have a direct through grease passage. Three lubricator fittings have a 1/8" pipe thread and all three have a built-in ball and spring check valve to prevent the grease from being pushed out through the inlet orifice. The water pump rear fitting has a removable cap made of brass. In this fitting, an inner spring loaded cylindrical phenolic plug was used instead of a steel ball. A special grease gun adapter must be used for all Model A grease fittings.

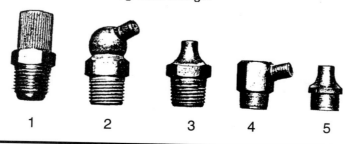

Type   1   2   3   4   5

LUBRICATION

EVERY 1000 MILES

Location	Quantity	Grease Fitting	Location
20. Generator (Oil Squirt -SAE 30)	2		Q

EVERY 2000 MILES

Location	Quantity	Grease Fitting	Location
Grease Gun			
21. Throwout Bearing Slider	1	3	R
22. Steering Sector Shaft (1928/1929)	1	3	S
600W Gear Oil			
23. Steering Gear Box	1		S
Vasoline			
24. Distributor Cam	1		T

EVERY 5000 MILES

Location	Quantity	Grease Fitting	Location
Bearing Grease			
25. Front Wheel Bearings (Packed Bearing Grease)	4		U
600W Gear Oil			
26. Differential	1		V
27. Transmission	1		W
Shock Fluid			
28. Shocks	4		X

Service Lubrication

LUBRICATION

LUBRICATION LOCATION CHART

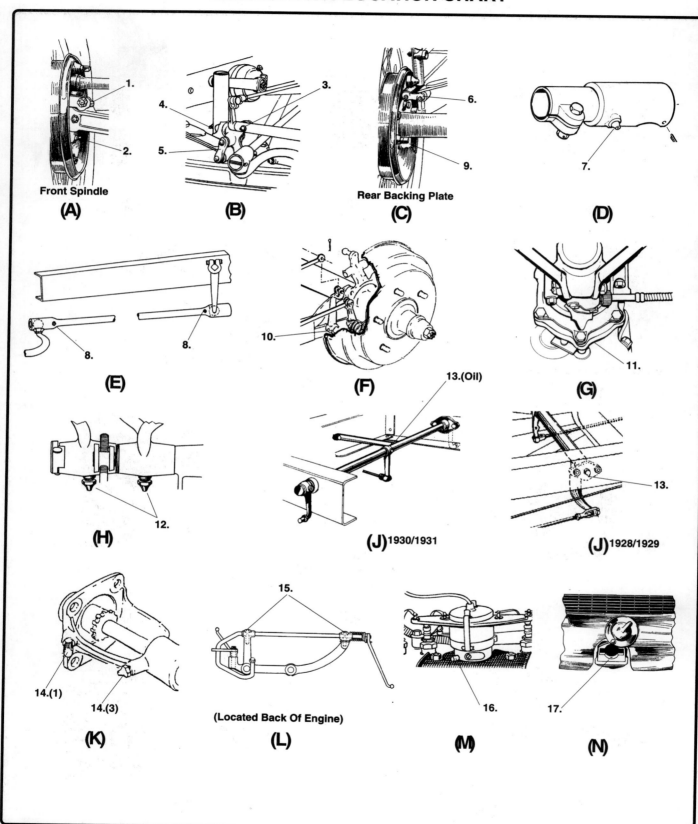

LUBRICATION

LUBRICATION LOCATION CHART

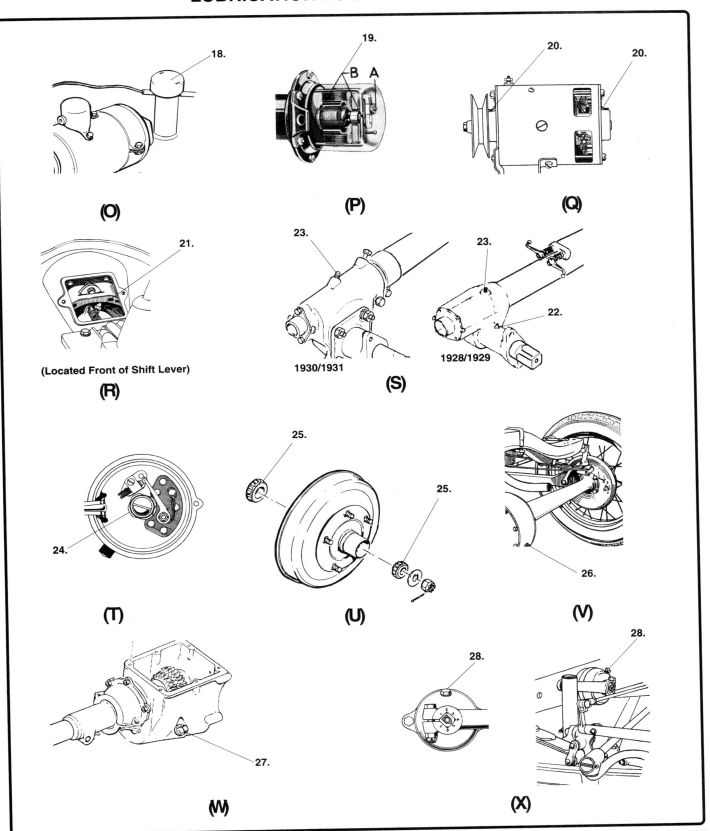

Service Lubrication

LUBRICATION

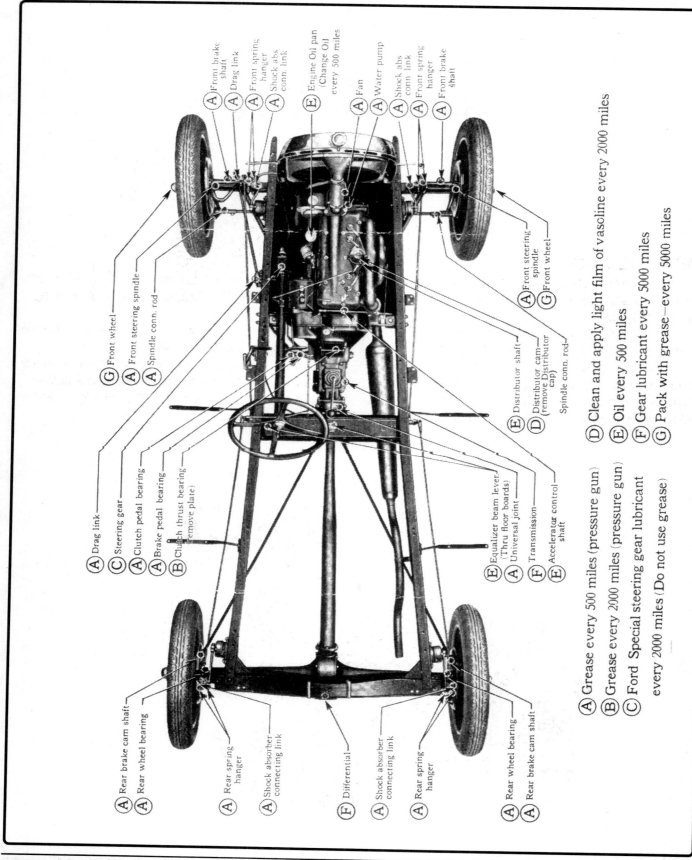

Service Lubrication

SECTION IV
TROUBLESHOOTING

INTRODUCTION

Troubleshooting is a method of isolating a problem (failure) to a specific system, circuit or failed component. The Model A can be divided into five (5) independent circuits for the purpose of troubleshooting and fault isolation.

The first step is to determine which of the five major circuits is causing the problem. The next step is then to trace the fault to a specific component in that circuit. The five (5) circuits include:

1) Cooling System, 2) Ignition System, 3) Fuel System, 4) Electrical System, and 5) Engine System. Troubleshooting chart 4-1 will aid in isolating the fault to one of the five major systems. Troubleshooting charts 4-2 through 4-6 include a description for each of the major systems and a troubleshooting chart to aid in isolating the faulty component.

TROUBLESHOOTING

Troubleshooting Chart 4-1
Major System Isolation

The following troubleshooting chart will aid in isolating the fault to one of the five major systems. Refer to charts 4-2 through 4-6 for a description of each system and corresponding troubleshooting chart.

Symptom	Probable Cause	Refer To
1. Engine Overheating	1. Incorrect ignition timing	Chart 4-3 Ignition System
	2. Blown Head Gasket	See Cyl. Head page 1-80
	3. Radiator - Insufficient Cooling Fan Belt - Loose Water Pump - Leaking	Chart 4-2 Cooling System
	4. Carburetor - Rich Mixture	Chart 4-4 Fuel System
2. Engine Won't Crank (Starter Does Not Turnover)	1. Battery Defective 2. Starter Defective 3. Battery Connections Loose 4. Starter Switch Inoperative	Chart 4-3 Ignition System
3. Engine Won't Crank (Starter Motor Turns)	1. Faulty Starter Bendix	See Starter page 1-285
	2. Faulty flywheel Ring Gear	See Engine page 1-147 (step 7)
4. Poor Idle	1. Faulty Carburetor	Chart 4-4 Fuel System
5. Loss of Power	1. Restricted Fuel Line	Chart 4-4 Fuel System
	2. Restricted Carburetor Jets 3. Carburetor Float Needs Adjusted	Chart 4-4 Fuel System
	4. Low Cylinder Compression	See Engine page 1-115
	5. Timing Retarded 6. Defective Coil	Chart 4-3 Ignition system
6. Engine Backfires	1. Faulty Condenser 2. Defective Distributor	Chart 4-3 Ignition System
7. Engine Backfires (Down Hill Coast)	1. Rich Carburetor Mixture	Chart 4-4 Fuel System

Troubleshooting

TROUBLESHOOTING

Symptom	Probable Cause	Refer To
8. Engine Intermittent (Rough Running)	1. Defective Distributor 2. Faulty Spark Plugs	Chart 4-3 Ignition system
9. Light Bulbs Burn Out (Frequently)	1. Poor Electrical Grounding 2. Generator Defective	Chart 4-5 Electrical System (See Addendum)
10. Starter Stuck (Will Not Move)	1. Starter Pinion Hung Up On Ring Gear	See Bendix page 1-20
11. Battery Discharges	1. Defective Battery 2. Defective CutOut Relay 3. Defective Electrical Wiring 4. Defective generator	Chart 4-5 Electrical System
12. Ammeter Shows Discharges	1. Defective Battery 2. Defective CutOut Relay 3. Defective Generator	Chart 4-5 Electrical System
13. Ammeter Reads Zero	1. Defective Ammeter 2. Defective CutOut Relay 3. Defective Generator	Chart 4-5 Electrical System
14. Engine Knocks	1. Main Bearing Clearance 2. Rod Bearing Clearance 3. Timing Gear Clearance. 4. Faulty Piston 5. Distributor Shaft Too Tight	Chart 4-6 Engine System

TROUBLESHOOTING

Troubleshooting Chart 4-2
Cooling System

The cooling system consists of the radiator, fan, water pump, fan belt, water hoses and engine block. The radiator is usually the main cause for overheating, although other conditions can cause overheating (See chart below.) The more obvious causes of radiator problems are clogged radiator, loose fins on the radiator tubes which prevent efficient transmission of heat from the tubes to the fins and hence to the air, and leaks in the radiator. The lack of a baffle plate or incorrectly installed baffle in the top of the radiator below the filler neck can cause water to be pumped out the overflow tube, constantly reducing the volume of water. Low oil level and engine tolerances too tight can cause excessive heat to be generated in the block. The following chart will identify probable causes for overheating and suggested corrective action.

Symptom	Probable Cause	Refer To
1. Engine Overheating	1. Incorrect ignition timing	See Section II, Adjustments, page 2-18
	2. Radiator Clogged	See Radiator page 1-235
	3. Leaking Water Pump	See Water Pump page 1-352
	4. Incorrect Fan Belt Adjustment	See Fan Belt Adjust page 2-9
	5. Blown Head Gasket	See Head Gasket page 1-80
	6. Carburetor Adjustment too Rich	See Carburetor page 1-57
	7. Cylinder Compression too High (Change to lower compression head)	See Cylinder Head page 1-80
	8. Low Oil Level In Crankcase	Add Oil
	9. Piston and Ring Fit Too Tight	See Engine Overhaul page 1-143, step 5.

Troubleshooting Chart 4-3
Ignition System

The Model A ignition system is very simple and easy to troubleshoot. The ignition system includes the battery, starter motor, starter switch, terminal box, ammeter, coil, ignition switch, ignition cable, distributor (which include points and condenser), and spark plugs. Troubleshooting the ignition system should start with the Preliminary Test. The five (5) steps in the preliminary test will take five minutes and can quickly isolate a defective wire or component. If the preliminary test passes and the fault remains, proceed to the chart below. PRELIMINARY TEST: (Refer to the ignition system diagram below)
(Ignition key OFF)
1. Test for 6 volts at battery connection on starter.
2. Test for 6 volts at both terminal box wing nuts.
3. Test for 6 volts at both coil terminals.
4. Place a piece of paper between the point contacts in the distributor to keep points open.
5. Turn ON ignition switch and test for 6 volts on the open point arm.

This test has checked all wiring connections from the battery to the points. If any of the Preliminary Test failed, trace the fault to a disconnected or broken wire in the circuit.

Symptom	Probable Cause	Refer To
1. Engine Overheating	1. Incorrect Ignition Timing	See Timing page 2-18
2. Engine Not Starting	1. Battery Voltage Low 2. Defective Coil 3. Defective Condenser 4. Open Ignition Switch or Cable	See Ignition Switch page 1-201
3. Loss Of Power	1. Incorrect Timing 2. Defective Coil	See Timing page 2-18
4. Engine Backfires	1. Defective Condenser	
5. Engine Intermittent	1. Defective Condenser 2. Defective Points 3. Defective Spark Plugs	
6. Engine Knock	1. Loosen Distributor Locking Screw 2. Distributor Shaft Bushing too Tight	See page 1-106 Note See page 1-103 Step 7 and 8

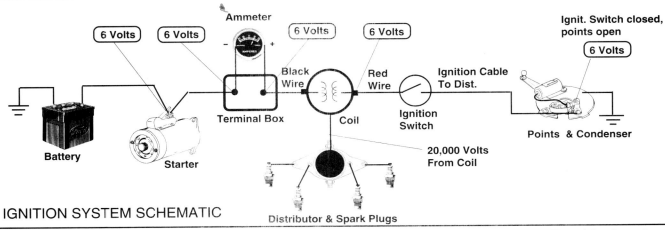

IGNITION SYSTEM SCHEMATIC

TROUBLESHOOTING

Troubleshooting Chart 4-4
Fuel System

The fuel system consists of the gas tank, gas shut off valve, gas lines (2), sediment bowl, and carburetor. The most common cause of fuel system failures is a dirty and rusted gas tank, resulting in dirty fuel to the carburetor. Gas tanks should be removed for cleaning and sealing. A restricted fuel line can cause loss of engine power. Restrictions are usually caused by the compression ferrules on the end of the fuel line from the sediment bowl to the carburetor. If the compression ferrule is placed further than 1/8" from the end of the line, the line is allowed to go too far into the connection, causing a restriction in the fuel flow. The other most significant failure is the carburetor. The carburetor should be cleaned and adjusted in accordance with the procedure in "Section I, Service and Repair, Carburetor", page 1-57.

Symptom	Probable Cause	Refer To
1. Engine Overheating	1. Rich Fuel Mixture	See Carburetor page 1-57
2. Engine Not Starting	1. No Fuel 2. Faulty (Dirty) Carburetor Jets 3. Manifold Air Leak	Add Fuel To Tank See page 1-57 Replace Gasket
3. Poor Idle	1. Faulty Carburetor 2. Adjust Idle Air Mixture 3. Carburetor Air Leak	See Carburetor page 1-57 See Idle Air Adjust page 2-7 See Carburetor page 1-57
4. Power Loss	1. Restricted Fuel Line 2. Restricted Carburetor Jets	
5. Engine Backfires (Down Hill)	1. Rich fuel Mixture	Adjust Float Level
6. Poor Gas Milage	1. Rich Fuel Mixture 2. Carburetor leaks	See Carburetor page 1-57

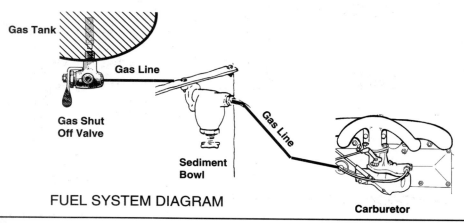

FUEL SYSTEM DIAGRAM

Troubleshooting Chart 4-5
Electrical System

The electrical system includes the battery, battery cable, terminal box, ammeter, generator, main wiring harness, horn rod, horn, stop light switch, and all lights. The electrical system is dependent on a fully charged battery and a good grounding system. Poor connection is the most common electrical problem. Check all connections at the battery terminals, terminal box connections, ammeter and generator connections. These connections must be clean and tight. Check for a clean (rust free) headlight ball socket. The weakest component in the electrical system is the cut out relay. For increased reliability, the cutout can be replaced with a diode. A fuse should be installed at point (A), mounted on the starter. This will protect the electrical system wiring. A fire can be started by a short in the system (it has happened).

Symptom	Probable Cause	Refer To
1. Light Bulbs Burn Out (Frequently)	1. Poor Grounds Between Generator and Battery.	See Addendum
2. Horn Inoperative	1. Dirty Armature 2. Poor Contact At Light Switch 3. Defective Horn Rod	See Horn page 1-194
3. Battery Discharges	1. Defective CutOut	Replace CutOut
4. Ammeter Shows Discharge	1. Defective Cut Out 2. Defective Generator	See Generator page 1-189
5. Ammeter Shows High Charge	1. Adjust Generator	See Generator Adjust page 2-10

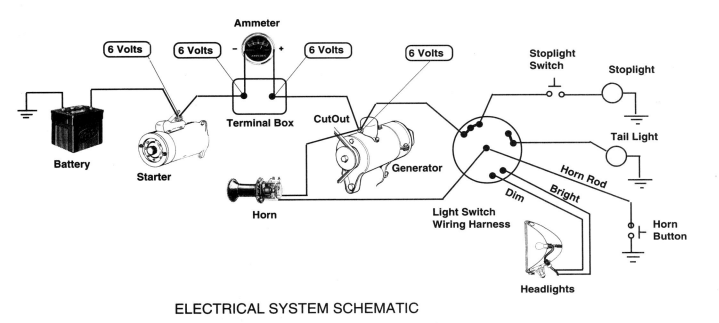

ELECTRICAL SYSTEM SCHEMATIC

TROUBLESHOOTING

Troubleshooting Chart 4-6
Engine Noises

A knocking sound in the engine is most likely caused by one of the following;

(1) Piston Slap Makes a sharp metallic noise. Idle engine and short out each cylinder spark plug. The noise will disappear when plug with bad piston is shorted. Noise will also disappear at acceleration. This can be caused by worn or out of round cylinder, or broken piston ring. Correct problem by reboreing cylinder and/or replacing piston.

(2) Valve Noise Makes clicking or rattle noise. Caused by excessive wear on valve stem or lifter, out of adjustment, or stuck valve. Correct by adjusting valve clearance, replace worn valve or lifter, regrind cam, replace valve guide and/or valve. A stuck valve can sometimes be loosened by passing oil through the carburetor while engine is running.

(3) Rod Bearing Knock Makes sharp metallic noise similar to a piston slap. Detection is opposite of piston slap. Rod knock is not heard at idle. Knock becomes louder as engine speed is increased. Caused by excessive rod bearing clearance. Correct by adjusting rod bearing clearance to .0015 inches by removing shims. May require repouring rod bearing.

4) Rear Main Bearing Knock Makes dull knocking or thud noise. Detected at speeds between 20 and 50 MPH. Knock will normally decrease or disappear while pulling or decelerating. Noise will be detected the loudest at normal driving speed, when not pulling or decelerating. Correct by adjusting bearing clearance to .001 to .0015 inches. If knock is excessive, crank should be checked for out of roundness. May need to repour all main bearings to correct.

(5) Timing Gear Knock Usually the most difficult to diagnose. If gear is loose or badly worn it will knock in all ranges. Run engine slightly above idle speed. Slowly open and close throttle. Knock will continue to be present, but just as engine slows down knock will become a slight rattle. Remove timing pin and reinsert into timing hole on timing gear cover. Press timing pin tightly against timing gear and accelerate slightly above idle. Knock will significantly be reduced or disappear. Correct by replacing both timing gear and crank gear as a matched set. The two gears should have a back lash clearence of .003 to .004". If more than .009 back lash, an over size (.005") timing gear should be installed.

(6) Wrist Pin Slap This cannot be detected by shorting out the cylinder plugs. Rapidly accelerate and decelerate the engine speed. The engine will pass through a certain speed range when the wrist pin will rattle at about the same pitch as a valve tappet noise. This can be corrected by installing a new wrist pin bushing in the rod or new wrist pin if badly worn. Wrist Pin should fit the piston and connecting rod with a tight metal to metal fit. The pin can be pushed into the piston and rod with a slight pressure of the hand. Pin to rod clearance is .0003 to .0005 inches.

ADDENDUM — TROUBLESHOOTING

MODEL A GENERATOR (CHARGING) CIRCUIT

The Model A electrical system is dependent on correct operation of the generator. The Model A generator is a 3-brush unit, using the 3rd (adjustable) brush to set the output voltage. Since the Model A generator has no voltage regulator, it depends on the battery connection to maintain a constant voltage output. A loss of battery connection or a poor terminal connection within the circuit between the generator and the battery will cause the generator output voltage to rise, as high as 20 volts. There are nine (9) connections between the generator and battery, as seen in the figure below. All nine (9) connection points must be tight and free of corrosion and rust to provide correct operation of the generating circuit. A poor connection at any one of the nine points, caused by loose connection, corrosion, paint, or rust, will create a resistance in the circuit, causing the generator to produce a higher than normal voltage (could go as high as 20 volts) to the lights and other electrical components in the electrical system. Depending on where the faulty connection is located, the ammeter may or may not indicate a change in current. A poor connection at the battery ground connection or a poor connection between the frame and engine can cause a high output to be produced from the generator. The Model A starting current is about 80 amps. This high starting current can get through a poor ground connection, enough to allow the car to be started, but the generator sees a poor ground connection as a high enough resistance to cause high voltage output from the generator. An indication of high generator voltage output is frequent burning out of light bulbs and ignition points burning.

The output of the generator should be checked with a volt meter. Set the engine idle speed fast enough to indicate a charge on the ammeter. Measure the generator output voltage at Cutout, point (9). Move the generator adjustable brush up or down to obtain 7.0 to 7.4 volts output. The ammeter should indicate approximately 8 amps. Measure the voltage at the battery terminal. There should not be more than .5 volts difference in the two voltage readings. If the reading at the generator is higher than the reading at the battery, check the nine connections for a poor connection. Many times, high generator output can be corrected by installing a secondary ground cable from the battery ground connection (at the frame cross member) to a bell housing bolt behind the starter motor. Check the output voltage of your generator before and after installing a secondary ground cable. You may see a considerable difference in output voltage. A secondary ground cable can also improve starter motor operation. The following table shows generator voltage output verses ammeter reading (these readings may vary slightly). Set the generator output at 8 amps (7.2 volts) for normal daytime driving. Night driving with headlights On requires about 12 Amps charge (this will drop to about 2 amps charge on the ammeter with the headlights ON.)

Generator Output Voltage	Ammeter Reading
7.8 volts	15 amps
7.5 volts	12 amps
7.2 volts	8 amps
6.5 volts	5 amps

When the generator CutOut becomes defective (will not close), eliminating generator output, be sure to ground the generator output terminal to prevent over heating the generator coils and burning up your generator.

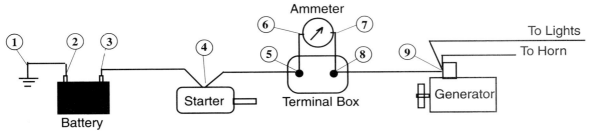

APPENDIX
PREVENTIVE MAINTENANCE CHECK LIST

EVERY FUEL STOP

- [ ] Check crankcase oil level
- [ ] Check radiator water level
- [ ] Check water pump packing
- [ ] Visual inspection of engine

MONTHLY

- [ ] Check water pump for leaks and end play
- [ ] Check carburetor and fuel lines for leaks
- [ ] Inspect fan for cracks
- [ ] Check battery water level
- [ ] Check tire air pressure -34 lbs.
- [ ] Check tires for breaks, cracks, and abnormal wear
- [ ] Check radiator water level
- [ ] Check water pump packing
- [ ] Visual inspection of engine

EACH 500 MILES

- [ ] Lubricate in accordance with 500 mile Lubrication Chart
- [ ] Change crankcase oil
- [ ] Tighten accessory mountings (windwings)
- [ ] Inspect radiator hoses
- [ ] Check fan belt adjustment (See Service Adjustments)
- [ ] Check wiper blade rubber
- [ ] Check generator charging rate, adjust as required (See Service Adjustments)
- [ ] Check carburetor and fuel lines for leaks

EACH 1,000 MILES

- [ ] Do all 500 mile checks
- [ ] Test front wheel bearings for looseness (See Service Adjustments)
- [ ] Oil generator bushings at each end of generator
- [ ] Tighten spring U-bolts, front and rear.
- [ ] Tighten all wheel lug nuts (64 ft. lbs torque)
- [ ] Test all lights (head, tail, stop, dash, dome)
- [ ] Inspect all cotter pins (See cotter pin list)
- [ ] Wipe out light switch (End of steering column)
- [ ] Lubricate door hinges, striker plate, dovetails
- [ ] Inspect entire fuel system for leaks
- [ ] Inspect exhaust system for leaks
- [ ] Check steering wheel free play (2" max, See Service Adjustments)
- [ ] Check specific gravity of battery, charge if needed (See service and repair, Battery)
- [ ] Check for tight electrical connections at all harness connections.
- [ ] Check for tight coil connections
- [ ] Check for tight connections at ammeter and terminal box
- [ ] Check distributor point gap (.016 - .018) See Service Adjustments
- [ ] Clean battery posts and clamps, tighten battery ground connection
- [ ] Clean horn commutator
- [ ] Drain fuel sediment bowl
- [ ] Check clutch pedal for 1" free play. See Service Adjustments
- [ ] Check tail light lens mounting screws

EACH 2,000 MILES

- [ ] Do all 1,000 mile items
- [ ] Lubricate in accordance with 2,000 mile Lubrication Chart
- [ ] Inspect starter commutator and brushes
- [ ] Examine tires for wear, cracks and damage
- [ ] Adjust Service Brakes (See Service Adjustments)
- [ ] Inspect front leaf spring for sagging and cracks
- [ ] Repack top end of shock links
- [ ] Tighten differential banjo bolts

EACH 5,000 MILES

- [ ] Do all 2,000 mile items
- [ ] Test engine compression
- [ ] Tighten rear wheel axle nut
- [ ] Rotate tires
- [ ] Lubricate in accordance with 5000 mile Lubrication Chart
- [ ] Flush cooling system
- [ ] Lubricate speedometer cable

EACH 10,000 MILES

- [ ] Do all 5,000 mile items
- [ ] Pull all brake drums, inspect brake linings, drums, and springs
- [ ] Polish headlight reflectors

APPENDIX

MODEL A SAFETY CHECK LIST

	Yes	No

Body
1. Doors close and latch securely.
2. Safety glass installed in all windows.
3. Rear view mirror state approved.

Engine
1. Carburetor free of leaks.
2. All gas lines free of leaks.
3. Gas gauge free of leaks.
4. Approved type gas lines installed.
5. Wiring free of bare areas and properly routed.
6. Fuse installed between starter connection and terminal box connection.
7. Fan hub and blades free of defects.
8. General condition of engine compartment neat and orderly.
9. Air filter / spark arrestor installed on carburetor.
10. Throttle linkage - no bends and returns freely.
11. Exhaust system - no leaks.

WHEELS
1. All lug nuts properly tightened - 64 ft. lbs.
2. Tire pressure - 34 lbs.
3. Tire condition - acceptable tread, no breaks.
4. All four (4) shocks installed and working.
5. No front wheel shimmy.

LIGHTS
1. High beam and low beam operational
2. Taillights and stoplights operational (no burned out bulbs)
3. Directional indicators operational (if installed)

STEERING
1. Tie-Rod correctly installed and tightened. No excessive wear and properly lubricated.
2. Drag link correctly installed and tightened. No excessive wear and properly lubricated.
3. No excessive play in steering wheel (2" maximum).

BRAKES
1. Properly adjusted on all four wheels.
2. Emergency brake properly adjusted (Locks at 3rd notch).
3. Brake pedal travel properly adjusted (See Service Adjustments)
4. Brake rods and clevis pins correct with cotter pins.

MISCELLANEOUS
1. Registration and insurance papers in vehicle.
2. Safety flares and first aid kit in vehicle.
3. Horn and windshield wiper operational.
4. Tool kit and flashlight in vehicle.
5. Seat belts installed and functional.

_____
CAR OWNER

_____
CHIEF INSPECTOR

Date Inspected _____

MODEL A COTTER PIN USAGE CHART

Qty.	Location

1/16 X 1/2"
- 4   Equalizer operating shaft pin cap - 28 only
- 4   Brake cross shaft frame bracket
- 2   Hand brake lever bracket - 28 only
- 1   Hand brake lever retract spring - 28 only
- 6   Rear engine support pads

3/32 X 1/2"
- 1   Hand brake lever pawl - 28 only
- 1   Hand brake lever rod
- 1   Hand brake lever pawl pin - 28/29 only
- 1   Front radius rod retaining pin
- 1   Clutch pedal shaft collar pin

3/32 X 5/8"
- 3   Front brake plate assembly
- 2   Emergency brake toggle connection link
- 1   Hand brake lever arm - 28 only
- 1   Hand brake lever sector
- 1   Hand brake lever arm - 28 only
- 5   Universal joint outer cap
- 1   Tail pipe clamp
- 8   Engine connecting rods
- 1   Throttle bell crank
- 4   Shock arm bolts

1/8 X 5/8"
- 1   Brake pedal to equalizer shaft - 28 only
- 1   Brake pedal clevis pin
- 1   Brake pedal rod to cross shaft
- 8   Brake rod adjusting clevis
- 1   Hand brake lever pawl pin
- 2   Emergency brake lever to cross shaft rod
- 1   Emergency brake cross shaft to rear end
- 1   Cutch pedal to release shaft arm trunion

3/32 X 3/4"
- 2   Operating wedge stud assy
- 2   Brake cross shaft guide - 28 only
- 2   Spindle bolt locking pin - 29/29 only
- 2   Spindle connecting rod end
- 1   Steering gear housing bolt
- 1   Steering gear arm
- 1   Fan shaft
- 6   Main engine bearings
- 1   front engine support
- 8   Front and rear spring shackles
- 4   Rear bolts on rear radius rod

1/8 X 3/4"
- 16   Brake shoe roller pins
- 8   Rear brake plate assembly

3/32 X 1"
- 2   Front radius ball cap

1/8 X 1"
- 2   Front spring perch
- 2   Spindle arm
- 2   Rear axle and gear shaft
- 1   Rear radius rod - front bolt
- 4   Rear spring retaining bar
- 1   Starter rod - 28 only

5/32 X 1"
- 2   Spindle assembly

1/8 X 1-1/4"
- 2   Side mount arm support
- 4   Shock link plug

1/8 X 1-1/2"
- 2   Spindle connecting ball plug
- 2   Drag link ball plug
- 2   Transmission main drive gear - 28 only

APPENDIX

BOLT - GRADE / TORQUE COMPARISON

Grade Markings on Head				SAE 2 ⬡		SAE 5 ⬡		SAE 8 ⬡	
BOLT SIZES				TORQUE (ft.-lbs.)					
Bolt Dia.	Threads per in.	Bolt Head	Nut	Dry	Lub	Dry	Lub	Dry	Lub
1/4	20	3/8	7/16	66 *	20 *	8	75 *	12	9
1/4	28	3/8	7/16	76*	56*	12	9	14	10
5/16	18	1/2	9/16	11	8	17	13	25	18
5/16	24	1/2	9/16	12	8	24	18	25	20
3/8	16	9/16	5/8	20	15	30	23	45	35
3/8	24	9/16	5/8	23	17	35	25	50	35
7/16	14	5/8	3/4	32	24	50	35	70	55
7/16	20	5/8	3/4	36	27	55	40	80	60
1/2	13	3/4	13/16	50	35	75	55	110	80
1/2	20	3/4	13/16	55	40	90	65	120	90
9/16	12	7/8	7/8	77	55	110	80	150	110
9/16	18	7/8	7/8	80	60	120	90	130	175

* Torque values expressed in inch-lbs.

Common Lubricants	Percent of Torque Reduction Required
Never-seize	Reduce std, torque 45 %
Grease	Reduce std, torque 40 %
Heavy oils	Reduce std, torque 40 %
Graphite	Reduce std, torque 30 %
White Lead	Reduce std, torque 25 %

SPECIFICATION CARD

FRONT END
Caster : 5°
Toe-In : 1/16" ±1/32"
Spindle Bolt (King Pin) : Dia. .8125"±.0005"
Spindle Bolt Bearing : Timken T83
      Bolt to Bearing Clearance : .001"±.0005"
Front Wheel Bearings:
    Inner Bearing : Timken 15118, Race: 15250
    Outer Bearing: Timken 09074, Race: 09196

REAR END
Gear Ratio : 3.78:1, 3.70:1(early 28), 3.54:1, 4.11:1
Pinion Bearing: Timken 28156 (2 ea.)
Race, Double Cone : Timken 28317
Axle Shaft : Dia. 1-1/8"
          1.128" to 1.130" @ Wheel Bearing
Rear Wheel Bearing :
   O.D. of Axle Housing Race: 2.061" to 2.0635"
   I.D. of Wheel Hub: 3.188" to 3.190" - Min 3.185"
Axle and Drive shaft Grease Seal: CR10296
Rear Drum Grease Seal: CR20112
Differential Lube : 600W or 160W

BATTERY
Voltage: 6 Volt
Positive Terminal : Ground Connection
Capacity : 80 Ampere Hours, Group 1
Charging Rate : 10 to 12 Amps

BRAKES - SERVICE
Braking Power: 40% Front, 60% Rear
Drum Diameter: 11"±.010"
Brake Shoe Lining Thickness: 3/16"
  Material: Woven Wire or Asbestos Composition
Brake Rod Length: 51-7/16" to 51-1/2"

BRAKES - EMERGENCY
Drum Diameter : 9-5/8"
    Lining Thickness: 3/16"

CAMSHAFT
Shaft Dia. : 7/8"
Bearing Dia. : 1.560"
Block Bore Dia. : 1.561"
Bearing Clearance (Max) : .003"
Cam Lift : .303"
Duration : 236°
Timing Gear Cover Spring: Tension 35 lbs.
Timing Gear Backlash : .003 to .005" (max. .009")
Camshaft Straightness : .0005" to .001"

CAPACITIES
Cooling System : 3 gallons
Gas Tank ; 1928/29 - 10 Gal., 1930/31 - 11 Gal.
Oil Pan (Empty) : 5 Qts., Oil Change : 4-1/2 Qts.
Transmission : 1-1/2 Pints
Steering Gear : 7-Tooth 7-3/4 oz., 2-Tooth 4-1/2 oz.
Differential ; 2-1/4 Pints

CARBURETOR
Throat Size : 1"
Float Level :
      1" from Float Ring to Machined Surface
Main Jet : No. 63 Drill Bit
Cap Jet : No. 63 Drill Bit
Comp Jet : No. 65 Drill Bit
Idle Jet : No. 75 drill Bit

CLUTCH
Pressure Plate Weight : 15 lbs.
Clutch Disc Weight : 2-1/2 lbs.
Clutch Pressure : 1100 lbs.
Foot Pedal Pressure : 30 lbs.
Clutch Dia. : 9", Thickness : 9/64
Clutch Pedal Clearance (Free Play) : 1"
Clutch Release Bearing Hub : 2.065" Dia.
Clutch Throwout Bearing : Bower 2065

CONNECTING RODS
Weight : 1 lb., 6 oz.
Balance Weight : 552 grams ±1 gram, Crank End
                  198 grams ± 1 gram, Pin End
Crankshaft Bearing : 1-1/2" Dia.
Piston Pin Bearing : 1" Dia.
Bearing Side Clearance : .008" to .012"
Piston Pin Clearance : .0005"
Crankshaft Clearance : .001"
Bearing Cap Bolt Torque : 40 - 50 lbs.
 Assembled with oil dippers facing camshaft.

COOLING SYSTEM
Water Pump Shaft : 5/8" Dia.
Water Pump Shaft End Play : .006 to .010"
Radiator Hoses :
    1928/29 - Upper 2" Dia., 6-1/4" Long
    1930/31 - Upper 2" Dia., 8" Long
  Lower (Two Pieces) 1-3/4" Dia., 2-3/4" Long
Radiator Capacity : 3 Gal.
Radiator Flow Rate : 38 GPM

SPECIFICATION CARD

CRANKSHAFT
Weight : 28 lbs.
Main Bearings : 1.624" Dia.
Crank Pins : 1.499" Dia.
Crank Pin Taper and Roundness : .0005" to .001"
Rear Flange Thickness : 3/8"
End Clearance : .004" to .007"
Main Bearing Clearance : .001"
Crankshaft Straightness : .0005"
Main Bearing Cap Torque : 80 - 100 lbs.

CYLINDER BLOCK
Cylinder Bore : 3.875" to 3.876"
Valve Guide Bore : .594" to .595"
Flatness On Top Of Block : .003"
Cylinder Bore Perpendicular to Top : .001" to .002"

DRIVESHAFT
Spline Inner Dia. : .901" to .911"
Spline Outer Dia. : 1.090" to 1.091"
Pinion Bearing Torque : 15 to 20 inch lbs.

ENGINE
Rated Horsepower : 24.03 SAE
Brake Horsepower : 40 HP
Firing Order : 1-2-4-3
Compression Ratio : 4.22:1
Piston Displacement : 200.5 Cu. In.
Bore : 3.876"
Stroke : 4.250"

EXHAUST
Exhaust Pipe : 2" I.D.
Tail Pipe : 1-5/8" I.D.

FLYWHEEL
Weight : 63 lbs., 4 Oz.
Balance : within .15 In/oz
Flywheel Bolt Torque : 65 Ft./lbs.
Clutch mounting surface and clutch disc surface must run true to crankshaft within .005" TIR.
Clutch mounting shoulder diameter must be concentric with crankshaft flange diameter within .005"TIR
Pilot Bearing GMN6203 DV

GAS TANK
Capacity : 1928/29, 10 Gallons; 1930/31, 11 Gallons

GENERATOR
Type : Two Pole
Brushes : Three (one adjustable)
Max. Normal Charging Rate : 12 Amps
@ 1600 Armature RPM
Brush Spring Tension : 35 to 40 Oz. Ea.
Field Current Draw : 6.3 Amps @ 7 volts
Generator Motoring : Draws 5.75 Amps @ 7 Volts
Maximum Current : 18 to 22 Amps @ 6 Volts
Motoring Freely : 5 Amps @ 6 Volts
Field Test : 5.2 Amps @ 6 Volts

HEAD
Compression Ratio : 1928; 4.3:1
1929/1931; 4.22:1
Head Nut Torque : 55 Ft./lbs

IGNITION
Rotor Rotation : Counterclockwise
Point Gap : .016" to .020"
Condenser Capacity : .20 to .25 MFD
Spark Plugs : Champion 3X, 7/8-18 Thread
Spark Plug Gap : .035"
Spark Manual Advance : 20°
Rotor To Distributor Body Terminal : .025"

LIGHTS
Headlights : 32-50 cp. Double Contact Base
Cowl Light : 3 cp. Single Contact; Mazda 63
Parking Light : 3 cp. Single Contact; Mazda 63
Tail Light : 3 cp. Single Contact; Mazda 63
Stop Light : 21 cp. Single Contact; Mazda 1129
Inst. Pnl Light : 3 cp. Single Contact; Mazda 63
Dome Light : 3 cp. Single Contact; Mazda 63

LUBRICATION
Oil Pump Type : Gear
Pump Capacity : 9 Pints/Min @ 1300 RPM
Pump Gear Teeth to Housing Clearance : .001 to .002"
Cover to Gear Face Clearance : .001" to .002"
Drive Gear to Camshaft Gear Clearance : .003 to .005"

SPECIFICATION CARD

PISTONS
Displacement : 200.5 cu. Inches
Weight : 1 lb. 1-7/8 oz. (476.8 grams)
Variance in Weight : ± 2 grams
Diameter : 3.8745" (Bore 3.875)
Variation in Piston Compression Height : .003" to .005"
Piston Pin Bushing : I.D. .992", O.D. 1.0675"
Pin Fit in Rod Bushing : .0003" max.
Pin Fit in Piston : .0002" to .0005"
Piston fit in Cylinder : .002"
Ring Clearance in Groove : .001" to .002"
Ring End Gap : Top - .012 to .015";
    Middle - .010 to .012"; Bottom - .008 to .010"

RADIATOR
Tubes : (1928) Round, 1/4" Dia.
Number of Tubes : 94 in 4 Rows
    (1929) Round, 1/4" Dia.
Number of Tubes : 100 in 4 Rows, or 87 in 5 Rows
Tubes : (1930/31) Flat, 5/32 X 1/2"
Number of Tubes : 102 in 3 Rows
Flow Rate : 38 GPM

SPRINGS
Front, Free Length : (10 Leaf) 30-5/8" to 30-13/16"
Rear, Free Length : Tudor/Fordor 38-7/8" to 39"
    Phaeton, Roadster, Coupes 39-1/8" to 39-1/2"

STEERING
Turning Radius : 17 Ft.
Gear Ratio : 1928/29 11-1/4:1; 1930/31 13:1
Steering Wheel Dia. : 1928/29 17-1/2"; 1930/31 17"
Sector Shaft Bearing Clearance : .001" to .0015"
Bearings : 7-Tooth T83; 2-Tooth Timken 3571

TRANSMISSION
Gear Ratios : High 1:1; Second 6.9:1; Low 8.75:1
Bearings : Main Shaft Front Ball -1208
    Main Shaft Rear Ball - 1306
    Counter Shaft Short - Bower J 241256
    Counter Shaft Long - Bower J 241246
    Pilot Bearing - SKF 2RSJ

VALVES
Lift : .287" with .015" Clearance
Seat Angle : 45°
Seat Width : 3/32"
Stem Dia. : .311"
Valve Length : 5.677"
Head Diameter : 1.537"
Valve Opening Dia. : 1-3/8"
Port Dia. : 1-3/8"
Valve Guide Clearance : Exhaust .002";
                              Intake .001 to .0015
Lifter Clearance : Exhaust .015"
                Intake .013"
Valve Guides : I.D. .3135"; O.D. .5938"
Valve Spring : O.D. 1.022";
    Free Length : 2-15/16"
    Compressed Length : 2.250" (57-64 lbs.)
Valve Timing :
    Intake Opens 7-1/2° Before TDC
    Intake Closes 48-1/2° After BDC
    Exhaust Opens 51-1/2° Before BDC
    Exhaust Closes 4-1/2° After TDC

WEIGHTS (Approximate)
Roadster -2155 lbs
Std. Coupe -2257 lbs
Spt. Coupe -2283 lbs
Cabriolet -2273 lbs
Tudor Sedan -2375 lbs
Fordor (2 wdw) -2467 lbs
Fordor (3 wdw) -2462 lbs
Town Sedan -2475 lbs
Phaeton -2212 lbs
Dlx Delivery -2282 lbs
Taxi Cab -2500 lbs
Pickup (Open Cab) -2073 lbs
Pickup (Closed Cab) -2215 lbs
Panel Delivery -2416 lbs
Station Wagon -2482 lbs
Roadster Body -465 lbs
Coupe Body -591 lbs
Spt Coupe Body -596 lbs
Cabriolet Body -575 lbs
Tudor Sedan Body -726 lbs
Fordor (2wdw) Body -782 lbs
Fordor (3wdw) Body -786 lbs
Town Sedan Body -810 lbs
Phaeton Body -549 lbs

SPECIFICATION CARD

MODEL A MOTOR NUMBERS

1927
October 20, 1927	1		137
November	138		971
December	972		5275

1928
January	5276		17251
February	17252		36016
March	36017		67700
April	67701		109740
May	109741		165726
June	165727		224276
July	224277		295707
August	295708		384867
September	384868		473012
October	473013		585696
November	585697		697829
December	697830		810122

1929
January	810123		983136
February	983137		1127171
March	1127172		1298827
April	1298828		1478647
May	1478648		1663401
June	1664302		1854831
July	1854832		2045422
August	2045423		2243920
September	2243921		2396932
October	2396933		2571781
November	2571782		2678140
December	2678141		2742695

1930
January	2742696		2826649
February	2826650		2940776
March	2940777		3114465
April	3114466		3304703
May	3304704		3509306
June	3509307		3702547
July	3702548		3771362
August	3771363		3883888
September	3883889		4005973
October	4005974		4093995
November	4093996		4177733
December	4177734		4237500

1931
January	4237501		4310300
February	4310301		4393627
March	4393628		4520831
April	4520832		4611921
May	4611922		4695999
June	4696000		4746730
July	4746731		4777282
August	--		--
September	4777283		4824809
October	4824810		4826746
November	4826747		4830806
December	--		--

MODEL A BODY TYPES

Body Types	Name	Year
35-A	Std. Phaeton	1928-29
35-B	Std. Phaeton	1930-31
40-A	Std. Roadster	1928-29
40-B	Std. Roadster	1930-31
40-B	Dlx. Roadster	1930-31
45-A	Std. Coupe	1928-29
45-B	Std. Coupe	1930-31
45-B	Dlx. Coupe	1930-31
49-A	Special Coupe	1928-29
50-A	Spt. Coupe	1928-29
50-B	Spt. Coupe	1930-31
54-A	Business Coupe	1928-29
55-A	Tudor Sedan	1928-29
55-B	Std. Tudor Sedan	1930-31
55-B	Dlx. Tudor Sedan	1931
60-A	Fordor Leather Back-Briggs Seal Brown Top	1928-29
60-B	Fordor Leather Back-Briggs Black Top	1929
60-A	Fordor Steel Back-Briggs	1929
68-A	Cabriolet	1929
68-B	Cabriolet	1930-31
68-C	Cabriolet	1931
135-A	Taxi-Cab	1928-29
140-A	Town Car	1928-29
150-A	Station Wagon	1928-29
150-B	Station Wagon	1930-31
155-A	Town Sedan -Murray	1929
155-B	Town Sedan- Briggs	1929
155-C	Town Sedan - Murray	1930-31
155-D	Town Sedan -Briggs	1930-31
160-A	Std. Fordor Sedan	1931
160-B	Town Sedan	1931
160-C	Dlx Fordor Sedan	1931
165-A	Std. Fordor Sedan- Murray	1929
165-B	Std. Fordor Sedan -Briggs	1929
165-C	Std. Fordor Sedan -Murray	1930-31
165-D	Std. Fordor Sedan - Briggs	1930-31
170-A	Std. Fordor Sedan 2/w Briggs	1929
170-B	Std. Fordor Sedan 2/w Briggs	1929-30
170-B	Dlx. Fordor Sedan 2/w Briggs	1930-31
180-A	Dlx. Phaeton	1930-31
190-A	Victoria	1930-31
400-A	Convertiable Sedan	1931

COMMERCIAL

66-A	Dlx. Pickup	1931
76-A	Open Cab Pickup	1928-30
76-B	Open Cab Pickup	1930-31
78-A	Pickup	1928-31
78-B	Pickup	1931
79-A	A Panel Delivery	1928-30
79-B	A Panel Delivery	1930-31
82-A	Closed Cab Pickup	1928-30
82-B	Closed Cab Pickup	1930-31
85-A	AA Panel Delivery	1928-30
85-B	AA Panel Delivery	1930-31
130-A	Dlx. Delivery	1928-30
130-B	Dlx.I Delivery	1930-31
130-B	Dlx.I Delivery (Drop Floor)	1930-31

ORDER FORM

Please send me _____ copies of **Model A Ford Mechanics Handbook**

Name _____
Address _____
City _____ State _____ Zip _____

METHOD OF PAYMENT

Check for $ _____ payable to :
Cottage Hill Publishing
22126 Cottage Hill Dr., Grass Valley, CA. 95949

☐ Credit Card; Charge my account ☐ MasterCard ☐ VISA

Exp. Date: _____ Signature _____

Qty	Unit Cost	Extended
	32.95	
Calif. Residents Only Add 7.25% Tax		
Sub Total		
Shipping & Handling U.S.A. (PRIORITY) $ 5.50 CANADA (AIR) $ 9.00		
Order Total		

ORDER FORM

Please send me _____ copies of **Model A Ford Mechanics Handbook**

Name _____
Address _____
City _____ State _____ Zip _____

METHOD OF PAYMENT

Check for $ _____ payable to :
Cottage Hill Publishing
22126 Cottage Hill Dr., Grass Valley, CA. 95949

☐ Credit Card; Charge my account ☐ MasterCard ☐ VISA

Exp. Date: _____ Signature _____

Qty	Unit Cost	Extended
	32.95	
Calif. Residents Only Add 7.25% Tax		
Sub Total		
Shipping & Handling U.S.A. (PRIORITY) $ 5.50 CANADA (AIR) $ 9.00		
Order Total		

ORDER FORM

Please send me _____ copies of **Model A Ford Mechanics Handbook**

Name _____
Address _____
City _____ State _____ Zip _____

METHOD OF PAYMENT

Check for $ _____ payable to :
Cottage Hill Publishing
22126 Cottage Hill Dr., Grass Valley, CA. 95949

☐ Credit Card; Charge my account ☐ MasterCard ☐ VISA

Exp. Date: _____ Signature _____

Qty	Unit Cost	Extended
	32.95	
Calif. Residents Only Add 7.25% Tax		
Sub Total		
Shipping & Handling U.S.A. (PRIORITY) $ 5.50 CANADA (AIR) $ 9.00		
Order Total		